ELEVATING PRODUCTIVITY WITH **GENERATIVE AI**

The

REVOLUTION in PROJECT MANAGEMENT

VIJAY KANABAR, PhD | **JASON WONG**

Foreword by **Ricardo Viana Vargas, PhD**

The AI Revolution in Project Management:
Elevating Productivity with Generative AI
Vijay Kanabar, PhD and Jason Wong

Pearson
www.informit.com

To report errors, please send a note to errata@informIT.com

Executive Editor: Laura Norman
Development Editor: Margaret Anderson
Senior Production Editor: Tracey Croom
Tech Editor: Anish Kanabar
Copy Editor: Liz Welch
Compositor: Danielle Foster
Proofreader: Dan Foster
Indexer: Rachel Kuhn
Interior Design: Danielle Foster
Illustrations: Vived Graphics
Cover Design: Chuti Prasertsith
Cover Illustration: TechSolution/Shutterstock

ISBN-13: 978-0-13-829733-6
ISBN-10: 0-13-829733-9

1 2023

Dedications

We want to dedicate this book to our mentors, colleagues, project management practitioners, and students who have shaped our thinking and work in project management over the years. Your insights, opportunities, and partnership have made us better professionals and educators, and your support guided us successfully to where we are today.

I dedicate this book to my family—my wife Dina, daughter Meera, and son Anish, the loyal companions of the past, and the present "Hail Caesar!" Additionally, my sincere gratitude to my mom Chandrika, who keeps asking if the book is done yet ("Yes Mom, it is done!"), and my sisters Rekha and Bina and their families. I would like to extend my deepest gratitude to my mother-in-law, Manjula, and the supportive extended families in Vancouver. Finally, my dozen-plus cousins and friends—please don't forget me simply because I am not active in the WhatsApp group.

—Vijay Kanabar

I would like to dedicate this book to the aspiring and current project managers looking to navigate our AI future. May this book equip you with the knowledge to effectively lead projects and teams in our ever-evolving technological landscape. My hope is that through these pages you will gain the understanding to harness AI as a tool and partner in delivering successful initiatives that make a difference in the world. I also want to extend gratitude to my friends who have supported me along the way. Last but not least, I want to dedicate this book to my family: my mother Kristina; my father Peter; my sister Jennifer; and my loyal companion, Sophie. They have cheered me on, and I wouldn't have been able to do it without them.

—Jason Wong

Pearson's Commitment to Diversity, Equity, and Inclusion

Pearson is dedicated to creating bias-free content that reflects the diversity of all learners. We embrace the many dimensions of diversity, including but not limited to race, ethnicity, gender, socioeconomic status, ability, age, sexual orientation, and religious or political beliefs.

Education is a powerful force for equity and change in our world. It has the potential to deliver opportunities that improve lives and enable economic mobility. As we work with authors to create content for every product and service, we acknowledge our responsibility to demonstrate inclusivity and incorporate diverse scholarship so that everyone can achieve their potential through learning. As the world's leading learning company, we have a duty to help drive change and live up to our purpose to help more people create a better life for themselves and to create a better world.

Our ambition is to purposefully contribute to a world where:

- Everyone has an equitable and lifelong opportunity to succeed through learning.
- Our educational products and services are inclusive and represent the rich diversity of learners.
- Our educational content accurately reflects the histories and experiences of the learners we serve.
- Our educational content prompts deeper discussions with learners and motivates them to expand their own learning (and worldview).

While we work hard to present unbiased content, we want to hear from you about any concerns or needs with this Pearson product so that we can investigate and address them.

- Please contact us with concerns about any potential bias at www.pearson.com/report-bias.html.

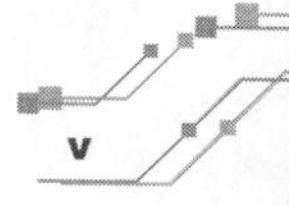

Contents

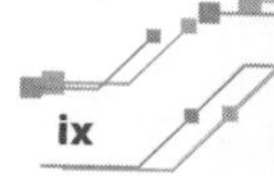

Acknowledgments

Heartfelt gratitude is extended to the executive editor, Laura Norman, for the unwavering support and encouragement that were instrumental in bringing this book to fruition. Your dedication to investing both time and expertise has had a profound effect on the success of this project. Your commitment and guidance were paramount in propelling this work to its completion swiftly and efficiently.

Thanks are also due to the development editor, Margaret Anderson. Her insights, perspectives, and patience contributed significantly to the book's quality and depth.

Additional recognition to the rest of the publishing team: production editor Tracey Croom for managing the production team, copy editor Liz Welch for refining the content, and Danielle Foster for both the interior design and composition, enhancing the book's visual appeal. Laura Robbins of Vived Graphics is acknowledged for the book's illustrations, while thanks are extended to Dan Foster for proofreading and to Rachel Kuhn for indexing.

The leadership of the Project Management Institute (PMI) continues to exert a tangible influence, inspiring the drive necessary for projects of this kind to reach fruition and advance the profession and literacy of AI.

Special mention is reserved for the team, colleagues, and students at the Metropolitan College at Boston University. Their dedication, commitment to research, and excellence shaped this work and paved the way for academic and professional opportunities. To the faculty, our thanks for the collaborations, discussions, and shared knowledge that cultivated a space for development and creativity in project management.

About the Authors

Dr. Vijay Kanabar is an associate professor and the director of Project Management Programs at Boston University's Metropolitan College. In recognition of his outstanding contributions to the field, he was honored with the PMI Linn Stuckenbruck Teaching Excellence Award in 2017. He has a track record of advising organizations such as Blue Cross Blue Shield, Staples, United Way, and Fidelity Investments on training and technology needs. As a distinguished author, he delved into AI research three decades ago, developing AI expert systems that aided project practitioners in cost estimation. Additionally, he holds certifications such as PMP, PMI-ACP, and CSM.

Jason Wong is an IT leader at a Boston-based hospital and an adjunct professor at Boston University, where he teaches project, program, and portfolio management and shares his profound understanding of generative AI with students, guiding them to master the methods necessary for developing generative AI systems. He imparts his deep knowledge of generative AI to students, ensuring they grasp both the foundational concepts and advanced techniques essential for creating cutting-edge artificial intelligence models. He lends his expertise as a practitioner in leading, managing, and overseeing diverse IT projects and products, with a specialized focus on electronic health records (EHR) and picture archiving and communications systems (PACS). He holds a masters in computer information systems and is a certified PMP, PMI-ACP, and CSPO.

Foreword

A New Era in Project Management

I've spent most of my professional life navigating the intricate world of project management, from being an entrepreneur to leading humanitarian projects at the United Nations, and from sharing insights through my podcast to being a volunteer leader in PMI. During this journey, I've seen the field evolve in countless ways. But until now, nothing has been as transformative in my own experience as the advent of artificial intelligence (AI).

AI is not just a buzzword; it's a tool reshaping how we manage projects and engage with stakeholders. Imagine a world where AI can sift through mountains of data to understand stakeholder needs better than ever before and better than any human being could do.

This is not a future perspective. This is happening right now! Generative AI can help us identify, engage, and communicate with stakeholders in ways we never thought possible. It can automate the mundane, freeing our time to focus on strategic issues requiring human insight.

But let's not forget that technology is a tool, not a replacement for our human skills. While AI can help us in many ways, from team building to decision-making, it has its pitfalls—and they are not little. Issues like ethical considerations, bias, and nuanced decision-making remind us that human oversight is irreplaceable. We must use AI responsibly, ensuring it aligns with our ethical standards and complements our human skills. This is what our organizations expect from us and what society expects from responsible human beings.

In *The AI Revolution in Project Management*, Vijay Kanabar and Jason Wong help us drive this intricate machine, showcasing real-world scenarios such as Walmart, which is already leveraging AI to make their procurement processes more efficient.

Another relevant aspect of the book is about Agile and AI. Integrating AI with adaptive project management approaches such as Agile and Scrum is particularly exciting. AI can help create detailed product backlogs and even articulate a project's vision. It's like having a super-powered assistant that understands your project's needs intimately.

These examples are clear indications of how the future can be bright, but it's up to us to steer the ship correctly.

Artificial intelligence is powerful, but, like any tool, it has limitations and drawbacks. One of the biggest concerns people have regarding AI is bias in the decision-making process. For instance, an AI system designed to screen résumés and select the best candidates could inadvertently favor individuals from specific backgrounds. This is a severe concern that responsible project managers need to be aware of, especially when using AI in recruitment or stakeholder engagement. In project management, building trust and rapport with stakeholders is crucial.

Another limitation is the absence of the "human touch." While AI can analyze data and generate responses, it can't understand the nuances of human emotion or the subtleties of interpersonal relationships. Let's not forget: AI does not have feelings.

Data privacy is another area that requires our attention and is covered by Vijay and Jason in this book. As we feed more and more data into AI systems, the question of who owns this data and how it's used becomes increasingly essential. Project managers must ensure that data is stored securely and its usage complies with privacy laws and ethical standards.

Finally, as we stand on the brink of this AI revolution in project management, I am filled with both hope and caution. Hope for the incredible efficiencies and insights that AI promises, and caution for the ethical and practical considerations that come with it.

So, as you turn the pages of this book, I invite you to explore this brave new world. Let's learn together, apply our knowledge responsibly, and lead our projects to success in this exciting era of AI.

Our organizations and society deserve that.

Ricardo Viana Vargas, Ph.D.

Ricardo is an experienced leader in global operations, project management, business transformation, and crisis management. As founder and managing director of Macrosolutions—a consulting firm with international operations in energy, infrastructure, IT, oil, and finance—he managed more than $20 billion in international projects in the past 25 years.

As former chairman of the Project Management Institute (PMI), Ricardo created and led the Brightline Initiative from 2016 to 2020 and was the director of project management and infrastructure at the United Nations, leading more than 1,000 projects in humanitarian and development projects.

He wrote 16 books in the field, has delivered 250 keynote addresses in 40 countries, and hosts the "5 Minutes Podcast," which has reached 12 million views. His course on LinkedIn Learning, "Generative AI in Project Management," has more than 52,000 students.

Ricardo holds a Ph.D. in Civil Engineering, a master's in Industrial Engineering, and an undergraduate degree in Chemical Engineering.

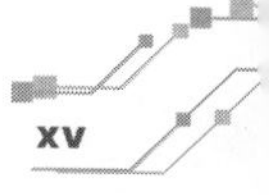

Prologue

The Intersection of Project Management and AI

Project management, at its core, is a discipline of orchestrating complex tasks, managing resources, and ensuring the successful completion of projects within set parameters of scope, time, cost, and quality. Over the years, tried-and-true methodologies have been established, shaping how industries approach and execute projects. From the predictive model's linear approach to the adaptive agile approach, project management has continually evolved to address the changing needs of industries and organizations.

Enter the world of generative artificial intelligence (AI)—a realm where machines mimic human intelligence processes, such as learning, reasoning, and self-correction. The fusion of AI with project management offers an exciting promise: the ability to harness vast computational powers to streamline processes, anticipate risks, and optimize resources in unimaginable ways.

With AI, project managers like you can tap into deep data reservoirs of knowledge, glean insights from patterns invisible to the human eye, and make rapid, informed decisions previously unfeasible. Imagine a scenario in which an AI tool could predict potential project bottlenecks weeks in advance or suggest optimal resource allocations based on historical data and current project dynamics. Such capabilities can transform the very fabric of project management, making it more proactive than reactive.

Moreover, integrating AI into project management signals a broader cultural shift in organizations—a move toward embracing innovation and staying agile in a rapidly changing technological landscape. Organizations willing to harness the combined might of project management and AI stand to gain a competitive edge, delivering projects with greater efficiency, reduced costs, and enhanced quality.

Navigating This Book

The journey of knowledge is often as critical as the destination. As readers embark on this exploration of the confluence of project management and AI, they will find the structure of this book meticulously designed to facilitate a seamless and enriching learning experience.

The emphasis of our narrative in this book, based on our research, is on text generation by AI tools. While AI's capabilities extend to various modalities, such as video and image generation (e.g., DALL-E), this book focuses on text generation. This concentration allows for a deeper understanding and exploration of how AI can be applied effectively to textual data in project management practice.

Each chapter can be thought of as multilayered tapestry. The fictional case studies are used to ground each chapter in real-world possibilities. We illustrate scenarios where AI tools such as ChatGPT, Google Bard, and Claude could play pivotal roles in planning, organizing, and managing project outcomes. All generative AI responses seen in the text are produced by ChatGPT, unless otherwise specified by a source notation. These narratives serve dual purposes: they paint a vivid picture of AI's capabilities and highlight the nuances and intricacies of prompt engineering with such tools.

The book goes beyond passive reading; immerse yourself in the unique tripartite dialogue—where authors, AI, and readers can participate in dynamic conversations. It's an opportunity for readers to actively question, ponder, and challenge the unfolding narrative. The entire book is written by humans who use AI-generated examples to illustrate how project managers can leverage AI in their work.

Interspersed within this dialogue, a technical guide in each chapter offers a deeper dive on one or more topics for those keen on the "how-to." These guides demystify AI tools, providing practical insights, step-by-step instructions, and tangible examples. These guides ensure that you not only understand the theoretical potential of AI but also have an opportunity to practice with the tools and techniques and harness their practical applications.

Understanding the Tools and Terminology

The world of AI is as vast as it is intriguing. As with any specialized field, it has unique tools, terminologies, and nuances. It might appear daunting to a newcomer, but a closer look reveals a structured ecosystem designed for diverse applications.

AI products such as ChatGPT, Google Bard, or Claude, introduced in this book, each possess different strengths and serve distinct needs. While they all fall under the umbrella of generative AI tools, the subtleties in their functionalities, algorithms, and interfaces can significantly impact their application in project management.

Consider the difference between a hammer and a screwdriver. Both are tools, but their design and functionality are determined by their specific uses. Similarly, while a prompt might be designed for ChatGPT, its outcome in Google Bard could differ due to the underlying differences in how these AI products have been trained and developed.

The diverse array of tools reflects professionals' varied challenges and requirements. Some tools might excel in data analysis, whereas others could be optimized for natural language processing or predictive modeling. Professionals must understand these nuances, ensuring they select the right AI tool for the task.

> **AI TOOLS** See Chapter 10, "AI Tools for Project Management," for some selected recommendations. A comprehensive coverage of AI tools for project management can be found at the Pearson website: *www.informit.com/AIforPM*.

Some content or features highlighted in our chapters and technical guides may be exclusive to paid services. For instance, ChatGPT Plus operates on a subscription model. Its advanced features, such as GPT-4 capabilities, plug-ins, and advanced data analysis tools, are available solely to subscribers.

Beyond tools, the terminology of AI also plays a crucial role. Terms like "token" or "context window" aren't mere jargon; they are fundamental concepts that define how AI interacts, understands, and responds. Grasping these concepts is essential for anyone looking to integrate AI effectively into their workflows. It equips them with the knowledge to anticipate AI's behavior, understand its limitations, and fully harness its capabilities.

It may also be useful to clarify a couple of software terms:

- **Plug-ins:** Within this book, we refer to ChatGPT plug-ins exclusively. However, another AI, Bard, also recently introduced plug-ins.
- **Extensions:** These refer to Internet browser extensions commonly found in popular web browsers such as Google Chrome, Firefox, and Edge.

Interactive Learning and Application

Traditional books provide knowledge in a linear format, with the author imparting wisdom and the reader passively consuming the content. However, in the age of interactive technologies and the dynamic realm of AI, we believe that the learning experience can—and should—be more immersive.

This book is not just a compilation of information; it's an interactive platform. It is designed to foster a multidimensional learning experience, blurring the lines between passive reading and active engagement. We have striven to create an environment where readers are not just consumers of content, but active participants in the unfolding narrative.

At the core of this interactive approach are the fictional case studies, which provide both illustrative examples and catalysts for thought. As you navigate these narratives, you are invited to engage with the scenarios, question the AI's responses, and even experiment with your own prompts. It's a hands-on approach, allowing readers to witness the capabilities of AI in real time and in realistic settings.

Complementing these case studies is the unique tripartite dialogue. This three-way conversation between the authors, the AI, and the readers serves multiple purposes. It demystifies complex concepts, provides diverse perspectives, and encourages you to challenge and validate your understanding. This dynamic interaction ensures that learning is not a one-way street but a collaborative journey.

Lastly, the technical guides at the end of each chapter act as deep dives into the practical implementation of AI. They provide a transition from theoretical understanding to practical application, ensuring that the knowledge gained is conceptual and actionable.

Ethical and Practical Considerations

Navigating the world of AI is not merely about understanding its capabilities but also about being keenly aware of its limitations and ethical considerations. AI, with all its predictive might, remains a tool. It can't replace the human touch, intuition, and experience seasoned professionals bring to the table.

From a practical standpoint, understanding AI's capabilities is paramount. While the allure of AI's potential can be captivating, it's crucial to approach it with a discerning eye. AI tools, regardless of their sophistication, have limitations. These limitations are not just in terms of computational capabilities but also in the form of inherent biases, context windows, and the occasional "hallucinations." A seasoned professional knows that AI can provide invaluable insights and augment decision-making, but it should not be the sole decision-maker. Human intuition, experience, and judgment, remains irreplaceable.

But beyond the practical lies the domain of the ethical. In an age where data breaches and privacy concerns make headlines, the ethical use

of AI is non-negotiable. When feeding project or company data into AI systems, one must tread carefully and be fully aware of the implications. This awareness extends beyond the immediate concerns of data privacy to the broader impact of AI-driven decisions. For instance, if an AI tool recommends resource allocation that might lead to layoffs, the ethical implications of such a decision need careful consideration.

Moreover, the data-sharing policies of AI platforms warrant scrutiny. Different platforms have varied approaches to data usage, and understanding these nuances is critical. For example, while ChatGPT might refine its model based on user interactions, other platforms like Claude might adopt a different stance.

Furthermore, understanding the "currency" of AI is crucial. Tokens, or word chunks, form the basic units that AI understands and processes. Just as a project manager might allocate resources judiciously, understanding token limits and context windows becomes paramount when engaging with AI. These constraints mean that AI can "forget" during lengthy interactions, necessitating occasional reminders from the user.

Equally important is the understanding that AI can "hallucinate."

> **AI HALLUCINATION** **This term simply means AI might sometimes generate inaccurate outputs based on factual data and reasonably good prompts.**

Because of this, it's essential to approach AI-generated content discerningly, cross-referencing and validating when necessary. For instance, if you are not confident about a response generated by the AI, consider copying the response just generated and pasting it into a new chat session and asking the same AI to verify its accuracy. If the AI has web access—whether through plug-ins or incorporated natively—you can explicitly ask for citations in your prompts. Additionally, leveraging traditional sources, such as a quick Google search or a scholarly journal review, provides a layer of validation, ensuring the information generated is accurate and reliable.

Data Privacy and User Responsibility

In the digital age, data is often equated to currency. Its value is immense in terms of the insights it can offer. The potential risks associated with its misuse continue to be a concern even with newer generative AI applications. The intersection of AI and data privacy is a critical area of focus, and understanding the intricacies of data handling by AI platforms is paramount. Every piece of data fed into an AI system leaves a digital footprint. Whether it's project timelines, resource allocations, or financial data, the sensitivity of this information varies, and so do the potential repercussions of its exposure.

You must also understand the broader ecosystem in which AI platforms operate. Different AI tools have varied policies on data retention, sharing, and usage. For instance, while some platforms might use user interaction data to improve and refine their algorithms, others might prioritize user anonymity and not store interaction data.

NOTE Currently, ChatGPT uses your input prompts and data and outputs for future training unless the user turns off data sharing. However, Claude won't use your interactions for training its model.

To conclude, data privacy and user responsibility stand as twin pillars. Together, they ensure that the adoption of AI is effective, secure, and responsible.

Embarking on the Journey

The journey into the confluence of project management and AI is not a mere exploration of tools and techniques. It's a voyage into the future of how projects are conceptualized, executed, and delivered. As the chapters of this book unfold, they paint a picture of a world where traditional project management methodologies meld seamlessly with the capabilities of generative AI.

This journey requires both curiosity and caution: curiosity to explore the myriad ways AI can augment human capabilities, offering new insights and solutions, and caution to navigate the landscape carefully, always prioritizing ethical considerations.

One of the undeniable truths of the generative AI domain is its rapid evolution. The pace at which advancements are occurring is staggering, and new features and capabilities are constantly emerging. Recognizing this, we have provided readers with an accompanying online repository to access the most current information and tools. This repository will be periodically updated with information on new technology as it becomes available.

By the conclusion of this book, you will have gained a comprehensive understanding of various competencies and generative AI capabilities essential in the discipline of project management, such as project planning tools, task management tools, collaboration and communication tools, document management tools, risk management tools, budgeting

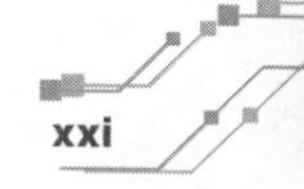

and cost management tools, performance monitoring tools, resource management tools, quality management tools, and project management software enhanced by AI.

Specifically, as you review the chapters, you will uncover the excellent capabilities of AI as illustrated in the following table for specific competencies.

COMPETENCY	CAPABILITY				
PM Tasks	Explaining Concepts	Communications	Creativity, Brainstorming, & Decision-Making	Rehearsing & Role-Playing	Summarizing and Reporting
Stakeholder Management	✔	✔	✔	✔	
Project Planning	✔	✔	✔		✔
Risk Assessment	✔	✔	✔		✔
Resource Allocation	✔	✔	✔		✔
Task Prioritization	✔	✔	✔		✔
Meeting Agenda and Minutes		✔	✔		✔
Leadership & Communication	✔	✔	✔	✔	✔
Monitoring and Control		✔			✔
Change Management	✔	✔	✔	✔	✔
Knowledge Management	✔	✔			✔

The best way to start is to dive in. You can learn the prompt engineering that is relevant to you as the need arises. We suggest you simply download the app and start right away. Give AI your scenario and ask it to address your problem or opportunity. Brace yourself for astonishment!

Supplemental Content

AI is a fast-changing field with new developments and features every day. To help readers keep up with the latest trends and tools, the authors have provided supplemental content where you can find the most up-to-date information.

1. Go to www.informit.com/AIforPM and either sign in to your account or create an account.
2. Click Submit to register your product.
3. In your account on the Registered Products page, you will see your registered products.
4. Click the Access Bonus Content link to go to the Downloads page for this product.
5. Click the link(s) to download the desired files.

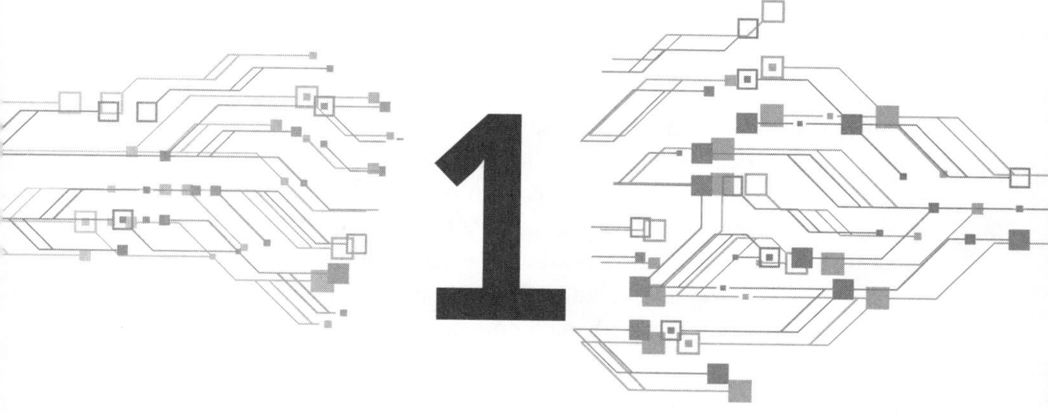

1 Dawn of a New Era

In the coming years, projects will be planned, executed, and managed like never before. Generative artificial intelligence (AI) excels at content creation, it will offer project managers advanced capabilities such as quickly building a project plan based on simulated scenarios, rescheduling plans easily, predicting risks, and providing rapid real-time solutions to issues.

Modern project management began to take root in the early 1960s, when industrial and business organizations began to value the benefits of organizing work around projects. Ambitious projects from NASA, such as sending human explorers to the moon, required effective project management. Globally across industries, organizations began to embrace and implement systematic project management tools and techniques to ensure success and efficiency. This period saw the establishment of standards and best practices, encapsulated by formal education and credentials in project management from dedicated project management organizations.

Global collaboration, professional development, and academic research led to the advent of technological tools and techniques, all of which collectively positioned project management as a distinct and necessary discipline crucial for the efficient execution and success of complex projects in the modern era.

Integrating AI into the realm of project management signals a transformative shift and the dawn of a new era for project management. AI tools will help optimize resource use, anticipate project bottlenecks, and automate mundane tasks. This enables project managers to concentrate on devising strategies, delivering value, and managing stakeholders and their concerns.

Not Robots

Many of us grew up in a world in which AI was the stuff of science fiction experienced on the movie screen. It was possibly a humanlike robot that was novel, fun, and fascinating, and that impressed us with its capabilities. These characters captivated our imagination, making us wonder about a world where machines might think and act like us someday. However, these robots never actually came to work and did not help us plan and organize projects or enhance our productivity.

More recently, interactive technology—such as Siri, Alexa, and related impressive voice or chat assistants—has intrigued us with the possibilities that AI technology could bring to the table. There is a certain awe in asking a question out loud and receiving a relevant answer from a nonhuman entity. These interactions felt novel and were very useful: What is the weather today? What is my commute time to work today? What is on my calendar today? Due to integration with data, these AI assistants could provide something real and practical.

But while these AI assistants introduced us to communication with devices and traditional chatbots, the experience was missing an in-depth, persistent, and continuous "humanlike" interaction with an entity we could recognize as a peer, if not a true expert.

Enter *generative* AI—and contextual language models based on an architecture that generates perfect humanlike text.

> **GENERATIVE ARTIFICIAL INTELLIGENCE TOOLS** These AI models use computer algorithms to create new text content in response to a prompt. Many types of generative AI products are emerging that can create various types of content, such as audio, programming code, images, and videos. For project management applications, this is what we mean by AI.

Designed to converse with humans in natural language, the outcome from AI products such as ChatGPT is coherent and engaging. ChatGPT is an expert on various subjects, capable of understanding and generating humanlike text based on the prompts it receives. It can answer questions, assist in various tasks, and maintain natural conversation across topics ranging from medicine to project management. Such tools are always available, very fast in response time, and appear eager to help.

Tools like ChatGPT represent an evolution in conversational AI. They are designed to understand context very well, assist with tasks, or engage in conversations as if you were genuinely talking with another human being. The experience of talking with such tools is distinct. It's as though you're chatting with a true expert who knows all.

A note of caution. Like the warning on cigarette boxes, every conversation with ChatGPT must start or end with a warning saying, "Hey, I am not a real human." Reid Hoffman's book, *Impromptu*, which uncovers his conversations in the latest version of ChatGPT, GPT-4, is worth quoting within this context:

> *I hope that you, as a reader, will keep the fact that GPT-4 is not a conscious being at the front of your own wondrously human mind. In my opinion, this awareness is key to understanding how, when, and where to use GPT-4 most productively and most responsibly.*[1]

1 Hoffman, R. (2023). *Impromptu: Amplifying Our Humanity Through AI.* Dallepedia LLC.

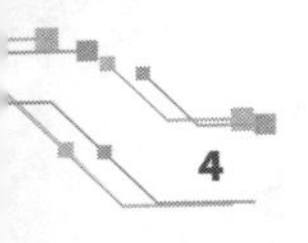

A quick note on comparison with traditional chatbots, which many of us might have experienced as customer service assistants. These often felt robotic and overly scripted. In many cases, such chatbots cannot answer our questions and therefore frustrate us. In contrast, generative AI tools are adaptable and possess vast knowledge and capabilities beyond what a conventional chatbot is designed to handle. This results in a more human-like conversation experience, reducing user frustration and offering more accurate and nuanced answers.

The impact of ChatGPT goes beyond just answering questions. It's also redefining the way we perceive AI. No longer are we limited to perceiving AI as a programmed entity—such as a robot programmed to walk, lift, or build. Instead, we're entering an age when AI can be a valuable tool—a coach, a companion, a mentor, a collaborator in various spheres of life and work and in disciplines such as project management. This modern AI has the potential to understand context, provide insights, and augment the human capabilities of project managers and enhance their productivity.

Let's demonstrate such capabilities using a semifictional case study in which we draw upon our real-world experience with project management and AI practitioners, altering some details and identifying information to illustrate AI's transformative impact on project management.

AI IN ACTION: SWIFT PROJECT TURNOVER

This example is based on our experience with an insurance company we'll call New Era Insurance, in Hartford, Connecticut. Project managers in this organization faced obstacles, and projects underperformed in specific key metrics involving cost and schedule. The senior leadership assumed that this was due to a lack of the ability to estimate projects accurately. However, a conversation with the project managers and other team members revealed that the root cause for the problem was poor change management practices and staff turnover. The latter point was a significant source of stress for project managers; we aim to demonstrate how AI can alleviate this issue and assist with recruitment of team members.

There is a high risk of wasted time and loss of productivity when a team member departs from the project team or exits the organization. Elevated turnover in projects can lead to reduced efficiency, heightened costs for recruitment and training, and a drop in the spirits of the existing team, potentially affecting the project's final results. Moreover, turnover puts more pressure on project managers as they grapple with integrating new members and maintaining project consistency. Can AI assist in addressing turnover by expediting the rehiring process? Let's consider an example.

ImageFlow/Shutterstock

At New Era Insurance, Ellen, a seasoned project manager, was in a quandary. Jen, a key team member, decided to leave midway through a pivotal project. The departure threatened to derail their timelines and disappoint the stakeholders. However, equipped with the new capabilities of their generative AI-driven HR system, Ellen was optimistic about handling the turnover and facilitating a quick return to normalcy.

When Jen submitted her resignation, Ellen logged into the company's enterprise AI platform, code-named "HR-GPT." She entered the job role and project specifics. Within minutes, HR-GPT pulled up a list of potential candidates from both internal databases and external job platforms. The AI system screened résumés, matching candidates with the required skills and expertise for the project.

Ellen received notifications of top candidates, complete with AI-generated interview schedules based on Ellen's availability, that of the candidates, and available conference rooms. HR-GPT even prepared a set of interview questions tailored to assess the candidates' skills in relation to the project's needs. This saved Ellen hours of preparation.

After the interviews, Ellen felt a bit torn between two candidates. She turned to HR-GPT again, which provided an analysis comparing the candidates based on their responses, past job performances, and fit with the company culture. This made Ellen's decision more straightforward.

Fastforward: once the new employee, Max, was selected, HR-GPT moved into onboarding mode. Max received a series of personalized tutorials about the project. These tutorials, generated by the AI, came from documentation, past team discussions, and actual code snippets to help him understand the project's current state. Such onboarding can take a significant amount of time away from the project team.

On Max's first day, he didn't wander around looking for supplies or access permissions. HR-GPT had already set up his workstation, granted him access to necessary files, and even scheduled a virtual meet-and-greet with the team.

Ellen watched with satisfaction as Max quickly integrated into the team, armed with insights and knowledge that typically took weeks to accumulate. The project not only stayed on track, but also thrived with fresh energy.

Many practitioners estimate that up to 90 percent of a project manager's time is dedicated to oral and technical communications, a significant portion of which might be not the best use of their time. Let's study this further, looking first at the time Ellen would take without HR-GPT and then with HR-GPT (**Table 1.1**). In this scenario, AI saved Ellen approximately 25 hours on recruiting, interviewing, decision-making, and onboarding tasks. Given that these tasks are primarily communication-related, we can infer that a significant proportion of a project manager's time is spent on communications management. You can see how generative AI can be a highly effective tool for recruiting new employees when a project faces unexpected staff changes.

TABLE 1.1 Time Saved with HR-GPT

ACTIVITY	TRADITIONAL	WITH HR-GPT
Job posting and candidate search	Researching and writing a job description, posting on multiple platforms, and manually reviewing the CVs Estimated time: 8 hours	One hour to input the role and project specifics. Time saved: 7 hours
Interview scheduling	Coordinating with candidates and rescheduling when conflicts arise Estimated time: 4 hours	One hour for automated scheduling Time saved: 3 hours

continues

ACTIVITY	TRADITIONAL	WITH HR-GPT
Interview preparation	Crafting tailored interview questions and reviewing candidate backgrounds in detail Estimated time: 6 hours	One hour for AI-generated questions tailored for the role Time saved: 5 hours
Candidate comparison and decision	Reviewing interview notes, deliberating, and possibly discussing with colleagues Estimated time: 4 hours	One hour to review AI's instantaneous comparison and analysis Time saved: 3 hours
Onboarding preparation	Preparing documentation, setting up a workstation, granting access to files, and organizing a meet-and-greet Estimated time: 8 hours	One hour (mostly automated) Time saved: 7 hours

AI and Brook's Law

Suppose we trust that AI can efficiently manage project turnovers and efficiently handle project transitions. In that case, we may be ready to question one of the most recognizable tenets of project management practice, Brooks Law.

BROOKS' LAW Adding manpower to a late software project makes it later.

Fred Brooks coined this in his 1975 classic book *The Mythical Man-Month.*[2] The validity of Brooks' Law is evident intuitively. The communication overhead increases when more new people are added to a project. More time is spent onboarding the new team members and coordinating and resetting communications between team members. Such changes will leave less time for the planned development tasks for the existing team members and will result in further slippage in the schedule.

2 Brooks, F. (1975). *The Mythical Man-Month*. Addison-Wesley.

Let's see how ChatGPT understands Brooks' Law.

Prompting is a straightforward process. You ask a question, widely called a *prompt*, and ChatGPT provides a response. If you have experience with ChatGPT, you may already be familiar with its AI chat interface (**Figure 1.1**).

What is Brook's Law?

Brooks's Law is a principle in software engineering which posits that "adding human resources to a late software project makes it later." It was introduced by Frederick P. Brooks in his 1975 book, "The Mythical Man-Month: Essays on Software Engineering."

The law emphasizes the often counterintuitive nature of managing software projects. One might assume that adding more people to a project that's running behind schedule would accelerate progress, but Brooks argues otherwise. Here are some reasons why:

1. **Ramp-up Time**: New personnel need to be trained and brought up to speed, requiring time from existing team members.
2. **Communication Overhead**: As the team size increases, the number of channels for communication among team members increases combinatorially. This leads to more time spent in meetings and in communications rather than actual development.
3. **Task Partitioning**: Some tasks are indivisible, meaning they can't be effectively broken down further for multiple people to work on simultaneously.
4. **Interpersonal Dynamics**: Larger teams can lead to more complex interpersonal dynamics, including potential conflicts, that can slow progress.

FIGURE 1.1 ChatGPT interface with a prompt and response

The first-time user might notice that ChatGPT functions like a web page with a search bar but with an uncluttered and clean look. So, what is so distinctive about ChatGPT?

To begin with, the response you see in Figure 1.1 is a unique, well-written answer to the prompt. You will possibly not find the same response anywhere else in printed literature or on a website. As such, ChatGPT does not natively offer citations or sources for the information presented in response to the prompt. Every time you prompt, generative AI tools produce a unique response tailored to that prompt. You're likely to encounter diverse output variations even when using the same prompt a second time.

It's important to note that this doesn't guarantee the accuracy of the response. Later in this chapter, we will delve into the fundamentals of generative AI and its potential to produce misleading, or "hallucinated," information.

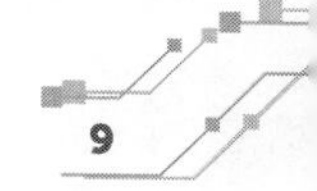

To continue, ChatGPT understands the context from one query to another; we do not see such behavior from search engines. To illustrate, let's ask ChatGPT a question based on our New Era Insurance case study.

For a fresh and nuanced viewpoint, let's gather some thoughts from ChatGPT and see what it says about that?

PRESENTATION OF PROMPTS AND RESPONSES The style of set-apart text you see below indicates (in this book) an exchange with an AI tool such as ChatGPT, with the prompt in quotes.

"ChatGPT, imagine AI is assisting a project manager in integrating a new team member to ensure timely project completion. There's a case to be made here that AI has the potential to diminish the traditional constraints outlined by Brooks' Law."

Your analysis of how generative AI can help mitigate the challenges Brooks' Law poses is insightful. Let's break down the reasons for that.

- **Automated Onboarding:** Using AI for onboarding is a promising idea. It ensures consistency and speed, as well as 24/7 availability. It can drastically reduce the time it takes for a newcomer to become productive, although it might not completely replace the nuances of human-to-human interaction during onboarding.
- **Enhanced Communication:** While AI can streamline communication, human nuances, emotions, and intent might not always be captured accurately by AI. However, for straightforward communications, AI can be very effective.
- **Task Allocation:** AI can use data to optimize task distribution, but it's important to note that not all tasks are quantifiable. Some tasks require creativity, human touch, or other intangibles that an AI might struggle to understand.
- **Predictive Analysis:** AI-driven insights can be valuable for project management, but they're only as good as the data they're based on. They should be used as one of many tools in a manager's decision-making arsenal.
- **Documentation and Knowledge Transfer:** While AI can help keep documentation updated and suggest relevant information, creating meaningful, in-depth documentation often requires human insight, especially in complex projects.
- **Routine Automation:** This is one of the most straightforward benefits of AI. Automating routine tasks can help maintain project momentum and ensure that human resources are allocated to more complex, value-added tasks.

Notice how fluid our conversation flows from confirming what we know about Brooks' Law to testing a hypothesis about its validity if AI is used. The response is friendly, helpful, and insightful. Several key factors contribute to this behavior. Unlike search engine responses, the advanced natural language processing of AI systems analyzes and understands human language and requests.

Additionally, large training datasets have exposed the AI product to diverse conversations and writing styles, which helped the AI to generate more humanlike responses. Finally, between the first and second prompts, we notice contextual awareness—ChatGPT considers earlier parts of the conversation when formulating responses rather than reacting to the second prompt in isolation.

AI tools can help in virtually all aspects of project management, from ideation and execution to project closing. It offers insights, generates content, and assists in project-related problem-solving.

Let's illustrate a few snippets of its ability, starting with the initiating phase.

"We need to implement an RSVP system so that we know how many employees will attend events planned by HR at New Era Insurance. What project ideas and features come to mind? Present a concise version of a possible project solution."

Here's a concise version of the project solution for the RSVP system:

- Web-based RSVP Application:
  a. Employees create profiles, view event listings, and RSVP.
  b. Event reminders and notifications are sent out automatically.
- Mobile App Integration:
  Develop a mobile-friendly version with push notifications.
- Calendar Integration:
  Allow syncing of RSVP events with personal calendars such as Google Calendar and Outlook.
- Feedback & Analytics:
  a. Post-event feedback for attendees.
  b. HR dashboard showing attendee numbers and event ratings.

- Waitlist System:

  For events with maximum capacity, create an automated waitlist.
- Security & Accessibility:

  Ensure data protection and make the system accessible for all employees.
- Communication Features:

  HR announcements related to events and a platform for employee queries.

This solution is honed from its vast training data. While the recommendations provide valuable insights for a project solution, the final decision requires human intuition, experience, and judgment.

Diverse Expertise

ChatGPT is versatile. The following query demonstrates its depth of knowledge in business analysis and tools and techniques, such as must-have, should-have, could-have, won't-have (MoSCoW), to prioritize features.

"A business analyst comes into the picture to help the project manager with the RSVP project. We also need to work with HR and IT to prioritize the features. We need to set up a meeting."

Here's a proposed approach to how the business analyst (BA) can collaborate with HR and IT, and use ChatGPT to prioritize the features for the RSVP system:

1. Requirement Gathering with HR:
    a. Objective: Understand the primary needs of HR for event management.
    b. Action: BA schedules a brainstorming session with the HR team to list all desired features. Using ChatGPT can help facilitate this by generating potential features based on industry standards.
2. Technical Feasibility with IT:
    a. Objective: Assess which features are technically feasible and what resources are required.
    b. Action: BA collaborates with the IT team to evaluate the proposed feature list. This will involve understanding the current IT infrastructure, any potential integration needs, and any constraints.

3. User Experience (UX) Consideration:
   a. Objective: Ensure the system is user-friendly and meets employee needs.
   b. Action: BA can use ChatGPT to generate user stories or simulate potential user interactions. This helps in understanding the employee perspective and prioritizing features that enhance UX.
4. Prioritization Session:
   a. Objective: Rank the features based on importance, feasibility, and impact.
   b. Action: BA facilitates a workshop involving representatives from HR and IT. Features are ranked using methods like the MoSCoW technique (must-have, should-have, could-have, won't-have) or by assigning numerical values. ChatGPT can assist by providing insights into the potential impact of each feature based on similar projects or industry standards.
5. Set Up a Meeting:
   a. Objective: Finalize the prioritized list and kickstart the development phase.
   b. Action: BA schedules a meeting with the project manager, HR, and IT leads. During this meeting, the prioritized feature list is presented and approved. Any adjustments can be made based on further inputs from the stakeholders.
6. Documentation:
   a. Objective: Ensure that all requirements and their priorities are well documented.
   b. Action: Post meeting, BA creates a detailed document outlining each feature, its priority, and any specific notes or instructions related to it. This document serves as the primary guide for the development and implementation phase.

"Using a table structure, display features using any prioritization technique, and prepare the project team for the prioritization session."

You can structure the prioritization session using the MoSCoW method. This method helps stakeholders focus on the most critical requirements.

Here's the table for the prioritization session:

FEATURE	DESCRIPTION	PRIORITY (MOSCOW)	STAKEHOLDER COMMENTS
Web-Based RSVP Application	Allows employees to view events and RSVP.	Must-Have	
Mobile App Integration	Mobile-friendly version with push notifications.	Should-Have	
Calendar Integration	Sync RSVP events with personal calendars.	Should-Have	
Feedback and Analytics	Post-event feedback and HR dashboard.	Must-Have	
Waitlist System	Automated waitlist for full events.	Could-Have	
Security and Accessibility	Data protection and accessibility for all employees.	Must-Have	
Communication Features	HR announcements and a platform for employee queries.	Should-Have	

Procedure for Prioritization Session:

1. Introduce the MoSCoW Method: Before diving into the table, give a brief explanation of the MoSCoW method, ensuring all team members understand each category.
2. Present the Feature and Description: The BA will walk through each feature and its description.
3. Stakeholder Voting: After each feature is discussed, stakeholders will vote on its priority. They can either agree with the initial suggestion or provide an alternative.

4. Stakeholder Comments: This column allows stakeholders to provide reasoning for their votes or add additional thoughts.
5. Revisiting and Finalizing: After all features have been discussed and voted on, revisit any contentious points or features with mixed votes. Discuss and finalize the priority.
6. Documentation: Post-session, the BA should document and distribute the finalized priorities among the project team for reference.

This prompt illustrates how generative AI can help prioritize and create a tutorial for the project team.

"The project scope was identified successfully. We need to manage stakeholders well. Can you identify risks with any specific stakeholders within the RSVP project? One risk we know for sure is that there is a difference of opinion about the value of using AI to generate code for the project.

Select risks where the probability is high, and impact is high. Present the information in a tabular format."

RISK	DESCRIPTION	POTENTIAL OUTCOME
Diverging Opinions on AI Integration	Stakeholders differ on AI code generation.	Developmental delays, increased costs, underutilized AI.
Resistance to Change from End Users	Employees resist the new RSVP system due to its complexity or unfamiliarity.	Reduced system effectiveness, decreased event participation.
IT Department's Technical Limitations	IT concerns over integrating AI due to inexperience or perceived complications.	Technical glitches, project delays, incomplete system.
HR's Functional Expectations	HR's specific needs might conflict with IT or other department visions.	System misalignment with primary user needs, reduced utility.
Data Security and Privacy Concerns	Worries about AI system's handling and processing of employee data.	Privacy breaches, noncompliance, potential legal issues.

The next step for the project manager is to request a risk response strategy for each of the identified risks. Prompts for this can be quickly executed similarly as demonstrated. We do not cover this aspect here. However, this topic is addressed in Chapter 8, "The Role of AI in Risk Management." Now let's look to see how AI can assist a project manager with utilizing soft skills.

Projects often fail if there is a communication breakdown, especially within the context of poor interpersonal skills with the project team members or stakeholders. Developing interpersonal skills by studying responses from AI is a valuable opportunity.

Let's describe an example and see how ChatGPT provides guidance and tips to a developing scenario that might result in a valuable employee suddenly quitting.

"Here is a scenario that played out at work today. Tell me if I did something wrong as a project manager:

Me: I'm sorry, but you have to fly to Atlanta. The customer wants an in-person meeting.

Team Member: I'm afraid of flying. I haven't taken a plane ride since the pandemic.

Me: You want me to tell the customer my business analyst is afraid to fly?"

In this scenario, there are a few aspects that could have been handled differently:

1. **Empathy and Understanding:** When your team member mentioned their fear of flying, it's essential to respond with empathy and understanding. Expressing sympathy for their concerns would have been a more appropriate initial reaction. You could have said something like, "I understand that flying can be a source of anxiety, especially after the pandemic. Let's discuss this further and see if we can find a solution that makes you comfortable."
2. **Open Communication:** Rather than immediately suggesting canceling the project, engaging in an open and constructive conversation would have been better. You could have asked your team member about their concerns and explored potential solutions or alternatives.
3. **Maintain Professionalism:** Telling the customer that your team member is afraid to fly may not be the most professional approach. Protecting your team member's privacy and addressing their concerns internally is essential.

A more effective response might have been:

"I'm sorry to hear about your fear of flying, especially given the current circumstances. I understand the customer prefers an in-person meeting, and we want to honor that request. Let's work together to find a solution that makes you comfortable with the travel. Are there any specific concerns you have about flying that we can address? Perhaps we can explore options like scheduling a direct flight, providing additional support, or arranging for someone to accompany you. Your well-being is important to us, and we'll do our best to make this trip as stress-free as possible."

This response is genuinely empathetic. Not only is ChatGPT possessing technical competencies, but also soft or "power skills." The outcome will likely be positive, and trust and respect for the project manager is bound to grow after such a conversation as opposed to what transpired earlier in the scenario.

This ability of ChatGPT is not unique to project management. Peter Lee, in *The AI Revolution in Medicine*, makes a similar note after documenting his first contact with AI:

> *Never, amid all my high expectations for how artificial intelligence could improve medical care, did I imagine that among its power would be teaching human beings to be more empathetic.*[3]

Artificial Intelligence

In this section, we define artificial intelligence (AI) and related key terms and introduce its significance within the context of Generative AI. This introduction, even though it is technical, provides essential context and clarifies the terminology relevant to our discussion of AI in project management.

History of AI

AI, as a discipline, dates to the Dartmouth Summer Research Project on Artificial Intelligence, organized by John McCarthy in 1956. McCarthy is credited with coining the term "artificial intelligence" to describe how machines could be made to simulate aspects of human intelligence. Nevertheless, the underlying ideas can be traced back to

3 Goldberg, C, Kohane, I, and Lee, P. (2023). *The AI Revolution in Medicine: GPT-4 and Beyond*. Pearson Education.

Bayesian probability and even Aristotelian logical reasoning. Arguably, the most influential of AI's founders was Alan Turing, whose 1950 essay "Computing Machinery and Intelligence" explores how intelligence might be tested and how machines might automatically learn.

Subsequent work, such as Marvin Minsky's 1960 paper "Steps Toward Artificial Intelligence," laid the mathematical foundation for AI, including gradient-based optimization. Another seminal contribution was Frank Rosenblatt's implementation in 1958 of the perceptron, an algorithm for learning a binary classifier and now known as the simplest type of neural network. But following criticism—by Minsky, among others—of the ability of Rosenblatt's connectionism to solve more complicated problems and limitations in computing power, data, and funding, AI experienced its first "winter" in the 1970s.

Connectionism would be revived, however, in the 1980s due to advancements in neural network training devised by Geoffrey Hinton and David Rumelhart, among others. Although a second AI "winter" would occur in the 1990s, the groundwork had been laid for deep learning, in which multiple layers between input and output allow for learning more complex relationships. Today, AI often refers to deep learning as the ability to collect and store vast amounts of data and train models using advanced processors, making it feasible to build neural networks with millions of trainable parameters capable of humanlike speech and vision.

See **Table 1.2**, which provides a historical overview with key milestones for AI.

TABLE 1.2 Key milestones in the history of AI

Birth of AI (1956)	The term "artificial intelligence" was coined, and the field was officially born.
Early AI Programs and Initial Optimism (1956–1974)	AI research flourished in the late 1950s and throughout the '60s, with machines playing checkers and proving mathematical theorems.
Robotics and Vision (1956s–present)	The first industrial robot was used for manufacturing in 1956. Both robotics and computer vision continue to play essential roles in the ongoing evolution of AI.

continues

Natural Language Processing (NLP) (1960s–present)	ELIZA—An early natural language processing computer program. Subsequent rise of NLP is truly transformative due to machine learning and deep learning models leading to LLMs.
Speech (1962–present)	The earliest speech recognition systems, such as IBM's Shoebox. Due to multimodal AI models, the integration with NLP is more pronounced today.
Expert Systems (1980–1987)	AI makes a comeback with the development of expert systems. These programs answer questions or solve problems about a specific domain of knowledge.
Machine Learning (1993–present)	Machine learning is a type of AI that allows computers to learn without being explicitly programmed.
Development of Generative Models (2014–present)	Generative adversarial networks (GANs) were developed. Involves two neural networks—a generator, which creates new data instances, and a discriminator, which tries to distinguish between real and fake data.
Development of Transformers and Attention Mechanisms (2017–present)	The "Attention Is All You Need" paper presents the Transformer model, enhancing language understanding. By focusing on specific input parts for output, it excels in numerous NLP tasks.[4]
Large Language Models (LLMs) (2018–present)	OpenAI introduces GPT (Generative Pretrained Transformer), a large-scale, unsupervised, language prediction model. This leads to GPT-2, GPT-3, and GPT-4, each progressively larger and more capable.

4 Vaswani, A., Shazeer, N., Parmar, N., Uszkoreit, J., Jones, L., Gomez, A. N., Kaiser, L., & Polosukhin, I. (2017). "Attention Is All You Need," *Advances in Neural Information Processing Systems* 30.

AI Applications

We will briefly introduce core terminology and AI concepts (**Figure 1.2**) before turning to ChatGPT (or other LLMs), the application most relevant to project management.

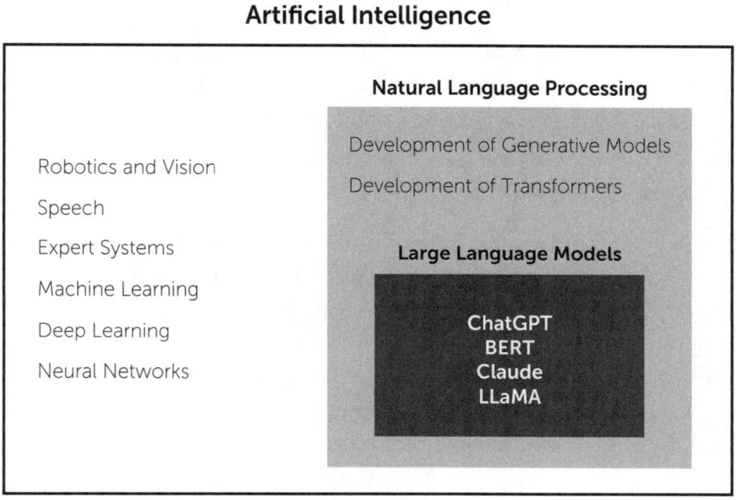

Artificial Intelligence

Robotics and Vision
Speech
Expert Systems
Machine Learning
Deep Learning
Neural Networks

Natural Language Processing

Development of Generative Models
Development of Transformers

Large Language Models

ChatGPT
BERT
Claude
LLaMA

FIGURE 1.2 AI technologies

Expert Systems

Expert systems are computer programs designed to mimic the decision-making abilities of human experts by leveraging predefined rules and knowledge bases. They provide solutions to specific problems within certain domains—the conclusion and explanations for the decision and reasoning behind them are readily traced to a knowledgebase. Expert systems are like experienced advisers that can provide specialized guidance on specific topics. Just as a financial adviser leverages their knowledge of markets and investing, expert systems apply predefined rules to reach conclusions or solutions within a particular domain. The reasoning behind the expert system's recommendations can be traced back to its knowledgebase, much like following an adviser's logic back to their financial expertise.[5]

5 Kanabar, V. (1993). "Integrating Project Planning Tools into the CASE Architecture." In T. J. Bergin (Ed.), *Computer-Aided Software Engineering*. Idea Group Inc.

One of this book's authors, Vijay Kanabar, designed an AI application called Project Factors Expert System (PFES) to perform the expert task of assessing a project's complexity for estimating its cost.

The knowledgebase of the AI program was modeled after the wisdom of expert cost estimators with practical experience and knowledge of critical factors that impact cost estimates.

The legacy of expert systems regarding knowledge representation, interpretability, and the integration of domain knowledge continues to inform and influence the development and applications of generative AI.

Machine Learning

Machine learning (ML), a core AI component, empowers computers to learn from and make decisions based on data without being explicitly programmed. It involves algorithms that iteratively learn from data, enabling models to improve their performance over time. Traditionally, software was programmed with instructions to perform a task. However, with ML, systems can analyze vast amounts of data, identify patterns, and make predictions or decisions autonomously. ML algorithms can analyze data to find patterns and make predictions without being explicitly programmed for each scenario. For instance, consider email filtering. Instead of manually defining rules to classify emails as spam or not, an ML system can be trained on a dataset of emails, learning to distinguish spam from legitimate messages based on patterns.[6] As it processes more emails, its accuracy improves—similar to a student becoming more skilled as they practice more exam questions.

Deep Learning

Deep learning, a subset of machine learning, has gained immense popularity due to its effectiveness with capabilities such as image recognition, natural language processing, and speech recognition.[7] It utilizes neural networks with multiple layers called "deep" networks. It wasn't until the 2000s, when computational power, abundant data, and algorithmic improvements were available, that deep learning became practically

6 Alurkar, A. A., Ranade, S. B., Joshi, S. V., Ranade, S. S., Sonewar, P. A., Mahalle, P. N., & Deshpande, A. V. (2017). "A Proposed Data Science Approach for Email Spam Classification Using Machine Learning Techniques," 2017 Internet of Things Business Models, Users, and Networks, 1–5.

7 Raaijmakers, S. (2022). *Deep Learning for Natural Language Processing*. Manning.

viable. This innovation has revolutionized areas like image and speech recognition. To illustrate, deep learning is like a child learning to recognize animals. Initially, the child learns to recognize basic features like colors, shapes, and textures. This is like the low-level layers in a neural network detecting simple attributes in images. As they grow older, the child learns to combine these basic features into recognizable parts like legs, tails, ears, and so forth.

Given sufficient examples and practice, deep neural networks can master complex tasks such as image and speech recognition, similar to the way children develop skills like animal identification through everyday experience.

Neural Networks

Neural networks, a name inspired by the human brain's architecture, are foundational to deep learning and artificial intelligence. A numerical parameter called weight notes the connection strength between two neurons. A neural network consists of layers of *neurons*, which you can think of as little processing units. Each of these neurons in the network takes in some information, does a little computation, and then passes on the results. The magic of neural networks lies in their ability to adjust these weights based on the data they're trained on, optimizing their performance. A key innovation with neural networks is an algorithm, which trains neural networks by adjusting weights based on the output. Let's explain this with an example:

- Imagine you're trying to learn to recognize rabbits. Rabbits have four legs, fur, big ears, and a small stubby tail. The house rabbits are disciplined. They come in different sizes and colors.
- A neural network is like the brain and works similarly when trying to understand and remember all these hints to recognize a rabbit.
- When you're learning to recognize rabbits, neurons' first layers might focus on basic features like identifying colors or shapes. The successive layers combine those basic features to identify parts like ears, legs, fur, or a tail. Then, further layers combine those parts to recognize a whole rabbit.
- The final layer that recognizes the whole rabbit from the input is called the *output layer.*

The learning part happens as the network adjusts itself based on the experience it gains. Suppose it wrongly identified the rabbit as a cat. Upon correction, the network would slightly tweak the weights of certain features like ear shape, size, and length. Over time, and with enough examples, the network improves and will recognize rabbits reliably.

Natural Language Processing

Natural language processing (NLP) is a field of artificial intelligence that focuses on how computers can understand, interpret, and respond to human language in a valuable way. Between humans, this is simple and noncomplicated. Even babies seem to quickly learn and understand a basic version of our language. By the time we are adults, we have experienced a lifetime of communication. NLP is a challenge when it comes to AI. It needs to integrate computational linguistics, computer science, and cognitive psychology to analyze the complexities of human language.

To help put this into perspective, natural language processing is like a foreign exchange student immersed in a new culture and language. At first, they struggle to follow conversations and understand idioms. But with time and exposure, they grasp the nuances of the language. Similarly, NLP algorithms must make sense of the complexity and context of human communication. Using statistical and linguistic techniques, NLP allows machines to parse sentences, determine meaning, and generate valuable responses—akin to a student developing fluency in a new language. Just like learning a language comes naturally to humans, NLP aims to impart machines with similar communication abilities.

NLP is increasingly integrated into various applications, from virtual assistants to sentiment analysis tools, revolutionizing how we interact with technology. For example, Siri and Alexa use NLP to understand voice commands and answer questions. Finally, the advancements in NLP enable the recent successes in generative AI capabilities that we notice in tools like ChatGPT.

Transformers

Transformers are a type of neural network architecture used in NLP and AI systems like ChatGPT. Once you train a transformer using large amounts of data, it can create completely new data by improvising. Consider a chef preparing a new soup. They taste the broth and realize it needs more salt. So they add some, taste again, and adjust the seasoning further. This iterative process allows the chef to dynamically focus their attention based on the soup's evolving needs. Google discovered the transformer neural network architecture in 2017.

Technically, it gauges the relevance of words in predicting subsequent ones, enhancing language understanding and generation. Since 2017, transformers and their attention mechanisms have driven AI advancements, including translation, chatbots, and writing aids.

Generative Pretrained Transformer

Generative pretrained transformer (GPT), developed by OpenAI, is an AI model designed for NLP tasks. It operates on the transformer architecture, which excels at handling sequential data, making it ideal for text generation. GPT is "pretrained" on vast amounts of text, enabling it to grasp context, semantics, and intricate language patterns.

- "Generative" implies producing coherent and contextually relevant text based on given prompts. Drawing an art class analogy, generative implies GPT's ability to craft new text or images like students creating unique art.
- "Pretrained" indicates its extensive prior learning. Unlike traditional models that require task-specific training such as playing chess, GPT can be fine-tuned for various applications, from text completion to question-answering.
- "Transformer," as indicated earlier, is the ability to simultaneously grasp various concurrent dimensions and respond aptly.

Foundation Model

A foundation model refers to a large-scale ML model that is trained on vast amounts of data and can be fine-tuned for specific applications. OpenAI, for instance, used the term *foundation model* to describe models like GPT-3 and GPT-4. These models, once pretrained, serve as a foundational base and can be adapted for various tasks with smaller amounts of specialized data. The idea is to leverage the general capabilities of the foundation model and tailor it to specific needs.

Technically, newer GPT versions possess more neural network parameters, enhancing their learning capacity. This progression has led to advanced applications in writing and creativity.

For instance, GPT-3 has 175 billion parameters, and the more powerful GPT-4 has 1.76 trillion.[8] We consider ChatGPT in detail as an one example of a popular generative AI tool that's useful to project managers.

ChatGPT

ChatGPT is a popular large language model developed by OpenAI, an AI research and deployment company. As you just learned, GPT stands for generative pretrained transformer. It is a contextual language model based on transformer architecture to generate humanlike text. Designed to converse with humans in natural language, the outcome is coherent, informing, and engaging.

ChatGPT is only one example of generative AI technology. In this chapter, we also introduce you to Claude and Bard. Other AI products create content other than language responses, such as audio, code, images, and videos.

TECHNICAL GUIDE **See the Technical Guide at the end of this chapter to understand how to use ChatGPT and related AI tools.**

How It Works

Here's a brief overview of the architecture of ChatGPT and how it works:

1. **Architecture:** ChatGPT is based on the transformer architecture, which we introduced earlier.
2. **Pretraining:** The model undergoes a pretraining phase in which it is exposed to vast amounts of text from the Internet.
3. **Fine-tuning:** After pretraining, the model is fine-tuned on narrower datasets, often generated with the help of human reviewers.
4. **Safety and Scaling:** OpenAI has made efforts to ensure that ChatGPT is safe to use and minimizes biases. OpenAI also actively seeks feedback from users to improve and address any shortcomings.

8 Caelen, O., and Blete, M. A. (2023). *Developing Apps with GPT-4 and ChatGPT*. O'Reilly Media.

During the initial training phase, the model learns by predicting the next word in a sentence, aiding in understanding grammar and world facts. However, it can also absorb biases from the training data. To address this and enhance the model's output, OpenAI uses human reviewers. Following OpenAI's guidelines, these reviewers evaluate model responses. Their continual feedback refines and improves the model over time.

Five Steps

Let's understand how ChatGPT works when it answers the simple prompt, "Define the role of a project manager." Five steps are completed before you see the response:

1. **Tokenization:** This is the process of converting a sequence of characters (like a sentence or paragraph) into a sequence of tokens, or simply word chunks. The goal is to break down text into pieces that are meaningful for the model to process. The input, "Define the role of a project manager," is split into tokens like ["Define," "the," "role," "of, " "a," "project," "manager"]. Tokens are mapped to integer IDs (such as 27) which are then mapped to numerical vectors. These vectors become the model's initial word representations. See **Table 1.3** for an example.

TABLE 1.3 An example of tokenization

TOKEN	TOKENIZED FORM	NUMERICAL VECTOR
Define	"Define"	[0.56, −1.22, 0.9 ...]
the	"the"	[−0.12, 1.47, −0.56, ...]
role	"role"	[1.23, 0.03, −0.77, ...]
of	"of"	[−1.10, 0.82, 0.45, ...]
a	"a"	[0.67, −1.15, 0.50, ...]
project	"project"	[0.90, 0.11, −0.36, ...]
manager	"manager"	[−0.45, 0.78, 1.12, ...]

2. **Contextual Understanding:** The vectors sequentially pass through the model's neural layers. For instance, seeing the token "Define" might make the model anticipate a subsequent description.

3. **Token Prediction:** Post-processing, the model predicts the next token using the transformed vectors. For example, after "Define", it might favor "a" or "the" due to frequent training patterns.
4. **Sequence Building:** After predicting "The", the model might foresee the tokens "role of a project manager is". Likely, the next tokens could be "to", then "lead". Predicted tokens are looped back into the model, influencing further predictions—for example, "Prompt response: The role of a project manager is to lead."
5. **Completion:** The model continues until an end-of-sentence token emerges or after generating a predetermined number of tokens. It could conclude with "is responsible for planning, executing, and finalizing projects to ensure timely and on-budget completion." For example, "Prompt response: The role of a project manager is to lead a team."

Attention Mechanisms and Constraints

ChatGPT uses *attention mechanisms* to weigh the influence of different words when predicting the next word in a sentence. The main idea behind the attention mechanism is that it allows the model to focus on the most relevant parts of the input when producing an output. This selective focus allows the model to consider the entire context of a sentence or passage of text, leading to much more accurate conversation.

Attention mechanisms can answer this tricky question correctly: "Is the king a man and the queen a woman?" The attention mechanisms of the language model result in word embeddings and representations to suggest that (a) in the context of monarchy, a "king" is a title given to a male monarch, whereas "queen" is a title given to a female monarch—for instance, Queen Elizabeth, the UK's longest-serving monarch; (b) but this might not be entirely accurate. Given the recent changes in monarchy, the language model must clarify that the terms can be used in various contexts with different meanings. For instance, a "queen" can also refer to the wife of a king, in addition to playing the role of a female sovereign. In the context of language models, the word "king" being associated with "man" and "queen" with "woman" is based on their usage patterns found in the data used for training.

AI models such as ChatGPT contain a *context window*, which refers to the amount of information you can input into the model at one time. Due to computational constraints, there's a maximum number of tokens a model can handle in a single input. This limitation means that extremely long texts might need to be truncated or split to fit within ChatGPT's context window. For example, if you need an AI model to summarize a 10-page project report, this might be too large for ChatGPT to process.

Language models like ChatGPT are not database-driven in the conventional sense. While they're designed to generate coherent and relevant text, they can sometimes "hallucinate" or predict the wrong words. There are various reasons for these inaccuracies. One is that the data they were trained on might contain conflicting information. Additionally, if a specific topic wasn't adequately represented or included during training, the model might provide incorrect or uninformed responses.

Prompt Engineering

Prompt engineering is an important skill you'll need to develop to make the most of AI tools as a project manager. You'll learn to craft specific instructions or prompts to guide AI language models to produce responses that fit your needs. It's a technique to optimize the performance of models like ChatGPT by providing more precise context or specifying the expected answer format. Effective prompt engineering can enhance the accuracy and relevance of a model's responses, making it a crucial step in harnessing the full potential of LLMs for specific tasks or applications.

Here's some terminology associated with prompt engineering:

- **Zero-Shot Prompting:** This approach involves giving the model a task it hasn't seen during training and expecting it to perform adequately.
- **Few-Shot Prompting:** The model has a few examples (or "shots") to guide its response. It's akin to teaching someone by showing them a few instances of a task and then asking them to replicate or extend that knowledge.
- **Chain-of-thought:** This method uses several prompts to lead the model through a series of related thoughts or steps to arrive at a desired answer, like guiding someone step-by-step through a thought process. An evolved version of this method involves more intricate and complex prompting strategies through multiple layers of reasoning to derive a sophisticated output.

A template can be used to structure a prompt. Here's a breakdown of the template elements:

1. **Act as or Persona:** This approach is a way to guide the AI model's behavior and set the tone they should assume or context for the interaction. The idea is to get the model to generate responses as if it were embodying the role or persona specified.
2. **Objective:** The outcome or goal of the prompt.
3. **Context:** Provides background or situational information to guide the model's response.
4. **Constraints:** These are specific limitations or guidelines to shape the output.
5. **Instructions:** Clearly define what you want. Examples include "Summarize the following text" or "Translate the sentence into French."

A prompt based on the template might look like this:

"Act as a project manager. Describe a day in the life of a project manager. The individual works in the construction sector and uses traditional, not agile, methodology. Describe the results in two paragraphs using bullet format."

ATTRIBUTE	PROMPT COMPONENT
Act as or Persona	Project manager
Objective	Describe a day in the life of a project manager
Context	Works in the construction sector
Constraints	Uses traditional, not agile, methodology
Instructions	Describe the results in two paragraphs using bullet format

Here are the different examples of prompts, all structured using this template as a structure.

Act as or Persona: Project manager
Objective: Explain the challenges faced by a project manager.
Context: Oversees projects in the health-care sector.
Constraints: Must comply with strict regulatory guidelines.

Act as or Persona: Project manager
Objective: Detail the communication strategies a project manager uses with stakeholders.
Context: Works in a multinational corporation.
Constraints: Communicates across different time zones and cultures.

Act as or Persona: Project manager
Objective: Describe how a project manager handles team conflicts.
Context: Leads a diverse team in the finance sector.
Constraints: Must maintain project deadlines while resolving disputes.

Our output quality is excellent if we document the context and constraints clearly.

The following is a sample of prompts that you can ask generative AI tools:

- **Define Clear Objectives:** How can you ensure all stakeholders and team members understand and align with the project's goals?
- **Scope Management:** How do you plan to define and control the project scope to prevent scope creep?
- **Risk Management**: What strategies will you implement to identify, assess, and mitigate potential project risks?
- **Resource Allocation:** Describe your approach to allocate and monitor human and material resources effectively.
- **Regular Status Reporting:** How do you plan to provide consistent status updates to stakeholders and the project team?
- **Budget Control:** Describe your approach to monitoring project costs and ensuring they remain within the approved budget.
- **Quality Assurance:** What benchmarks and metrics will you establish for quality, and how will you ensure they are met or exceeded?
- **Team Engagement and Motivation:** How do you plan to keep the project team engaged, motivated, and recognized for their performance?
- **Conflict Resolution:** What steps will you take to address and resolve conflicts constructively?

In each case, the output from the prompt will be very high-level, and you will need to prompt further to uncover valuable project management knowledge.

You'll see examples of well-crafted prompts throughout this book, as well as tips for how to improve your prompts to fit your needs. Specifically, the rest of the book will introduce prompts related to these topics:

- Chapter 2, "Stakeholders and Generative AI," will provide prompts to assist you with critical stakeholder identification and engagement, ensuring key stakeholders are involved throughout the project.

- Chapter 3, "Building and Managing Teams Using AI," will offer prompts focused on building effective teams and demonstrating strong leadership skills, critical components of successful project delivery.
- Chapter 4, "Choosing a Development Approach with AI," will present prompts to assist you in determining the right development approach for your project, whether predictive, adaptive, or a hybrid model, setting the stage for project success.
- Chapter 5, "AI-Assisted Planning for Predictive Projects," will supply prompts to guide you through initiation and planning activities for predictive projects, enabling thorough early planning.
- Chapter 6, "Adaptive Projects and AI," will furnish prompts specifically targeted for managing adaptive projects that require greater flexibility and responsiveness to change.
- Chapter 7, "Monitoring Project Work Performance with AI," will deliver prompts on monitoring project work performance, including execution, controlling, and managing quality, providing oversight to keep projects on track.
- Chapter 8, "The Role of AI in Risk Management," will provide prompts addressing risk management head on, arming you with tools to identify and mitigate risks.
- Chapter 9, "Finalizing Projects with AI," will offer prompts to steer you through verifying, validating, transitioning, and closing projects, bringing them to successful completion.

Ethical Considerations and Professional Responsibility

Ethical considerations and professional responsibility in artificial intelligence are paramount, given AI's profound impact on society. Here's a list of some key considerations:

- **Transparency:** AI systems, especially decision-influencing ones, should be clear about how they function to prevent biases and unfounded conclusions.
- **Data Privacy:** AI's reliance on vast datasets necessitates strict adherence to data protection and informed consent.
- **Bias Mitigation:** Addressing and reducing biases in AI models is essential for ensuring fairness in their outputs.

- **Accountability:** AI systems must be reliable. When mistakes occur, clear responsibility lines—whether it's the tool provider, developers, users, or deploying organizations—should be established.
- **Environmental Considerations:** The considerable resources for training AI models emphasize the need to assess their environmental footprint.
- **Regulatory Oversight:** As AI integrates into various sectors, robust regulatory frameworks are imperative for its ethical use.
- **Human Augmentation:** The line between AI augmenting versus replacing human roles, especially in sensitive sectors, warrants thoughtful evaluation.
- **Hallucinations and Data Accuracy:** AI models, especially ones like ChatGPT, might produce inaccuracies, or "hallucinations," due to limited or conflicting training data. You must be aware of this potential risk and always fact-check information provided by AI.
- **Data Ownership and Training Implications:** You should learn the data sharing policies of your AI providers. Some models might use your proprietary data for further training, while others might not.

Key Points to Remember

Throughout this chapter, we've explored how the emergence of artificial intelligence marks a transformative moment in the realm of project management. As a project manager, you must acknowledge and adapt to this evolving landscape.

- AI tools are rapidly evolving to augment key project management competencies such as planning, organizing, and controlling projects.
- AI has a rich history; the culmination of this led to the current state of the art in natural language processing (NLP).
- NLP allows AI systems such as ChatGTP, Bard, and Claude.ai to converse naturally by understanding the context of conversation very well.
- Generative AI like ChatGPT produces remarkably humanlike content but still has limitations around accuracy.
- Evaluate risks thoughtfully before integrating AI into your organization.
- AI tools in the hands of project managers as decision-makers will outperform those who do not plan to leverage such tools.
- You must be cautious about data input, fact-check AI outputs, and understand the implications of sharing data with AI systems, especially regarding data use for further model training.

Technical Guide

1.1 Using ChatGPT

Instructions

1. Go to **https://chat.openai.com** to access the ChatGPT interface. You'll need to create a free OpenAI account if you don't have one.
2. The chat interface is simple, with a text prompt box at the bottom. Start by typing or speaking your question, conversation topic, or anything you want the AI to respond to (**Figure 1.3**).

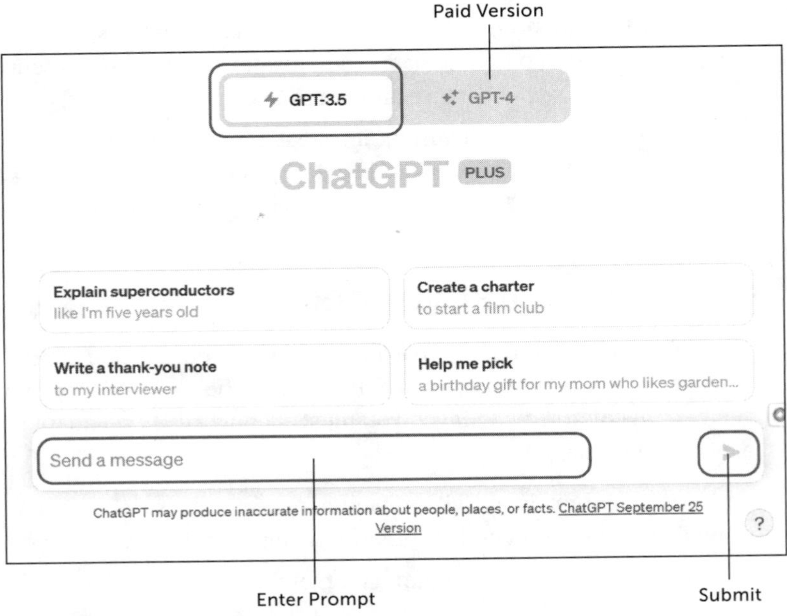

FIGURE 1.3 ChatGPT Plus interface

3. Press **Enter** or click **Submit** to send your prompt. ChatGPT will process the request and generate a response.

Tips and considerations:

- Chat naturally as you would with a person. Ask questions, share information, and ask for explanations or clarification.
- You can change subjects or move the conversation in different directions at any time. The bot will follow along.
- Rephrase your original prompt for clarity if the response is unclear or inaccurate. You can also ask ChatGPT to explain or expand on its answers.

- Please don't treat it as a search engine by asking only one-off, simple questions. Have an actual back-and-forth discussion to get the most value.
- Chat histories and responses are stored in the cloud and by default could be used for ChatGPT's future training. However, you can change the settings so that the response is deleted.
- There are different functionalities, features, and limitations depending on whether you use the free or the paid version of ChatGPT.
- A smartphone version is available for both iOS and Android.
- GPT Plus allows you to browse *current* data, using Bing.

1.2 Using Bard

Starting a Chat

1. Navigate to **bard.google.com**. This will open a chat interface (**Figure 1.4**).
2. Type a prompt in the chat box at the bottom. You can ask questions, request information, or start a conversation.
3. Click **Send** or press **Enter** to submit your request to Bard.

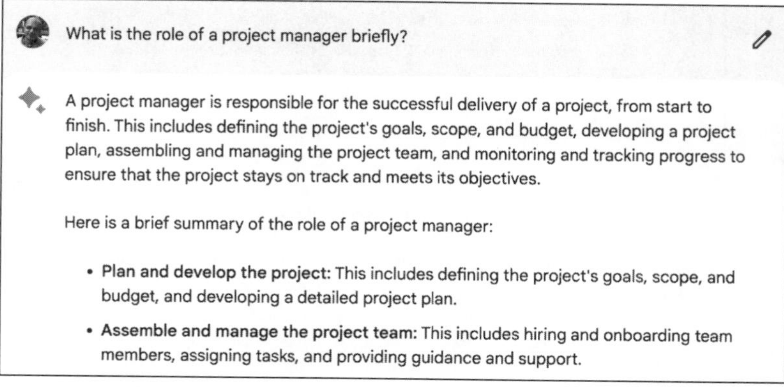

What is the role of a project manager briefly?
A project manager is responsible for the successful delivery of a project, from start to finish. This includes defining the project's goals, scope, and budget, developing a project plan, assembling and managing the project team, and monitoring and tracking progress to ensure that the project stays on track and meets its objectives.
Here is a brief summary of the role of a project manager:
• Plan and develop the project: This includes defining the project's goals, scope, and budget, and developing a detailed project plan.
• Assemble and manage the project team: This includes hiring and onboarding team members, assigning tasks, and providing guidance and support.

FIGURE 1.4 Bard interface

Conversing with Bard

1. Chat naturally in a conversational way, as you would with a person.
2. Bard will process your request and generate response text in its chat bubbles.
3. Follow up with clarifying questions if its response is unclear or inaccurate.
4. Change topics or shift the conversation by simply starting a new line of discussion.

1.3 Using Claude.ai

Access at the Claude.ai site might not remain consistent. Once you gain access, the rest of the steps guide you to entering your first prompt:

1. Go to **www.claude.ai** in your web browser.
2. Enter your email address and select **Continue with email**.
3. You will be sent a Login code to your specified email address. Find and copy the **login code**.
4. Paste or enter the login code. Click on **Continue with login code**. You will be taken to the Claude chat interface.
5. Type your prompt in the chat box at the bottom. For example: "What is the role of a project manager?"
6. Press **Enter** or click the **Send** icon to submit your prompt. You will see output such as that shown in **Figure 1.5**.

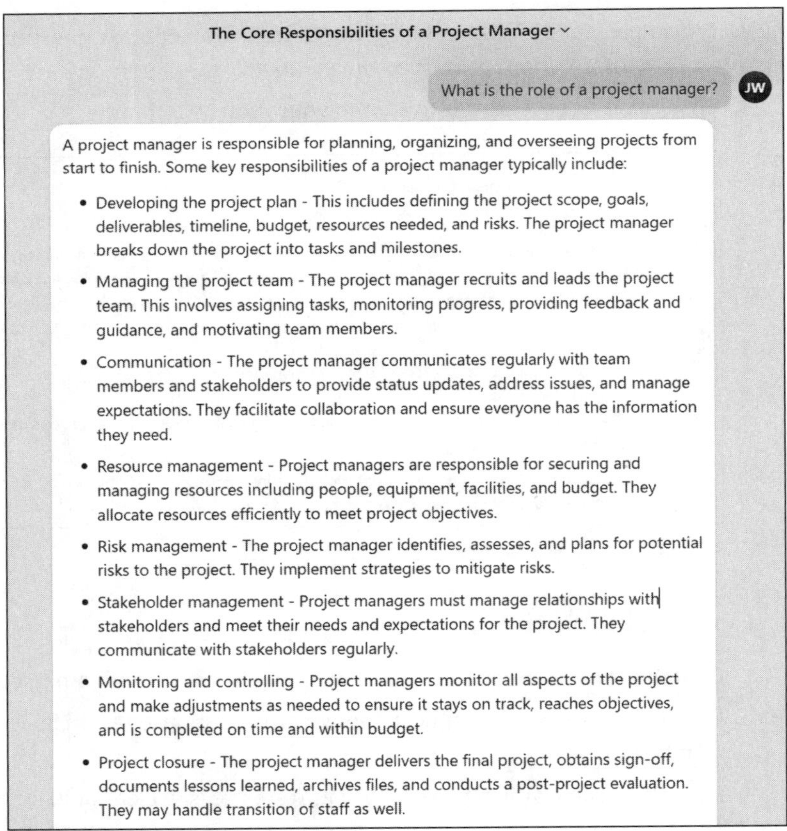

FIGURE 1.5 Claude interface

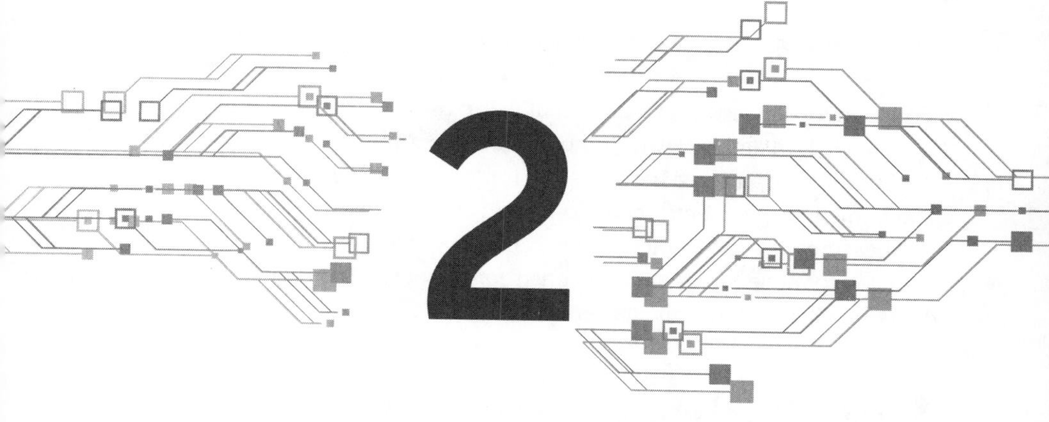

Stakeholders and Generative AI

Projects succeed if you as the project leader successfully identify and engage stakeholders, constantly communicating with them and meeting their expectations. Stakeholder management is more than just a valuable skill—it's a necessity. Generative artificial intelligence (AI) is a precious tool in this effort. Whether you're a novice or an experienced project manager, you can benefit by leveraging AI throughout the project delivery life cycle. AI technologies will significantly enhance productivity and efficiency, from identifying and engaging stakeholders to maintaining effective communication.

AI IN ACTION: LML HOME IMPROVEMENT

For each topic, we will present a real-world use case of an AI model such as ChatGPT, in action. LML Home Improvement Inc. was founded by Luiz M. Lorenzo, originally a carpenter by trade. After a successful start in the home improvement sector, completing small projects such as building basements, rooms, and garages, Luiz sought to grow his business. He decided to move into the home construction sector. He'd heard of AI tools like ChatGPT and quickly mastered using ChatGPT at a basic level.

LML Home Improvement Inc.

Luiz needed to identify stakeholders for his new construction project in a small neighborhood in the outskirts of Acton, Massachusetts. Using a ChatGPT app on his phone, he was quickly presented with a list of eight stakeholders. He was fully aware of most of the stakeholders, such as those listed here:

- Architect/designer
- Subcontractors
- Suppliers
- Finance providers
- Local government/regulators

But it was the list of stakeholders that he had not been aware of that proved to be valuable. Luiz had no experience with issues that could arise when a large project is planned. The AI models have information about projects, both small and large, and ChatGPT listed three additional stakeholders he had not considered:

Neighboring Community: Neighbors may have a stake, particularly regarding disruption during the construction process.

Real Estate Agents: Real estate agents could assess the home's potential value.

Insurance Companies: LML Home Improvement had insurance, but the fact that AI prominently identified insurance companies got Luiz thinking about whether his insurance was sufficient.

Luiz wrote a letter to the neighboring community and informed them about the disruption. He proactively contacted a real estate agent to get ideas for designing and furnishing. Finally, Luiz increased his liability coverage after talking with his existing insurance company.

Identifying Project Stakeholders

In this section, we will consider how AI can facilitate identifying the stakeholders for any given project. Later in the chapter, we will illustrate how you can keep your stakeholders engaged by keeping them better informed, involved, and appreciated.

Understanding Stakeholders

Stakeholders. We've all heard the term. Let's consult the *Project Management Body of Knowledge* (PMBOK):

> *A stakeholder is an individual, group, or organization who may affect, be affected by, or perceive itself to be affected by a decision, activity, or outcome of a project.*

Basically, a stakeholder in project management is anyone interested in the project's outcome and who is impacted by the project. These could be individuals, groups, or even organizations. Stakeholders can be internal or external to the project.

RESOURCE The PMBOK is a global standard from the Project Management Institute (PMI) leveraged by professionals worldwide. *The Process Groups: A Practice Guide*, is a useful companion to PMBOK that offers practical guidance.[1]

1 www.PMI.org

The PMBOK guide identifies eight project performance domains: groups of related activities critical for effectively delivering project outcomes. The first and possibly the most important domain is the *stakeholder performance* domain.

There are different kinds of stakeholders in the project environment (**Figure 2.1**), and they all need to be identified, rated for their impact, and managed.

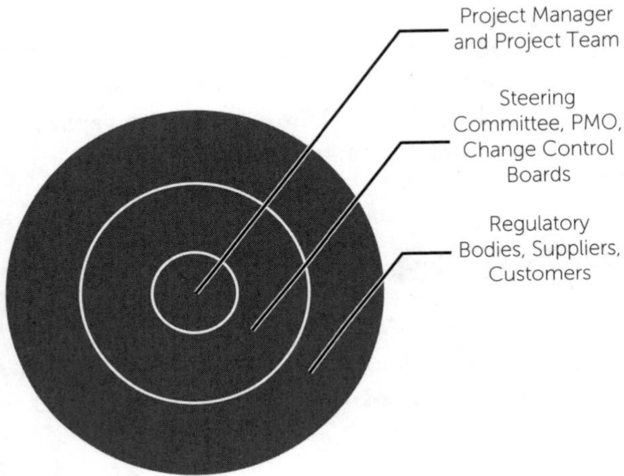

FIGURE 2.1 Stakeholders in the project environment

Throughout this book, you will see examples of the project team—developers, designers, clients, and sponsors—interacting with AI tools. This might include project management software and automation tools. In this chapter, we focus specifically on using an AI tool such as ChatGPT to streamline various aspects of the project with stakeholders.

Leveraging AI to Identify Stakeholders

Identifying stakeholders is a critical aspect of project management. So, how can you leverage AI to streamline this process?

Here's where a tool like ChatGPT comes in handy. Its ability to quickly process large volumes of data can help identify stakeholders based on their interactions and engagements. To begin with, such language models have learned lessons from millions of projects across industries of all types. Additionally, with training, these models can analyze additional project data such as active or historic email communications and identify individuals who are involved in project-related conversations and who might be stakeholders. AI tools can delve into organizational data to identify relevant parties, depending, of course, on the training or learning documents provided. AI can identify stakeholders from various sources, including project documentation, emails, and social media. ChatGPT, for example, understands the context and frequency of these communications. These techniques can help you, as a project manager, quickly and accurately identify the relevant stakeholders.

A fictional case study can clarify this. Say you are working with Global Health Inc., a start-up in a highly digitized industry. Let's see how AI can help you with activities associated with the stakeholder performance domain. Global Health has several email threads about the project. Consider the following prompt:

> ***"ChatGPT, can you analyze these email threads and help me identify potential stakeholders for our project?"***
>
> I'd be happy to help, but as an AI language model, I'm unable to directly access or analyze your emails due to privacy and security concerns. However, I can guide you on how to do this analysis yourself or with a supervised AI tool that complies with your organization's data security guidelines. Typically, you'd look for individuals frequently involved in the email conversations, those with decision-making power, and those impacted by the project.

This conversation highlights the critical aspect of data privacy and the role of responsible AI use in project management. Before utilizing AI tools like ChatGPT, ensure you are fully aware of and compliant with your company's data privacy guidelines. If you're granting AI access to your emails or manually pasting email content into ChatGPT, it's paramount that you're not violating any company rules or regulations. An interaction might look like this

> ***"I have been rummaging through all these email threads for our Global Health project, and it's making my head spin. We need to identify our stakeholders, but there are so many emails! Could you lend me a hand?"***
>
> I get where you're coming from, and I'd be thrilled to help! Based on what we understand about the project and its correspondence and the emails you provided, I noticed a chain of emails between John Doe, the Director of Global Health Operations, and Sarah Brown, the Head of Finance, deep in discussing the project's budget.
>
> There are also multiple threads where Mike Green, a Regional Director, juggles resources and timelines with the project team.

There are also emails from Emily White, a Senior Analyst, voicing concerns and sharing insights about how the project might unfold.

Now, what could you infer from this?

- John Doe, the Operations Director, is likely to be one of your key stakeholders. He's right in the thick of things, especially regarding financial decisions.
- Sarah Brown is equally crucial. As the person holding the purse strings, she's a stakeholder who would significantly influence the project's financial standing.
- And let's remember Mike Green. His input as a Regional Director in project planning and resource allocation suggests that he's an operational stakeholder who can directly influence project execution.
- Emily White, too, deserves a mention. She might not have a managerial role, but as a Senior Analyst, her insights about the project's impact make her a stakeholder to be considered.

By playing out this scenario, you can see how an AI tool can help you sift through all that data and identify your stakeholders. All four individuals could be stakeholders based on their involvement and influence. Remember, this is a simplified example, but it gives you an idea of how AI works.

Let's see a few more prompts to ChatGPT as examples. First, a prompt to get started on the list of stakeholders:

"ChatGPT, I have a list of people I have engaged in email conversations about the Global Health website project. Can you review my emails and help me identify other key stakeholders and their role in these interactions?"

Sure, I can help you analyze the frequency and context of these interactions. However, please note that while I can provide suggestions based on data, the final decision should also consider qualitative factors like their influence, interest, and impact on the project. Here is a table that might address your needs:

STAKEHOLDER	ROLE
John Smith	Director of Business Analysis
Mary King	Director of IT
Das Pear	Director of Marketing

Isn't it incredible how AI can transform the working day of a project manager? The possibilities of AI being able to scan through heaps of data to identify potential stakeholders are endless.

The beauty of AI lies in its ability to dive deeper. For instance, AI can analyze the tone, sentiment, and context of email conversations and other forms of communication. This level of analysis goes beyond just identifying who is involved to discerning how they're involved, their potential impact, and their interest in the project.

Consider a prompt like this:

> ***"Analyze the sentiment and context of interactions with Jane from the IT department regarding the Global Health website project. Could you provide an estimate of her potential influence and interest?"***

ChatGPT will scan the data, look for patterns and contextual cues, and might respond with something like this:

> Based on my analysis, Jane frequently discusses the technical aspects of the project and often proposes innovative solutions. This suggests she has considerable technical influence and seems highly invested in the project's success. The overall sentiment of the interactions with Jane appears positive.

Now, you've identified a stakeholder and gained insights into her potential influence and interest. These insights can be invaluable in strategizing stakeholder engagement.

Engagement, too, can reach new heights of personalization with AI to solidify someone's role as a stakeholder. Let's say you ask,

> ***"Could you draft an engaging, personalized update for Jane acknowledging her contributions and encouraging her continued involvement?"***

ChatGPT might respond with a draft saying:

> Dear Jane,
>
> Just wanted to take a moment to acknowledge the remarkable work you've been doing on the Global Health website project. Your knack for technical problem-solving and innovative suggestions have really lit up the way forward for us. Your dedication is appreciated, and we look forward to your continued involvement.

Updating the Stakeholder List

Consider the complex dynamics of a project: multiple teams, various roles, shifting priorities, and an evolving environment. In this context, you must keep updating your stakeholder list, acknowledging that new significant participants may emerge while others may recede into the background.

AI can play a critical role in this dynamic stakeholder identification. By continuously monitoring and analyzing communications and interactions, AI can alert you to new potential stakeholders as they emerge. Here's another hypothetical conversation with ChatGPT:

> ***"Are there any emerging stakeholders in the Global Health website project based on the recent email communications?"***
>
> After analyzing the recent interactions, I have noticed that Alex from the Legal department has started actively participating in the discussions. Although not previously identified as a key stakeholder, Alex's increasing involvement and legal expertise might make him a significant stakeholder moving forward.

This continuous monitoring allows you to keep your finger on the pulse of the project, ensuring that no potential stakeholder is overlooked.

The Impact of AI on Stakeholder Expectations

Stakeholders in the era of AI also have different expectations. With technology advancing at breakneck speeds, stakeholders expect more transparency, faster responses, and personalized interactions—areas where AI can excel.

As a project manager, you can meet and exceed these high expectations using AI, such as ChatGPT. Real-time reporting, for instance, is a task that you can automate with AI. This way, you keep your stakeholders informed and foster transparency. Additionally, ChatGPT can help provide instantaneous responses to stakeholder queries or concerns, improving stakeholder satisfaction.

Consider this example in our case study: Global Health is working on a tight deadline, and your stakeholders are anxious about the progress.

> ***"Could you please generate a progress report for the website project to share with our stakeholders?"***

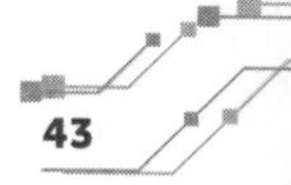

Of course. Here's a draft of the progress report:

Project Name: **Global Health Website Development**

Current Phase: **Design Stage**

Key Accomplishments:

1. Completed user interface design
2. Established color scheme and branding
3. Developed site structure and navigation

Upcoming Milestones:

1. Begin front-end development (Expected start date: 9/1/2025)
2. User testing (Expected start date: 11/1/2025)

Risks and Issues:

Potential delay in front-end development due to dependency on external vendors.

Please note that these are projected dates and may be subject to change. We appreciate your understanding and continued support.

Remember to customize this template based on your actual project details.

That was good practice. While ChatGPT provides an initial draft, it's up to you as the project manager to fine-tune and customize the message to suit your stakeholders. The initial prompt provided was very generic, but if we'd given more project context in the prompt, ChatGPT would have generated more specific and tailored information.

As we push further into the age of AI, not only are stakeholders expecting faster responses and increased transparency, but they are also seeking deeper engagement and more proactive communication. They want to feel like they're part of the conversation and not just passive recipients of updates. And this is where AI's predictive and analytical capabilities can be leveraged.

Imagine, for instance, asking ChatGPT to predict your stakeholders' potential questions after seeing the latest progress report. With its ability to process large volumes of data and predict patterns, ChatGPT can help anticipate and prepare for stakeholder reactions.

Based on the data provided, stakeholders might ask about the following:

- What are the specifics of the dependency on the external vendor, and how might it cause a delay?
- What steps are we taking to mitigate this risk?
- Are there any budgetary implications associated with the potential delay?

By proactively addressing these anticipated concerns in your communications, you'll be meeting the stakeholders' need for a deeper level of engagement, thus building their trust and support.

Beyond generating reports and answering queries, AI can also help manage stakeholder expectations regarding project risks. By analyzing project data, AI can identify risk patterns and potential pitfalls, enabling you to proactively communicate these risks to your stakeholders.

Assuming ChatGPT already has access to customized datasets of a company or organization, think about a prompt like this:

"Based on past project data and our current progress, what potential risks should we communicate to our stakeholders?"

Alternatively, you can use this prompt if you need to input some context to ChatGPT to better understand your project.

"Act as an expert in project management, risk analysis, and stakeholder communication. Use your capabilities to analyze the project information provided. Review our current project progress, the resources involved, potential hurdles, and our existing risk mitigation strategies. From this, generate a report that includes a current status update, identified risks, progress made, potential stakeholders who should be informed, and strategic advice on next steps. This report should be in semi-formal language and structured in a way that is easy to comprehend for all stakeholders involved. Information to consider includes:

Project Description: We're currently developing a new AI model to optimize our recommendation system.

Progress Details: We're halfway through our timeline with major milestones achieved on time.

Known Risks: Potential data bias and resource allocation.

Current Risk Mitigation Strategies: Regular bias testing and reallocation of resources as needed.

Stakeholder Information: Includes a team of data scientists, business executives, product managers, and end users."

As we utilize AI in managing stakeholder expectations, another crucial aspect that's rapidly gaining prominence is AI's role in stakeholder *sentiment analysis*. Understanding how stakeholders feel about a project can be instrumental in managing their expectations effectively. AI can analyze stakeholder communication for sentiment, providing valuable insights into their emotional state and overall attitude toward the project.

Let's consider a scenario. You ask ChatGPT,

> ***"Based on the recent communications, how does the design team feel about the recent changes we've implemented?"***

> Based on recent emails and messages analysis, the design team appears to have positive sentiment toward the changes. Positive language and expressions suggest they are satisfied with the recent implementations.

Armed with this information, you can craft your messages and responses more accurately, keeping the positive sentiment alive and addressing any concerns promptly.

Additionally, as you navigate this new landscape, you'll notice an increasing demand for AI that doesn't just respond to commands but that also offers suggestions and recommendations proactively. Stakeholders could expect this level of initiative from AI, further influencing the dynamics of project management.

Imagine a scenario in which ChatGPT notices a pattern of recurring issues during a particular phase of your projects. It might proactively suggest:

> In the past few projects, there have been noticeable delays during the testing phase due to unexpected bugs. To mitigate this risk, I recommend incorporating a more robust debugging process in the project plan.

Such proactive insights from AI can significantly improve your preparedness, allowing you to manage stakeholder expectations more effectively.

Moreover, with AI's data analysis and predictive modeling capabilities, you can now give your stakeholders more realistic project forecasts, reducing the gap between expectations and reality. This level of predictive accuracy can go a long way in maintaining stakeholder confidence and ensuring their continued support.

For example,

> ***"Based on past projects of similar scale, what is the most realistic timeline for the testing phase of our project?"***

With a response from ChatGPT, you'd be better equipped to set more accurate timelines and manage stakeholder expectations more effectively.

And as you continue to explore this terrain, you must focus on practical and empathetic communication, stakeholder engagement, and respect for data privacy. In each chapter, we include a section that specifically addresses ethical situations, including transparency about data privacy. It's clear that as we harness the power of AI in managing stakeholder expectations, we are not just evolving our methodologies but also redefining the boundaries of what is achievable in project management.

Stakeholder Analysis with AI

Once you have identified your stakeholders, it's time to delve deeper into their interests, needs, and preferred communication channels—this is *stakeholder analysis*. Stakeholder analysis is a crucial step in any project management process, as it helps you to understand the various parties involved, their interests, needs, and preferred communication channels. This analysis enables organizations to develop effective strategies for stakeholder engagement, ensuring that all parties are informed, involved, and satisfied with the project's progress and outcomes. A problem we face is that there are differing personal and political interests. AI is able to provide out-of-the-box solutions to such dilemmas.

Understanding Stakeholder Interests and Needs

After identifying your stakeholders, you must develop a full understanding of their interests and needs to manage their expectations and ensure the project's success. Stakeholders are the heart and soul of any project. Understanding their needs and interests is crucial to managing their expectations and ensuring project success. Traditional methods of stakeholder analysis can be time-consuming and complex. AI can add a whole new dimension to this process.

AI models like ChatGPT can assist you in understanding your stakeholders by analyzing textual data such as emails, project briefs, and even meeting transcripts. This information can effectively tailor project plans and communication strategies to address stakeholder needs and interests.

For example, in our Global Health example, assume you have a project brief and some initial conversations recorded. You can ask ChatGPT for an analysis:

"All right, we've done a great job identifying potential stakeholders. But understanding them is a different ball game. We need to grasp their interests and needs for this project, and we have a project brief and a bunch of initial conversations with them. Could you help me determine what our stakeholders might be interested in?"

I'm with you, and it sounds like a fascinating challenge. Based on the information you've given me, let's create another hypothetical scenario:

Project Quality: From what we know, our stakeholders seem keen on a high-quality website. They're looking for something comprehensive that covers all of Global Health's services. But it's not just about information—the website must be user-friendly, accessible, and visually appealing. They're not going to compromise on the quality!

Time Crunch: There's also this undercurrent of a tight deadline. There might be upcoming marketing campaigns or events that hinge on this project. Time is of the essence here.

Budget Constraints: Amidst all this, there are murmurs about budget constraints. The stakeholders need cost-efficient solutions that will ensure the quality of the website is maintained.

NOTE ChatGPT's interpretation is based on the information provided. It's essential to confirm the analysis with the stakeholders themselves. Human judgment is essential when it comes to understanding nuanced human needs and interests.

Next, ask ChatGPT for specifics about individual stakeholders that have been identified:

"That's great to start with. Can you help us delve deeper into some of the specific stakeholders' interests and needs?"

You're right, and I'd be glad to help! Let's build upon our earlier conversation and dive deeper into those stakeholder needs and interests.

John Doe, the Director of Global Health Operations, likely has a vested interest in the project's overall success, ensuring all operations are running smoothly and aligning with the organization's strategy.

Sarah Brown, as the Head of Finance, might be particularly interested in the cost-efficiency of the project, closely monitoring the budget and looking for ways to optimize spending.

{Response continues with the other stakeholders, truncated for brevity and relevance.}

Imagine using an AI model to sift through textual data—emails, project briefs, meeting transcripts—to pinpoint stakeholders' interests and needs. It could analyze linguistic patterns, frequency of topics, sentiments, and more. Such insights will allow you to tailor your project plans and communication strategies more effectively. You could proactively address stakeholder needs and interests, leading to better engagement and, ultimately, a more successful project.

Ranking Stakeholders by Power and Interest

As a project manager, you can consult ChatGPT to help assess stakeholders' power and interest levels, using a tool from the PMBOK:

"Could you please generate a Power Authority vs Interest Matrix for your identified stakeholders?"

Sure, I'd be happy to help you generate a Power vs Interest Matrix for these stakeholders. In a Power vs Interest Matrix, we plot stakeholders based on their level of interest in the project against their level of power or influence over the project.

Given the information provided in the conversation, here's how you might plot the stakeholders:

John Doe, Director of Global Health Operations: High Power, High Interest. As the Director, John Doe likely has significant influence over project decision-making. Given his role, he's likely to have a high interest in the overall success and efficiency of the project, aligning it with the organizational strategy.

Sarah Brown, Head of Finance: High Power, High Interest. Sarah, being in charge of the finances, can influence project decisions based on budget and cost concerns. She is likely to be interested in optimizing spending and maintaining cost efficiency.

{Response continues with the other stakeholders, truncated for brevity and relevance.}

Please remember that this is an approximate classification, and these stakeholders' actual power and interest levels could vary based on many factors, including organizational culture and personal commitment. This information is based on historical data and job titles, but in many cases, the job title might not accurately reflect power or authority.

It is also important not to publicly show this information to the stakeholders. Although this document is a vital project plan document, it should be kept in a private notebook. Case in point: Emily might not be pleased that she is classified as a low-power and low-interest stakeholder.

For quick reference, ChatGPT can generate a table and matrix to help you better visualize this information:

"Hey ChatGPT, can you please put that information in table format?"

Of course, here's the Power vs Interest Matrix in a table format

STAKEHOLDER	POWER	INTEREST
John Doe	High	High
Sarah Brown	High	High
Mike Green	Medium	High
Emily White	Low	Medium

TECHNICAL GUIDE **Refer to Technical Guide 2.3 for a step-by-step guide to uploading an attachment to allow ChatGPT to create a visual presentation of the data.**

Remember that the classifications of power and interest as low, medium, or high can vary based on the specific circumstances and dynamics within your organization. They are approximations that can serve as a guideline for how much attention and management each stakeholder might require during the project.

"That was great! Can you please put that in a grid or quadrant please?"

Certainly!

Figure 2.2 shows how, based on the description of the job titles of these stakeholders, ChatGPT Advanced Data Analysis (Code Interpreter) has inferred their power levels in a grid.

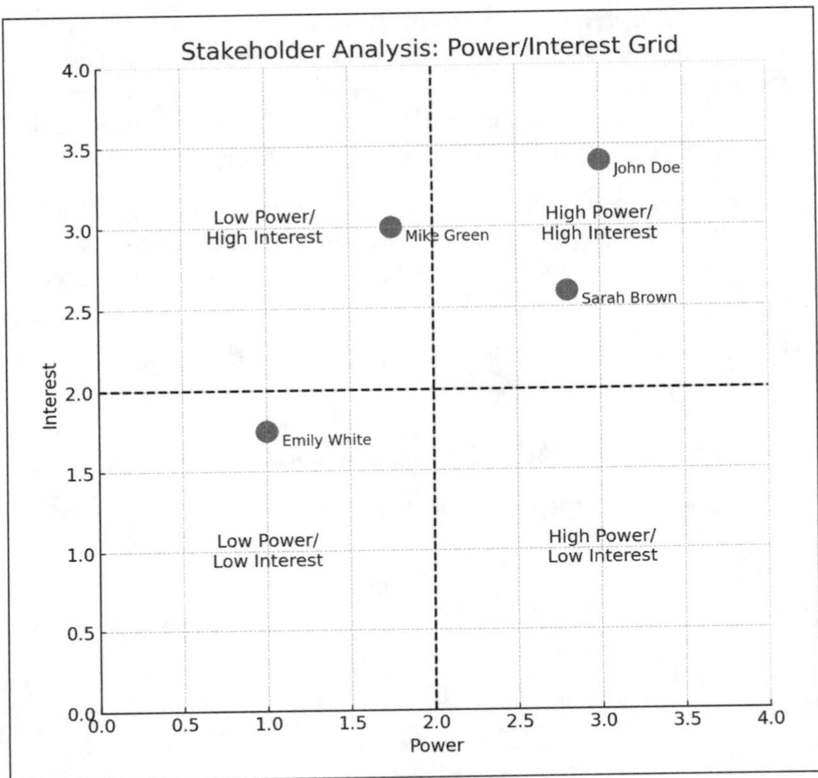

FIGURE 2.2 Power vs. Interest grid generated by ChatGPT Advanced Data Analysis

Of course, as with any tool, AI has its limitations. Real-world decision-making calls for human judgment, empathy, and an understanding of cultural and emotional nuances that AI might not fully grasp. But it's undeniable that AI offers a valuable support system, helping you navigate stakeholder management challenges with greater ease and confidence.

Stakeholder Communication Preferences and Channels

Effective communication is critical to successful stakeholder engagement, and understanding stakeholder preferences for communication channels is crucial to achieving this. AI can analyze stakeholder interactions to determine whether they prefer email, phone calls, or face-to-face meetings, and their selected frequency and style of communication. You can then use this information to develop tailored communication plans that meet the needs of each stakeholder.

For instance, a stakeholder who is highly engaged and responsive to visuals might receive a dynamic project dashboard, where we used ChatGPT

Advanced Data Analysis tool to add visual aids to communications. Another stakeholder, who prefers detailed reports, might receive an in-depth written analysis. Similarly, messages to stakeholders can be tailored to address their specific concerns, whether those are about cost, quality, schedule, or other aspects of the project. By understanding, addressing, and personalizing each stakeholder's unique needs and preferences, AI can help foster stronger, more effective stakeholder relationships to better manage their expectations and foster their engagement and support.

In the context of our case study, if Global Health has previous projects with similar stakeholders, you could use AI to analyze communication patterns:

> ***"How would I go about identifying the preferred communication channels of our stakeholders?"***
>
> Sure. Look for frequency and responsiveness across different channels (such as email, Slack, and Teams). Stakeholders who respond quickly on a certain channel likely prefer that one. Also, consider the formality and complexity of the information being shared. Complex or formal information is often better suited to email or face-to-face meetings, while casual or urgent updates may be better for chat apps.

This example provides some general strategies for determining the best communication method. However, as companies adopt AI and integrate their datasets, AI can sift through massive quantities of data to unveil patterns and connections that might otherwise be missed. And because AI constantly learns and adapts, it can provide even more accurate and timely insights into stakeholder needs.

> ***"Based on historical communication data, can you help identify the preferred communication channels of our stakeholders?"***
>
> Absolutely, I can help you understand the communication preferences of your project stakeholders based on the fictional historical data available. Here's what the analysis suggests:
>
> Jane from IT, for instance, tends to respond most quickly and effectively when contacted via Slack. She is typically active during regular business hours, and her concise responses indicate a preference for direct, short communication. She also frequently uses emojis to convey her reactions, suggesting that she appreciates a certain level of informality in digital communications. However, Jane usually prefers emails for more formal and complex topics, particularly when discussing system upgrades or significant IT decisions.

Then there's Bob from Marketing. He prefers face-to-face meetings or video calls on Zoom for detailed discussions. He is more likely to respond to emails when a session is requested or to confirm details. His communication style indicates a preference for personal interaction and in-depth conversation.

{Response truncated for brevity and relevance}.

Understanding these preferences can significantly enhance your communication efficiency with stakeholders. Remember that stakeholders' preferences can change over time and with changing circumstances, so it's always a good idea to review and ask for feedback regularly.

If you continually engage with an AI tool like ChatGPT, it progressively refines its understanding based on the feedback and additional information provided. Jane from the IT department prefers direct, concise communication rather than lengthy updates. If we feed this preference back into the AI, it can adjust its communication style when interacting with Jane, making future messages more tailored to her liking.

Consider a prompt like this

"Remember that Jane prefers concise updates. Can you provide a short but comprehensive update on the project status for her?"

NOTE AI models like ChatGPT operate based on *tokens*, which can be thought of as words, characters, or slices of text. Each conversation has a token limit, a maximum amount of information the model can hold at once. In extended chats, if the token limit is reached, earlier tokens might be dropped, making it seem like the AI has forgotten a detail. If that happens, it's perfectly okay to jog its memory with a reminder!

ChatGPT would then adjust its response:

Sure, here's a brief update: Dear Jane, ...

AI's ability to learn and evolve makes it a dynamic tool in stakeholder engagement that becomes more attuned to stakeholder preferences the more you interact with it.

In essence, AI encourages a shift from a one-size-fits-all approach to a nuanced, personalized strategy centered on understanding and respecting individual stakeholder preferences. As you adopt and integrate AI into your project management practices, you'll be better equipped to foster meaningful, productive relationships with your stakeholders.

Benefits of AI in Stakeholder Analysis

In our Global Health example, you've seen how AI has helped identify stakeholders, understand their needs, and determine their communication preferences. Now let's consider the benefits of AI in stakeholder analysis.

AI can quickly analyze vast amounts of data, which is particularly helpful for large-scale projects involving numerous stakeholders. This capability enables you to quickly identify potential risks, opportunities, and areas requiring attention.

Another benefit of AI in stakeholder analysis is its ability to identify patterns and trends, which can help predict stakeholder behavior and preferences. By understanding these patterns, you can better tailor your communication strategies and engagement efforts to maximize stakeholder satisfaction.

"Could you provide more insight into how AI can help predict stakeholder behavior?"

Certainly! AI can analyze historical data and previous interactions with stakeholders to identify patterns in their behavior, preferences, and concerns. By leveraging machine learning algorithms, AI can predict how stakeholders react to certain situations or decisions. This information empowers project managers to proactively address potential issues, adapt communication strategies, and foster stronger relationships with stakeholders.

That's quite impressive! Another notable advantage of AI in stakeholder analysis is the ability to learn and improve continuously. As AI systems are exposed to more data and interactions, they can refine their understanding of stakeholder dynamics and provide more accurate insights. This continuous improvement can lead to documenting a sound relationship strategy, better project outcomes, and increased stakeholder satisfaction.

AI has the potential to revolutionize stakeholder analysis by providing valuable insights, predicting stakeholder behavior, and continuously learning and improving. As AI continues to advance, it will be crucial for project managers to strike the right balance between leveraging AI's capabilities and maintaining a human-centric approach to stakeholder engagement. AI assistance allows project managers to focus on strategic planning and relationship building, ultimately leading to more successful projects.

Engaging Stakeholders through AI-Driven Communication

It's time to actively engage our stakeholders. This is where AI can add significant value. AI-driven communication can help project managers engage stakeholders more effectively by generating personalized content, targeting specific groups, and measuring engagement levels through sentiment analysis.

Personalized engagement goes beyond disseminating information; it builds relationships and fosters dialogue. Automated reports generated by AI can offer real-time updates, ensuring stakeholders are always in the loop. This kind of timely transparency can significantly boost stakeholder confidence and engagement.

AI-Generated Content and Messaging

Let's see what ChatGPT has to say about this topic:

"Could you explain how AI-generated content and messaging can help engage stakeholders?"

Absolutely! AI-generated content and messaging can help project managers create tailored messages for stakeholder groups. By analyzing the interests and needs of each stakeholder, AI can generate relevant and engaging content that resonates with them. This can save time and effort for project managers while ensuring that the communication is effective and well-received by the stakeholders.

"Thank you, ChatGPT. That's an interesting point."

AI-generated content can help you save time and effort while creating engaging messages. AI can aid in generating clear, concise, and compelling messages tailored to the communication preferences of different stakeholders.

Suppose Global Health needs to send its stakeholders an email update about the website project. You can use ChatGPT to generate a draft by providing relevant details:

"Help me draft an email update about the website project. The development phase is complete, and we're entering the testing phase. We are on track to meet our deadline."

Subject: Global Health Website Project: Progress Update

Dear [Stakeholder's Name],

I hope this message finds you well. I'm writing to provide an update on the Global Health Website Project.

I'm delighted to share that our dedicated team has completed the development phase and is now transitioning into the testing phase. This crucial stage involves rigorously checking all functionalities and features to ensure optimal performance.

Rest assured, we are on track to meet the previously communicated project deadline, affirming our commitment to delivering quality work promptly.

We look forward to presenting you with a user-friendly, accessible, visually appealing website that aligns with Global Health's esteemed reputation.

Thank you for your ongoing support and trust in our team. We will continue to keep you informed as we progress further.

Best regards,

[Your Name]

AI-generated messaging can also extend to more immediate channels such as Slack or Teams, creating regular, concise updates tailored to those platforms.

Personalized and Targeted Communication

AI-driven communication can help project managers deliver personalized and targeted messages to stakeholders. By understanding each stakeholder's communication preferences and needs, AI can help tailor the message format, tone, and content to better resonate with them. This personalized approach can lead to more effective communication, stronger relationships, and better project outcomes.

"Can you provide an example of how personalized and targeted communication can work?"

Sure! A project manager needs to update stakeholders on the project's progress. AI can analyze the preferences of each stakeholder and segment them into groups, such as those who prefer visual presentations, written reports, or short updates via email. The AI can then generate appropriate content for each group, ensuring that each stakeholder receives the information in their preferred format. This personalized approach can lead to increased engagement and satisfaction among stakeholders.

That's a great example of how AI can help project managers deliver personalized and targeted communication to stakeholders.

Personalization is a crucial benefit of AI in communication. Language models like ChatGPT can help craft messages that consider each stakeholder's unique needs and interests.

For example, the tech-savvy stakeholders at Global Health may appreciate more detailed updates about the technical aspects of the project, whereas others may prefer high-level progress updates.

> ***"Could you help me craft a detailed technical update about the website project for our tech-savvy stakeholders."***
>
> Hi, team,
>
> We've wrapped up the development phase of the Global Health Website Project, and we're now transitioning into testing. Here's a quick rundown of what that involves:
>
> We'll perform unit tests on individual components, integration tests to ensure all parts of the site work together smoothly, and usability tests to provide a top-notch user experience.
>
> Our tech stack [mention the technologies used] has proved robust and efficient so far, and we're making sure our code is clean and well-documented to facilitate future updates.
>
> We are on track with our timeline, and we'll keep you updated with any significant milestones or roadblocks.
>
> Thanks for your support and do let us know if you have any questions or need further details.
>
> Best,
>
> [Your Name]

When it comes to engagement, AI's capacity for personalization truly shines. Different stakeholders might prefer different modes of communication—some might prefer a brief text message, others a comprehensive email, and others might appreciate a visual representation of data. AI can adapt to these preferences, tailoring each stakeholder's communication medium and style.

Let's see how ChatGPT can tailor a communication mode to the design team that prefers visual updates:

> ***"Since the design team comprises individuals who typically learn and process information visually, could you please communicate the project's progress to them in a visual format? I will upload an Excel file for you to review. It would be helpful if you could create a project update using pie charts and bar graphs given the data provided, as these are effective visual aids that will assist the team in comprehending the information more effectively."***
>
> Absolutely. I can create a visual representation of the current project status for the design team. I will create a bar graph to show the progress of each design stage and a pie chart to showcase the distribution of tasks among the team members given the file you uploaded.

With ChatGPT Advanced Data Analysis, you have the capability to upload a file containing data, which can then be interpreted and represented visually using both a bar graph and a pie chart (**Figure 2.3**). In this case, ChatGPT was able to work with the data tables in the uploaded Excel file without having to touch Excel. The bar graph showcases the progress of each design stage. The y-axis represents the percentage of completion, and the x-axis represents different design stages such as Concept Development or Prototyping. Each bar provides a visual representation of the current progress in each stage.

The pie chart in Figure 2.3 showcases the distribution of tasks among the team members. Each slice represents a team member, and the size of the slice corresponds to their level of involvement in the project. Such personalized engagement helps stakeholders feel valued and acknowledged, which can significantly enhance their involvement and commitment to the project.

AI's potential in stakeholder identification and engagement extends beyond mere efficiency. It offers the capability to keep the stakeholder list dynamic, aligns communication with stakeholder preferences, and adds a layer of personalization. As we fully embrace AI's potential, we move toward a more nuanced, practical approach to stakeholder management.

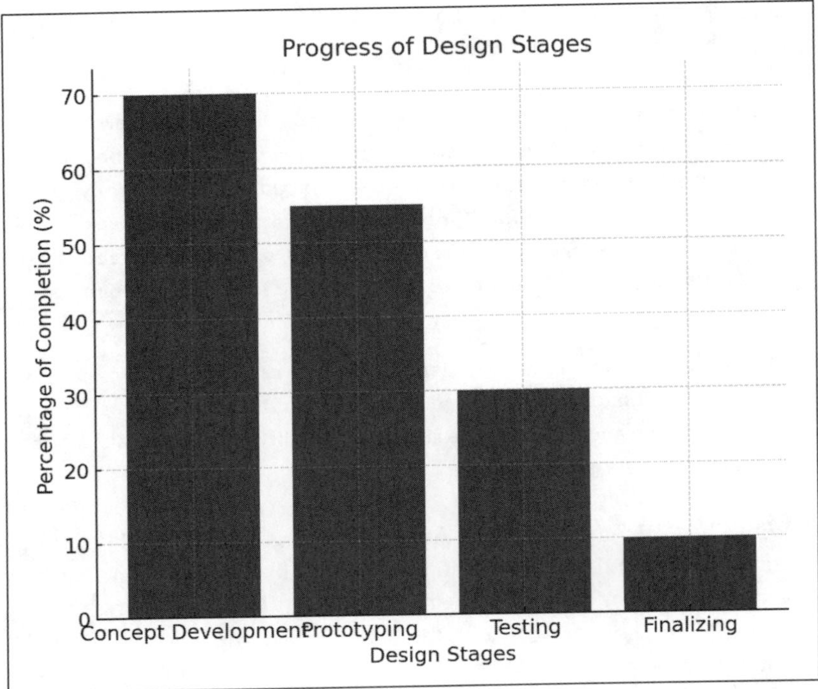

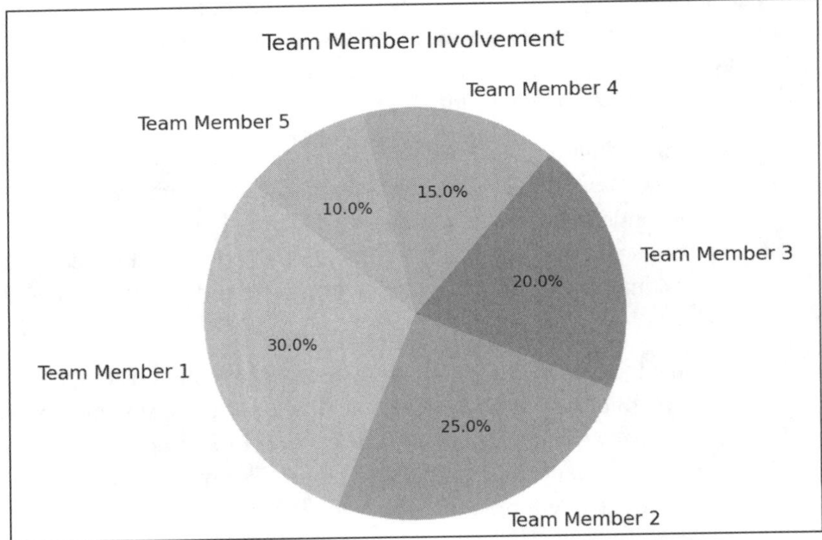

FIGURE 2.3 Bar chart and pie chart generated by ChatGPT Advanced Data Analysis

A NOTE OF CAUTION Project managers must consider the company policy and work with IT to ensure that email communications are kept confidential.

TECHNICAL GUIDE Refer to Technical Guide 2.3 to see how to use ChatGPT Advanced Data Analysis tool (formerly Code Interpreter) to upload an attachment and instruct ChatGPT to present data visually.

Measuring Stakeholder Engagement and Sentiment Analysis

AI can also help you measure stakeholder engagement and analyze their sentiments toward the project. By tracking metrics such as email open rates, click-through rates, and social media engagement, AI can provide insights into how effectively the communication reaches and engages stakeholders. Additionally, sentiment analysis can help you understand your stakeholders' emotions and opinions, allowing them to proactively address any concerns or issues.

"Could you give me an example of how sentiment analysis can be used in stakeholder engagement?"

Certainly! Sentiment analysis can gauge stakeholders' reactions to project updates, announcements, or other communications. For example, suppose a project manager shares a significant milestone update on social media. In that case, AI can analyze the comments and reactions to determine whether stakeholders are generally positive, negative, or neutral about the news. This information can help the project manager identify issues requiring further attention or communication, ensuring stakeholders feel heard and valued.

Sentiment analysis can provide valuable insights into stakeholders' emotions and opinions, helping you proactively address concerns. With this information, you can take appropriate actions to enhance stakeholder engagement.

"Could you provide some examples of how these insights can improve engagement?"

Absolutely! Insights from engagement metrics and sentiment analysis can be used in various ways such as identifying communication gaps, addressing concerns, tailoring content, and monitoring trends.

Beyond AI-driven stakeholder engagement, we're now entering a new era where AI is not only a tool but a potential partner and stakeholder.

Furthermore, AI tools can also assist in measuring stakeholder engagement. AI can identify positive, negative, or neutral sentiments through sentiment analysis in stakeholder communications. It can analyze email responses, feedback surveys, or even social media posts related to the project, helping you understand stakeholder sentiment and engagement levels in real time.

For example, you could ask,

> ***"Could you analyze the sentiment of the feedback received from stakeholders about the latest project update?"***

The AI could then provide a sentiment analysis report, shedding light on how well the update was received and where improvements might be needed.

Through our Global Health case study, we've illustrated the practical application of AI in project management and how prompt engineering plays a significant role in the interaction between you and the AI tool. Now, you can see the capabilities of AI and how using tools like ChatGPT can save time and ensure consistent, engaging communication with stakeholders.

> **NOTE** Global Health project managers must consider the company policy and work with IT to ensure that email communications are kept confidential.

In conclusion, AI-driven communication can significantly enhance stakeholder engagement in a project. You can used AI responsibly and transparently to foster stronger relationships with your stakeholders by generating personalized content, targeting specific stakeholder groups, and measuring engagement levels

AI as a Stakeholder for Project Management?

As AI continues to evolve and play increasingly vital roles in project management, it raises the question: should AI, even though a tool, be considered a key stakeholder? This provocative idea challenges the conventional perspective on stakeholder management, as we acknowledge AI's learning capabilities and potential impact on project outcomes.

Admittedly, it is difficult to pinpoint the specific needs an AI system like ChatGPT would have in comparison to human stakeholders. However, its learning capabilities enable it to improve over time, becoming more efficient and accurate in its tasks. This autonomous evolution distinguishes AI from traditional project management tools.

Consider the Global Health case study, where ChatGPT's continuous improvement in drafting email updates is evident. The more you use it, the more it learns to align with your style, making its responses more personalized and precise. This adaptability is an asset but requires the user to continually review AI's performance and provide feedback, just as you would with any other team member.

Beyond AI-driven stakeholder engagement, we're now entering a new era where AI is not only a tool but a potential partner and stakeholder. While this perspective is still in its infancy and we've yet to fully comprehend the ramifications, it raises thought-provoking questions about AI's role in project management and its potential to shift our understanding of stakeholders.

Ethical Considerations and Professional Responsibilities

Think about being a project manager as you'd think about coaching a sports team: every player has an impact. It's the same when using AI tools like ChatGPT to work with stakeholders. These tools can make a real difference when chatting with stakeholders, planning, and monitoring risks. So, you must keep a close eye on how the AI is doing to ensure it's working properly, being used effectively, and not causing any problems. Always be aware that real-world decision-making calls for human judgment, empathy, and an understanding of cultural and emotional nuances that AI might not fully grasp. In addition, AI has limitations: one notable gap is its inability to understand or interact with the world in real time. Let's look at Global Health again. Assess how ChatGPT's email drafts and stakeholder analysis are helping (or not helping) with stakeholder engagement. Are the stakeholders happy with the emails the AI is writing?

Powerful models like ChatGPT can completely change how we manage project stakeholder engagement, but it's also essential to consider the ethical issues around using ChatGPT in stakeholder engagement. This includes keeping data private, avoiding bias, being transparent, and ensuring that someone is accountable and responsible for data practices.

Data Privacy and Security

When an AI product such as ChatGPT is used in stakeholder engagement, it handles sensitive data. Keeping that data safe from anyone who shouldn't have it is essential. You should know how the AI handles privacy and data and ensure it sticks to the rules. For example, if you upload emails for AI to learn from, can you trust that AI will keep them confidential?

It is also important to get *explicit* consent for data processing and storage when using AI systems. Let stakeholders know precisely how ChatGPT will be used and what that means for their data privacy. In addition, allow your stakeholders to change their minds at any time about how their data will be used and stored.

Bias and Discrimination

AI models like ChatGPT learn using loads of data, and they might pick up and continue any bias that is present in that data. This could lead to biased or offensive content in the responses from the AI, which could damage relationships with your stakeholders and throw a wrench in the works for your project.

To reduce the risk of bias, keep a close eye on what the AI product is producing and give feedback to the AI provider so that the software can keep improving. Aim for diversity and inclusivity in stakeholder engagement, involving stakeholders with different backgrounds and views. This can help prevent the AI from accidentally reinforcing existing biases or creating new ones.

> **NOTE** AI's understanding of ethics and legality is limited to the training data it has received.

Depending on its training, AI might unintentionally generate inappropriate or harmful content, which could be a significant issue in a management context.

Transparency and Explainability

Being transparent is also important when using ChatGPT for stakeholder engagement. Stakeholders should know when they are interacting with an AI tool and understand its potential limitations and risks. Being open about what's happening helps build trust and credibility, which are key to good stakeholder engagement.

> **EXPLAINABILITY** AI's ability to provide understandable reasons for its predictions or recommendations.

It's key that the system explain *why* it's giving the outputs it is. You must ensure that stakeholders have some understanding as to why the AI is saying what it is. You can do so by providing clear explanations and context to back up what the AI is saying.

Accountability and Responsibility

Finally, having accountability and responsibility is essential when using ChatGPT in stakeholder engagement. Be clear about who's responsible for what the AI says and how it affects the engagement process. Also be ready to handle any issues or worries stakeholders might have about using AI.

By thinking about data privacy, bias, transparency, and accountability, as project managers we can make sure we're using ChatGPT responsibly and ethically, helping to build trust and cooperation among stakeholders and contributing to the success of their projects.

Key Points to Remember

As we have journeyed through this chapter, we have come to understand that the advent of artificial intelligence represents a particularly significant shift in the landscape of stakeholder management. It's a shift we need to embrace as project managers.

- The powerful analytics and communication capabilities of AI allow it to quickly process large volumes of data.
- AI can streamline stakeholder identification and analysis.
- Using AI, we can personalize stakeholder communications efficiently to more effectively meet stakeholder expectations and foster stronger engagement.
- Real-world decision-making calls for human judgment, empathy, and an understanding of cultural and emotional nuances that AI might not fully grasp.

One notable gap is AI's inability to understand the world in real time. For instance, the project manager upon learning from a colleague that a stakeholder is a keen golfer would naturally recall that and leverage this information to build a good relationship.

Technical Guide

Here's a step-by-step guide to set you up to use the ChatGPT Advanced Data Analysis tool (formerly Code Interpreter) to create graphs and visual data in status reports for stakeholders.

2.1 What Is the ChatGPT Advanced Data Analysis Tool?

ChatGPT Advanced Data Analysis is a powerful feature developed by OpenAI that allows the AI model, ChatGPT, to execute Python code. This feature is integrated into the chat environment in a stateful Jupyter notebook, providing an accessible and user-friendly way to perform real-time code execution, data analysis, and visualization tasks.

Advanced Data Analysis has many potential use cases, especially in project management. Beyond Python code, it can interact with a variety of data sources such as Microsoft Excel and comma-separated values (CSV) files. It can generate a wide range of visuals, including bar graphs and pie charts, making it an incredibly versatile tool to generate data-driven insights.

NOTE You need to be a ChatGPT Plus Subscriber to access Advanced Data Analysis.

2.2 Enabling Advanced Data Analysis for ChatGPT

1. To access Settings, find your username on your ChatGPT account. **Click the ellipsis icon** (three dots) and then click **Settings**.
2. On the Settings page, click **Beta Features**.
3. In the Beta Features section, you'll see the option **Advanced data analysis**. Click the toggle switch to turn it on (**Figure 2.4**).

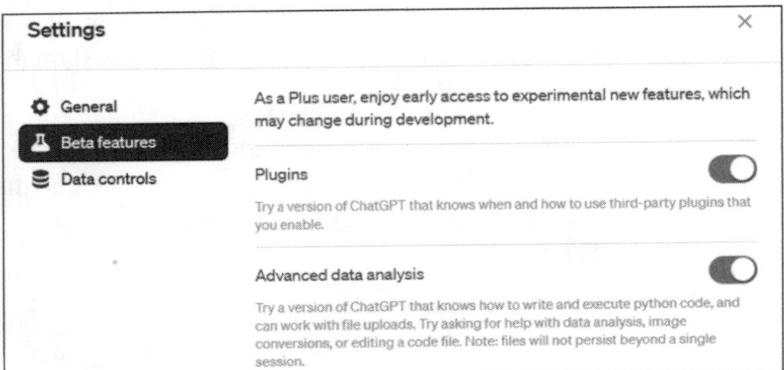

FIGURE 2.4 Enabling Advanced Data Analysis under Beta Features

2.3 Uploading a File with Advanced Data Analysis

As a project manager, you're likely dealing with a lot of data, stored in Excel files or other similar formats.

ChatGPT can analyze this data directly. All you need to do is upload your Excel file containing the project data to ChatGPT. Once the file is uploaded, ChatGPT can read the data and begin the analysis process.

1. Start a New Chat. Choose GPT 4 as your AI model. From the drop-down menu that appears, select **Advanced Data Analysis** (**Figure 2.5**).

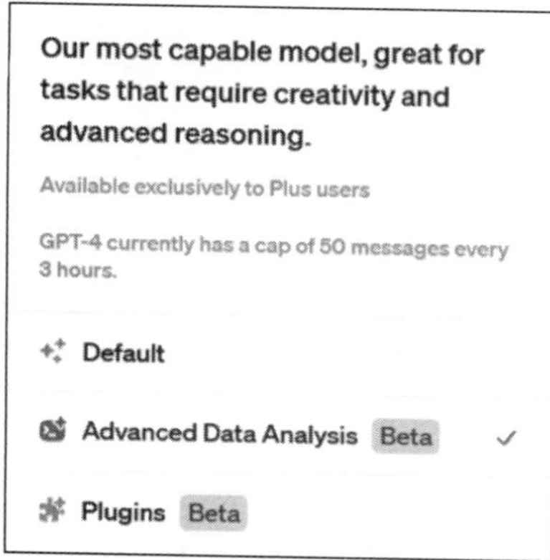

FIGURE 2.5 Selecting Advance Data Analysis (formerly Code Interpreter) in a new chat

2. In the chat window, click the button that looks like a plus sign (+) to upload a file that contains your project data (**Figure 2.6**).

FIGURE 2.6 Uploading a file

3. To create a prompt, type your request for ChatGPT. For example, you might ask it to make a graph or chart from the data that you have uploaded.

From this uploaded data, ChatGPT can generate various types of data visuals, including bar graphs and pie charts.

Bar graphs are excellent for comparing different groups or tracking changes over time. For example, you might want to compare the number of tasks completed by each team member. All you need to do is tell ChatGPT what you want to compare, and it can generate a bar graph for you.

Pie charts are ideal for showing the proportions of a whole. For instance, you might want to see how your project budget is distributed across different areas. Again, simply tell ChatGPT what you want to visualize, and it can create a pie chart based on your project data.

Building and Managing Teams Using AI

In this chapter, we explore the transformative role of AI in team management. We begin by examining how AI is reshaping recruitment onboarding, providing a swift, fair, and personalized experience. Then, we look at how AI can augment leadership, facilitating communication, and providing early warning of issues. Next, we discuss AI's role in fostering collaboration, especially in cross-functional teams. Finally, we investigate how AI can support conflict resolution and decision-making.

AI IN ACTION: WALMART MANAGING BUYER–SELLER NEGOTIATIONS

For our real-world case in this chapter, we look at how Walmart Inc. uses artificial intelligence-powered software to negotiate contracts with its suppliers. Project procurement management involves successfully handling negotiations between buyers and sellers for goods and services. The project manager is involved with planning, conducting, and controlling procurements. Their role in procurement management varies depending on the organization and size of the project, but invariably there is support from both the procurement staff and legal department.

When a decision is made about the resources or services for a project, the project manager becomes actively involved in documenting the procurement plan and identifying suitable sellers. This process can be time-consuming. However, AI can make it a less tedious process for both buyers and sellers.

Walmart customized Pactum, a text-based AI interface that negotiates with human suppliers on behalf of Walmart. Pactum can analyze historical data, identify patterns, and present procurement needs and proposals. Historical data includes information such as the offers and counteroffers made, reasons for agreement or disagreement, and factors influencing the outcome. Walmart's AI system uses this data to identify patterns and trends. This information has successfully generated alternative proposals that are more likely to be accepted by the sellers.

Walmart sellers have been very satisfied with these results.[1] In addition to experiencing faster response time, they feel that AI is functioning quite satisfactorily as a non-partial mediator. Additionally, AI systems can flag risks. If the chosen supplier has experienced supply chain disruptions in the recent past, the AI system would alert the buyer about this risk.

Considering the case above, let's think about how AI can assist in mediating:

Communication: Facilitate open and transparent communication between the buyer and the seller and discuss concerns and expectations regarding the terms and conditions of the contract.

1 Tobin, Ben (April, 2023). "Walmart Is Using AI to Negotiate Prices with Suppliers, Report Says—And the Suppliers Are Loving It." *Business Insider.*

Clarification of the Agreement: Review the initial agreement to identify any misunderstandings or miscommunications leading to a conflict and involve legal experts if necessary.

Negotiation: Engage in negotiations to find a mutually satisfactory resolution, addressing specific terms and potential compromises.

Agreement and Implementation: Document the agreed-upon resolution, signed by all parties involved, and promptly communicate to all stakeholders.

The Walmart case study is a great example of the points we will cover in this chapter: how AI can assist with communication, conflict management, negotiation, and related challenges.

AI-Assisted Recruitment and Selection

In today's competitive business environment, effective recruitment is crucial to successful team management. We've found through conversation with project managers and other technical leaders that recruitment consumes a significant amount of time. As a project manager you are already tasked with many responsibilities, and including the recruitment process on this list puts additional strain on your already busy schedule.

But for your project to be successful, you must attract, identify, and secure the right talent to build strong and successful teams. These days, the recruitment process has become more competitive, complex, and dynamic, and it requires sophisticated solutions. This is where artificial intelligence comes in. AI-assisted recruitment has emerged as a game changer, promising to transform traditional hiring processes by automating repetitive tasks, reducing bias, and enabling more informed decision-making.

The Role of AI in Recruitment and Selection

When you're working on a project, assembling the right team often involves a significant amount of tedious labor—from sorting through numerous résumés, to conducting preliminary screening interviews, to assessing candidates based on the information they provide. The process can be time-consuming, susceptible to human errors, and stressful.

But the emergence of AI technology has started to change this landscape. Let's imagine you're setting up a project team for a new initiative at a tech company. You can leverage a tool like ChatGPT to recruit and select potential team members. Here's a prompt that can get you started:

> ***"I would like to recruit team members for my project. How can you assist me in the recruitment process?"***
>
> As an AI model, I can assist in multiple ways. I can help parse and screen resumes to identify candidates with the specified qualifications and relevant skills and experience. This makes the process quicker and reduces the chances of overlooking a promising candidate. Also, I can help you design a structured interview protocol to assess the crucial competencies for your project.

That's a good start and sounds impressive! But can AI guide you further by helping assess a candidate's suitability for the team dynamics and project culture, analyzing their responses and gauging their cultural fit? Here are some comments on this aspect from ChatGPT:

> An AI model can analyze responses provided by candidates during the interview process and compare them to the desired team culture or company values. It identifies patterns and language usage and can compare responses to successful past candidates or employees. Using AI in recruitment and selection has the potential to reduce some forms of bias in the process. AI will likely ignore age, gender, and race while evaluating candidate profiles. This helps reduce some forms of unconscious bias that can creep into the recruitment process and helps ensure compliance with corporate and state laws.

But will AI be entirely free of bias?

Let's ask ChatGPT:

> ***"Can you talk about the potential limitations and challenges we might encounter while trying to achieve a bias-free recruitment process using AI?"***
>
> While AI models can be designed to ignore factors such as age, gender, and race, they can still reflect biases present in their training data or in the decisions they are trained on. It's important to regularly check and validate AI models for potential biases and maintain transparency about how AI's decisions or recommendations are being made.

For example, consider the specifics of AI's interpretation of "cultural fit" and how it might introduce bias in favor of "similar" people. In short, you must understand both AI's potential benefits and limitations in recruitment and selection.

As we delve further into the different stages of AI-assisted recruitment and selection in the following sections, we'll uncover more about how AI transforms this critical aspect of project management (**Figure 3.1**).

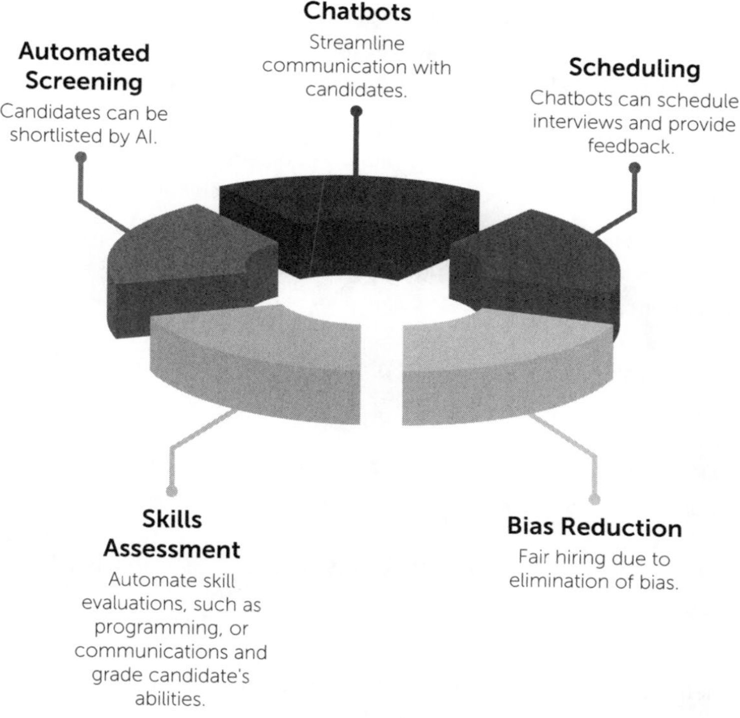
Chatbots
Streamline communication with candidates.
Automated Screening
Candidates can be shortlisted by AI.
Scheduling
Chatbots can schedule interviews and provide feedback.
Skills Assessment
Automate skill evaluations, such as programming, or communications and grade candidate's abilities.
Bias Reduction
Fair hiring due to elimination of bias.

FIGURE 3.1 The role of AI in recruitment provides insights into how AI can contribute to this function.

Benefits of AI in Recruitment and Selection

Perhaps the project you're working on is a significant technology transformation project for a global corporation. We're talking about overhauling legacy systems, implementing cloud infrastructure, and integrating state-of-the-art cybersecurity protocols. A project of this scale needs a team that's not only technically competent but also adaptable and able to navigate the complex landscape of a large-scale transformation.

Let's explain this scenario to ChatGPT:

> ***"We've got this massive tech transformation project coming up. How can AI assist in ensuring we recruit and select the right team for such a demanding project?"***

Here are a few ways AI can be instrumental in this context:

Speeding Up the Recruitment Process: AI can quickly scan and evaluate thousands of resumes to identify the most qualified candidates. This significantly cuts down the time spent in the initial stages of recruitment.

Finding the Right Skills: AI can be programmed to understand the specific skills, qualifications, and experience needed for the project. It can then match these requirements with the information in the resumes to find the right fit.

Assessing Cultural Fit: The AI can analyze a candidate's responses to understand their mindset and alignment with the company's culture. This helps ensure that you're building a team that's not only skilled but also harmonious.

Minimizing Bias: By focusing only on the relevant qualifications, skills, and experience, the AI can reduce unconscious biases that might creep into the recruitment process. This helps create a more diverse and inclusive team.

Take a moment to think about your projects. Where could these AI benefits have the most significant impact?

TECHNICAL GUIDE **See Technical Guide 3.1 to understand AI's role in identifying a list of preliminary tools to help with recruitment.**

Pitfalls and Challenges in AI-Assisted Recruitment and Selection

Like any technology, AI is not without its limitations, and you must recognize them before considering using AI for recruitment and selection. Let's prompt ChatGPT to obtain some insight:

"Can you help us understand the potential challenges or pitfalls in AI-assisted recruitment and selection?"

Bias in AI: While AI can help reduce unconscious bias, it's not entirely free of it. AI learns from data, and if the data is biased, the AI might amplify these biases.

Lack of Personal Touch: AI can efficiently sift through thousands of applications, but it might miss nuances that a human recruiter would catch. There's a risk of overlooking good candidates who may not look great on paper but could excel in the role.

Data Privacy Concerns: AI systems handle a lot of personal data. This raises legitimate concerns about data security and privacy.

Over-Reliance on Technology: AI can make the recruitment process more efficient, but over-reliance on it could lead to a lack of human judgment in decision-making. It's important to find the right balance between AI and human input.

These are excellent points to consider. **Figure 3.2** reminds us that we must critically examine the role of AI before making any radical changes to current practices.

Bias in AI
System can unintentionally amplify existing biases if they learn from biased data.

Lack of Personal Touch
AI may miss subtle nuances in applications that a human recruiter might notice.

Data Privacy Concerns
Significant concerns about data in the hands of bots—privacy and security risks.

D

Reliance on Technology
Decision-making is now in the hands of AI.

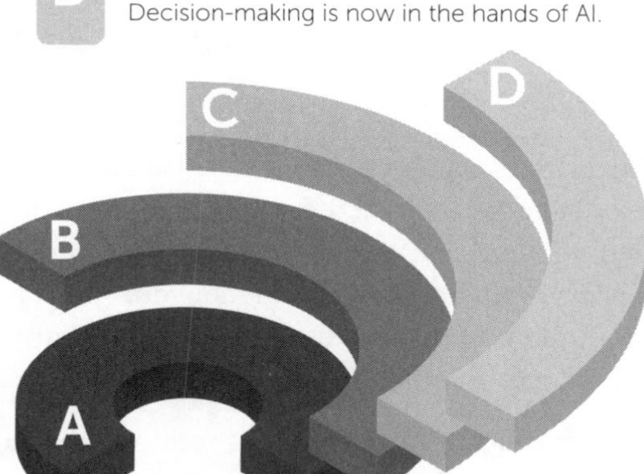

FIGURE 3.2 Pitfalls and challenges of AI

Future of AI-Assisted Recruitment and Selection

The future of AI in recruitment is teeming with potential. The rapid advancement of AI products, integrations with existing systems, and services in the market advancements are reshaping the recruitment landscape, making the process more efficient and inclusive. Let's ask Chat GPT to probe this aspect:

> ***"How do you think AI will shape recruitment and selection in the future?"***
>
> Automation Expansion: AI's role in automating mundane tasks will likely expand. More sophisticated AI could handle higher-level tasks such as conducting initial interviews or even negotiating job offers.

Better Candidate Experience: AI can offer a more engaging, interactive candidate experience. For example, AI could guide candidates through the application process or provide real-time feedback, making the process more transparent and less intimidating.

Bias Reduction: There's ongoing work to reduce bias in AI systems. In the future, we might see AI that's better at recognizing and mitigating bias, leading to more fair and equitable recruitment.

Increased Data Privacy: As data privacy concerns grow, there will be more emphasis on secure AI systems that protect candidate data.

It's essential that you, as a project manager, remain adaptable, learn about these advancements, and apply them responsibly in your projects. Balancing AI's capabilities with the human touch is crucial, leveraging personnel or AI where they shine the most.

AI-Driven Team Onboarding, Training, and Development

Once the talent acquisition phase concludes, you need onboarding, training, and development to integrate these new members effectively into the team. However, standard one-size-fits-all onboarding processes often miss the mark, lacking the personal touch that individual employees need to acclimate and grow within their roles. Here's where AI-driven approaches can create a significant difference.

By using artificial intelligence, you can tailor onboarding and training initiatives to match your individual employees' unique needs, skills, and learning styles. AI can make these processes more engaging, efficient, and, most importantly, personalized.

Onboarding and Training

Imagine the first day of new team members on your project—the flurry of introductions, the avalanche of information, the apprehension mixed with excitement. An organization can demonstrate its mission, values, and unique characteristics through a well-executed onboarding process. Onboarding provides new hires with access to essential systems and an overview of successful team culture.

Can a friendly AI guide them through this process, answering questions and providing personalized training and guidance? Let's ask.

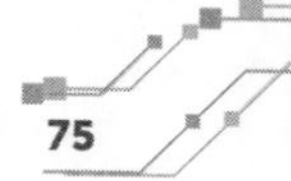

"We have a new team member joining our Global Health website project. As a project manager, I'm curious to know how AI could help in onboarding and training. Can you walk me through the basics?"

AI has tremendous potential in onboarding and training, making them more efficient, personalized, and engaging. Here's a basic outline of how it works:

Efficiency: AI can automate mundane onboarding tasks such as filling out paperwork, freeing up human resources to focus on more important tasks.

Personalization: AI can provide personalized training modules based on the new member's role, background, and learning style.

Engagement: Interactive AI tools can make the training process more interactive and engaging, improving knowledge retention.

Support: AI can provide 24/7 support, answering queries and assisting whenever the new member needs it.

This is a broad overview. The specifics would depend on project needs, support available from human resources, and the AI tools at your disposal. Let's delve deeper into how AI can enhance team onboarding.

The Role of AI in Team Onboarding

Onboarding is often a time-consuming process involving a lot of paperwork and scheduling. What role could AI play for a company like Global Health?

"Can you explain how automation can be used during onboarding?"

Paperwork Processing: AI can automate the processing of necessary paperwork. This can include forms for personal information, tax documents, and policy acknowledgment. For example, let's say Lisa has to fill out her tax information. AI can pre-fill the form with the details Lisa provided during the recruitment process.

Onboarding Schedule: AI can automatically generate an onboarding schedule based on the new hire's role, department, and other key factors. This can include introductory meetings, training sessions, and check-ins.

For Lisa, this means she doesn't have to guess what her first week will look like, as she will have a detailed schedule outlining her tasks. Let's see how AI can help with further personalization.

"How can AI personalize the onboarding experience for new hires like Lisa?"

Personalization can make the onboarding process engaging and relevant. Here are a few ways AI can help:

Role-Specific Content: AI can analyze Lisa's role and responsibilities in the Global Health project and provide her with relevant content. This might include briefs on previous projects, critical documents, and introductory materials about her job.

Learning Style Adaptation: People have different learning styles. AI can assess how Lisa interacts with the onboarding materials and adjust the content to fit her learning style. For instance, if Lisa seems to engage more with visual content, AI could provide more infographics, diagrams, and videos.

Nudges for Next Steps: AI could also anticipate what Lisa needs to know next and provide timely nudges. If Lisa is reviewing a document on the project's objectives, AI might suggest she look at the timeline next.

With AI, you have a tailored journey for Lisa.

AI can also be instrumental in helping new hires like Lisa gain the knowledge they need. **Figure 3.3** describes the roles for AI, including on-demand support, learning pathways, and performance feedback.

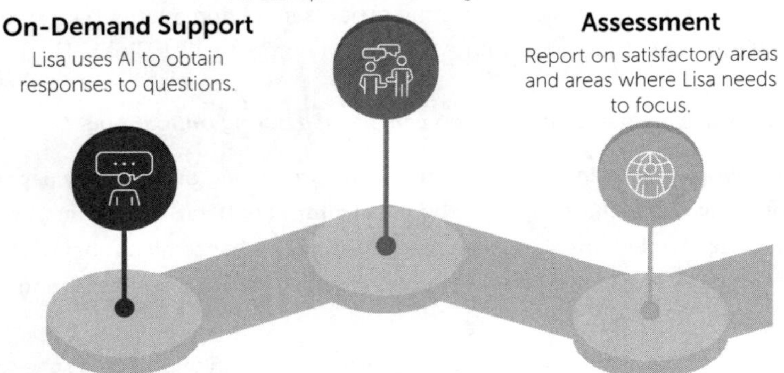
Learning Pathway
Training modules are recommended based on the role—for example understanding Scrum.
On-Demand Support
Lisa uses AI to obtain responses to questions.
Assessment
Report on satisfactory areas and areas where Lisa needs to focus.

FIGURE 3.3 Tailored journey for knowledge acquisition

Now let's look at this from the perspective of Lisa, who will start working as a project coordinator on the product development team. She could use a prompt like this:

"I could use some help in my role as project coordinator in the Product Development team. I will coordinate project activities, maintain project documentation, liaise with stakeholders, and ensure project timelines and quality standards are met in the tech industry. My key performance indicator this quarter is successfully delivering two product enhancements on time and within budget. Could you generate a 30-60-90-day onboarding plan? Use the SMART framework. Please match each SMART goal with a metric to measure my success objectively. Provide this output in table format."

AI would reply with an output such as the following:

> Welcome aboard, Lisa! Let's craft your 30-60-90-day onboarding plan based on your given role and responsibilities. Here's a bit of background to get us started:
>
> You've just started a new job as a Project Coordinator in the Product Development team. You'll coordinate project activities, maintain project documentation, liaise with stakeholders, and ensure project timelines and quality standards are met in the tech industry. Your key performance indicator this quarter is to successfully deliver two product enhancement projects on time and within budget. The SMART onboarding plan is shown below.

SMART GOALS	METRICS
Specific: Acquire a full understanding of the two enhancement projects, the team, and the stakeholders. **Measurable:** Successfully lead a kickoff meeting for both projects. **Achievable:** With support from the team lead and adequate project documentation. **Relevant:** Directly related to your role as Project Coordinator. **Time-bound:** To be achieved within the first month.	Kickoff meeting held, feedback from team members and stakeholders, and self-assessment of understanding.

continues

SMART GOALS	METRICS
Specific: Streamline the project plan and process based on the project understanding. **Measurable:** Implement process improvements improving weekly progress. **Achievable:** With feedback from the team and approval from the project manager. **Relevant:** This will directly impact the delivery of the projects. **Time-bound:** To be completed by the end of the second month.	Project plan updated, process improvements documented, and measure of progress efficiency (time saved).
Specific: Successfully manage project execution to stay on schedule and within budget. **Measurable:** Both projects are on track without any major issues. **Achievable:** With the help of the refined project plan and collaboration of the team. **Relevant:** Meeting project deadlines and budgets are KPIs for your role. **Time-bound:** To be accomplished by the end of the third month.	Project status reports, budget reports, stakeholder feedback, and project timeline tracking.

Obtaining stakeholder feedback on the plan is essential, and with that adjustment, this tailored onboarding plan is a good starting point for Lisa.

TECHNICAL GUIDE Technical Guide 3.2 provides an opportunity for you to experiment with the onboarding prompt template.

AI's Impact on Team Development and Training

Let's imagine the scenario where our Global Health project is moving along well. Lisa, who was recently onboarded, is now transitioning into the training phase of her team integration. AI can make this process more efficient, targeted, and engaging.

"We have managed to get Lisa on board with our project, but now comes a critical phase: training. How can AI make this process more effective?"

Two recommendations provided by ChatGPT appear relevant:

> Continuous Learning and Up-Skilling: AI can identify gaps in team members' skills and suggest suitable learning resources. It ensures team members like Lisa continue to grow and develop their skills, staying up-to-date in an ever-evolving field.
>
> Training Effectiveness Assessment: AI can monitor progress, analyze the performance of training modules, and provide feedback. This means the effectiveness of Lisa's training can be assessed, and necessary adjustments can be made.

AI can help Lisa apply her learning.

> ***"Can you explain how AI can facilitate bridging the gap between learning and application?"***
>
> Scenario-Based Learning: AI can create real-life scenarios or simulations where Lisa can apply what she's learned. This could include handling conflict within the team, solving project-related issues, or making strategic decisions. It provides a safe environment to learn, make mistakes, and learn from them.
>
> Real-Time Assistance: AI tools can provide real-time support while Lisa works on tasks. If she is unsure how to proceed, AI can provide suggestions based on the training she received.
>
> Performance Tracking: By monitoring Lisa's work, AI can assess how well she is applying the learned skills and provide constructive feedback.

The value AI brings extends beyond personalized learning paths and interactive training. It has the potential to guide team members through various project management methodologies, assist with software training, and provide mentorship in complex project scenarios.

Lisa might need to learn about different project management methodologies and understand the software tools. Should Lisa recommend a predictive approach, the adaptive approach, or Lean? AI can help guide Lisa through various project management methodologies' principles, processes, and best practices (discussed further in Chapter 4, "Choosing a Development Approach with AI"). It can provide resources, explain complex concepts, and even quiz Lisa to ensure she's grasping the concepts.

AI can provide step-by-step guidance, answer questions, and offer troubleshooting assistance. Suppose Lisa is learning how to use project management software such as Jira. In that case, AI can guide her in creating and assigning tasks, tracking project progress, or setting up notifications.

In both these scenarios, AI provides a safe, low-pressure environment for Lisa to learn at her own pace and can also serve as a mentor. Here's how ChatGPT explains it:

> Question and Answer: Lisa can ask AI any questions she has about her role, a task, or a concept she's learned. AI can provide detailed, easy-to-understand answers. Think of it as a knowledgeable colleague who's always available to help.
>
> Scenario Discussions: AI can discuss complex project scenarios with Lisa, helping her understand different perspectives and approaches. It can present similar past scenarios, discuss potential strategies, and assess the pros and cons of each.
>
> Reflective Practice: AI can prompt Lisa to reflect on her experiences, her decisions, and their outcomes. By encouraging Lisa to articulate her thoughts and reasoning, AI can help Lisa develop critical thinking and decision-making skills.

We've seen that AI can help create dynamic onboarding plans, assist with ongoing training, and even act as a coach for professional development. All this leads to improved performance, higher job satisfaction, and lower employee turnover rates.

Enhancing Leadership with AI

Effective team leadership is pivotal to project success. An adept leader can coordinate efforts, foster collaboration, maintain morale, and guide the team toward their common goal. However, team leadership is an intricate endeavor that involves managing diverse personalities, skill sets, and communication styles. Balancing this diversity while ensuring efficient progress can be a daunting task. This is where AI-enhanced team leadership comes into play. **Figure 3.4** describes some of the areas where AI can help.

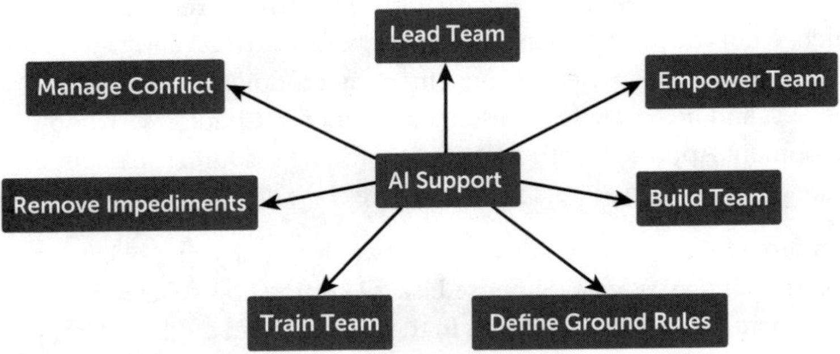

FIGURE 3.4 AI-enhanced leadership

Artificial intelligence, coupled with human leadership, can profoundly transform team management dynamics. AI can help leaders streamline communication, boost productivity, personalize engagement, and identify areas for team improvement.

Using AI for Setting Vision and Direction

The success of any project ultimately ties back to the vision and direction set forth by its leaders. You might ask, how does the project fit in with the broader mission and vision of my organization? How can you ensure alignment between the project goals and your organization's strategic objectives? Let's consider these important questions, using our ongoing Global Health project as a case study.

The first step in setting the vision and direction for a project is understanding the "why." In the case of Global Health, the project's objective is to build a website to increase awareness and engagement for the organization. But the *why* goes deeper—it's tied to the larger mission of Global Health, which is to enhance global access to health-care information and resources.

As a project manager, you can leverage AI tools like ChatGPT to break down this broader organizational mission into specific, actionable project goals.

> ***"I'm trying to understand how the Global Health website project aligns with the organization's larger mission. How can we break down this mission into specific goals for our project?"***
>
> Based on the mission of Global Health, some achievable project goals could be:
>
> Increase accessibility: The website should be designed in a way that's accessible to all, regardless of geographical location or technological proficiency.
>
> Enhance engagement: The website should provide interactive resources, tools, and content to engage visitors and encourage them to be part of the health-care conversation.
>
> Foster collaboration: The website should provide platforms for stakeholders to collaborate on health-care initiatives, share information, and support each other.

These project goals reflect the broader mission of Global Health well. They ensure alignment between the project and the organization's strategic objectives.

The next step is communicating these goals and the broader *why* to the project team. You can again leverage AI to help articulate these goals and the *why* clearly and engagingly.

> ***"Can you help me communicate these goals and the broader 'why' to the team?"***

The AI response is brief and relevant.

> Team, our project has a vital role in realizing the broader mission of Global Health, which is to enhance global access to health-care information and resources. We're not just building a website; we're creating a platform that increases accessibility, enhances engagement, and fosters collaboration in the health-care space. Our project is a crucial piece in the larger mission puzzle, and each one of you plays an essential role in bringing this mission to life.

Lastly, you can use AI to monitor progress toward these goals, providing real-time updates with the ability to adjust the direction as necessary. AI can analyze data, flag potential roadblocks, and suggest possible course corrections. AI is a valuable tool, but the leadership, empathy, and judgment you bring are irreplaceable.

It's also important to create an exciting project or product vision that aligns with your organization's strategic goals. The vision serves as the North Star, inspiring and guiding your team as they navigate through the challenges of the project.

The project vision for your Global Health initiative could be:

> *We aim to create a digital platform that will democratize health-care information, making it accessible, engaging, and collaborative for everyone, regardless of geographical location or technological proficiency.*

This vision aligns with the broader mission of Global Health and its strategic objectives, providing a clear direction for your team. However, creating such a vision is just the start. The real challenge lies in communicating it effectively to the team and maintaining focus on this vision throughout the project's life cycle.

Here is where AI tools like ChatGPT can prove invaluable:

> ***"How can we effectively communicate this vision to our team and ensure we stay true to this vison throughout the project?"***

A compelling vision should be communicated as a story that inspires and motivates. Here's a possible way to share it with your team:

As a team, we are embarking on a journey that has the power to change lives around the world. We are not just building a website; we are creating a platform that will break down barriers, ensuring that quality health-care information is no longer a privilege but a right that everyone can access regardless of where they live or their level of technological skill.

Our vision is to democratize healthcare information, make it engaging, and foster global collaboration. We're not just aiming to create a functional, user-friendly website; we're striving to build a platform that resonates with everyone who interacts with it. Every line of code we write, every design decision we make, should be guided by this vision.

To ensure you stay true to this vision, I suggest regular check-ins at key milestones to revisit the vision and assess how well your decisions and progress align with it.

As the leader, you will be communicating the vision effectively, demonstrating commitment through your actions, fostering a positive team culture, and aligning individual roles and tasks with the vision. By accomplishing this, you can lead your team to believe in the vision and work toward it.

The ability to effectively communicate the vision, its importance, and the alignment of project goals is one of the most crucial leadership skills a project manager must possess. As the project manager, you can leverage AI, but the inspiration and motivation that drive a team toward the vision come from your leadership.

Motivating Teams with AI

Motivating a team relates closely to the work you've done on the vision. When team members understand how their work contributes to the larger picture, they're more likely to be motivated, engaged, and committed to the project's success.

Motivating your team involves learning what drives each team member, aligning their individual goals with the project's objectives, recognizing their efforts, and fostering a positive and supportive work environment. Today, AI can lend a hand in these areas, making the process more efficient, personalized, and effective.

Individual Goals

Determining what drives each team member is not a straightforward task. Everyone has different intrinsic and extrinsic motivators; understanding them can take time and patience. This is where AI can be a valuable tool.

Suppose you want to understand what motivates your team in the Global Health project. Assuming the team completed a survey, the following prompt could provide good insight:

> ***"I need to understand what motivates my team. We've recently completed a survey where each member shared what drives them in their work. Can you analyze the responses and help me identify common themes and individual motivators?"***

Based on this prompt, ChatGPT could analyze the survey responses and provide insights into the different motivators present within the team. This could range from intrinsic motivators like learning opportunities and achievement to extrinsic motivators like bonuses or salary. Knowing these, you can craft personalized motivation strategies to drive each team member to perform their best.

Alignment

When team members see how their work contributes to the project's success and aligns with their personal and professional goals, their engagement and motivation levels rise.

Once again, let's consider our Global Health project. If you wanted to align team members' goals with the project objectives, you could ask AI to help map these out:

> ***"I have the project objectives for the Global Health project, and I also have a list of personal and professional goals from each team member. Can you help me align these goals with our project objectives?"***

By identifying individual goals and project objectives, ChatGPT can provide a roadmap on how these two can intersect, creating a win–win situation where team members feel their work contributes to their personal growth and the project's success.

Staying Positive

Every project, including the Global Health project, inevitably faces challenges. During these turbulent times, team morale can dip and motivation levels can wane. A project manager's role is not just to navigate through these difficult times, but also to keep the team motivated, ensuring they remain focused and productive.

You could consult AI like ChatGPT to brainstorm motivational strategies in challenging scenarios:

> ***"We've hit a rough patch in our Global Health project. The team's morale is low, and I need some creative ideas to motivate them. Can you help?"***

AI would generate various responses, from suggesting specific team-building activities to proposing personalized words of encouragement for each team member based on what it has learned about their motivations and personality.

Celebrating project milestones is vital for acknowledging the team's hard work and progress. However, after the celebration, there is often a risk of a lull in momentum. Ensuring your team remains motivated and focused on the next set of goals is key to maintaining the project pace. You could write a prompt like this:

> ***"We've just hit a significant milestone with our Global Health project, and the team is thrilled. However, I want to ensure we maintain this momentum. Can you suggest strategies for doing so?"***

In response, you might see the following:

> Set the next set of clearly defined short-term goals.
>
> Develop a "post-win" plan that includes recognizing individuals' contributions and reaffirming how these wins align with the overall project objectives and individual team members' goals.

In summary, whether it's understanding individual motivators, aligning personal goals with project objectives, supporting the team through challenges, or maintaining momentum after wins, AI can be a powerful tool in a project manager's motivational arsenal. But keep in mind that AI is a good tool for augmenting human leadership, not replacing it. The human touch, empathy, and interpersonal skills that you bring are still paramount in motivating and successfully leading a team.

Understanding and Influencing Stakeholders with AI

Negotiating and influencing plays a critical role in successful project outcomes. Project managers constantly navigate situations in which they must engage and influence various stakeholders, such as team members, sponsors, executives, and customers. This influence is not just about manipulation; it's about creating alignment, driving understanding, and fostering buy-in for a shared vision or direction.

How can AI software help project managers improve in this human, interpersonal aspect of their work? Using our Global Health project as a case study, let's consider this topic again.

First, the power of influence often lies in the quality of the information you can bring to bear. Here, various tools that work with ChatGPT can provide you with critical data, insightful analytics, and objective evidence.

> ***"ChatGPT, we have a challenging meeting coming up with our stakeholders, who seem quite skeptical about our proposed website design. They have expressed reservations about its user-centric approach, fearing it may compromise the professional look they envision for the website. Could you help me gather evidence and arguments to support our perspective?"***

You can expect a response such as the following:

> It's well established in the UX/UI field that user-centric design improves user engagement and can significantly enhance a site's professional image. Here are some specific points you might want to consider...

ChatGPT's ability to retrieve and summarize relevant information from vast amounts of data is invaluable in these circumstances. It equips you with robust evidence to support your perspectives and can help you influence stakeholders more effectively.

Second, AI tools like ChatGPT can aid in the communication process itself. Effective communication is a cornerstone of influence, and AI can assist you in conveying your messages in clear, compelling, and persuasive ways.

"I'm preparing a presentation to our team about why we should adopt a new project management software. Some of the team members are quite attached to our current system and might resist the change. Can you help me draft a persuasive argument on why this shift will be beneficial in the long run?"

One of the main benefits of switching to the new software is its superior feature set, which includes...

In this way, ChatGPT can provide guidance and suggestions for effectively communicating the benefits and rationale behind proposed changes, thus helping you influence your team's openness to new ideas.

Finally, influence is about building relationships, understanding others, and being able to see situations from different perspectives. Although AI does not replace the human ability to connect with others emotionally and empathetically, it can provide quantitative insights into human behaviors and preferences, helping you tailor your approach to different individuals and groups.

"I have some stakeholder feedback data from our last project. We've conducted an anonymous survey with our stakeholders about our performance. Here's some data:

Communication (rated on a scale of 1–10): [8, 7, 6, 7, 8, 7, 7, 9, 9, 7]

Deadline Management (rated on a scale of 1–10): [7, 8, 7, 6, 7, 6, 7, 8, 9, 7]

Quality of Outputs (rated on a scale of 1–10): [9, 8, 8, 7, 7, 9, 9, 9, 8, 9]

Stakeholder Engagement (rated on a scale of 1–10): [8, 7, 8, 7, 6, 8, 9, 7, 7, 8]

Additionally, we have received written feedback. Here are some selected comments:

'The team communicated well, but there were times when I felt left out of the loop.'

'Deadlines were met, but it often felt last-minute.'

'The final output was of high quality, though I had concerns about the process.'

'Overall engagement was good but can be improved.'

Can you help me analyze this data to better understand their concerns and preferences?"

The results are displayed graphically in **Figure 3.5**.

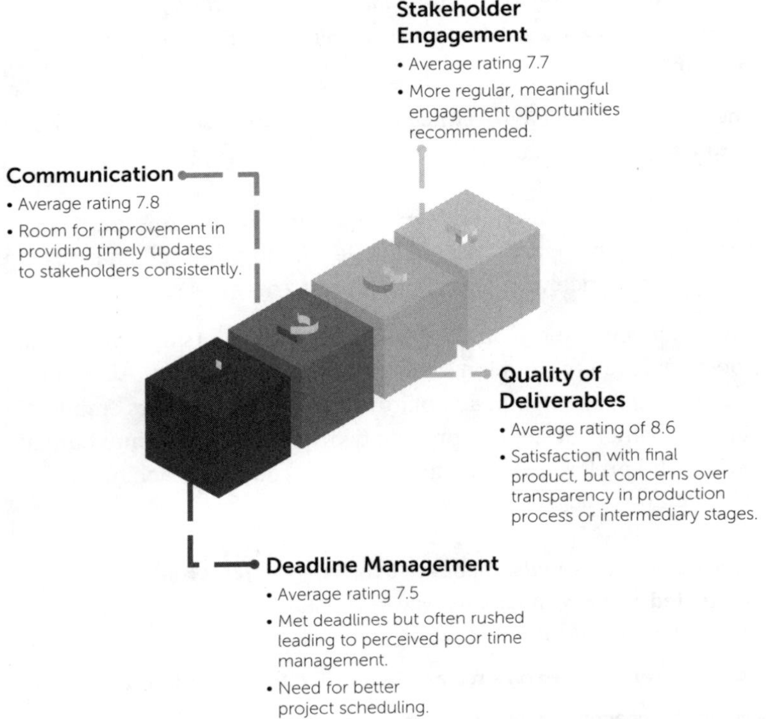

Stakeholder Engagement
• Average rating 7.7
• More regular, meaningful engagement opportunities recommended.
Communication
• Average rating 7.8
• Room for improvement in providing timely updates to stakeholders consistently.
Quality of Deliverables
• Average rating of 8.6
• Satisfaction with final product, but concerns over transparency in production process or intermediary stages.
Deadline Management
• Average rating 7.5
• Met deadlines but often rushed leading to perceived poor time management.
• Need for better project scheduling.

FIGURE 3.5 Team communications: graphic of survey results tabulated by AI

Based on this analysis, you could focus on the following areas for improvement: more consistent and detailed communication, better project schedule management, more transparency in the project execution process, and consistent and meaningful stakeholder engagement. Remember, every project is a learning opportunity.

These insights can help you strategize your approach and make stakeholders feel more valued. AI successfully assists you, as the project manager, to better understand your stakeholders and engage them to be more effective leaders.

Emotional Intelligence and AI

Emotional intelligence (EI), the ability to recognize, understand, and manage our own and others' emotions, is a key aspect of effective leadership. In a project management context, a leader with a high EI can foster a more empathetic, understanding, and thus productive work environment.

Figure 3.6 illustrates the components of EI, which are defined as follows:

- **Self-Awareness:** Recognizing and understanding your own emotions and how they influence your behavior.
- **Self-Management:** Controlling your emotions and adapting to changing circumstances. Involves goal setting and achieving.
- **Social Awareness:** Understanding others' emotions and needs, empathizing with them, and grasping group dynamics.
- **Social Skills:** Nurturing social relationships, managing conflicts, exerting influence, and working effectively in a team.

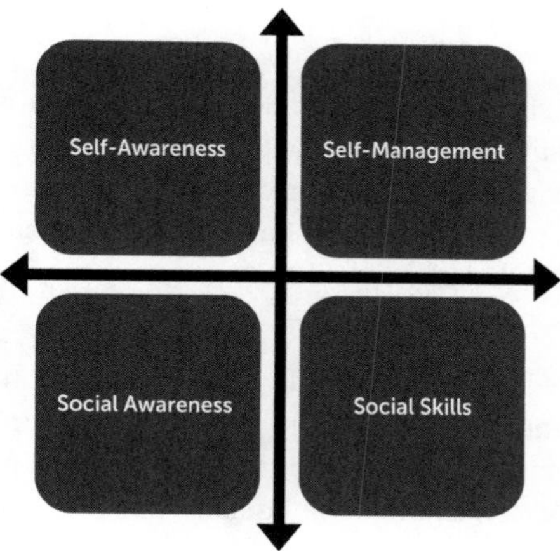

FIGURE 3.6 Quadrant illustrating components of emotional intelligence

Now, how can artificial intelligence help us with emotional intelligence, you may ask?

On the surface, AI, being inherently nonhuman, may seem far removed from the world of emotional intelligence. However, AI tools can offer surprising avenues to boost our emotional intelligence capabilities, especially understanding and managing emotions in a team setting.

Assume you've conducted a team meeting in which some key decisions were made. You've recorded the meeting minutes, and you want to analyze the emotional undertone of the meeting to understand your team's sentiments better. A good starting point would be the following prompt:

> ***"I have the minutes of our recent team meeting. It was a pretty intense one with a lot of important decisions. Can you help me understand the overall emotional tone of the discussion?"***

AI analysis is based on the text provided and doesn't account for nonverbal cues or context outside of the text. Here's a broad overview of the output:

> Positive Sentiments: Several phrases indicated optimism and agreement, such as "exciting potential," "brilliant idea," and "great teamwork." These suggest a sense of enthusiasm and collaboration in the team.
>
> Negative Sentiments: There were also some expressions of concern or disagreement, like "unrealistic expectations," "tight schedule," and "budget worries." These reflect some apprehensions within the team.
>
> Neutral Statements: Most of the text involved factual statements or logistical discussions. These are crucial for the project but do not indicate strong emotions.

The above emotional tone analysis suggests that while the team is generally enthusiastic and collaborative, there are concerns about project expectations, schedules, and budgets. AI recommends that addressing these concerns in the next team meeting might be helpful to ensure that everyone is on the same page and that any apprehensions are openly discussed and managed.

As the project manager, with the help of AI, you can gauge the emotional climate of your team. Such insights can guide you to manage your team's emotions effectively, ensuring that concerns are addressed, positive sentiments are reinforced, and, ultimately, team morale remains high.

Let's look at how AI can aid in gaining these insights using the Global Health project as our continuous case study.

Self-awareness is about understanding your emotions and how they impact your actions. As a project manager, you could use ChatGPT to facilitate self-reflection by prompting you to consider your responses to certain situations.

> ***"I had a tough interaction with a team member today, and I think I reacted poorly. Can you help me reflect on this?"***
>
> Of course! Let's start by identifying what happened. Can you describe the interaction and how you responded?

Through this conversation, AI can help you reflect and gain insight into your own emotional reactions.

Once you recognize your emotions, the next step is managing them effectively (**self-management**). As a project manager, you can use ChatGPT to explore different strategies for emotion management.

> ***"I feel quite stressed about the upcoming project deadline. Can you suggest some strategies to help me manage this stress?"***
>
> Certainly! Stress can be challenging to manage, especially with looming deadlines. Here are some strategies that might help...
>
> *{Response truncated for brevity and relevance.}*

AI can provide a range of suggestions, from practical time management techniques to mindfulness exercises, to help you navigate your emotions effectively.

Social awareness involves understanding and empathizing with the emotions of others. In this regard, ChatGPT can help analyze team communication to identify potential emotional undercurrents, as you've already seen.

To prepare for a difficult conversation with a team member, you can role-play the conversation with AI to practice your approach. Use a prompt such as the following to get going:

> ***"I need to have a difficult conversation with one of my team members about their performance. Can we role-play this conversation?"***
>
> Absolutely. Would you like to start, or shall I?

By role-playing with ChatGPT, you can explore different ways of addressing the situation, thus improving your interpersonal skills and ultimately managing the relationship more effectively.

To conclude, AI can help you work on your EI, but it can't fully comprehend the depth and complexity of human emotions. Therefore, face-to-face interactions, open dialogues, and empathetic understanding remain vital for effective leadership and team management.

Using AI Tools to Enhance Team Collaboration

In today's increasingly connected and dynamic workplace, effective team collaboration forms the backbone of successful project outcomes. The complexity and diversity of tasks necessitate seamless communication, coordination, and collaboration among team members. To manage these challenges, AI tools are revolutionizing how we collaborate, making the process more efficient, engaging, and productive.

AI-driven project management and collaboration platforms can provide various services. These include providing project updates, scheduling and coordinating meetings, facilitating brainstorming sessions, and ensuring transparent and consistent communication. AI tools can dynamically adapt to your team's needs, fostering an environment of effective collaboration.

In this section, we'll consider the many ways AI can facilitate cross-functional collaboration, as well as address the possible challenges and solutions in implementing AI for team collaboration.

Enhancing Team Communication with AI

In a complex, multifaceted project like the Global Health project, it becomes increasingly essential to maintain clear and effective communication channels. Misunderstandings or miscommunications can result in project delays, cost overruns, or even a project failure. With AI tools, the landscape of team communication has transformed.

Providing Quick Answers

In our Global Health project, a team member might ask this question:

> ***"Could you provide a quick overview of the latest developments in our initiatives?"***

Here, ChatGPT could provide a detailed summary of the major Global Health initiatives up to its training data cutoff date:

> Up until September 2021, significant Global Health initiatives include efforts to manage and understand the COVID-19 pandemic better, the push toward achieving universal health coverage, addressing climate change–related health issues, and combatting antimicrobial resistance, among others... *{Response truncated for brevity and relevance.}*

This response gives the team member a concise summary and can aid further research efforts.

Improving Communication

As a project manager aiming to stress the importance of adhering to the project timeline, you might ask the following:

> ***"How can I communicate the importance of adhering to the project timeline more effectively to the team?"***
>
> Here's a draft of a suggested approach:
>
> Dear team, I want to emphasize the critical nature of our project timeline. It serves as our roadmap, keeping us aligned and focused. Each milestone we meet directly impacts our success. While I understand our challenges, I believe in our collective ability to meet these deadlines. Let's continue to support each other in this endeavor. If you encounter issues affecting your timelines, please reach out so we can address them together...

Collaboration and Brainstorming

In a brainstorming session, you might seek innovative ideas for community engagement by asking this:

> ***"We're brainstorming ways to increase community engagement for our Global Health project. Can you provide some innovative ideas?"***

The AI response could include a comprehensive list of strategies. Here are some excerpts:

> Certainly, here are some innovative ways to increase community engagement: 1. Organize online forums and webinars to educate the community about the project... 2. Partner with local influencers or leaders who can help spread the word... 3. Utilize social media platforms to share project updates and engage with the community... 4. Develop an app or website feature that allows the community to track the project's progress and contribute ideas...

Enhancing Writing Skills

A team member seeking to improve their project report might make this request:

> ***"Please provide feedback on this report."***

AI could offer feedback on multiple aspects, including content, structure, language use, and more:

> Certainly, here's some feedback: Your report is detailed and informative. However, the structure could be improved for better clarity. I suggest following a more linear approach to present your findings... Your language is clear, but some sentences are too long, which might confuse the reader... Consider using more bullet points and subheadings to break up the text and make it more readable...

Such a detailed response can significantly help your team members improve their writing skills and produce higher-quality reports.

Analyzing and Summarizing Meetings

Consider a scenario where you've just concluded an essential meeting with multiple project stakeholders, and you have collected several action items, decisions, and key takeaways. Analyzing and summarizing this information manually can be a daunting task. However, you can use AI to simplify this process:

> ***"We've had a significant project update meeting today, and I need your assistance to extract the key points. Here's the meeting transcript. Can you help?"***
>
> Due to unforeseen server issues, the project timeline has been pushed back slightly. However, the technical team anticipates these problems will be resolved by the end of the week.
>
> The marketing team has finalized their strategy for the project launch and plans to share it with the team next week.
>
> The beta testing phase has garnered mostly positive responses, with some minor changes suggested for the user interface. The development team will make the necessary changes.
>
> The next review meeting is set for the end of the month, where all team leads are expected to present their progress updates.

By having an AI like ChatGPT summarize the meeting, you ensure that no key point is missed and keep everyone on the team on the same page. Also, you can update any team members who could not attend the meeting about the proceedings.

Next, consider the often vast language gap between team members from different areas of expertise. It's not uncommon for a technical expert to have to convey complex, specialized information to a nontechnical stakeholder. ChatGPT can serve as a bridge in such situations:

> ***"Our technical lead has provided an update that reads, 'The back-end refactoring for better async handling is complete. The API endpoints are more performant now, and the front-end team will have an easier time working with them.' I need to convey this to a nontechnical stakeholder. Can you simplify this for me?"***
>
> Here's a more accessible version: "Our tech team has made significant upgrades to the behind-the-scenes infrastructure of our project. As a result, the project's website or app will perform more efficiently, and it should make the work of our other teams easier as well."

While we've used ChatGPT as an example here, it's worth noting that the AI market offers many similar tools. For instance, some tools can join virtual meetings, listen in, and summarize the meeting, highlighting key points, decisions, and action items. Such technology can greatly improve the efficiency and effectiveness of team communication, contributing to a more streamlined and coordinated project management process.

As generative AI advances and matures, additional products are arriving in the marketplace. They can join virtual meetings, listen in, highlight key points, summarize meeting minutes, generate action items based on transcripts, and more. Products currently include Microsoft Teams Premium, Slack GPT, and Zoom AI Companion. These tools are cloud-based platforms that allow users to chat, call, share files, and collaborate on projects. However, they also have some unique features that make them stand out from other communication tools.

By enhancing communication, these AI tools ensure that the project team, stakeholders, and project managers are aligned toward the common project goals, leading to improved project outcomes. They bring clarity, save time, and help maintain project momentum—crucial aspects of successful project management.

Facilitating Cross-Functional Collaboration with AI

Cross-functional collaboration is a defining characteristic of many project teams, involving members from different areas of expertise working toward a common goal. This diversity can provide a wellspring of innovation and problem-solving capacity, but it can also present challenges, especially regarding effective communication and collaboration. Artificial intelligence, particularly AI conversational models like ChatGPT, can significantly facilitate this process.

Suppose in the Global Health project you are preparing for a critical phase in which the engineering and marketing teams must collaborate closely. As the project manager, you could prompt:

> ***"Our engineering and marketing teams need to collaborate on the prototype's design for our Global Health project. What strategies can we implement to ensure effective and efficient cross-functional collaboration?"***

ChatGPT might suggest:

> Ensuring efficient and effective collaboration across different teams is pivotal for the success of your project. Here are some strategies that could help:
>
> Set Common Goals, Communication Plan, Regular Sync-ups, Use Project Management Tools, Create a Collaborative Environment, Bridging the Gap with a Lexicon

Now, ChatGPT brings up a great point about "bridging the gap." In cross-functional teams, it's common for different teams to have different jargon, terminologies, and ways of thinking. The engineering team, for instance, might have a very technical language filled with acronyms, whereas the marketing team might use more industry-specific phrases and concepts. This discrepancy in language can lead to misunderstandings and slow the progress of the project.

This is where an AI tool like ChatGPT can make a substantial impact. ChatGPT can assist in the creation of a shared lexicon—a common language—that can help bridge the gap between different functional teams. You might ask the following:

> ***"Can you help us create a lexicon that bridges the language gap between our engineering and marketing teams?"***

ChatGPT, processing this request, will respond with a general strategy for proceeding:

> Extraction of Terms: Initially, we can analyze the conversations, documents, emails, and other communication from both teams. From this analysis, we can identify and extract each team's most commonly used terms and their contextual meanings.

Creating Analogies: Next, we can create a list of analogies that relate the terms used by the engineering team to concepts that are familiar to the marketing team and vice versa. This process can help team members quickly understand the terminology of the other domain. For instance, an analogy could be: "Think of the software architecture (engineering term) as the storyboard (marketing term) for our software product. It outlines the overall structure and flow, just as a storyboard outlines the key scenes in a movie."

Sharing the Lexicon: Once the lexicon and analogies are created, we can share them with both teams. They can then use this lexicon as a reference during their communications, thereby minimizing misunderstandings and facilitating smoother collaboration.

We can ask AI to go deeper and provide some analogies between the two cross-functional teams, this time using technical terms:

"Can you please show more examples of the extraction of terms and analogies between the two teams?"

To extract terms, allow AI to analyze a week's worth of communication from both the engineering and marketing teams. After AI sifts through the data, it might identify the following terms as crucial in each team's communication:

Engineering Team:

- Agile development
- API (Application Programming Interface)
- DevOps
- Version control
- CI/CD (Continuous Integration and Continuous Delivery)

Marketing Team:

- SEO (Search Engine Optimization)
- User persona
- Content strategy
- Engagement metrics
- Conversion funnel

With this information, AI can then generate a list of analogies to help bridge the understanding between both teams. Here's how that might look:

> **Engineering to Marketing Analogies:**
>
> Agile development: Think of agile development like a flexible content strategy. We plan, create, and improve our software iteratively, much like how you plan, publish, and optimize content based on its performance.
>
> API: APIs are like collaboration partners for our software. They help our software interact with other applications, similar to how influencers help your content reach a broader audience.
>
> DevOps: DevOps is our way of ensuring that the development and operations teams work smoothly together, similar to how you aim for seamless collaboration between content creators and social media managers.
>
> **Marketing to Engineering Analogies:**
>
> SEO: SEO is a set of practices that make a website more visible on search engines, similar to how well-written code makes a software application more efficient.
>
> User persona: A user persona is a representation of our ideal customer, much like a use-case scenario represents an ideal path for our software's functionality.
>
> Conversion funnel: The conversion funnel is a way to visualize the journey of a customer, much like a data flow diagram visualizes the journey of data through our software.

By creating such a shared lexicon and using these analogies in communication, both teams can better understand each other's roles, leading to enhanced cross-functional collaboration and fostering smoother and more effective cross-functional collaboration.

AI in Conflict Resolution and Decision-Making

People and teams are complex, and when we bring in dimensions such as different cultures or virtual teams, there will inevitably be misunderstandings and conflicts—every project will present its own challenges. One of the inevitable obstacles that will arise in every team is miscommunication and internal conflict. Whether it's a clash of ideas, differences in approach to deliver a solution, or disagreements on priorities, conflicts can disrupt the harmony and productivity of the team.

But not all conflicts lead to disasters. When managed effectively, the conflict resolution process can lead to innovative solutions and a deeper camaraderie among team members. AI can play a transformative role in mitigating conflicts. It is impartial and has a rich set of solutions learned from previous conflicts that can help with decision-making.

AI can assist in conflict resolution by providing an unbiased perspective, identifying the root causes of the conflict, and suggesting potential resolutions. The AI model, being neutral, can mediate between the conflicting parties, encouraging dialogue and fostering a resolution that respects the views of all parties involved.

Problem-solving is a key part of the conflict resolution process. AI can significantly enhance the decision-making processes in a team to come up with innovative solutions and solve conflicts. Decision-making, especially in complex projects, often involves considering many factors, analyzing large amounts of data, and predicting potential outcomes. AI can simplify this process by providing data-driven insights, forecasting outcomes, and recommending solutions employing its vast data-handling capabilities and risk analysis.

Using AI to Facilitate Conflict Resolution

In any project environment, conflict is virtually inevitable. Whether it's a minor misunderstanding over responsibilities or a major disagreement over project objectives, these instances can interrupt workflow, dampen team morale, and, if left unresolved, jeopardize the project's success. Here's where AI models like ChatGPT can assist in facilitating a resolution.

AI can't replace human involvement in conflict resolution, especially when there is a need for professional interpersonal intervention, understanding emotional nuances, or dealing with cultural issues. However, it can support the process by providing impartial inputs, promoting objectivity, suggesting resolution strategies based on vast knowledge and past similar scenarios, and even identifying potential conflict points before they escalate.

Consider a scenario where your team members disagree on prioritizing tasks. One group believes that Task A should be tackled first due to its higher perceived value, whereas another group advocates for Task B because it's a prerequisite for several other tasks.

> ***"Our team disagrees about task prioritization. Group 1 insists on starting with Task A due to its higher perceived value, while Group 2 argues that Task B should be prioritized as it's foundational for other tasks. Can you guide how we can come to a resolution?"***

AI will suggest a few steps to consider:

> Define the Criteria: Clearly outline what criteria you're using to prioritize tasks. It could be urgency, ROI, effort needed, or how foundational the task is to other tasks. Make sure the criteria are clear, fair, and agreed upon by everyone.
>
> Rank Tasks Using the Criteria: Independently rank Task A and Task B using the agreed criteria. If possible, use a numerical system for objectivity.
>
> Discuss Rankings in a Team Meeting: Have each team present their case with the rationale behind their rankings. This open discussion can lead to mutual understanding and even compromise.
>
> Vote if Necessary: If the disagreement persists, consider a democratic approach where each team member votes after the discussion. This can help ensure everyone feels heard and part of the decision-making process.

As project manager, you should ensure the team understands that the goal is not about winning an argument but about finding the best way forward for the project.

The first step is to confront the issue. When an issue is identified and confronted as promptly as possible, it can promote collaboration. This will foster a space where all parties can openly discuss their differences and work toward a resolution that satisfies everyone. Delay in confronting an issue typically escalates tension and can significantlly impact project success.

Consider our Global Health project case study. As a project manager, you might pose the following question:

> ***"I want to set up a collaborative meeting to resolve a conflict between our data analysis and field research teams. They are having issues agreeing on the best way to collect data. Can you give me a structure for this meeting?"***

AI might provide the following, or something similar, on how you could structure your meeting:

> Introduction: Start by emphasizing the importance of collaboration and explain the purpose of the meeting. Creating an environment where everyone feels safe to express their opinions is crucial.
>
> Understanding the Issue: Allow each team to present their viewpoints about the best data collection method. Ensure everyone listens and tries to understand the other side.

Discussion: Encourage a constructive dialogue between the teams. Try to identify common grounds and areas of disagreement.

Brainstorm Solutions: As a group, brainstorm possible solutions. Aim for options that address the concerns of both teams.

Decision-Making: Review the suggested solutions collectively and decide on an action. The decision could be reached by consensus or, if necessary, a vote.

TECHNICAL GUIDE See Technical Guide 3.3. The above solution deals with confronting issues head-on and is the recommended approach. Since conflict management is an important topic, we provide additional information and prompts about other conflict management approaches in the Technical Guide.

Using AI to Support Decision-Making

From setting strategic directions to choosing between alternative paths, project managers often face complex decisions that can impact the outcome of the project. AI can assist in this process by providing data-driven insights and facilitating informed decision-making

For instance, ChatGPT can be utilized to explore different scenarios and their potential outcomes based on its knowledge of similar situations or understanding decision-making strategies. Let's consider a decision in our case study, the Global Health project.

"Some of us believe we should focus our efforts on developing a robust health-care infrastructure, while others believe we should prioritize educating the local population about health practices."

Upon requesting input on this prompt, we see the following response from AI:

Both approaches have their merits, and the choice ultimately depends on the specific context of your project. Here are some things to consider for each approach:

Developing Health-care Infrastructure: This strategy could provide a more immediate and visible impact on the community. It could enable faster and more effective treatment and prevention of diseases. However, it would require substantial resources and a longer implementation timeline.

Educating the Local Population: This approach might have a slower impact but could provide a more sustainable long-term solution. Knowledge and awareness about health practices can lead to behavioral changes that could decrease the prevalence of certain diseases over time. It might require fewer resources and could be implemented faster.

Ideally, a combination of both approaches could be the most effective. However, you need to consider your project's resources, timeline, objectives, and the specific needs of the community you're working with.

This gives you as a project manager objective, nuanced insights to inform your decision-making process. AI can also assist with decision-making in other ways. For example, when you're dealing with large amounts of data, AI can help summarize and interpret this data to facilitate understanding and decision-making. It can help draw out key trends, highlight significant findings, and provide an overall data summary, making it easier for you to make an informed decision.

"We have collected a lot of health data from our survey in the community. Can you help summarize it and highlight key findings?"

Absolutely, based on the data you provided, here are some key findings:

There is a high incidence of [disease X] in the [Y age group].

Most individuals lack access to [specific health-care service].

[Z percentage] of individuals are unaware of [particular health practice].

These findings suggest that there is a significant need for both health-care services and education in the community.

{Note that the brackets in the response would include the specific findings.}

"Based on your knowledge and understanding of similar projects, what are some potential risks we might face in our Global Health project, and how can we mitigate them?"

Several risks can potentially impact a global health project like yours. Here are a few, along with possible mitigation strategies:

Risk: Disease outbreak disrupting project activities. Mitigation: Develop a contingency plan that includes remote working arrangements and health and safety protocols.

Risk: Resistance from local communities. Mitigation: Ensure community engagement and awareness campaigns are part of the project to gain their acceptance and cooperation.

Risk: Resource limitations. Mitigation: Conduct regular resource planning and allocation reviews to ensure optimal use of available resources.

Scenario Planning: Project managers often need to consider multiple scenarios and their potential impacts on the project.

ChatGPT can help create or analyze these scenarios based on its vast knowledge:

> ***"Can you help me understand the possible scenarios if we decide to extend the project timeline by six months?"***
>
> Here are a few possible scenarios and their potential impacts:
>
> Scenario 1: The project scope is increased due to the extended timeline. While this could result in more comprehensive outcomes, it may also require more resources.
>
> Scenario 2: Stakeholders might express concerns over the delay, which could impact their commitment and support. Regular communication and updates could mitigate this.
>
> Scenario 3: The team might face fatigue due to the extended timeline, potentially impacting productivity. Regular team check-ins, breaks, and acknowledgment of their efforts could help maintain morale.

AI can aid in project performance analysis to help you make informed decisions. Using ChatGPT, you can ask for insights based on the performance data:

> ***"Our project progress seems to be progressing slower than expected. Could there be any reasons for this based on similar projects you know?"***
>
> Project delays can happen due to a variety of reasons. Here are a few potential causes:
>
> Scope Creep: Frequent changes or additions to the project scope can slow down progress.
>
> Resource Constraints: Insufficient resources or unoptimized resource allocation can impact project speed.
>
> Communication Breakdown: Delays can occur due to miscommunications or lack of clarity among team members.

Such insights can assist you in identifying potential problems and engage in a conversation with stakeholders. The outcome will hopefully result in an informed decision and steer the project in the right direction.

Using AI in Tuckman's Model

In 1965, psychologist Bruce Tuckman presented a model often referred to when discussing team development.[2] Tuckman's model consists of stages that every team goes through as it matures and strives for success:

1. **Forming:** It's a time of uncertainty and apprehension as team members are just getting to know each other and their roles. An AI tool can help organize and facilitate initial team meetings, clarify roles and responsibilities, and provide project information in an easily accessible manner.
2. **Storming:** This stage is characterized by conflicts as team members start to express their opinions. It's normal for team members to have different views, but conflicts must be managed constructively.
3. **Norming:** During this stage, team members start to resolve their differences, appreciate each other's strengths, and establish workflows.
4. **Performing:** This is when the team is effectively and efficiently working toward project goals.
5. **Adjourning:** This is the stage where the project is coming to an end, and the team members begin to move on to different projects.

Next, let's examine how AI can assist project managers in each stage.

Forming

"I am forming a team. Can you help me draft an email to the team, providing an overview of the project, and clarifying their roles and responsibilities?"

Here's a suggestion from AI describing how you might structure the email:

> Dear Team,
>
> I am excited to announce the commencement of Project X, aimed at developing an innovative software solution for our client, ABC Corp. This project is crucial to our ongoing commitment to providing top-notch software solutions.
>
> To ensure the project's success, each team member has been assigned specific roles and responsibilities:
>
> John, as the Project Lead, you'll be overseeing the project's progress and providing guidance to the team. Mary, as the Lead Developer, your expertise will be essential in developing the software. Ali, as the Business Analyst, you'll be in charge of understanding and incorporating the client's

2 Tuckman, B. W. Developmental sequence in small groups. *Psychological Bulletin*, 1965, 63(6), 384–399.

requirements into our design. Priya, as our Quality Assurance Lead, you'll be responsible for ensuring that our solution meets the quality standards set by our client and our company.

Each one of you plays a crucial role, and I'm confident that together, we can successfully deliver this project. Please feel free to contact me if you have any questions or need clarification about your roles.

Best,

[Your Name]

Storming

Consider the scenario where we're facing some conflicts in the team, particularly around design decisions.

"Can you help me draft a message that acknowledges everyone's perspectives and encourages collaborative resolution?"

Here's a suggested draft:

Dear Team,

I've noted that there have been some differences of opinion concerning our design decisions. I would like to commend you all on your passion and dedication to ensuring we deliver the best solution for our client.

As you all know, healthy debate can lead to innovative solutions. It's imperative to remember that we share a common goal—the success of Project X. I would like to call a meeting next week where we can openly discuss these ideas. Everyone's perspectives will be heard, and I believe that together, we can resolve these conflicts and find a design direction that aligns with our client's needs and our team's strengths.

Thank you for your ongoing commitment to this project.

Best,

[Your Name]

Norming

AI can help you communicate to encourage your team and acknowledge progress.

"Can you help me draft a message to the team, acknowledging the progress we've made in our recent discussions and encouraging further collaboration?"

Absolutely! Here's a draft for you:

Dear Team,

Over the past few weeks, we've had some intense discussions about the direction of Project X. I want to take a moment to appreciate the progress we've made.

I've noticed a renewed sense of unity and shared understanding among us. Our recent meeting has helped us align our ideas and expectations, and the dedication each one of you has shown is commendable.

Let's keep this momentum going. As we move forward, I encourage you to continue to share your ideas and feedback, no matter how big or small. Let's remember, it's our collective insights and collaboration that will lead us to success.

Thank you once again for your hard work and commitment.

Best,

[Your Name]

Performing

As part of ongoing communication, celebrating success is as important as solving problems.

"The team's really been hitting their stride and we're making excellent progress. Can you help me draft a message celebrating their success and encouraging continued effort?"

Of course! Here's a draft for your message:

Dear Team,

I'm writing this message with a sense of great pride and joy. Over the past few weeks, our team's performance on Project X has been nothing short of outstanding.

Each one of you has made significant contributions to our shared goals. Your continuous collaboration, initiative, and dedication have led us to this point of success, and for that, I am extremely thankful.

However, let's not forget that we still have milestones to reach. I am confident that with the same level of effort and cooperation, we can successfully complete this project and exceed our client's expectations.

Once again, congratulations on the excellent work. Let's keep up this momentum!

Best,

[Your Name]

Adjourning

It can be challenging to end an intense period of work and go separate ways. What does ChatGPT advise?

> Of course, wrapping up a project is just as critical as the initial phases, and I'm glad you're looking at it with such importance. Your project completion report should of course include a project summary, listing project achievements and challenges, but that's not all. Be sure to include:
>
> Lessons Learned:
>
> a. Highlight the key lessons learned throughout the project.
>
> b. Detail changes to be implemented in future projects as a result.
>
> Team Acknowledgments:
>
> a. Thank your team for their efforts.
>
> b. Acknowledge any standout performances.
>
> c. End with some optional social connection time.

Let's get into the lessons learned:

> ***"Based on the project notes, emails, and meeting transcripts, can you help me identify some of the key lessons learned from this project?"***
>
> Given the hypothetical data provided, here are a few possible lessons learned:
>
> Communication: There were several instances where clearer communication could have prevented missteps. Moving forward, we could benefit from implementing more structured communication strategies, such as weekly check-ins and detailed project updates.
>
> Resource Allocation: At times, resources were stretched thin, causing delays. Future projects could benefit from a more conservative approach to resource allocation, ensuring there's a buffer for unexpected needs.
>
> Risk Management: Some risks weren't fully anticipated, leading to surprises along the way. A more comprehensive risk management strategy could help us anticipate and mitigate risks better in the future.

> **TECHNICAL GUIDE** **We have also created a prompt template that you can adapt for your scenarios; see Technical Guide 3.4.**

AI can provide invaluable support in each stage of Tuckman's model of team development. ChatGPT's ability to generate clear, nuanced, and context-specific responses allows it to effectively assist you in guiding your teams through the various stages of development.

Ethical Considerations and Professional Responsibility

With the significant advantages AI tools bring to team management, they also present important ethical considerations and professional responsibilities that must be navigated wisely. From recruitment and onboarding to leadership, collaboration, conflict resolution, and decision-making, each involvement of AI carries its own set of ethical considerations. Also, it's essential to regularly evaluate the performance of AI and monitor for any negative impact. The use of AI may need to be adjusted or restricted.

AI-Assisted Recruitment and Onboarding

When you use AI tools in the recruitment process, it's essential to ensure fairness and objectivity. Bias can inadvertently be introduced through the training data provided to the AI model, which could result in unfair hiring practices. A preference for candidates who are similar to past successful candidates can perpetuate homogeneous teams. Ethical use of AI in this context means actively taking measures to avoid such biases, ensuring equal opportunity, and respecting diversity.

Similarly, in AI-driven onboarding, it's crucial to ensure that the use of AI doesn't isolate new team members or replace valuable human interaction. While AI can assist with providing information and answering queries, the human aspect of welcoming and integrating new members into the team should remain a priority.

AI in Team Leadership and Collaboration

AI tools can be excellent aids in team leadership, providing insights and suggestions based on vast data and knowledge. However, leaders remain accountable for their decisions and actions. AI outputs should be treated as aids, not replacements for human judgement, wisdom, and empathy in leadership.

In facilitating team collaboration, it's important to use AI responsibly and transparently. This includes ensuring that team members are aware of and comfortable with how their communications are being used and that their privacy is respected. It also involves validating AI insights with real-world context and judgment to avoid miscommunication or misunderstandings.

AI in Conflict Resolution and Decision-Making

AI can provide valuable assistance in conflict resolution and decision-making processes, but the ultimate responsibility lies with the human leaders. AI outputs should be considered as one of many inputs in these sensitive areas, and human judgment should always play the deciding role. Ethical considerations include treating AI advice with caution and considering the emotional and interpersonal aspects that AI might not fully understand.

In summary, while AI tools such as ChatGPT can revolutionize many aspects of team management, their use must be navigated with a strong ethical compass. Don't compromise when it comes to ensuring fairness, objectivity, and transparency when using AI in recruitment, onboarding, and team management. That said, there are ways to adhere to ethical standards while levering the many powerful advantages of AI to support leaders and enhance team management.

Key Points to Remember

Artificial intelligence tools, specifically products like ChatGPT, are revolutionizing the realm of recruitment, onboarding, and team management. When utilized effectively, AI can streamline processes, mitigate biases, and enhance decision-making. However, its integration must be approached with caution and vigilance. Here are the key points to consider:

- AI can optimize recruitment and onboarding but cannot replace the nuances of human interaction.
- Leadership and decision-making should leverage AI for data insights, but human judgment remains paramount.
- It's vital to ensure fairness, transparency, and accountability when employing AI, and to continually monitor its performance and impacts.
- Respect for data privacy and the importance of obtaining informed consent are essential.
- In any AI-related processes, human leaders hold the ultimate responsibility for outcomes and decisions.

Technical Guide

3.1 Using AI to Identify Recruitment Tools

First, let's look at the outcome from a search engine query for chatbots using this query.

"For purposes of recruitment, what chatbots are available?"

The results are presented in **Table 3.1**. Note that the first four are sponsored results.

TABLE 3.1. Search engine results for chatbots

RANK	TITLE	SNIPPET
1	NICE AI Chatbot Solution	Brings together NICE's highly specialized AI models for CX with cutting-edge generative AI. Put AI power to work for you...
2	Ada	Discover the benefits of investing in accessible AI-powered chatbots for ROI-driving CX. Take your CX efforts to the next level...
3	Indeed	Are You Looking for the Ideal Candidate? Start Your Search on Indeed.com Now!
4	TELUS International Chatbots	Leverage our winning combination of people, process & technology when building a chatbot. Recruitment Chatbot Ultimate Guide...
5	Recruiteze	Job Bot is a leading recruitment chatbot that helps recruiters source and screen hourly workers. It is an AI-based platform that...
6	Select Software Reviews	An HR Chatbot is one major category within AI recruiting software that allows job seekers and employees to communicate via...

In contrast, when AI is used, the same prompt produces different results, precise and to the point as shown in **Table 3.2**. (Note that for this example we made no attempt to present a current list of chatbots. The results are from ChatGPT's historic database, rather than the up-to-date ChatGPT Plus and Bing.) It is apparent that the AI summary is more useful than the search engine results page.

TABLE 3.2 ChatGPT response for recruitment chatbots

CHATBOT	KEY FEATURES
Mya	Mya engages with job applicants through a conversational AI platform, automating up to 75% of the recruitment process. It can prescreen candidates, answer their questions, and schedule interviews.
Olivia	Olivia simplifies tasks such as answering candidate queries, screening applications, scheduling interviews, and providing updates on application status. It's accessible through various platforms, including web, mobile, and social media.
Xor	Xor uses AI to automate recruitment tasks like screening, interview scheduling, and candidate reengagement. It's available in over 100 languages and can communicate via text, WhatsApp, email, or live chat.
Arya	Arya uses machine learning to automate the sourcing, shortlisting, and engagement of candidates. It interacts with candidates to understand their qualifications, skills, and experiences.
JobPal	Now owned by Outmatch, JobPal's chatbot automates communication with candidates via various channels, including career sites, social media, and messaging apps. It can screen candidates, answer their questions, and schedule interviews.

3.2 Onboarding Prompt Template

You will have an opportunity to experiment with the onboarding template. Replace the variables in the brackets <> with details about your personalized scenario:

> ***"Act as an experienced manager. You will help me onboard new hires successfully and as quickly as possible.***
>
> ***I just started a new job in <your job> in the <your team>. I will be responsible for <your responsibilities and job duties> in the <your job industry>. My key performance indicator is <KPI and metric for company or project it is trying to accomplish> this quarter.***
>
> ***You will generate a 30-60-90 day onboarding plan using the SMART framework (Specific, Measurable, Achievable, Relevant, and Time-Bound).***
>
> ***Please match each SMART goal with a metric so my success can be objectively measured. Please provide this output in table format."***

3.3 Conflict Management Prompt Template

Earlier we discussed confronting issues head-on. Since conflict management is an important topic, we have provided additional information and prompts. In the following template, you can choose to specify your preferred conflict resolution style from this list.

Confrontation: Often termed as problem-solving or collaboration, confrontation is a win–win approach where conflict is addressed directly with the goal of reaching a mutually beneficial solution. It's ideal for complex issues that need thorough discussion. ChatGPT can help guide effective confrontations, fostering open communication and collaborative problem-solving.

Compromise: Another conflict management strategy is compromise. This is generally regarded as a lose–lose solution but is a common temporary outcome in some conflicts. Sometimes, it's necessary to find a middle ground that all parties can accept, even though it means not everyone gets everything they want. In the case of a compromise situation, ChatGPT can provide insights into the art of negotiation and reaching a mutually acceptable solution.

Accommodation: There may be situations where one party chooses to give in to the demands of the other. This could be when the issue is not of high importance or when preserving the relationship is deemed more significant than the conflict itself. ChatGPT can assist in guiding such a process with empathy and understanding.

Avoidance: There are times when it's best to sidestep the conflict, especially when the issue is minor or when there are more pressing matters to address. ChatGPT can assist in identifying when avoidance might be the most suitable strategy and provide suggestions for doing so in a manner that doesn't exacerbate the situation.

Competition: In some situations, a win–lose approach to conflict resolution is necessary, especially when the stakes are high or a quick decision must be made. In such scenarios, the decision typically falls to the project manager or a higher authority. ChatGPT can offer advice on how to handle such a resolution effectively while minimizing potential fallout.

Given the various conflict management strategies, we have provided a Conflict Scenario Template that you can apply to your projects and situations. Simply provide ChatGPT with specifics by completing variables within the prompt, and it will help guide you in suggesting a conflict management strategy.

Instructions:

1. Type or copy this prompt:

   "ChatGPT, I am <👤 Your Role> and I'm faced with a conflict involving<👥 Involved Parties>. The situation is as follows: <💥 Conflict Description>. My aim is to reach <🎯 Desired Outcome>. Could you suggest the most effective conflict resolution strategy for this situation? If I've indicated a preference for a particular style of conflict resolution <⚖️ Preferred Style of Conflict Resolution>, could you also consider that in your response?"

2. Fill in the angle-bracketed variables in the prompt with specifics that apply to your situation:

   - <👤 Your Role>: Describe your position and involvement in the project.
   - <👥 Involved Parties>: Specify who else is involved in the conflict (teams or individuals).
   - <💥 Conflict Description>: Give a clear, neutral summary of the issue at hand.
   - <🎯 Desired Outcome>: What do you aim to achieve by resolving this conflict?
   - Optional: <⚖️ Preferred Style of Conflict Resolution>: If you have a preferred style of conflict resolution, state it here. If not, leave it blank for an unbiased suggestion from ChatGPT.

3.4 Tuckman Model Prompt Template

Earlier, we described how AI can be used during the stages of the Tuckman model of forming, storming, norming, performing, and adjourning. We have provided a template for prompts that you can adopt for your specific needs.

Instructions:

1. Type or copy this prompt:

   "I am a <👤 Your Role> and I'm working with a team that's currently experiencing <🚧 Team Dynamics>. The specific issues we're facing are < 💥 Challenges>, and I'm aiming for <🎯 Desired Outcome>. Based on our current situation and considering Tuckman's model stages (forming, storming, norming, performing, and adjourning), can you suggest which stage we might be in and provide some strategies to help us progress?"

2. Fill in the bracketed variables in the prompt with specifics that apply to your situation:
   - <👤 Your Role>: Describe your role (such as project manager, team leader).
   - <🚧 Team Dynamics>: Describe the current dynamics or interactions in your team (such as conflict, lack of clear roles).
   - <💥 Challenges>: Describe the specific issues your team is facing.
   - <🎯 Desired Outcome>: Describe your goals for the team's development or resolution of the issues.

Once you've filled in the details, use the prompt to interact with ChatGPT to receive customized advice on your team's possible stage and strategies for progression.

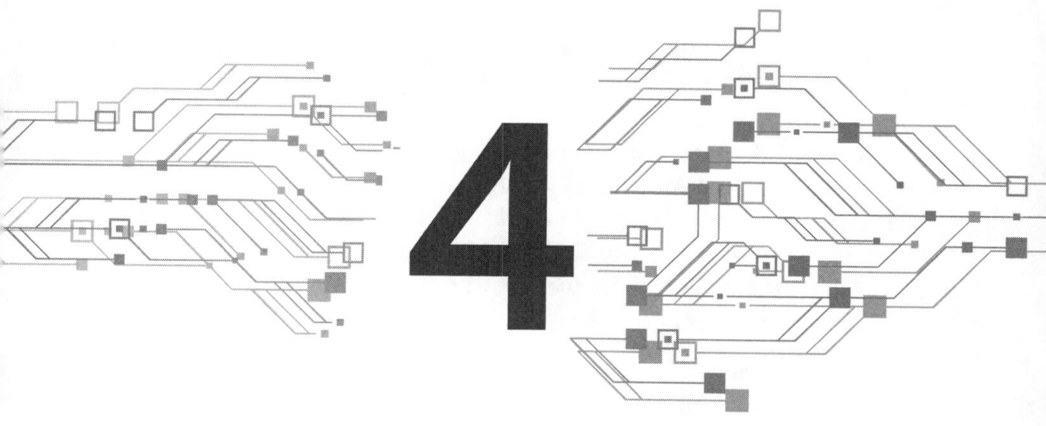

Choosing a Development Approach with AI

This chapter delves into the interplay between various project development approaches and the integration of generative artificial intelligence (AI), focusing on ChatGPT once again to help determine the approach to optimize the project management life cycle. Given the unique organizational context, we explore the core methodologies—predictive, adaptive, and hybrid—and walk you through the decision-making process of project managers getting the most out of using AI.

AI IN ACTION: HEALTHCARE.GOV

This brief real-world case scenario deals with HealthCare.gov, a website that the U.S. federal government operates to facilitate health insurance enrollment under the Affordable Care Act (ACA). The legislation is also referred to as "Obamacare" in literature. Significant technical and operational issues impacted the launch of the Healthcare.gov project in 2013. The health insurance exchange website was plagued with slow load times and back-end data services issues.

A lack of clear leadership, poor scope management, inadequate testing, and insufficient infrastructure planning characterized the project. A root cause for the failure was possibly *poor selection of the project approach* and *inadequate tailoring* of the development approach. The project was executed linearly, sequentially, following a waterfall or predictive project management approach. Think of a "big bang" style with predictive delivery where all components are developed in parallel and integrated simultaneously at the end. This approach is inflexible and does not readily accommodate changes or unexpected technical challenges. In addition, complexity of the project and the apparent lack of fully defined requirements at the outset contributed to the project's challenges and substantial scope creep.

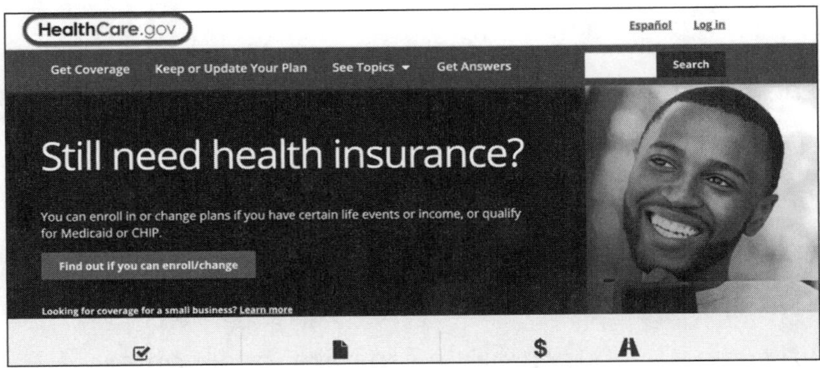

HealthCare.gov website

Given the complexity and evolving nature of the HealthCare.gov project requirements, let's consider whether AI could have been leveraged to deliver the project successfully.

We'll make a retrospective argument that AI could have significantly changed the disastrous initial launch of the HealthCare.gov project. An AI tool such as ChatGPT could have provided valuable guidance on selecting a suitable project management methodology and offering ongoing support throughout the project.

Let's see how.

We asked AI to conduct a forensic analysis and provide key recommendations it would have considered to ensure the successful delivery of the HealthCare.gov project. Here are the key recommendations that ChatGPT provided:

- **Project Management Approach:** Strongly consider agile or hybrid methodologies to handle the project's complexity and evolving requirements.
- **Testing:** Emphasize the importance of continuous testing throughout the project to detect and resolve issues early.
- **Leadership:** Establish clear leadership and governance structures for effective decision-making among the sponsors, vendors, and the project team.
- **Ongoing Guidance:** Provide real-time assistance to escalate risks, navigate issues, manage scope, and prioritize work based on business value.

AI has shed light on the selected delivery approach, questioned the predictive "big bang" single delivery approach, and recommended an adaptive project delivery approach. Based on data from similar projects (that AI is aware of) and an analysis of their success and failure, AI would have helped HealthCare.gov identify an appropriate and successful strategy. Given the complexity of the project and the apparent uncertainty of the requirements, an agile or hybrid approach might have been recommended rather than the predictive approach used.

As you will see in this chapter, adaptive approaches, hallmarked by iterative development, constant testing, and regular customer feedback, act as a buffer against product quality problems. With the HealthCare.gov project, regular testing and feedback from stakeholders could have led to early detection and rectification of issues, reducing the risk of significant problems cropping up at launch.

In this chapter, we'll focus on selecting and supporting your approach, but AI can be a constant guide throughout the project development process. We have started seeing AI play a significant role in project planning and organizing as a *consultant*, successfully helping teams navigate the day-to-day project management challenges effectively.

Understanding Predictive, Adaptive, and Hybrid Life Cycle Approaches

The world of project management is one of constant evolution and learning. In this era of rapid change, project managers must choose the most suitable approach for their projects, with a spectrum of methodologies to choose from. We'll focus on the popular predictive, adaptive, and hybrid life cycle approaches (**Figure 4.1**). A review of these approaches will provide a foundation for examining the role of AI using our Global Health example from the previous chapters.

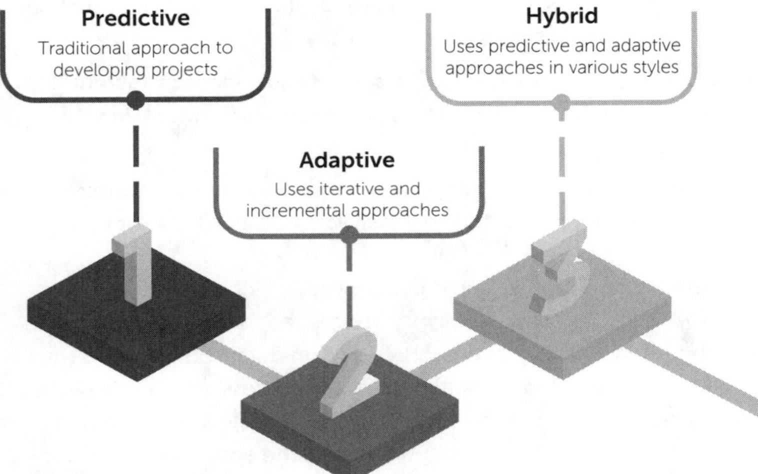

FIGURE 4.1 Consider a predictive, adaptive, or hybrid approach.

Predictive Life Cycle Approach

The predictive life cycle approach, often referred to as the waterfall model, is characterized by a linear and sequential design where progress flows in one direction—like a waterfall (**Figure 4.2**). Iteration is not feasible. There is emphasis on up-front planning and control of the steps. This approach is favored when a low degree of innovation, requirements certainty, and scope stability are present. It's called "predictive" because it relies on the premise that requirements, scope, cost, and timeline can be predicted with certainty. Because predictive approaches rely on constraints, there is an attempt to restrict and tightly control change. Predictive life cycles are best suited for organizational environments with high compliance requirements, a structured hierarchy, and a culture favoring predictive approaches.

In the context of our Global Health website revamp case study, let's say the project has a high degree of requirements certainty and scope stability. Global Health wants a new user-friendly, visually appealing, and comprehensive website, and they have a clear picture of the final website's structure and the functionalities.

During analysis and planning, the project team takes the time to develop a detailed project plan outlining the tasks, timelines, and resources required. Documentation plays a critical role in predictive methodologies. Requirements are defined in detail and documented at the beginning of the project. This documentation provides a clear roadmap for the project and serves as a reference point throughout the project life cycle. For Global Health, this could mean deciding on the website's architecture, choosing the right technologies, allocating tasks to the team, and setting a clear timeline.

The real work is executed in the design and development phases, with team members working on their assigned tasks, such as designing and coding, creating content, and integrating functionalities.

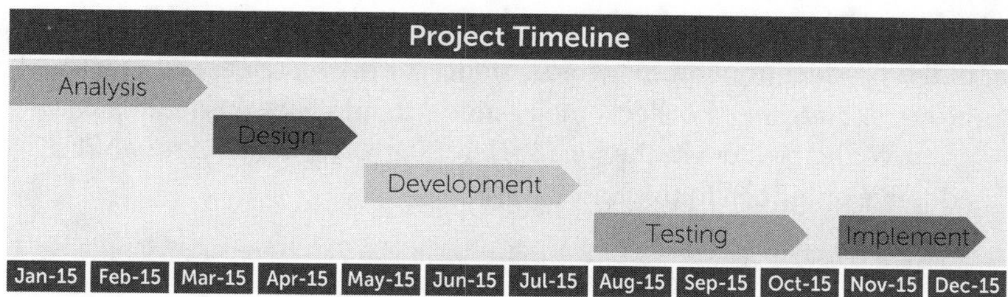

FIGURE 4.2 Predictive life cycle approach

During the development phase, the website project's performance is tracked and measured to ensure everything goes according to plan. Any deviation from the initial plan is managed through formal change control procedures to minimize disruptions and keep the project on track. When the project is finalized, all the deliverables are handed over to the client. This includes ensuring that the new website is live and functioning as intended and that all project documentation is complete.

In a predictive approach, each phase is distinct, and a phase cannot start until the previous one has been completed. This strategy works for projects with well-defined and stable requirements.

In a predictive setting, stakeholders usually give their inputs at key stages; they're not deeply involved in day-to-day tasks. The timeline is firm and features well-defined milestones. Organizations using this approach have a traditional structure, with clear roles from top to bottom. The culture values structure, planning, and completing a scope within the budget and on schedule.

Adaptive Approach

The adaptive approach comes in three flavors: iterative, incremental, and agile. If a project is *iterative*, a specific phase, such as design, can be revisited as many times as needed, even after the development phase has started. If a project is associated with *incremental* delivery, it is not released all at once but as multiple deliveries of viable but not complete products. The combination of both iterative and incremental delivery is exhibited in the *agile* development approach. This approach is designed to deal with high levels of uncertainty. Rather than planning the entire project in detail from start to finish, work is done in short iterations, or *sprints*. The analysis, design, development, and testing will occur incrementally for minimally viable deliverables, and the requirements can evolve throughout the project.

Imagine a scenario in which Global Health explores a completely new market with an innovative website. The team starts with a basic version of the product (minimum viable product, or MVP), releases it to a small group of customers, collects their feedback, and uses this feedback to improve the product in the next sprint. **Figure 4.3** walks through the adaptive approach in this case:

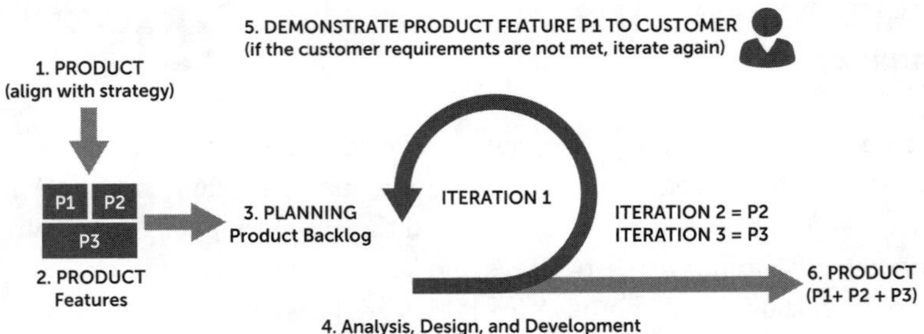

FIGURE 4.3 Iterative, incremental, and agile approaches

1. The product is defined as a website.
2. The website has three product features—P1, P2, and P3.
3. Upon planning and brainstorming, the team decided that, due to the complexity of the new website, the project would benefit from an adaptive approach.

4. The analysis, design, and development stages will occur several times—at least once for each product feature.
5. Upon demonstrating the product feature P1 to the product owner and customers, analysis, design, and redevelopment might occur again if the customer requirements are not met. The customer can use feature P1 in its current state if they believe that it provides value—such as a website that has information but no available forms or interactive functionality. Incrementally, P2 and P3 go through the same process.
6. When all features are complete and content is approved, the product is released to the customer.

Key characteristics of the adaptive approach include:

- Emphasis on collaboration and customer engagement
- Adaptive planning
- Change welcomed
- Continuous improvement

Both incremental and iterative approaches allow Global Health to adapt and respond to changes quickly.

Adaptive projects work best when stakeholders are active participants, deadlines are flexible, and funding is based on the project's needs. Ideally, the organizational structure is fluid, and the culture values flexibility, innovation, and continuous learning. Global Health must be agile and have the know-how to support such a flexible approach.

Hybrid Life Cycle Approach

The hybrid life cycle approach combines both the predictive and adaptive approaches. It's used when some parts of the project are well known and can be planned in detail (predictive), and other parts are uncertain and require flexibility and iterations (adaptive).

The hybrid life cycle approach balances flexibility and predictability. It's especially suitable when the product environment culture and the project or organization environment vary, calling for different methodologies to be used concurrently.

A hybrid approach tries to blend the best of both worlds. Stakeholders are engaged as needed; deadlines have certain fixed points and room for flexibility. Funding is generally fixed but can wiggle a bit depending on the project's needs. Project managers can take care of compliance issues early to avoid problems later. The organization structure can be rigid in some parts and flexible in others. The culture, likewise, embraces a mix of stability and innovation.

Using AI to Select the Right Development Approach for Projects

Finding the right development approach for a project is crucial to determining its overall direction and success. It's worth emphasizing that no single approach is universally superior. Instead, the most effective approach will depend on the unique circumstances of each project and the nature of the environment in which it is being implemented.

AI can provide insights, analysis, and recommendations for project managers. For instance, AI could assess project briefs, emails, and other documentation to help assess the degree of innovation, requirements certainty, scope stability, and ease of change. These attributes could then be compared to organizational characteristics such as stakeholder involvement, schedule constraints, funding availability, and compliance. Using this information, AI can make an informed decision as to whether a project is better suited to a predictive, adaptive, or hybrid approach.

At the simplest level, AI can create a simple multiple-choice questionnaire to help you decide which approach is best. This quick questionnaire should guide the team's decision on an agile versus hybrid versus waterfall approach.

"Can you create a brief questionnaire to help the team decide whether they should adopt agile, hybrid, or waterfall?"

1. How clear are the project requirements and scope at this stage?
   a. Unclear (favors agile)
   b. Somewhat defined (favors hybrid)
   c. Highly specific (favors waterfall)
2. How flexible is the deadline for project completion?
   a. Flexible (favors agile)
   b. Moderate flexibility (favors hybrid)
   c. Rigid, non-negotiable (favors waterfall)

3. How comfortable is the team with changing requirements during development?
    a. Very comfortable (favors agile)
    b. Somewhat comfortable (favors hybrid)
    c. Prefer locked-down requirements (favors waterfall)
4. Does the project involve a lot of new/untested technology or techniques?
    a. Yes (favors agile)
    b. Somewhat/in parts (favors hybrid)
    c. No, proven technology (favors waterfall)
5. How important is it to deliver working software frequently?
    a. Very important (favors agile)
    b. Moderately important (favors hybrid)
    c. Not as important (favors waterfall)

TECHNICAL GUIDE We have provided a prompt template that you can adapt for your own projects in Technical Guide 4.2.

Consider Selecting a Predictive Approach with AI

Let's imagine a scenario. You're a project manager who has collected information about your upcoming project. You have a clearly defined scope, and the stakeholders have detailed expectations. You have also noted that the organization is quite stable, and you're using well-known technology. The time has come to decide which project management approach to take.

In such a situation, an AI tool like ChatGPT can be incredibly beneficial. It can analyze the data you've gathered and provide insights on the best project management approach for you. Let's start with this prompt:

"I am unsure about our development approach for our upcoming project. Here's some information: our project is to build a new bridge. The stakeholders have provided detailed requirements. We're using construction methods that we're very familiar with, and our organization doesn't experience many sudden shifts. We have a clear budget and an initial plan. Can you help me determine the best approach?"

Certainly, based on the data you've provided, I have a few initial thoughts. However, to give you a more accurate recommendation, could you tell me more about how well you understand the requirements? And are these requirements expected to change significantly throughout the project?

"The requirements are quite thorough and are based on a strategic decision made by top management. They shouldn't change significantly unless there's a big shift in our company's direction."

Thank you for the additional details. Based on the information, it appears that your project could benefit from a predictive approach. This approach is often advantageous when you have a clear understanding of the requirements at the beginning of the project, a stable organizational environment, and familiarity with the technology being used. Since your project aligns well with these conditions, a predictive approach may lead to a higher likelihood of success. This approach will enable you to plan out the majority of the project from the beginning and execute according to that plan."

"That makes a lot of sense, ChatGPT. I was leaning toward a predictive approach, but I wasn't sure. Your analysis helped confirm my thoughts. Could you also provide some advice on implementing a predictive approach effectively?"

Absolutely! There are several key elements to implementing a predictive approach successfully. First, you'll want to develop a detailed project plan at the beginning of your project. This plan will include clear milestones, deliverables, and timelines. Regular progress tracking against this plan will be critical. Second, since changes can disrupt the schedule and increase costs, a strong change management process should be in place. Finally, regular communication with stakeholders is vital to ensure expectations are met, and any potential changes are managed proactively.

Next, let's see what happens when you give AI specific project documents and artifacts to provide even more helpful insight:

"I have a project charter and some additional documents that give more context about the project. Could they be useful for further analysis and advice?"

Absolutely, reviewing those documents can provide additional insights and refine the advice I can give you. If you upload those files, I can help analyze the content to extract more information about the project.

"That sounds helpful. However, I'm not sure about the best way to upload these files. Could you guide me?"

Certainly! If you're using an interface that supports file uploads, you can simply upload the files directly. If not, you could use a plug-in or Advanced Data Analysis to read the contents of the file and then share that content with me. Either way, I'll be able to analyze the contents of the files to provide you with more tailored advice.

CONFIDENTIALITY Be aware of any sensitive, proprietary, or confidential data. Consult with your employer or organization before uploading anything.

Let's see how ChatGPT can help provide additional guidance on managing a predictive project so that you can feel confident in choosing that route.

"I'll look into that and come back to you with the documents. Meanwhile, could you provide some more general advice on how to manage a predictive approach project effectively?"

With a predictive approach, it's important to monitor and control the project closely to ensure it stays on track. Regularly check the project against your initial plan and adjust as necessary. Keep your stakeholders informed of the progress and any changes. Also, encourage open communication among your team members to spot potential issues early and address them promptly. It's also beneficial to have a risk management plan in place because uncertainties can still exist even in well-planned projects.

"Great advice, ChatGPT. I'm feeling more confident about implementing a predictive approach for my project."

I'm glad to hear you're feeling more confident! Along with guidance, I can help you manage and monitor various aspects of your predictive project. For instance, I can assist with:

Resource Allocation: I can analyze your resource needs based on the data you provide and suggest optimal ways to allocate resources to meet your project's objectives while maintaining efficiency.

Risk Identification and Mitigation: With a thorough understanding of your project's specifics, I can help you identify potential risks and propose mitigation strategies, increasing your project's chances of success.

Project Scheduling: Given the data about the tasks, dependencies, and timelines, I can help create a realistic and efficient project schedule.

Stakeholder Communication: I can aid in drafting clear and concise status updates, meeting notes, and other communication items, ensuring that all stakeholders stay informed and aligned.

Performance Monitoring: I can guide you in setting up key performance indicators (KPIs) and help you track them throughout the project. This enables you to make data-driven decisions and adjust your approach as needed.

Would you like to explore any of these areas further?

ChatGPT has provided good suggestions here. It has highlighted some of the key aspects related to predictive projects that are prevalent to making sure waterfall projects stay on track as they pertain to scope, time, and cost. The following prompt asks if AI can help with scheduling:

"Could you help me understand how we could create a project schedule for this predictive approach project?"

For a predictive project, the schedule is typically detailed and established up front. Here's a simplified example of how we might create a schedule:

Let's start by looking at the broad categories of tasks your project involves. Typically, in a bridge construction project like yours, we might have tasks related to design and planning, site preparation, substructure construction, superstructure construction, and finalization and testing. Do you have any details on these? If you could give me a list of tasks with their estimated times and dependencies, I can help draft a preliminary schedule.

Great, so ChatGPT can work from a list of tasks or activities.

NOTE In Chapter 5, "AI-Assisted Planning for Predictive Projects," we will show how ChatGPT can brainstorm tasks and activities for you and actually help create a work breakdown structure (WBS), schedule, and Gantt chart.

"I don't have a detailed breakdown of tasks yet, but I know we have to cover all those stages. For example, in the design phase, we need to create blueprints, choose the construction materials, and determine the load calculations. In the construction stage, we have to build the foundations and pillars as outlined in our requirements."

That's a great start! Even if we don't have the detailed tasks yet, having a broad idea of the project stages and their activities helps plan the project's progression. Later, you can refine and elaborate these tasks into a more detailed work breakdown structure. For now, we can create a high-level project schedule, setting indicative timelines for each stage based on typical bridge construction projects.

This discussion probably has you leaning toward predictive methodology, a rigid and well-structured approach with predetermined scope, budget, and timeline. However, the real-world context, details, and constraints should ultimately determine the optimal approach for each project. Assessing and interpreting such information from raw project data and documents can provide invaluable insights. ChatGPT, with its remarkable natural language processing capabilities, can facilitate this process, helping you make more informed decisions and navigate your projects with increased confidence and productivity.

Next, let's explore how AI can guide you in deciding when an adaptive approach may be better suited for your projects.

Consider an Adaptive Approach with AI

As a project manager, you are often faced with new projects, incorporating emerging technologies or requiring a fluid scope that will evolve based on user feedback as we saw in the HealthCare.gov project. AI can help you choose a development approach. Let's explore an illustrative example using ChatGPT:

"I'm starting a new project, and it's a bit of uncharted territory for us. We're developing a new software application using emerging tech we haven't worked with before. We plan to refine our scope based on user feedback continuously. The project needs to be responsive to fast-paced market changes. I have some project details and data here. Can you help me figure out a suitable project management approach?"

From what you've told me, it sounds like this project will be quite dynamic with likely changes in scope and direction. To guide you better, could you provide more information about the following?

- How defined are the project's outcomes at this stage?
- What's the level of user involvement you anticipate throughout the project?
- Does your team have any experience with iterative development or feedback loops?

"The project's outcomes aren't too defined yet because we want to incorporate user feedback as we go. Users are expected to be heavily involved throughout the project. As for my team, we have some experience with iterative development, and we're open to learning new ways to improve."

Thanks for sharing that. It seems like your project will benefit from a high degree of flexibility. To make sure I guide you correctly, can you also tell me more about:

The technology that you're using—how new or uncertain is it?

What is the level of tolerance for risk in your organization, particularly for this project?

"The technology is quite new and evolving rapidly, which adds some uncertainty to the project. As for risk tolerance, our organization is willing to accept a higher degree of risk for this project because they see it as a strategic investment."

I appreciate your comprehensive responses. Based on the details you've shared, an adaptive or agile approach might be suitable for your project. This approach allows for continuous refinement based on user feedback, handles uncertainties well, and suits projects with higher risk tolerance. Of course, this is a suggestion based on the information provided. You should always consider your team's capabilities and the specific context of your organization in making the final decision.

With ChatGPT, you can explore and examine possible options based on the provided data. It helps you make an informed decision, but ultimately, the final choice lies with you, as the project manager, and the team.

"Thank you, ChatGPT. So, an adaptive or, more specifically, an agile approach might be good for us. Can you help me understand what our project execution would look like under this approach?"

Certainly! In an adaptive or agile approach, you'll be working in small, iterative cycles called "sprints." These sprints usually last a few weeks. At the start of each sprint, the team plans out what they will work on, which is typically a portion of the overall project scope that has been prioritized based on user needs and feedback.

Throughout the sprint, the team develops and tests this piece of the project, and at the end of the sprint, they deliver a usable product increment. Then, they reflect on what worked well and what didn't in a "retrospective" meeting and use these learnings to improve their process for the next sprint.

"Sounds like a significant shift from our usual way of working. Our team can adapt, but I'm worried about how our stakeholders will react. How should we manage that?"

That's an excellent point. Change can be challenging. In agile, stakeholder engagement is often managed through regular reviews and demonstrations of the work completed in each sprint. These "review" meetings provide an opportunity for stakeholders to give feedback and for the team to adjust their plans for the next sprint based on this feedback.

Also, involving stakeholders in prioritizing the work for each sprint can help ensure that their most important needs are being addressed. This approach allows stakeholders to see regular, tangible progress, which can help build trust and buy-in.

Would you like to dive deeper into any particular aspect of managing stakeholder expectations or concerns under an Agile approach?

Remember, if you choose this approach, it would be essential to manage stakeholder expectations from the start, letting them know about the shift in methodology and highlighting the benefits it brings. These include flexibility, the ability to adapt to changes more rapidly, and the delivery of value in increments, rather than waiting until the end of the project.

This conversation with ChatGPT is helping you gain a deeper understanding of the suggested approach and its implications. Let's see if ChatGPT knows anything about how to win and convince stakeholders.

"Yes, I'd appreciate some guidance on how to explain this shift in methodology to our stakeholders, and how to manage their expectations effectively."

In explaining the shift to an adaptive approach, it may be helpful to focus on the benefits this methodology can bring, such as flexibility and more frequent delivery of value. Here are some points you might consider:

Incremental Delivery: Explain that instead of waiting for the complete project to be finished, they'll see workable increments at the end of every sprint. This means they can start using or benefiting from parts of the project sooner.

Flexibility: Unlike the traditional waterfall approach, where changes late in the project can be costly or problematic, an adaptive approach embraces change. It allows for regular adjustments to the project as we learn more or if their needs change.

More Collaboration: They'll have more opportunities to provide feedback and see their ideas incorporated into the project. This can lead to a product that more closely meets their needs and expectations.

In managing their expectations, remember to stress that while the adaptive approach has its advantages, it also requires their active participation and feedback. It's a collaborative effort that needs everyone's commitment.

One more thing to remember: even though we'll deliver working increments of the project at regular intervals, it's possible that not everything they want will be delivered in the early stages. We'll need to work together to prioritize what gets worked on in each sprint.

You can see that ChatGPT can help you address potential questions and concerns before they arise, ensuring a smoother transition to the new project management approach.

Let's see if ChatGPT can inform us of some of the various agile methodologies that project managers can adopt.

"ChatGPT, you've been tremendously helpful so far. I'm curious about the agile methodologies and how they fit into the adaptive approach. I've heard of Scrum, Kanban, and Lean, but can you tell me more about them?"

Absolutely, let's dive in.

Scrum: A popular agile methodology operates in small, time-boxed iterations known as sprints, which typically last two to four weeks. Each sprint aims to produce a potentially shippable product increment. Scrum involves three key roles: the Product Owner, who represents the stakeholders and manages the product backlog (a list of desired features); the Scrum Master, who ensures the team follows Scrum principles; and the Development Team, who executes the work.

Kanban: Kanban focuses on visualizing the workflow, limiting work in progress (WIP), and maximizing efficiency or throughput. It uses a Kanban board with columns representing different stages of the process, from "to do" to "done." This makes it easy to see bottlenecks and work that is stalled.

Lean: Lean is more a philosophy than a methodology, focusing on minimizing waste and maximizing value to the customer. It emphasizes continuous improvement and efficiency.

All these methodologies have some common ceremonies, such as planning meetings, daily stand-ups, reviews, or retrospectives. These events allow the team to plan, coordinate, and review their work regularly.

Also, there are numerous technologies and tools designed to support Agile methodologies. Project management tools such as Jira, Trello, or Asana can be used to organize and prioritize tasks. Communication tools such as Slack or Microsoft Teams can help teams stay connected and collaborate effectively.

Now, considering your project's context, are you leaning toward a particular methodology or do you need more guidance?

Now that we have an overview of some agile approaches, let's see how ChatGPT suggests applying these.

> ***"Based on the details I've provided about my project, could you help me understand how each of these methodologies might be applied?"***
>
> Certainly, let's explore this further:
>
> Scrum: Given the innovative nature of your project and its complex technical requirements, Scrum could be beneficial. It would allow you to divide your project into manageable sprints, focusing on delivering a tangible value increment in each sprint. This iterative approach could also be valuable in managing the change and uncertainty in your project. The frequent Scrum ceremonies, like daily stand-up meetings and sprint reviews, would also provide opportunities for regular communication and alignment within your team.
>
> Kanban: Considering your project's creative aspects and the necessity for continuous delivery, Kanban can be helpful. It emphasizes visualizing your workflow, which could enhance transparency and alignment in your team. Its focus on limiting work in progress might help your team focus and reduce multitasking.
>
> Lean: Given the resource constraints you've mentioned and the need to maximize customer value, Lean principles could guide your project. They could help you identify wasteful activities and focus on what truly delivers value to your customer. Lean's emphasis on continuous improvement could also promote an iterative, learning-oriented culture within your team.

Remember, these methodologies are not mutually exclusive and can often be combined in a tailored approach. The key is to stay flexible and open to adjusting your approach as you learn more about what works best for your team and project.

When faced with the task of choosing the right project management approach, you'll find AI a useful ally. It can guide you by analyzing the distinct characteristics of your project and aligning them with the ideal methodologies.

NOTE In Chapter 6, "Adaptive Projects and AI," we will look at how ChatGPT can help with setting priorities, planning, and estimating these projects.

Consider Selecting a Hybrid Approach with AI

Hybrid approaches to project management combine aspects of both predictive and adaptive methodologies, allowing you to strike a balance between structure and flexibility. There are two major types of hybrid methodologies, each with unique features: flexible with a single delivery and incremental and structured.

If you describe your project's characteristics, ChatGPT can provide an analysis, drawing on the given information and suggesting a suitable hybrid approach. ChatGPT provides a detailed breakdown for each hybrid approach, explaining how the methodology operates in practice. This exploration of the hybrid methodologies provides insights into how to choose and tailor your project approach.

AI Advice on the Hybrid: Flexible with Single Delivery Approach

This hybrid approach excels in flexible environments and is oriented toward a single delivery. Suppose you're faced with a project for which some parts are very well defined but others are vague and likely to change based on stakeholder feedback. You are not sure how best to approach such a project, so you turn to ChatGPT for assistance.

> ***"I'm a project manager for a digital product. We have some features fully designed and specified, but for many features, we're still gathering user feedback and researching market needs. Can you help me figure out an effective way to manage this project?"***
>
> Certainly! The nature of your project sounds complex, with some aspects very clear and others still being defined. But before I can suggest an approach, I'd like to ask a few more questions: What is your team's experience with project management methodologies? What's the nature of your relationship with your stakeholders? And how firm are the deadlines and budget?
>
> ***"Our team is diverse. We have people who've worked in very traditional, waterfall-style projects and others who are used to an Agile, iterative style of work. We are expected to have regular touchpoints with the stakeholders to discuss progress and get feedback. The deadlines and budget are moderately flexible."***

With this information, ChatGPT can offer a more tailored suggestion:

> Given your team's diverse background and the nature of your project, you might want to consider a Hybrid (Flexible & Single) approach. This approach lets you start with a plan-based or predictive methodology for the parts of the project that are well defined while allowing you to switch to an Agile approach as you gather more information and the requirements of the other features become clearer. This approach can help you manage the clear aspects efficiently while allowing room for flexibility and adaptation as more information becomes available.

AI Advice on the Hybrid: Incremental and Structured Approach

This incremental and structured hybrid methodology is well suited for structured environments and favors incremental delivery.

Let's ask ChatGPT what it knows about the characteristics of a project that follows the hybrid approach that is incremental and structured:

> ***"I'm getting a clear image of how the Hybrid (Flexible & Single) approach might work. However, I have heard there is another type of Hybrid approach—Incremental and Structured. Can you explain that to me?"***
>
> Certainly! Hybrid (Incremental & Structured) projects use a more structured approach for the larger, overarching project goals and an incremental, or iterative, approach for execution. This approach tends to work well when the main goals and vision of the project are well defined but the path to achieving those goals is not entirely clear or may need to be adjusted along the way.
>
> Imagine you're launching a new online store. The high-level project goals—like delivering a functioning, user-friendly website with specific features—may be well defined from the start. This is where the structured, or predictive, part comes in: you plan out the broad steps needed to achieve your goals, establish milestones, and create a project schedule.
>
> However, when it comes to the specifics of how to build the website—the exact design, the implementation of each feature, the layout of the product pages—there might be some uncertainty. This is where the incremental, or Agile, approach shines: you work in short sprints, implementing one small piece of functionality at a time. After each sprint, you have something tangible to show your stakeholders, and you can get their feedback and adjust your plans as needed.

It's like building a house. The structure and floor plan might be fixed, but the choice of materials, the exact placement of windows, and the color of the paint could change as you progress.

"So, in the context of our software upgrade project, the structured part could be the overall plan to upgrade the software and make it more efficient, while the incremental part could be the specific tasks of adding new features, fixing bugs, and optimizing the code?"

Exactly! The structured part sets the stage, giving everyone a clear picture of the finished project. The incremental part, meanwhile, allows for flexibility and adaptation as the project progresses. It helps manage risks, as you regularly check in with stakeholders and make course corrections as needed.

We can conclude that this development approach offers a good blend of structure and adaptability—which helps maintain the project's trajectory while providing opportunity for refinements and enhancements. Like any project management approach, it requires careful planning, good communication, and a willingness to adapt as conditions change.

As project managers, we need to appreciate the diversity of all these approaches and understand how to apply them effectively in different scenarios. AI, particularly tools such as ChatGPT, can provide valuable guidance in this area, helping you choose the right approach based on the specific characteristics and constraints of your project, how the approach could be implemented, and how AI can assist.

Tailoring Your Approach with AI

Selecting an approach is just the first step. Tailoring that approach to suit the specific needs of your project, product, or organization is crucial. No approach is one-size-fits-all; they are frameworks that need adjusting and refining to align with the context of your work.

As you'll see from our conversation with ChatGPT, even when you are certain about the approach, there can still be uncertainties about implementation. With AI's help, you can find ways to *tailor* the chosen approach to better serve the project's unique requirements. We'll consider a scenario for which you have chosen an agile approach but need guidance to adapt it to your organization's workflow and policies.

Tailoring isn't a one-time activity but is continuous and iterative. As the project progresses and conditions change, AI can reassess the project and organization environment and provide ongoing guidance on adjusting the development approach for maximum efficiency and success.

Let's suppose you are a project manager operating within a waterfall or predominantly predictive environment. You are interested in integrating agile practices—the adaptive approach—into your project management. AI can shed light on how to seamlessly blend Agile ceremonies into your existing predictive methodologies to achieve peak outcomes.

Now, let's get ChatGPT's insights:

"I want to venture into the Agile approach for my upcoming project, but the strict guidelines of my organization and the complex requirements of the project leave me perplexed. Can you help me customize the Agile approach to meet my project's needs?"

Certainly, I'm here to assist you. First, could you provide details about your organization's guidelines and the project's needs? Any relevant documents or policies you can share would be beneficial. Remember to use a compatible plug-in or a code interpreter for file uploads.

"Our organization functions within a structured hierarchy, whereas Agile promotes a high degree of interaction and autonomy. On top of that, our project revolves around the creation of an enterprise software system, notorious for its complex architecture and coordination needs."

Thanks for the details. We have two main challenges: the organizational structure and the nature of the project. Incorporating agile will necessitate a careful blend of Agile principles within these constraints.

As a starting point, you can incorporate agile ceremonies like regular stand-ups and iteration planning within your teams. At the same time, continue with formal reporting to fit within the hierarchical decision-making process. This blend allows teams to self-organize and adjust their work more frequently, true to the Agile spirit, while still aligning with your organization's structure.

To handle the project's complexity, consider combining Agile practices with software tools, such as Jira or Trello, designed to manage complex projects.

Does this approach sound feasible, or should we explore other avenues?

ChatGPT provided a good starting point here. The idea of maintaining some level of formal reporting while incorporating Agile practices within teams sounds appealing. What about managing scope changes, given that project requirements evolve over time? What suggestions does ChatGPT have for handling that with this hybrid method?

Here are some recommendations for managing scope changes:

Promote open communication about changes. This transparency is vital, whether it's a change in requirements, budget, or team.

Implement a role, like a Change Control Board, to evaluate the effect of significant changes on the project's cost, timeline, and other deliverables. Their decisions should be transparently communicated to all stakeholders.

Use your project management tools to track these changes. This tracking can be as simple as maintaining a "change log" to record all changes, their impact, and subsequent actions.

"Those are some great tips, ChatGPT! However, I am a bit apprehensive. The development teams are open to Agile practices, but higher management may not be as flexible. How can we ensure buy-in from all organizational levels?"

This is a common hurdle when implementing changes in traditional structures. Here are some strategies:

Demonstrate Value Early: Show early success with pilot projects or phases. These tangible improvements can help sway those skeptical about the new approach.

Training and Workshops: All organizational levels must understand the hybrid approach's benefits and functioning. Invest in training sessions and workshops. Consider bringing in an expert who is well versed in both Agile and traditional methods to mentor the teams and leadership.

Involve Everyone in Planning: Include all relevant stakeholders, including upper management, in the planning and decision-making process. This involvement not only imparts a sense of ownership but also helps them understand the project's progression.

Regular Reviews: Establish a rhythm of regular reviews when stakeholders can collectively assess project progress and make decisions. This practice promotes transparency and allows everyone to appreciate the new approach's benefits.

Keep in mind that these are broad guidelines. The specific implementation will depend on your organization and its culture. Change takes time, especially in larger, more traditional structures. It is key to remain patient, persistent, and positive. Resistance may arise, but consistent efforts and a demonstration of benefits will win buy-in.

Now let's look into integrating some agile components into an existing waterfall approach:

"ChatGPT, I've been contemplating blending some of the adaptive approach's aspects into our predominantly predictive project management style. I believe it could enhance our flexibility, particularly in project phases involving a lot of learning and experimentation. I'm unsure, though, how to manage this transition smoothly. Can you guide me?"

Definitely, I'm here to assist. First, it's commendable that you're considering a hybrid model, blending Agile's flexibility into your traditionally predictive environment. This model can offer the best of both worlds when implemented correctly.

Let's start by understanding where you want to introduce more flexibility. Are there certain stages or teams you feel would particularly benefit from an adaptive approach?

"Our projects usually involve a lot of back-and-forth, experimentation, and feedback-based revisions during the design and development phases. I feel these areas could benefit greatly from a more flexible approach. However, I am also concerned about preserving the predictive approach's clear structure and control, particularly for the management team."

That's an essential balance to maintain—leveraging the benefits of Agile without sacrificing the advantages of a predictive approach.

One way is to introduce iterative development within your project's design and development phases. You can set short work cycles or "sprints" during which the team works on certain tasks, and then review and make adjustments based on feedback.

This "Water-Scrum-Fall" or "Wagile" model introduces flexibility and adaptability within certain phases while the rest of the project follows a more structured, predictive approach. The successful implementation of this approach will require changes in teamwork and communication styles. You may need to incorporate agile ceremonies like daily stand-ups, sprint planning, and retrospectives within these phases.

How does this starting point sound to you?

This seems like an interesting approach. But you have some concerns. Let's ask ChatGPT:

> ***"How do I prevent the agile team from getting out of sync with the teams working predictively at the start and end of the project?"***
>
> Ensuring alignment between different phases and teams is key. The solution here is to create touchpoints or synchronization points.
>
> For example, the outcomes of design and development sprints could be presented and reviewed in predefined meetings with stakeholders from the other phases.
>
> This interaction allows for regular information exchange, maintains alignment, and enables timely adjustments based on feedback.
>
> ***"What about introducing agile ceremonies to the team?"***
>
> To introduce agile ceremonies, start small and gradually increase their use as your team gets comfortable with them. You could start with daily stand-up meetings, brief sync-ups where the team discusses what they accomplished yesterday, what they plan to do today, and any roadblocks they're facing.
>
> Sprint planning and retrospectives may require more of a cultural shift, as they require a different way of planning and reflecting on work. Provide training and ensure everyone understands the benefits of these ceremonies.
>
> It might also be helpful to invite an agile coach or experienced facilitator for the first few ceremonies.

In summary, tailoring a project approach requires careful consideration of multiple factors, including the characteristics of the project, the organization's culture, and the team's specific needs.

Regardless of the approach, whether predictive, adaptive, or hybrid, AI can significantly assist you in aligning these methodologies with your unique organizational and project contexts. Ultimately, it's about creating a tailored approach that works best for your project and your team, fostering greater efficiency, and enabling successful project outcomes.

Ethical Considerations and Professional Responsibility

Using AI in predictive and adaptive project management methodologies can significantly enhance project planning, risk management, schedule forecasting, and decision-making. However, this powerful tool also introduces many considerations regarding data quality, interpretation of AI outputs, continuous monitoring, and ethical use. There are different approaches, and it seems even AI models like ChatGPT haven't encountered all of them. This is where the traditional research approach—reviewing global standards, practice guides, and journals needs to occur concurrently with leveraging AI as a tool.

AI's predictions and suggestions depend entirely on the input data's accuracy, representation, and lack of bias. It is essential to ensure the quality of this data to avoid basing project decisions on misinformation, which could significantly impact the project's outcome.

Moreover, while AI can analyze vast quantities of data, the real value of its output lies in correct interpretation. Misunderstanding or misreading the AI's output can lead to incorrect project decisions. This point underscores the need for project managers to understand the AI's capabilities and limitations and frequently ask the AI product for clarifications. It's beneficial to provide training and education to project managers and teams about AI's uses, benefits, and limitations. This helps in the more informed and cautious deployment of these tools.

The dynamic nature of project management necessitates regular checks to ensure the AI's predictions remain accurate and relevant. This might mean updating the AI's training data, refining its model, or adjusting its parameters. Human-in-the-loop systems, in which humans work in conjunction with AI, can provide a valuable checkpoint in these instances, reinforcing accountability and harnessing the strengths of both humans and AI.

We've introduced the idea of explainability, which pertains to the model's ability to provide understandable reasons for its predictions or recommendations. However, providing a thorough explanation of how AI models, such as ChatGPT, generate responses might involve complex machine learning theories, which may not be understandable to non-technical stakeholders. A sensible course might involve providing high-level insights into how the model works for transparency and contextual explanations for specific predictions or suggestions for explainability.

In this chapter, we looked at the project context to choose the best development approach. Similarly, the appropriateness and usefulness of AI in project management will depend on the project context. Factors such as the project's scale, the organization's AI readiness, the complexity of the project, and even the industry sector can impact the suitability of using AI for project management.

In conclusion, AI can significantly aid in project management, evaluating scenarios to determine the best development approach for your project. However, AI's use in project management should always complement, not replace, human expertise and judgment.

Key Points to Remember

Throughout this chapter, we discussed that predictive, adaptive, and hybrid approaches have distinct strengths and weaknesses, and the choice of approach should be tailored to the specific requirements of the project and its organizational context.

- AI products such as ChatGPT can help project managers select the right project development approach based on organizational context, complexity, stability, and criticality of project requirements.
- In a more predictive-focused organization, AI can aid in integrating adaptive components. .
- In an organization more accustomed to adaptive approaches, AI models assist in adding predictive elements that can help bring structure and improve long-term planning.
- AI models should be used as a tool to support, not replace, human judgment in project management. AI can help inform decisions, but ultimate responsibility and accountability lie with human leaders.

Technical Guide

4.1 A Conversation with Claude

While we have used ChatGPT for our case study, addressing the output from another AI solution, Claude.AI from Anthropic, is worthwhile to illustrate for the HealthCare.gov case study.

"What were the three key reasons why the HealthCare.gov system was delayed?"

There were a few key reasons why the initial launch of Healthcare.gov was problematic in 2013:

A. Scope Creep—The scope and requirements for the website kept expanding during development, making it difficult to design and test everything properly in time. There were changing policy decisions that impacted technical requirements.

B. Insufficient Testing—Due to the tight deadlines and changing requirements, there wasn't enough time to properly test the fully integrated system before launch. Only minor testing was done on the full site before it went live.

C. Integration Issues—Healthcare.gov needed to integrate with many different systems across multiple government agencies. There were delays in finalizing these connections and getting the right data to populate the site. The complexity caused significant bugs.

The three main issues were constantly changing requirements, lack of end-to-end testing, and integration challenges with outside systems. The rushed political timeline made developing and launching a complex new system like Healthcare.gov difficult. The major technical issues were eventually resolved after reworking the website and spending more time testing it after the initial launch.

"Did the selection of a non-agile approach contribute to the initial failure?"

Yes, the lack of an agile approach likely contributed to the initial failure of Healthcare.gov. Here's why:

- No Iterative Development—With a traditional waterfall approach, all requirements are meant to be defined up-front before any coding starts. This doesn't work well for complex new systems with vague requirements.
- Lack of Flexibility—Agile allows for pivoting and re-planning as issues emerge. Healthcare.gov followed a rigid plan that couldn't adapt to changing political needs and technical discoveries.

- No Working Software Builds—Agile focuses on continuous integration and delivering working software in short iterations. Healthcare.gov didn't have any end-to-end software until very late, making testing difficult.
- Late User Testing—Agile builds in user testing from the start to guide development. With Healthcare.gov, user testing happened too late to address core issues.

Learning from project failures, whether they are within the organization or external to it, is valuable. In this chapter, we showed how valuable lessons learned from other public projects can help you understand how to better navigate your project in the future.

4.2 Selecting an Approach Questionnaire Prompt

In templates, replace the angle brackets <> with one of the listed options. So, within your prompt for a project with flexible scope, the item:

> ***Clarity of project requirements and scope: <Replace with (A) Flexible, (B) Moderate flexibility, or (C) Rigid, non-negotiable>***

would become:

> ***Clarity of project requirements and scope: Flexible***

Here we have provided a template that lets AI help you determine which approach (predictive, adaptive, or hybrid) would be best for your project.

> ***"Assist me in selecting the appropriate project management approach for my project. You will ask me for characteristics and attributes of my project and organization/company. The questions will be asked in a multiple-choice format, and when presenting the question, you will also provide short and succinct descriptions of what each question is asking. If I am unclear, I may ask for clarification. Once all the questions have been answered, you will suggest a project approach based on my responses.***
>
> ***Clarity of project requirements and scope: <Replace with (A) Unclear, (B) Somewhat defined, or (C) Highly specific>***
>
> ***Flexibility of project completion deadline: <Replace with (A) Flexible, (B) Moderate flexibility, or (C) Rigid, non-negotiable>***
>
> ***Comfort level of the team with changing requirements during development: <Replace with (A) Very comfortable, (B) Somewhat comfortable, or (C) Prefer locked-down requirements>***

Does the project involve a lot of new/untested technology or techniques? <Replace with (A) Yes, (B) Somewhat/in parts, or (C) No, proven technology>

Importance of delivering working components frequently: <Replace with (A) Very important, (B) Moderately important, or (C) Not as important>

Team's experience with Agile development practices: <Replace with (A) Yes, extensive experience, (B) Some experience, or (C) No experience>

Degree of innovation in this project: <Replace with (A) High, (B) Moderate, or (C) Low>

Stability of the project scope: <Replace with (A) Low, (B) Moderate, or (C) High>

Stakeholder involvement in the project: <Replace with (A) High, (B) Moderate, or (C) Low>

Schedule constraints for the project: <Replace with (A) Flexible, (B) Moderate, or (C) Rigid>

Level of regulation and compliance the project must adhere to: <Replace with (A) Low, (B) Moderate, or (C) High>

Organization's culture regarding change and innovation: <Replace with (A) Flexible, (B) Semi-flexible, or (C) Rigid>

Any additional context or details you would like to provide about your project: <Free text response)>"

5

AI-Assisted Planning for Predictive Projects

In this chapter, we journey into the compelling realm of generative artificial intelligence (AI) and its value in project initiation and planning projects using the predictive development approach. First, we examine how AI tools, such as ChatGPT, can assist with business case creation and drafting a project charter. Next, we delve into AI's assistance in defining the scope, developing a work breakdown structure (WBS), and formulating schedules and budgets.

We'll address the crucial ethical considerations and professional responsibility in AI-driven project planning, the irreplaceable value of human judgment, and the importance of transparency.

AI IN ACTION: TOM'S PLANNER

Tom's Planner is a web-based tool used for project planning, management, and collaboration. It enables users to create and share professional Gantt charts in minutes, making project planning more efficient and organized. Tom's Planner is designed to help teams of all sizes plan their projects, and it is available in five languages and used daily by thousands of users in more than 100 countries worldwide. Tom's Planner has an AI-powered feature that allows users to create project plans in minutes.

Tom's Planner is powered by OpenAI's ChatGPT. Users enter a short, high-level description of their project, and Tom's Planner returns a Gantt chart with a complete project plan.

Tom's Planner website

Working with AI, such as ChatGPT, is an iterative process. Tom's Planner has added extra functions that allow users to adjust the activities in a project phase by giving the AI additional instructions. Users can ask the AI to make the activities more actionable or better reflect some details that the AI might have missed.

Tom's Planner is collaboration-friendly, enabling high involvement of all stakeholders in the planning process. Tom's Planner can have unlimited team members, and sharing Gantt charts is free. This feature helps get everyone involved in project planning and reduces the number of status update emails and calls.

Tom's Planner with AI is a powerful tool for project planning, management, and collaboration. Its flexible and customizable interface makes it easy to adjust the Gantt chart to fit different requirements. The platform enables high involvement of all stakeholders in the planning process, and its freemium business model makes it accessible to users of all levels. For additional details, visit www.tomsplanner.com/ai-assist.

AI-Assisted Project Initiation

In predictive project management, the initiation phase is a foundational first step that formalizes the project's existence and sets its trajectory. This phase calls for identifying a project's value proposition, studying feasibility, formulating its scope, and formalizing it with a project charter. While needs assessment and business case formulation are traditionally associated with the broader scope of business analysis, their outcomes lay the critical groundwork for project initiation.

As a project manager, you can harness the power of ChatGPT to stimulate brainstorming, facilitate research, draft critical documents, and bolster communication among your stakeholders. In other words, AI boosts your team's capabilities and streamlines the process leading to the initiation phase.

The sections that follow will investigate how ChatGPT can be a crucial ally in conducting a needs assessment and creating a business case. While not exclusively a part of the initiation process as described by PMBOK, these are essential steps that establish a strong foundation for the creation of the project charter.

Perform a Needs Assessment with ChatGPT

One of the first steps in setting a solid foundation for any project is to perform a comprehensive needs assessment. This process allows you to articulate the problem or opportunity at hand, scrutinize the current state, envisage the desired future state, and map out the gap in between. Once this gap is defined, potential solutions can be explored, evaluated, and ranked.

ChatGPT can be a useful tool in assisting with the needs assessment, aiding with everything from identifying the problem to assisting in recommending viable solutions. Consider a fictional scenario in which you are initiating a project to implement a customer relationship management (CRM) system at Fictional Corp. to improve customer service and satisfaction rates. Here are some examples of how ChatGPT can assist with the needs assessment such as determining the desired future state, recommending options, and facilitating a high-level timeline.

Determine the Desired Future State

In the needs assessment process, determining the future state involves analyzing the gaps between the current situation and the desired goals of an organization. In our fictional case study, we will use AI to analyze company information that includes surveys, system data, customer service metrics, and usage metrics. This step includes exploring the changes needed to tackle the identified problem or opportunity. For Fictional Corp., you might ask the following:

> ***"Given the issues with our current CRM system and our goal to improve customer service, can you help us envision a desired future state?"***
>
> In the future state, the organization will employ a scalable and flexible CRM system capable of accommodating a growing customer base. It will have efficient features for ticketing, customer interactions tracking, and robust reporting capabilities. This system will facilitate faster response times, personalized customer communication, and in turn, improved customer satisfaction rates.

Determine Viable Options and Recommend Solutions

Once you've identified the future state, it's important to examine various potential options, such as software or a built/manufactured product that could help achieve the business goals and objectives. This process includes conducting comparative analyses of options and recommending the most beneficial solution. Let's see how ChatGPT can facilitate this for Fictional Corp.'s customer service needs:

> ***"Can you suggest some potential CRM systems that are known for their scalability and flexibility, and recommend the best one based on our needs?"***

Based on industry standards and your organization's needs, three potential CRM systems come to mind: Salesforce, Microsoft Dynamics, and HubSpot. Given your specific requirement for scalability, flexibility, and robust features, Salesforce appears to be the most suitable solution. Salesforce is recognized for its extensive customization options, AI-powered insights, and scalability to accommodate growth.

Facilitate a High-Level Product Roadmap

Upon selecting the best solution, developing a product roadmap outlines the high-level sequence of delivery, or timeline. This roadmap serves as a strategic plan that aligns the project teams on the product's direction over time.

"Given that we have decided to move forward with Salesforce as our new CRM system, can you help us draft a high-level product roadmap?"

Here's a tentative roadmap for the CRM system upgrade:

Month 1–2: Project Initiation & Planning—Define project scope, gather requirements, assemble project team.

Month 3–4: Procurement & Customization—Procure Salesforce licenses, customize CRM to suit our requirements.

Month 5–6: Data Migration & Testing—Migrate data from the old system, conduct comprehensive testing.

Month 7: Training—Train all end users on the new CRM system.

Month 8: Go Live—Deploy the new system, provide continuous support.

Upon completing the needs assessment process, you now clearly understand your desired future state, recommended solution (here, a new CRM), and a high-level product roadmap. This puts you in a great position to build a well-researched business case.

Creating the Business Case with AI

A business case helps an organization decide whether a proposed project is worth investing in. The business case documents the problem or opportunity identified, analyzes the situation, and offers a recommended solution supported by cost–benefit and feasibility analyses.

It's also important to include a plan for measuring the realization of benefits. Throughout this process, ChatGPT can be a significant asset in providing information and insights and generating documentation.

Problem/Opportunity

Let's start with a situation statement, which identifies the problem or opportunity.

"Given the issues we're facing with our current CRM system and our goals for improvement, can you help draft a situation statement?"

The organization is currently dealing with a CRM system that lacks scalability and flexibility, which hampers the effectiveness of customer service and, ultimately, customer satisfaction. The opportunity lies in implementing a CRM solution that can accommodate the growing customer base, improve customer service, and provide valuable insights for business growth.

Analysis of the Situation

Next, let's move to an analysis of the situation where ChatGPT uses the recommended solution to analyze its support for business goals and objectives.

"Can you analyze how the proposed CRM system (Salesforce) aligns with our business goals and objectives?"

Implementing Salesforce as the new CRM aligns with the organization's goals of enhancing customer service and accommodating growth. Salesforce's scalable and flexible solution provides an improved ticketing system, efficient customer interaction tracking, and robust reporting capabilities. These features support the objective of providing timely and personalized customer service.

Feasibility Analysis

Now, let's have ChatGPT present the results of the feasibility analysis of the chosen solution.

"Can you provide a feasibility analysis and recommendation for the implementation of Salesforce?"

The implementation of Salesforce is feasible, considering its alignment with your organization's needs. It's a scalable and flexible solution renowned for its ability to support growth. However, like any major change, it will require a significant investment of time and resources, as well as extensive training for end users. Given these factors, Salesforce is still recommended as the most suitable solution to address your CRM needs.

Cost–Benefit Analysis

ChatGPT can also assist in summarizing the cost–benefits for the recommended option.

> ***"Can you help us summarize a basic cost–benefit analysis for implementing Salesforce?"***
>
> On the cost side, implementing Salesforce would involve software licensing, customization, data migration, and training expenses. However, the benefits significantly outweigh these costs. With Salesforce, your organization can expect improved customer service efficiency, higher customer satisfaction rates, better customer retention, and increased revenue. Furthermore, Salesforce's powerful analytics can provide valuable insights for future business strategies.

Evaluation of Benefits

Finally, ChatGPT can help outline a plan for measuring benefits realization.

> ***"How can we measure the benefits realization of implementing Salesforce?"***
>
> The benefits realization of implementing Salesforce can be measured using various key performance indicators (KPIs). These can include response times to customer inquiries, customer satisfaction scores, customer retention rates, and revenue growth. Additionally, Salesforce's analytics can provide valuable insights into customer behavior and preferences, contributing to the effective planning of future business strategies.

This was quite general from ChatGPT. Let's get more information regarding the costs and benefits with some actual estimates and values.

> ***"Create a simplified cost–benefit breakdown and analysis for a CRM implementation project. What are some estimated cost and benefits values? Present the results in tabular format."***

COST/BENEFIT	DESCRIPTION	VALUE
COSTS		
Software Acquisition	Cost of purchasing or subscribing to a CRM software solution	$150,000
Hardware Acquisition	Cost of acquiring any hardware required to support the CRM system	$50,000
Software Customization and Integration	Cost of adapting the CRM to our business processes and integrating it with other systems	$100,000
Training	Cost of training staff on the new CRM system	$30,000
Support and Maintenance	Annual cost of maintaining and supporting the CRM system	$20,000
Total Costs		$350,000
BENEFITS		
Improved Customer Retention	Projected annual increase in revenue due to improved customer retention	$100,000
Increased Sales Efficiency	Projected annual increase in revenue due to streamlined sales processes	$50,000
Decreased Marketing Costs	Projected annual savings due to more targeted marketing campaigns	$30,000
Total Benefits (Year 1)		**$180,000**
Net Benefit (Year 1)		**–$170,000**
Total Benefits (Years 2–5)		**$720,000**
Net Benefit (Years 2–5)		**$370,000**

With the help of ChatGPT, you have compiled a comprehensive business case, including a situation statement, an analysis of the situation, a recommended solution, a cost–benefit analysis, and a plan for benefits realization.

Now let's ask ChatGPT to cleanly organize this information and summarize it into a table format.

> ***"Given the information we have generated so far, could you please help compile a business case summary in table form?"***

The response from ChatGPT is in the form of a table:

BUSINESS CASE COMPONENT	DESCRIPTION
Problem/ Opportunity	The organization is currently dealing with an outdated CRM system that is not equipped to handle the growing volume of customer interactions, lacks integrations with other tools, and offers limited insights into customer behavior. These limitations are reducing the effectiveness of customer service and negatively impacting customer satisfaction.
Analysis of Situation	Salesforce, a cloud-based CRM, provides scalability, integration, and analytics for growing customer needs. It supports the organization's goals of boosting customer satisfaction and revenue.
Recommendation	After assessing the business requirements, current CRM limitations, and the features offered by several CRM providers, Salesforce is recommended as the new CRM system. Salesforce offers the necessary features to address the current business problems, improve customer service, and support business growth.
Cost–Benefit Analysis	Implementing Salesforce has notable costs, including licensing, customization, data migration, and training. Yet, its benefits—like enhanced customer service, better marketing insights, and increased sales productivity—outweigh these costs. The organization should recoup costs within two years and project a net gain of $370,000 over five years.
Evaluation/ Benefits Realization	Implementing Salesforce's benefits will be gauged using KPIs like reduced response times, improved satisfaction scores, higher retention, and increased revenue. Additional metrics include daily customer interactions, marketing campaign success, and sales conversion rates. A study will be conducted six months post-implementation to evaluate the CRM's success and ROI.

In this way, AI (ChatGPT in this case) not only helps generate and compile all necessary components of a business case but also presents them in a clear, concise, and easily digestible format.

This business case now provides a solid foundation for creating the project charter, which we will explore in the next section.

Creating the Project Charter with AI

A project charter is a formal, typically short document that describes your project in its entirety—including the objectives, milestones, and stakeholders. It authorizes the start of the project and serves as a point of reference for all parties involved.

Given the comprehensive business case you have generated with the assistance of ChatGPT, you now have sufficient inputs to create a project charter. Let's instruct ChatGPT to assist in this process.

> ***"Based on the business case, help me draft a project charter for our CRM implementation project."***
>
> Project Title: Customer Relationship Management (CRM) Implementation
>
> Start: September 1, 2025. End: March 1, 2026
>
> High-Level Description and End Result:
>
> - The project involves selecting and customizing a CRM software solution to streamline sales and marketing processes, increase customer retention, and decrease marketing costs.
>
> Justification:
>
> - As the business case outlines, the CRM implementation project is expected to increase revenue and decrease costs, with an estimated net benefit of $370,000 over five years.
>
> High-Level Requirements:
>
> - CRM system with capabilities for contact management, sales management, and targeted marketing
> - Integration with existing systems and staff training
>
> Success Criteria:
>
> - Increase in customer retention rates by 10% within the first year
> - Increase in sales efficiency by 15% within the first year

Project Budget:

- The total estimated cost of the CRM implementation project is $350,000.

Milestones:

- Selection of CRM software solution: September 30, 2025
- Customization and integration of CRM system: December 31, 2025
- Deployment of CRM system: March 1, 2026

Assumptions, Constraints, and Risks:

- Assumptions: Staff will be available for training and will adopt the new system readily.
- Constraints: The CRM system must be operational by March 1, 2026.
- Risks: Possible resistance to change from staff; the selected CRM may not integrate seamlessly with existing systems.

Assigned Project Manager: Jane Smith

Stakeholder List:

- Sales and Marketing Team, IT Department, Customers (indirect stakeholders)

Signatures: Project Sponsor and Key Stakeholders

Iterating and Refining Prompts

This is a good place to emphasize one of the key strengths of AI: its ability to learn and adapt based on the inputs it receives. This means you can iteratively and incrementally build upon your prompts and responses to fine-tune the output to your needs. For instance, if the initial response from ChatGPT doesn't quite hit the mark, you can refine your prompt to provide more context or specify the information you need. Similarly, if the response is too broad or lacks detail, you can ask follow-up questions or add new prompts to get more granular information.

This iterative process helps you get the most out of AI tools and allows you to guide AI to learn and improve over time. As you continue to interact with ChatGPT, it becomes better at understanding your specific needs and provide more accurate and relevant responses.

AI-Assisted Planning

Once the project charter has been developed and the project has been formally initiated. This stage involves creating several plans to guide the project team and manage stakeholder expectations. **Figure 5.1** shows areas in which AI can play a role, which we will explore further.

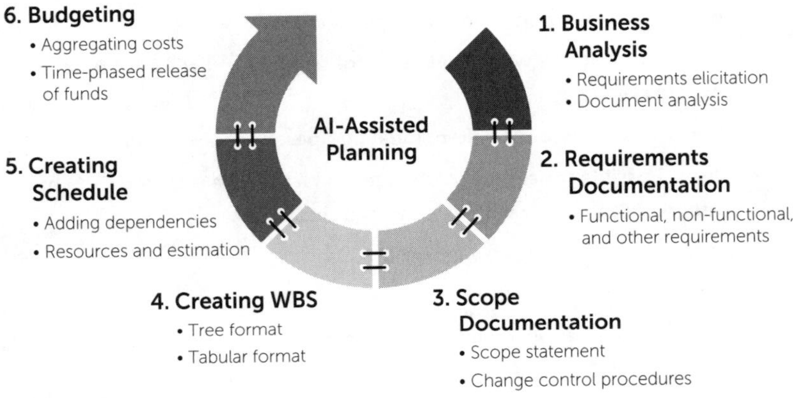
AI-Assisted Planning
1. Business Analysis
• Requirements elicitation
• Document analysis
2. Requirements Documentation
• Functional, non-functional, and other requirements
3. Scope Documentation
• Scope statement
• Change control procedures
4. Creating WBS
• Tree format
• Tabular format
5. Creating Schedule
• Adding dependencies
• Resources and estimation
6. Budgeting
• Aggregating costs
• Time-phased release of funds

FIGURE 5.1 AI-assisted planning

Business Analysis

Key aspects of planning include defining scope, gathering requirements, and analyzing them. These activities are called business analysis, a cognate project management discipline. One of the exciting aspects of generative AI is that it is specifically talented at requirements discovery, analysis, and documenting acceptance criteria. For example, ChatGPT can perform these tasks efficiently and accurately.

Using AI, project managers can save time and leverage the tool's predictive capabilities to anticipate potential challenges and devise appropriate strategies in response. We'll demonstrate how to use ChatGPT for requirements collection based on stakeholder inputs. We'll also demonstrate the role of AI in generating detailed project deliverables based on the project's objectives and constraints.

Role of AI in Requirements Collection

AI can be a beneficial tool in the requirements-gathering process. It can assist you in brainstorming sessions, creating interview questions or surveys for requirements elicitation, analyzing existing documents to gather information, and helping in requirements documentation.

Brainstorming with ChatGPT

Brainstorming is often used in requirements elicitation as it encourages expressing ideas without immediate judgment. AI can jump-start brainstorming even in a remote or individual setting. You can generate a prompt asking for brainstorming ideas on a specific topic, and it can produce a list of ideas, solutions, or features to aid you with free thinking. Additionally, if you're working in a group setting, you can feed the responses from team members to ChatGPT, which can help organize and refine the ideas.

> ***"Our team needs to brainstorm and gather our thoughts about the key features our new CRM system should have. Propose some ideas in a comma delimited list."***
>
> Integrated communication channels, advanced analytics, automated workflows, customer segmentation, mobile access, and intuitive interface. Please let me know if you would like me to elaborate any of the provided feature ideas.

This is a good base of ideas to start from. The team can then review the generated ideas, consolidate them, and refine them based on the organizational goals and constraints. The key is to jump-start the conversation based on a sound baseline of ideas, and AI helps facilitate that.

Document Analysis with AI

Document analysis is a critical part of requirements elicitation, which involves a deep dive into the existing document base. This could include a review of system specifications, user manuals, existing process descriptions, standard operating procedures, and system logs. This is a very time-consuming task, and it can be a challenge to review historical data and earlier product specifications.

Luckily, AI is good at reviewing documents and meaningfully summarizing information. You can input a document segment or a summary to obtain insights, and you might ask that ChatGPT's responses meet your needs: simpler, longer, shorter, or more professional.

A key strength of AI tools is filling in the blanks. For example, even if you provide incomplete information about a current system, AI can produce a well-rounded perspective of the system. Therefore, if you ask about the limitations of such an existing system, it will readily identify potential improvements.

"The user manual of our existing CRM system mentions limited reporting capabilities, a lack of integrated email marketing tools, and a nonintuitive contact management system. What potential improvements could we aim for in each of these areas for our new CRM system?"

Reporting Capabilities: An improved CRM system could include advanced analytics tools. This would provide comprehensive, customizable reports, and allow data-driven decisions based on real-time data. Users could tailor these reports to their specific needs, allowing for more personalized and effective use of the CRM system.

Email Integration: A CRM with built-in email marketing tools would greatly enhance the system's capabilities. This could include features like automated logging and tracking of customer interactions, scheduled emails, and integrated performance analytics. This would provide a more unified and streamlined approach to customer engagement.

Contact Management: For a more user-friendly experience, the new CRM could employ an automated data entry system and intuitive interface. This would reduce manual errors, improve data accuracy, and lead to better utilization of customer data. The interface should allow for easy navigation and quick access to necessary features to increase user efficiency.

NOTE For a large set of documents or complex information you can use OpenAI's enterprise version of ChatGPT to interact with databases and file systems for more advanced information extraction and analysis capabilities. Be sure to guard any sensitive information.

Requirements Documentation with AI

The requirements documentation process is the next crucial step. It involves the collation of all the requirements that have been identified. These could include functional, nonfunctional, business, solution, or stakeholder requirements.

AI can help systematically document these requirements. Based on the data from brainstorming sessions, document analysis, survey responses, and even images, you can prompt ChatGPT to draft a requirements document. You'll see that AI translates the raw information into specific, actionable requirements for each category.

Let's delve into using images for requirements documentation. For our CRM system, let's say we received a screenshot image illustrating desired functionality, and the image is the most accurate way to articulate the requirements to the project team and developers. Let's take this image from an image search on Google of Smartsheet, a popular project management vendor (**Figure 5.2**).

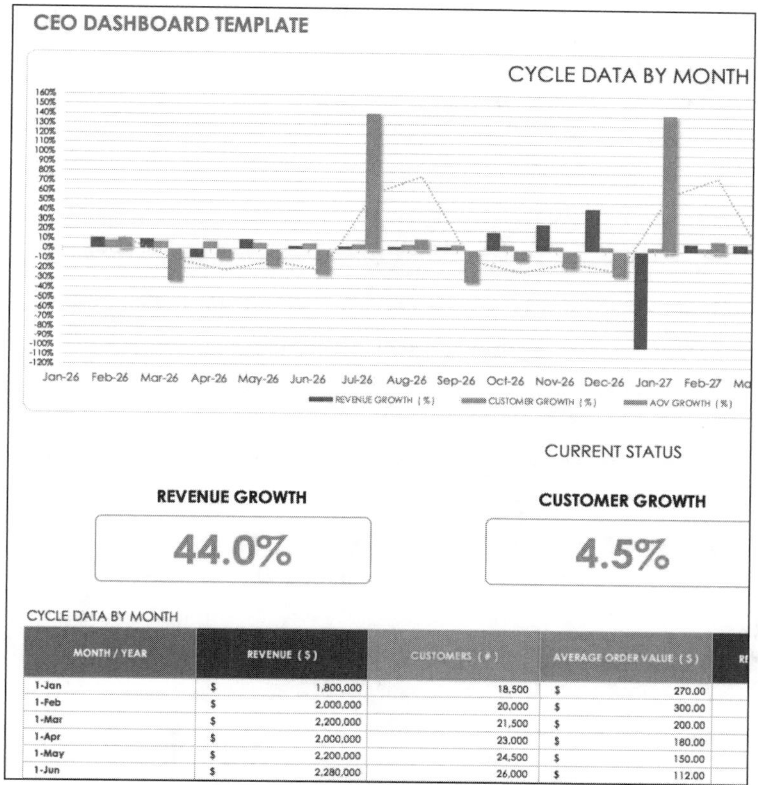

MONTH / YEAR	REVENUE ($)	CUSTOMERS (#)	AVERAGE ORDER VALUE ($)
1-Jan	$ 1,800,000	18,500	$ 270.00
1-Feb	$ 2,000,000	20,000	$ 300.00
1-Mar	$ 2,200,000	21,500	$ 200.00
1-Apr	$ 2,000,000	23,000	$ 180.00
1-May	$ 2,200,000	24,500	$ 150.00
1-Jun	$ 2,280,000	26,000	$ 112.00

FIGURE 5.2 A portion of the Smartsheet CEO dashboard capture showing functions

Here we should call upon the power of multimodal AI models. We can use AI products such as ChatGPT's Vision feature, Google's Bard and Microsoft's Bing AI to show the image and describe it, and then prompt the AI to show and explain it in terms that a builder or developer would understand.

> ***"Act as a business analyst. Review the attached image of an example CRM system dashboard. For our project, based on a meeting with stakeholders, we would like our system to provide the functions shown in the image. Please review it and extract requirements so that I can add it to the requirements documentation and so that I can use it to describe the system to our builders and development team."***

TECHNICAL GUIDE **Refer to Technical Guide 5.1 to see details of using image recognition with Bard.**

Here are the requirements for the CRM system dashboard based on the image:

The dashboard should be titled "CEO Dashboard."

The dashboard should display the following metrics:

- Revenue growth
- Customer growth
- Average order value (AOV) growth
- Current status of revenue growth, customer growth, and AOV growth
- Monthly data for revenue growth, customer growth, and AOV growth

Here are some other items that should be shown

- The dashboard should allow users to filter the data by date range, metric, or other criteria.
- The dashboard should be customizable so that users can add or remove metrics and change the layout.
- The dashboard should be easy to use and navigate.
- The dashboard should use a combination of charts, tables, and text to display the data.
- The dashboard should be visually appealing and easy to read.
- The dashboard should be customizable so that users can select the metrics they want to see.

"From the brainstorming session, document analysis, image analysis, and user survey, we've identified a set of requirements for our new CRM system. These requirements cover various functional, nonfunctional, business, solution, and stakeholder requirements. Could you help draft a requirements document based on these insights?"

Based on the information provided, here's a draft of the functional requirements for the new CRM system:

Functional Requirements: These are specific functions or tasks that the system should be able to perform:

- Integrated communication channels
- Automated workflows
- Customer segmentation capabilities
- Executive reporting and dashboards

Nonfunctional Requirements: These refer to the operational aspects of the system:

- Mobile access for continuous interaction with the CRM system
- Advanced analytics for real-time and customizable reporting capabilities

Business Requirements: These are high-level needs of the organization as a whole.

- Improving customer interaction
- Enhancing data-driven decision-making
- Automation of regular tasks to save time and reduce manual errors

Stakeholder Requirements: These are the needs or expectations of a stakeholder or a stakeholder group:

- Sales Team: Needs advanced analytics and automated workflows for better lead management
- Customer Service Team: Needs integrated communication channels for better customer interaction
- Marketing Team: Needs customer segmentation feature for personalized marketing campaigns

Solution Requirements: These depict how the solution must behave. This includes both functional and nonfunctional requirements that guide the development of the system.

- The CRM system must provide integrated communication channels.
- The CRM system should be mobile compatible.
- The CRM system should provide advanced analytics and reporting capabilities.

This categorization and structure can help teams understand the requirements from different angles, aiding in efficient project planning and execution.

After this, it can be helpful to create a RACI matrix, specifying who is Responsible, Accountable, Consulted, and Informed for each requirement to provide clarity on roles and responsibilities.

For instance, for the Advanced Analytics and Reporting feature, you, as project manager, might be *responsible* for overseeing its implementation, the head of the sales team might be *accountable*, the data analysis team might be *consulted*, and all other stakeholders might be *informed* about the progress.

AI can assist with creating a responsible, accountable, consulted, informed (RACI) matrix, a responsibility assignment matrix. This matrix helps you clarify roles and responsibilities in cross-functional/departmental projects and processes.

NOTE For some tables created by ChatGPT the layout has been adjusted to fit on these pages (column headings turned to fit).

"Let's introduce the topic of RACI matrix next. Given the documented stakeholder requirements and the stakeholders involved, create a RACI matrix for me please."

Here's a simple RACI matrix based on the stakeholder requirements mentioned:

REQUIREMENTS/ STAKEHOLDERS	SALES TEAM	CUSTOMER SERVICE TEAM	MARKETING TEAM	DATA ANALYSIS TEAM	PROJECT MANAGER
Advanced Analytics	C	C	C	R, A	C
Automated Workflows	R, A	C	I	C	C
Customer Segmentation	I	I	R, A	C	C

Key:

R (Responsible): Person or role that completes the task. The doer.

A (Accountable): Person or role that is the owner of the work.

C (Consulted): Person or role that needs to provide feedback and contribute to the task.

I (Informed): Person or role that needs to know of the action or decision.

In this scenario, the roles and responsibilities are fairly evenly distributed among the team. For instance, the data analysis team is both responsible and accountable for the implementation of the Advanced Analytics feature, while the sales team is both responsible and accountable for the Automated Workflows feature. For Customer Segmentation, the marketing team takes the lead as the responsible and accountable entity. You, as the project manager, play a more consultative role across these requirements.

AI-Assisted Project Scope Definition

Scope refers to the sum total of all the products, services, and results provided by your project. It defines the boundaries of the project, the breadth of its reach, and the extent of work that must be performed to deliver the project's end product or service. In essence, the project scope sets the stage for what the project will do—and equally important, what it won't do.

For instance, in our case study, the project scope for the CRM Implementation project at Fictional Corp. includes the selection of a CRM software solution, customization of this solution to suit the needs of Fictional Corp., integration of this solution with existing systems, and finally, training staff to effectively use this new system.

Understanding project scope is crucial for the following reasons:

- **Provides Clarity:** Clearly defining the project scope helps everyone understand what is expected, who is involved, what the project will deliver, and when it is expected to be delivered. It sets expectations for the project team, stakeholders, and clients, eliminating potential miscommunications or misunderstandings.
- **Guides Project Planning:** Provides a framework for planning, including the schedule, budget, resources, and risks.
- **Defines Success Criteria:** What it will look like when the project is complete and has achieved its goals.
- **Controls Cost and Prevents Scope Creep:** Scope creep is the unauthorized expansion of work, such as additional features or requirements, without consideration to time and cost. Scope definition prevents the tendency for the project scope to expand beyond its initial objectives.

Understanding project scope is one thing, but clearly articulating it in a Project Scope Statement can be time consuming—and that's where AI can lend a helping hand. Let's explore this in the next section.

AI in Creating a Scope Statement

The project scope statement builds on the brief scope overview in your project charter and transforms it into a clear, actionable document that guides your project management decisions.

AI can assist with the creation of the scope statement in a few ways.

Information Extraction

AI can sift through vast amounts of data from documents such as project charters, meeting transcripts, and emails to extract relevant details needed for a comprehensive scope statement.

> ***"ChatGPT, based on the project charter for the CRM Implementation at Fictional Corp., what are the major deliverables for this project?"***
>
> Based on the project charter you've provided, the major deliverables for the CRM Implementation project at Fictional Corp. appear to be:
>
> Selection of a CRM software solution.
>
> Customization of the selected CRM solution to fit the needs of Fictional Corp.
>
> Integration of the CRM solution with existing systems at Fictional Corp.
>
> Training for staff on the effective use of the new CRM system.
>
> *{Response truncated for brevity and relevance.}*

Scope Statement Drafting

Once the relevant information has been extracted, AI can assist in drafting the scope statement. This not only speeds up the process but can also help in maintaining consistency and completeness in the document.

> ***"ChatGPT, could you help me draft the Project Deliverables section of our scope statement based on the information you just provided?"***
>
> Of course! Here's a draft for the Project Deliverables section of your scope statement:
>
> The major deliverables of the CRM Implementation project at Fictional Corp. include the following:
>
> - Selection of a CRM software solution that aligns with the specific needs and objectives of Fictional Corp.
> - Customization of the chosen CRM solution to ensure it meets the unique demands of our organization, including integration with our existing systems
> - A comprehensive training program that empowers our staff to effectively use the new CRM system, thereby ensuring the system's successful deployment and adoption

Scope Management Procedures

AI can recommend standardized procedures for managing scope based on best practices from project management methodologies or from a database of past projects within the organization.

> ***"ChatGPT, based on best practices in project management, what steps should we take to control scope creep during the CRM Implementation project?"***
>
> Controlling scope creep is crucial for project success. Here are some steps you might consider:
>
> - Clearly define project scope: Make sure the scope is well defined and that all stakeholders have a shared understanding of what is included in the scope and what is not.
> - Implement a change control process: Changes to the scope should go through a formal change control process. This includes documenting the proposed change, analyzing its impact, and getting approval from the project sponsor or steering committee before implementing the change.
> - Regularly review and monitor the project scope: Regularly review the project status and compare it with the planned scope. If any deviations are noticed, take corrective actions promptly.
> - Communicate effectively: Ensure all stakeholders are informed about any changes to the project scope and their impacts on time, cost, and other project variables.

AI can assist in drafting the scope management plan, ensuring a structured, comprehensive, and organized document. ChatGPT could aid in preparing a section of the scope management plan, given our previous prompt asking about best practices and incorporating them as part of your standard procedures.

> ***"Based on your recommendations, could you help me draft a scope control plan?"***
>
> The CRM Implementation project will utilize a systematic approach to manage and control changes to the project scope. Here are the key steps we'll follow:
>
> - Clear Definition of Project Scope: We will start by defining a clear and detailed project scope to ensure everyone understands what the project includes.

- Change Control Process: We will implement a rigorous change control process. Any proposed changes to the project scope must be documented, and their impact on the project's timeline, cost, and quality must be analyzed. All proposed changes will need approval from the project sponsor or steering committee before implementation.
- Regular Scope Review: We will conduct regular reviews of the project's status and compare it to the defined scope. Any deviations will be addressed promptly through corrective actions.
- Effective Communication: All changes to the project scope and their impacts will be communicated to all stakeholders promptly.

AI in WBS Creation

A WBS (Work Breakdown Structure) is a critical project management tool used to define and organize the total scope of a project. This tool visually breaks down the project's entire scope into manageable chunks of work, or *work packages*, facilitating more accurate project planning, execution, and control. It is organized in levels, starting with the root level, which represents the entire project. This is then broken down into subsequent levels that detail the major deliverables and sub-deliverables. The lowest level of the WBS outlines the project's scope of work—these constitute the work packages.

The WBS is typically structured in a tree diagram, with each element assigned a unique identifier, often based on a decimal numbering system. This numbering, also known as the WBS code, helps in tracking and locating the WBS elements. The final level of the WBS, that is the work package level, outlines tasks that are small enough to be managed effectively when assigned to a specific team or individual.

To create a WBS, a project team typically considers several important documents:

Project Scope Statement: This specifies all the work to be included in the WBS, and no other work will be included.

Requirements Documentation: This key input helps identify and organize the tasks and subtasks in the WBS.

Organizational Process Assets: These can include policies, procedures, and templates from the organization such as those from previous similar projects.

Stakeholder Register: This provides information about who has interest or influence over the project. Their needs and expectations may determine some of the specific tasks that need to be included in the WBS.

The project team's knowledge and experience can guide the identification and organization of tasks and subtasks. They will have insights into what needs to be done, how long it may take, and how tasks may depend on each other.

Once these inputs are gathered and understood, the project team creates the WBS. This could be during a facilitated working session with the goal of identifying the major deliverables and then subdividing them into smaller, more manageable components. These components are the tasks that must be completed to create the deliverable.

This process is traditionally manual, requiring significant effort and collaboration. As we will see, AI has the potential to make the task more efficient and effective.

Using AI in WBS Creation

AI can play a significant role in creating a WBS by automating repetitive tasks, minimizing human errors, and providing insights based on historical data. Here's how an AI like ChatGPT could assist in WBS creation:

- **Creating WBS Templates:** ChatGPT could analyze previous project data to create WBS templates for similar current projects.
- **Automating Task Identification:** ChatGPT could review project documents such as the project scope statement and requirements to identify tasks to be included in the WBS.
- **Estimating Task Durations:** Based on historical data, ChatGPT could provide initial estimates of task durations, which can then be refined by the project team.
- **Identifying Dependencies:** ChatGPT could analyze the project requirements and tasks to identify potential dependencies, which can be critical in planning the project schedule.

To give a practical example, let's say you want to create a WBS for the CRM Implementation project at Fictional Corp.:

> ***"We're working on the CRM Implementation project, and we need to break down our tasks using a Work Breakdown Structure. Can you help us with that?"***

Absolutely! Based on the Project Charter you provided, and the typical tasks involved in a CRM implementation project, here is a high-level WBS you might consider:

CRM System Selection

1.1 Identify Requirements

1.2 Research Available Systems

1.3 Evaluate and Select System

CRM System Customization and Integration

2.1 Define Customization Requirements

2.2 Develop Custom Features

2.3 Integrate with Existing Systems

Staff Training

3.1 Develop Training Material

3.2 Conduct Training Sessions

3.3 Evaluate Training Effectiveness

CRM System Deployment

4.1 Prepare Deployment Plan

4.2 Execute Deployment Plan

4.3 Confirm System Operational

ChatGPT provided a very good starting point here. Notice that this is a high-level structure, and each item can be broken down further as needed. Let's have ChatGPT break it down into even more work packages:

"Thanks! Can you please decompose these into more work packages for me?"

ChatGPT: Certainly, let's break down the tasks:

1. CRM System Selection
    - 1.1 Identify Requirements
        - 1.1.1 Gather Input from Stakeholders
        - 1.1.2 Consolidate and Prioritize Requirements
        - 1.1.3 Finalize Requirements Document
    - 1.2 Research Available Systems
        - 1.2.1 Conduct Market Research

1.2.2 Shortlist Potential CRM Systems

1.2.3 Arrange Demonstrations/Presentations from Vendors

1.3 Evaluate and Select System

1.3.1 Define Evaluation Criteria

1.3.2 Rate Each System Against Criteria

1.3.3 Select Optimal System

2. CRM System Customization and Integration

2.1 Define Customization Requirements

2.1.1 Analyze Gap Between Chosen System and Business Needs

2.1.2 Define Custom Features Needed

2.1.3 Document Customization Requirements

2.2 Develop Custom Features

2.2.1 Design Custom Features

2.2.2 Develop Custom Features

2.2.3 Test Custom Features

3. CRM System Deployment

3.1 Pre-Deployment Checks

3.1.1 Conduct User Acceptance Testing

3.1.2 Perform System Backup

3.1.3 Prepare Deployment Plan

3.2 Deploy System

3.2.1 Install CRM System in Production Environment

3.2.2 Migrate Data to the New System

3.2.3 Perform Post-Deployment Testing

{Response truncated for brevity and relevance.}

This provides a more detailed plan for the remaining work packages. The granularity might vary depending on your project and your organization's specific policies and procedures. Using AI like ChatGPT to drill down further into the tasks not only helps in creating a detailed WBS but also prompts the project team to consider all necessary steps and potential challenges ahead. Thus, AI not only assists in task identification but also aids in comprehensive project planning.

Creating the WBS in Hierarchical Tree Form with AI

You previously had AI create your CRM Implementation project WBS in an outline or list format, but with the power of AI, you can have this information represented in various ways. Let's see it in tree form:

> ***"Can you please format the WBS in a tree or hierarchy format using plug-ins? Let's start with CRM System Selection first."***

ChatGPT will produce the graphic, which is too wide to show here. **Figure 5.3** shows the structure with details that would be legible if we had more room in this book to show it larger.

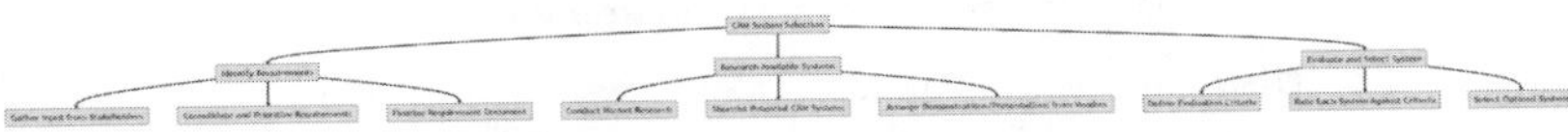

FIGURE 5.3 WBS for CRM system selection as created by ChatGPT

Remember, conversing and working with AI is an incremental and iterative process. While it created a good first pass, it still doesn't quite have everything you need. For instance, it is missing the WBS numbering. You might ask ChatGPT to fix that for you using the prompt: "The WBS hierarchy diagram is missing the WBS Codes. Can you please re-create it to include them?" ChatGPT would then produce the updated diagram.

You might then decide to ask AI to generate the rest of the WBS for you: "Can you please proceed with generating the rest of the WBS? Continue with using the WBS codes." The response will present diagrams for each section of the WBS. For the sake of brevity, we are not reproducing them here.

> **TECHNICAL GUIDE** See details on the ChatGPT plug-in in Technical Guide 5.3 used to generate diagrams such as the WBS in tree form.

Creating the WBS in Tabular Format with AI

The hierarchical tree form is excellent for understanding the breakdown of tasks and their relationships. However, it might also be useful to view the WBS in a tabular format. This format can provide a more straightforward, at-a-glance view of the work packages, their hierarchy, and the WBS codes.

> **NOTE** Small projects teams will want to bypass the hierarchical tree in favor of the tabular structure.

We'll ask ChatGPT to use the output from the previous conversation and transform the hierarchical tree into a tabular format. This capability can save time and ensure consistency.

> ***"We've created a hierarchical tree for our WBS. Now, we'd like to see this in a tabular format. Can you help us with this?"***
>
> Here's the WBS for the CRM Implementation project at Fictional Corp. in a tabular format:

WBS CODE	TASK NAME
1	CRM System Selection
1.1	Identify Requirements
1.1.1	Gather Input from Stakeholders
1.1.2	Consolidate and Prioritize Requirements
1.1.3	Finalize Requirement Document
1.2	Research Available Systems
1.2.1	Conduct Market Research
1.2.2	Shortlist Potential CRM Systems
1.2.3	Arrange Demonstrations from Vendors
1.3	Evaluate and Select System
1.3.1	Define Evaluation Criteria
1.3.2	Rate Each System Against Criteria
1.3.3	Select Optimal System
...	...

{Table truncated for brevity and relevance.}

The tabular format of the WBS provides a clear view of the tasks and their hierarchical structure. Your team can check the WBS for accuracy and edit the table as needed.

Remember, a WBS is not a project plan or project schedule and is not listed in chronological order. It is a tool that delineates the scope of the project into manageable chunks so that you and your team can best understand what tasks needs to be involved.

Creating a Schedule from the WBS Using AI

A project schedule is a timeline that includes start and finish dates for the project's activities, milestones, and deliverables. It is a visual representation of the project's timeline, depicting when and in what sequence the work packages (as identified in the WBS) need to be completed. It also identifies the dependencies between tasks and the resources assigned to each task.

The project schedule is a critical tool for project managers as it helps

- Track progress and performance against planned timelines
- Identify critical tasks that could impact your project's completion date
- Communicate the project plan and progress to your stakeholders

Creating a project schedule involves several steps:

1. **List Activities:** Identify all the specific activities needed to deliver the project. The WBS serves as the primary source for this list.
2. **Estimate Activity Duration:** Each activity's duration is estimated based on factors such as the complexity of the task, the resources assigned, and historical data from similar projects.
3. **Identify Dependencies:** Dependencies between tasks are identified. Some tasks can't start until others are completed, whereas others can be done in parallel.
4. **Assign Resources:** Resources (both human and material) are assigned to each task based on their availability and the task requirements.
5. **Create the Schedule:** A visual schedule is created, often using project management software, displaying the tasks' sequence and duration.

Creating a project schedule manually can be time-consuming, but AI can significantly streamline this process.

Using AI to Create a Project Schedule

Let's illustrate this with an example. Suppose you want to create a project schedule for the CRM Implementation project at Fictional Corp. You might interact with ChatGPT in the following way:

> ***"We've created a WBS for our CRM Implementation project. Now, we'd like to create a project schedule. Can you help us with this?"***
>
> Based on the WBS and the typical durations and dependencies involved in a CRM implementation project, here is a draft project schedule:

WBS CODE	TASK NAME	DURATION (DAYS)	PREDECESSORS
1	CRM System Selection	30	None
1.1	Identify Requirements	7	None
1.1.1	Gather Input from Stakeholders	3	None
1.1.2	Consolidate and Prioritize Requirements	2	1.1.1
1.1.3	Finalize Requirement Document	2	1.1.2
1.2	Research Available Systems	10	1.1.3
1.2.1	Conduct Market Research	5	1.1.3
1.2.2	Shortlist Potential CRM Systems	3	1.2.1
1.2.3	Arrange Demonstrations from Vendors	2	1.2.2
1.3	Evaluate and Select System	13	1.2.3
1.3.1	Define Evaluation Criteria	3	1.2.3
1.3.2	Rate Each System Against Criteria	7	1.3.1
1.3.3	Select Optimal System	3	1.3.2

{Table truncated for brevity and relevance.}

Notice that the AI added Durations and Predecessor columns in the WBS table without having you define those in your prompt. However, notice too that Start/End Dates aren't specified and Resources also need to be assigned to these tasks and work packages. Let's ask ChatGPT to add to it:

"Thanks. I noticed that you have not specified Start or End Dates. Can you please add those columns to the table? Assume the project starts on January 1, 2025. Can you also add a column called Resource Names and assign resources?"

WBS CODE	TASK NAME	DURATION (DAYS)	PREDECESSORS	START DATE	END DATE	RESOURCE NAMES
1	CRM System Selection	30		01/01/2025	01/30/2025	PM, Business Analyst
1.1	Identify Requirements	7		01/01/2025	01/07/2025	Business Analyst
1.1.1	Gather Input from Stakeholders	2		01/01/2025	01/02/2025	Business Analyst
1.1.2	Consolidate and Prioritize Requirements	3	1.1.1	01/03/2025	01/05/2025	Business Analyst
1.1.3	Finalize Requirement Document	2	1.1.2	01/06/2025	01/07/2025	Business Analyst

{Table truncated for brevity and relevance.}

As a project manager, you must factor in deadlines, key events, and other milestones while creating a project schedule. These elements provide significant checkpoints, help track progress, and ensure that the project is moving toward its objectives in a timely manner.

Milestones are significant events in your project schedule, often dictated by the sponsors. Common examples of milestones are the start and end of a project phase, the due date for a deliverable, or a scheduling decision point.

One key characteristic of milestones is that they have a duration of zero. In other words, milestones represent a point in time, and they do not consume any resources. In many project management information systems, such as Microsoft Project, milestones are represented by diamonds.

In your CRM Implementation case study, neither you nor ChatGPT have specified any milestones. Let's ask ChatGPT to help you identify some potential milestones for your project—a straightforward process.

> ***"We've been creating a project schedule for our CRM Implementation project. We realized we haven't identified any milestones yet. Can you help us with this?"***

In a CRM Implementation project, some milestones could be:

Milestone: CRM System Selection Completion

Milestone: CRM System Customization and Integration Completion

Milestone: CRM System Deployment

Milestone: Project Completion

These milestones represent significant events in your project and can serve as checkpoints to ensure your project is on track.

"Great, can you please add these newly identified milestones into the table? Please also update any milestones and task dependencies."

TASK ID	WBS LEVEL	TASK NAME	DURATION (DAYS)	START DATE	END DATE	PREDECESSORS	RESOURCE NAMES
...	...	...	...	...	...	...	...
1.2.2	3	Shortlist Potential CRM Systems	5	Jan 20, 2025	Jan 24, 2025	1.2.1	PM, IT Team
1.2.3	3	Arrange Demonstrations/ Presentations from Vendors	5	Jan 25, 2025	Jan 29, 2025	1.2.2	PM, IT Team
1.3	2	Evaluate and Select System	15	Jan 30, 2025	Feb 13, 2025	1.2.3	PM, IT Team
1.3.1	3	Define Evaluation Criteria	5	Jan 30, 2025	Feb 3, 2025	1.2.3	PM, IT Team
1.3.2	3	Rate Each System Against Criteria	5	Feb 4, 2025	Feb 8, 2025	1.3.1	PM, IT Team
1.3.3	3	Select Optimal System	5	Feb 9, 2025	Feb 13, 2025	1.3.2	PM, IT Team
M1	-	Milestone: CRM System Selection Completion	0	Feb 14, 2025	Feb 14, 2025	1.3.3	

{Table truncated for brevity and relevance.}

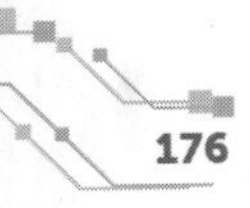

Note the inclusion of the milestone CRM System Selection Completion. ChatGPT correctly added it to the schedule and noted it with a duration of 0 days.

TIP Be sure to validate tasks and milestones—earlier versions of ChatGPT failed to show milestones and durations correctly.

Finally, as the project manager, you should consider external dependencies, specific deadlines, or other context-specific factors that AI may not know. These could include contractual deadlines, team meetings, coordination with other project teams, or key milestones, such as marketing milestones. You now have a project schedule!

TECHNICAL GUIDE In Technical Guide 5.3, you'll learn how to convert this table into a Microsoft Project File–compatible format.

AI-Enhanced Cost Estimation and Budgeting

In managing projects, the practice of cost estimation and budgeting plays a critical role in ascertaining the viability, scope, and potential success of the endeavor. Cost estimations and budgeting are crucial and indispensable components of project management. By knowing the costs associated with a project, you can plan accordingly, allocate resources, manage expectations, and avoid overspending. In this section, we'll delve into two fundamental approaches to cost estimation, top-down and bottom-up, and demonstrate how an AI model like ChatGPT can aid in these processes.

Top-Down Estimation

Top-down estimation allows you to create a high-level view of your budget based on the total cost of similar past projects. Let's say, for the CRM Implementation project at Fictional Corp., you have historical data suggesting that similar projects cost around $700,000. Because we already have a WBS, you could present this scenario to ChatGPT and ask

"Based on historical data from similar projects, our project should cost around $700,000. How can we distribute this cost across the different tasks outlined in our WBS?"

Given the historical budget of $700,000, the costs can be distributed based on the complexity and duration of each task, as well as the resources required. For example, if CRM System Selection represents about 20% of the project's work, it could be allocated $140,000 of the budget. We could continue this process for each task to ensure the total allocated budget aligns with the estimated project cost.

A top-down estimate is typically used for a quick and very rough approximate budget. This estimate essentially draws from projects of similar sizes in the past without spending too much time in determining what the project would entail. Top-down estimates would be more commonly used during the very early stages of a project.

Bottom-Up Estimation

In contrast to the top-down approach, bottom-up estimation begins with the smallest project tasks or packages and aggregates them into an overall project estimate. This method is more granular and precise, making use of the detailed WBS and the project schedule that you had AI create for you.

For example, with the CRM Implementation project, let's consider the Identifying Requirements task under the broader category of CRM System Selection. Here, the project manager is responsible for the task, which has a duration of 10 days. Considering your average daily rate, you can estimate the cost for this task.

This process can be streamlined using AI. ChatGPT, for instance, can take as input a detailed task list with associated resources and their rates, and then output a cost estimate for each task. Given its training on a diverse range of text materials, including project management literature, ChatGPT can handle this task efficiently, saving time and reducing the risk of human error.

As you proceed with your bottom-up estimation, let's add a Cost column to your project schedule and plan. This will enable you to see the costs associated with individual tasks. Here, the cost for each task is calculated based on the resources assigned to it, their respective rates, and the duration of the task.

"Given past historical project data, rates of our resources, and the duration of the tasks, please add a Cost column to our project schedule and plan."

Sure, here is the updated schedule and plan with a cost column:

TASK ID	WBS LEVEL	TASK NAME	DURATION (DAYS)	START DATE	END DATE	PREDECESSORS	RESOURCE NAMES	COST
...	...	...	...	...	...	...	...	...
1	1	CRM System Selection	44	Jan 1, 2025	Feb 13, 2025		PM, IT Team, Stake holders	$180,000
1.1	2	Identify Requirements	14	Jan 1, 2025	Jan 14, 2025		PM, IT Team, Stake holders	$56,000
1.1.1	3	Gather Input from Stakeholders	7	Jan 1, 2025	Jan 7, 2025		PM, Stake holders	$14,000
1.1.2	3	Consolidate and Prioritize Requirements	7	Jan 8, 2025	Jan 14, 2025	1.1.1	PM, IT Team,	$28,000
1.2	2	Research Available Systems	15	Jan 15, 2025	Jan 29, 2025	1.1.2	PM, IT Team,	$45,000
1.2.1	3	Conduct Market Research	5	Jan 15, 2025	Jan 19, 2025	1.1.2	PM, IT Team,	$15,000
1.2.2	3	Shortlist Potential CRM Systems	5	Jan 20, 2025	Jan 24, 2025	1.2.1	PM, IT Team,	$15,000
1.2.3	3	Arrange Presentations from Vendors	5	Jan 25, 2025	Jan 29, 2025	1.2.2	PM, IT Team,	$15,000
1.3	2	Evaluate and Select System	15	Jan 30, 2025	Feb 13, 2025	1.2.3	PM, IT Team,	$45,000
1.3.1	3	Define Evaluation Criteria	5	Jan 30, 2025	Feb 3, 2025	1.2.3	PM, IT Team,	$15,000

continues

TASK ID	WBS LEVEL	TASK NAME	DURATION (DAYS)	START DATE	END DATE	PREDECESSORS	RESOURCE NAMES	COST
1.3.2	3	Rate Each System Against Criteria	5	Feb 4, 2025	Feb 8, 2025	1.3.1	PM, IT Team,	$15,000
1.3.3	3	Select Optimal System	5	Feb 9, 2025	Feb 13, 2025	1.3.2	PM, IT Team,	$15,000
M1	-	Milestone: CRM System Selection Completion	0	Feb 14, 2025	Feb 14, 2025	1.3.3		$0

{Table truncated for brevity and relevance.}

One of the key advantages of using a WBS is its ability to both roll up and decompose costs. This means that if you want to see the total cost for an entire work stream or a higher-level task, you can simply roll up the individual task costs to see that subtotal. This feature provides you with a comprehensive view of your project costs, from the smallest tasks to the larger work streams. It allows you to manage your costs effectively and make informed decisions throughout the project life cycle.

The bottom-up estimation approach produces sound estimates and can ensure that the project remains on track and within budget.

Project Budgeting

Project budgeting is the process of allocating monetary resources to the different components of a project. It is crucial to release funds based on a calendar schedule in a timely manner so that the project delivers its objectives within the agreed financial parameters.

The budget is directly linked to the project's WBS and schedule—denoting when the expenses will occur. This is called a cost baseline or time-phased budget.

Total project cost is often divided into direct costs, those attributable to the project activities (like salaries of team members, costs of materials or services), and indirect costs that support the project activities (like overhead costs or administration costs). Given the level of complexity involved, it can be worthwhile to use AI to identify such categories and their estimated costs as a percentage of the overall budget.

The *direct costs* could include the licensing cost of the software, salaries of the project team, and costs of any hardware required. Since you've already broken down your tasks in the WBS and created a schedule, you can easily link direct costs to your project schedule, creating a time-phased budget. For example, the Deploy System task, which you estimated to take 5 days, might have a labor cost of $5,000 (assuming a daily rate of $1,000 for your team), a hardware cost of $2,000, and perhaps additional costs (such as electricity and Internet charges) of $500.

Indirect costs could include project management costs, administrative costs, and infrastructure costs. Indirect costs are often harder to assign to specific tasks because they support multiple or all tasks. For example, if you estimate project management and administrative overheads at 10 percent of total direct costs, and your direct costs total $50,000, indirect costs would be $5,000.

The sum of direct and indirect costs gives you the total project budget. It's important to note that a well-planned budget should also include a contingency reserve—an amount set aside to cover unexpected costs or overruns.

Given a budget, AI systems can break it down as shown with the prompt

"Create a project budget breakdown based on the details provided."

Personnel Costs: $315,000 (45% of budget)

- Project Manager: $45,000
- Business Analysts: $60,000
- Software Developers: $90,000
- Quality Assurance Engineers: $60,000
- UX/UI Designers: $30,000
- Systems Engineers: $30,000

Since not all funds are needed immediately, you might want some insights on releasing funds. Given a budget of $700,000, AI might recommend a time-phased release of funds, as shown here, based on its historical understanding of funds distribution of projects:

Here's an example of monthly allocation:

Month 1—Planning and Initialization: 30% of Budget—$210,000

This phase will involve heavy personnel involvement in terms of strategizing and planning, as well as setting up equipment and software.

Month 2—Execution and Monitoring: 50% of Budget—$350,000

This is typically the most resource-intensive phase. Hence a larger share of the budget is allocated here. This includes heavy involvement from all team members and the use of all planned resources.

Month 3—Closure and Reporting: 20% of Budget—$140,000

The remaining budget is used to wrap up the project, finalize reports, pay any remaining expenses, and handle any loose ends. The contingency fund is also fully available by this time in case it's needed.

AI can assist in calculating these costs, setting up the time-phased budget, and even analyzing various budget scenarios. For example, it can help answer questions like

"What would be the impact on our budget if the Deploy System task took 7 days instead of 5?"

"How much would we save if we managed to negotiate a 10% discount on our hardware costs?"

Remember, the project budget is a vital tool for project cost control. By comparing the budgeted cost of work scheduled with the actual cost of work performed, you can spot variances early and take corrective action if needed. This method, known as earned value management (EVM), is another essential aspect of project cost management that we will cover in Chapter 7, "Monitoring Project Work Performance with AI."

For our CRM Implementation project, let's assume the estimated cost is $700,000.

"We have cost estimates totaling $700,000. Could you help us create a plan to monitor the project spend against this budget?"

Monitoring your project spend against the budget is crucial for maintaining financial control. I suggest setting up a system that tracks costs as they occur in real time, categorized by each task. By comparing these real-time expenditures against your initial estimates, you'll be able to identify any variances quickly and adjust accordingly. For instance, if the Identifying Requirements task was budgeted at $5,000 but has so far cost $6,000, this discrepancy should be noted and addressed.

By utilizing AI products like ChatGPT in the cost estimation and budgeting process, you can more effectively predict and control project costs, contributing to the overall success of your project.

Ethical Considerations and Professional Responsibility

Navigating the evolving AI landscape for project planning demands addressing concerns like data privacy, transparency, inclusivity, and human oversight. Here are some key considerations for using AI in project planning:

Business Case Creation: AI can predict project outcomes based on past projects. It's crucial to explain how these predictions are made, ensure the data is unbiased, and avoid over-relying on AI, incorporating human judgment in final decisions.

Project Charter Creation: AI can facilitate project charter creation by analyzing the needs of stakeholders and the purpose of the project. However, sensitive information might be involved in this process. It is crucial to uphold data privacy and ensuring the AI model doesn't breach confidentiality.

Scope Creation: In defining the project scope, AI models can provide insights into scope creep from historical data. Ensure the data isn't biased, and incorporate human understanding for unique project nuances.

WBS and Scheduling: AI helps draft the work breakdown structure (WBS) and initial scheduling. However, the team should refine these drafts, balancing AI's data-driven insights with human expertise. Ethical considerations, like fair work distribution and acknowledging team input, remain paramount.

Cost Estimation and Budgeting: AI aids in cost predictions. However, it's vital to be transparent about AI's methods and remember that unforeseen events can impact costs. Combine AI's predictions with human and market insights.

In summary, as AI tools like ChatGPT become integral to project planning, the goal should be to complement, not replace, human expertise. This approach ensures ethical and responsible AI use in project management.

Key Points to Remember

In this chapter, we discussed how planning is incremental and iterative. Whether you're creating the WBS, schedule, or cost estimate, each step is built upon the previous one. This is true whether you're using traditional methods or AI. When using AI, it's crucial to revisit and refine the AI outputs as more information becomes available and as the project progresses.

- **Business Case Creation:** AI can assist in the analysis of a project's viability. It can help gather and process relevant data, like market trends, financial projections, and risk assessments.
- **Project Charter:** AI can help draft the initial charter based on the project's objectives, key stakeholders, and overall goals, but it should be reviewed and approved by project sponsors and stakeholders.
- **Project Scope Definition:** AI can generate a scope statement based on project details, but the project team should review and refine it.
- **Work Breakdown Structure (WBS):** AI can create an initial draft of the WBS, but this must be refined with the input and buy-in of the project team who are familiar with the actual work involved.
- **Project Scheduling:** AI can assist in generating project schedules based on dependencies and time estimates, but it should involve human oversight to ensure practicality and realism.
- **Cost Estimation and Budgeting:** AI can facilitate top-down and bottom-up estimation methodologies. However, cost details should be reviewed by human experts to ensure accuracy and reasonability.

Technical Guide

5.1 Multimodal Prompting with Google Bard Using Images

Google Bard can interpret images in prompts and generate text-based commentary on the image content. This can be used to extract requirements for stakeholders and the build team based on an image of features found in a product.

In the context of extracting requirements for the team from an image of product features, Bard can be used to

- Identify the features in the image
- Describe the features in detail
- Explain how the features work
- Identify any dependencies between the features
- Identify any potential problems with the features

The requirements extracted from the image can then be added to the Requirements Documentation for the build team to use.

Here are some examples of images that might contain features:

- An image of a new product feature
- An image of a user interface design
- An image of a wireframe
- An image of a prototype

How to Attach an Image Using Google Bard

1. Go to the Google Bard at **bard.google.com**.
2. In the text box, type your prompt.
3. Click the + icon next to the text box.
4. Select **Upload File** (**Figure 5.4**).

FIGURE 5.4 Google Bard Upload File

5. Choose the image you want to use from your computer.
6. Click **Open**.
7. Bard will interpret the image details based on its understanding of the prompt and its understanding of image shapes.
8. Bard will generate a response based on the image and the prompt. (If desired, AI can even produce code from an image.)

5.2 Create a WBS Diagram with ChatGPT Plugins

You can use ChatGPT Plus to create a WBS in hierarchy tree form:

1. Open a new conversation with ChatGPT.
2. Select **GPT-4** and select **Plugins** (**Figure 5.5**).

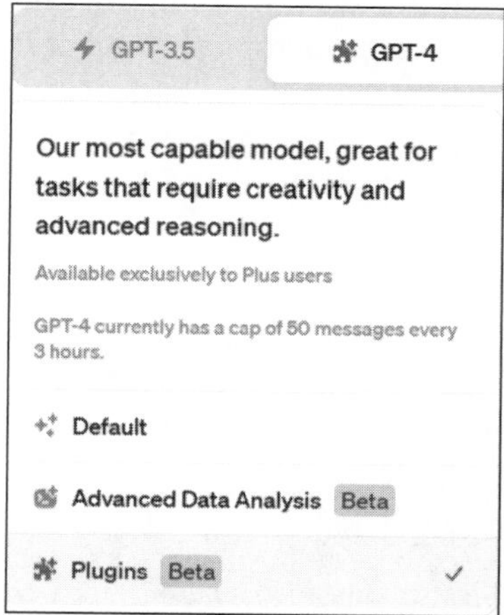

FIGURE 5.5 ChatGPT Plugins

3. Select a plug-in that allows for the creation of diagrams such as Show Me Diagrams (**Figure 5.6**). Note that the ChatGPT Plugin list is growing daily and that there are many plug-ins that can generate diagrams.

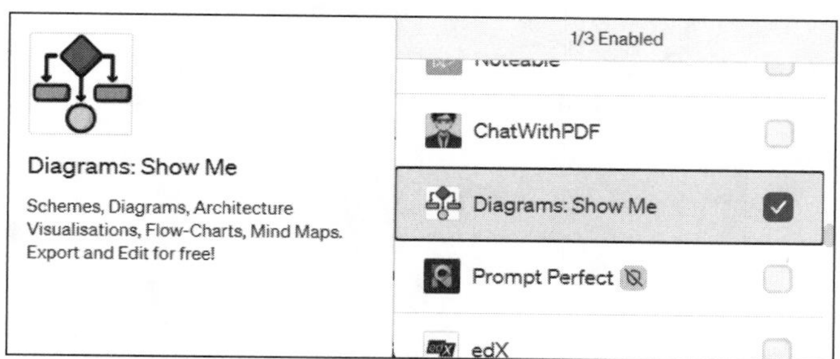

FIGURE 5.6 ChatGPT Show Me Diagram plug-in

4. Prompt ChatGPT to create a WBS in a list form—for example, "Please create a WBS for a home remodeling project in list form."
5. After ChatGPT creates the WBS for you, prompt ChatGPT to create a tree diagram of your WBS by saying, "Please show this WBS in tree form using the Show Me Diagram plug-in."
6. The plug-in will take a few seconds to generate a visual representation of your WBS.
7. Once the diagram is generated, you can download it as an image file or share it directly from the ChatGPT Plus platform.

5.3 Create a Project Plan and Gantt Chart Using ChatGPT and Project Plan 365 Browser Extension

A browser extension called Project Plan 365 integrates with ChatGPT to create project plans that can be opened using Microsoft Project or Project Plan 365. This extension allows users to quickly create a project plan using ChatGPT that can be opened online using Project Plan 365 or downloaded as a MPP file.

How to Install the Extension:

1. Open your Chrome or Edge browser.
2. Go to the Chrome Web Store or Microsoft Edge Add-ons store.
3. Search for **Project Plan 365 Assistant**.
4. Click **Add To Chrome** or **Get** to install the extension.
5. A pop-up will appear—click **Add Extension** to confirm.
6. The Project Plan 365 Assistant extension icon will now show up near the top right of your browser window.

How to Create a Project Plan:

1. With the extension installed, go to **http://chat.openai.com**.
2. In the chat box, type a request like **Create a project plan for a kitchen renovation** and press **Enter**.

3. Once ChatGPT generates the plan, click the **Format Text** button in the extension's pop-up (**Figure 5.7**).

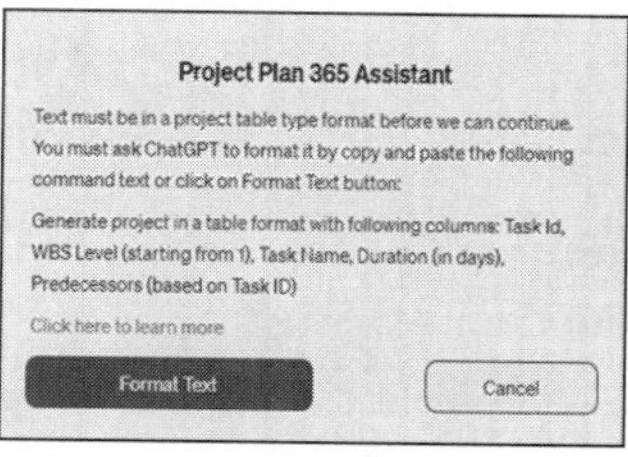

FIGURE 5.7 Project Plan 365 Assistant Format Text

4. This will reformat the plan into a table. Review the table and make any edits to the plan by typing new instructions in the chat box.
5. When ready, click the **Open Online** button to open the plan in Project Plan 365, or click **Download MPP** to download it (**Figure 5.8**).

FIGURE 5.8 Open the project plan

How to Edit the Project Plan

1. To add a task, type something like **Add a task called "Meet with contractor" after task 5**.
2. To change a task name, type **Change the name of task 10 to "Cabinet installation."**
3. To add a start date, type **Add a Start Date column** and then **Set start date of task 5 to 1/5/2025**.
4. To assign resources, type **Add a Resource Name column** and **Assign John to tasks 1–5**.
5. To remove a column, type **Remove the <*column name*> column**.
6. Review changes in the chat and repeat steps to continue editing.

How to Use an Existing WBS Table from ChatGPT

If you already have a WBS table created in ChatGPT, you can use the extension to open or download it.

The WBS table must have at least these columns:

- Task ID
- WBS Level (must be in full integers, not decimal)
- Task Name
- Duration
- Predecessors

Once you have the WBS Table generated in ChatGPT:

- When ready, click **Open Online** to open the plan directly in Project Plan 365 (**Figure 5.9**) or click **Download MPP** to download the plan as a MPP file to your computer.

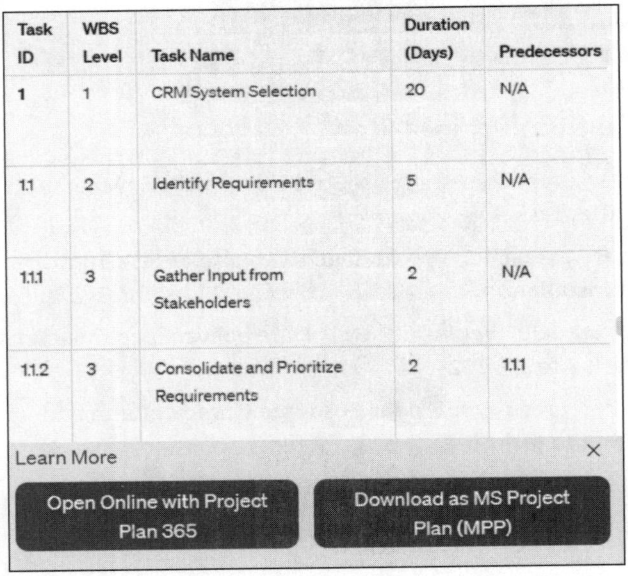

Task ID	WBS Level	Task Name	Duration (Days)	Predecessors
1	1	CRM System Selection	20	N/A
1.1	2	Identify Requirements	5	N/A
1.1.1	3	Gather Input from Stakeholders	2	N/A
1.1.2	3	Consolidate and Prioritize Requirements	2	1.1.1

Learn More ×

Open Online with Project Plan 365

Download as MS Project Plan (MPP)

FIGURE 5.9 Opening the project plan from ChatGPT

- If the WBS Level is not an integer, ChatGPT may not format the levels correctly. In that case, edit the chat to convert the WBS Level to an integer before exporting.

For additional step-by-step details on how to use this extension, please visit Project Plan 365's support website here: www.projectplan365.com/articles/project-plan-365-assistant-browser-extension

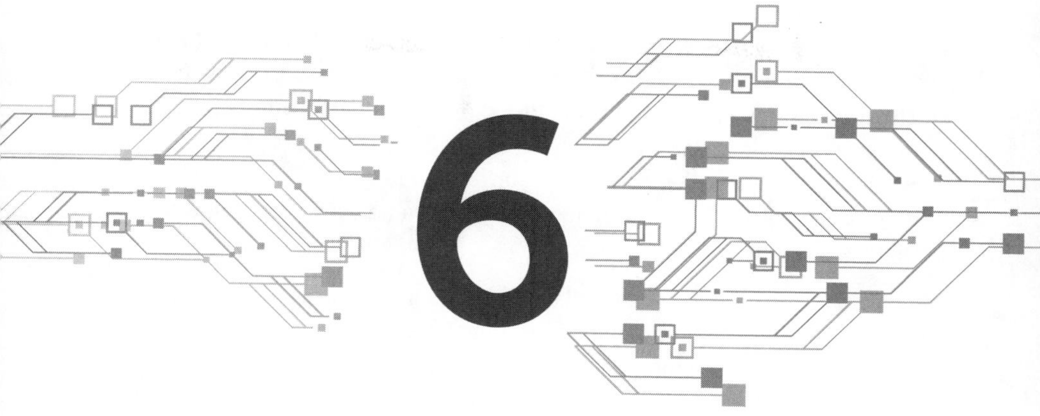

6 Adaptive Projects and AI

This chapter explores the adaptive approach, focusing on agile project management. We use Scrum, the most prevalent adaptive framework today for projects to introduce the role of generative artificial intelligence (AI) in project management. Scrum encourages teams to work iteratively and incrementally toward a common goal, facilitating adaptive planning, early delivery, and continuous improvement. With roots in the software sector, today it is used across industries and has wide-ranging applications.

AI IN ACTION: TRANSFORMING THE TRAVEL INDUSTRY

The travel industry is on the brink of a significant digital transformation. Integration of generative AI, such as OpenAI's ChatGPT and Google's Bard, by online travel agencies and startups promises to revolutionize trip planning and booking experiences and breathe new life into an industry that can benefit from such tools.

Travel industry players such as Expedia, Booking.com, and Kayak were early to invest in AI and machine learning because personalized online experiences are extremely popular in travel planning. Now, with the emergence of ChatGPT in November 2022, the industry has embraced it even further.

CHATGPT PLUG-INS OpenAI has plug-ins for ChatGPT that provide an enhanced and more immersive experience.

The plug-in initiative allows companies to train ChatGPT with current, industry-specific data, integrate it with their database, and provide customers with the latest and most relevant information. This process enables users to ask ChatGPT for travel advice or trip recommendations and seamlessly refer to the appropriate company for booking options.

Let's examine an implementation of ChatGPT by Expedia in its iOS app that integrates conversational AI and travel planning. This opens new possibilities in the travel industry, eliminating the need for customers to go through separate manual research and booking processes.

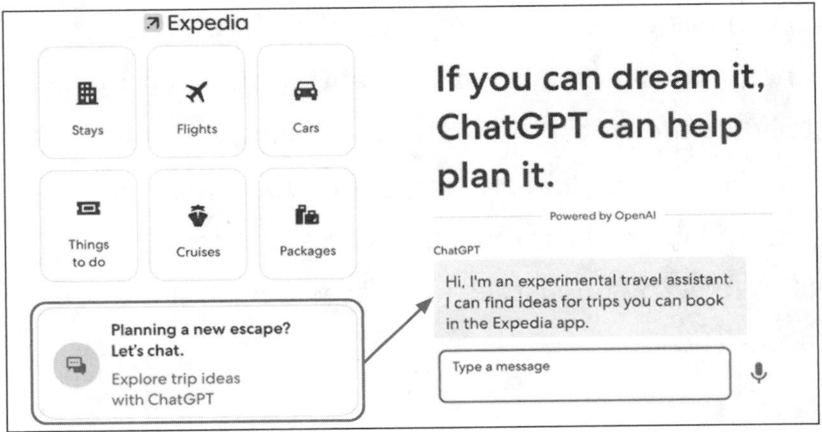

The first image shows how to activate ChatGPT in the Expedia app and begin conversational trip planning to Toronto, Canada, where customers interact with ChatGPT and receive recommendations. **Figure 6.1** illustrates how a conversation is saved in the trip planner. The trip planner can be accessed anywhere, even on a separate device like a desktop, to continue the booking process.

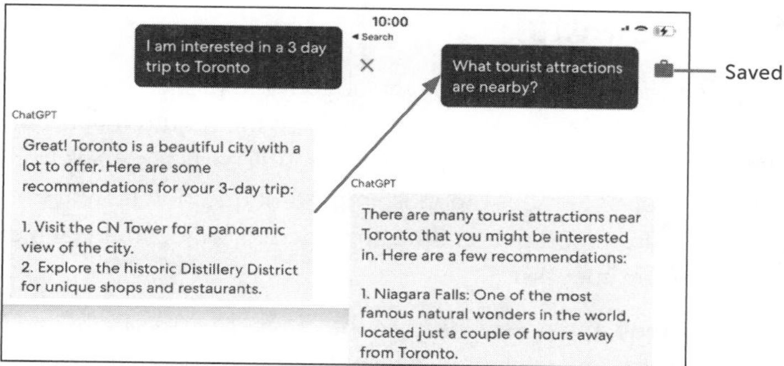

FIGURE 6.1 Trip to Toronto and saved conversation

Figure 6.2 illustrates the flexibility of the conversation, such as the weather in Toronto on a particular date. (This data is coming from ChatGPT's historical database.) Recommended activities and hotel suggestions with images and price ranges are saved to the customer's Trip Planner, allowing the customer to extend trip research beyond a single session.

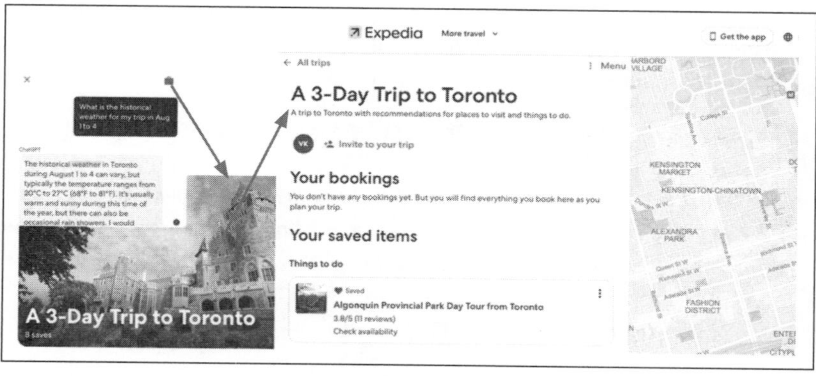

FIGURE 6.2 Integration of ChatGPT with the travel agency system

Customers can revisit and continue past conversations with ChatGPT at any point, enabling them to resume their trip-planning activities right where they left off. They can then book hotels or tourism packages from their existing accounts. This integration facilitates seamless research and booking of customers' trips, saving time and effort, setting the stage for a transformative shift in the future of trip planning with the help of AI.

AI applications such as this require an adaptive approach to complete the project in a timely manner. The most valuable features are introduced first from a prioritized backlog of requirements.

Adaptive Projects

The primary considerations for using the adaptive approach stem from affirmative answers to key questions such as: Are the requirements not well defined? Will they evolve with discovery? Will early feedback from customers be helpful? Perhaps the most important question is: Will the organizational culture permit a unique approach to project management and adapt to ensure success?

No project is unique, the possibility of scope creep is always high, and the best-laid plans must bow to change. It's not surprising that many practitioners and experts today favor the adaptive approach—but now you can call upon AI to assist with the challenges of this approach.

NOTE In this chapter, we will use the term *agile approach* interchangeably with *adaptive approach*.

Getting Organizational Support

For adaptive projects to succeed, agile project managers know three things are important: top management support, team involvement, and organizational willingness to be bold and experiment with new practices.

Let's see how ChatGPT responds to these issues via a query:

"I plan to use an agile approach to manage my next project; what guidance can you give me as I seek top management support, inclusiveness, and willingness to experiment with new practices?"

Here's the response from ChatGPT:

- Top Management Support: ChatGPT can assist in crafting concise presentations or documents advocating for agile transformation, including agile principles, benefits, and overcoming potential challenges. It can also help draft updates for management, showcasing the progress and benefits of the transformation.
- Team Involvement: ChatGPT can help create communication for teams explaining agile and its benefits. It can also suggest ways to engage

everyone in the process, such as through workshops or training sessions that promote agile principles.

- Experimentation and Feedback: ChatGPT can offer insights into agile practices and their implementation, suggesting context-based experiments. It can also recommend effective methods to gather and integrate feedback, such as designing retrospectives or feedback loops.

Case Study: Pioneering a Fitness Haven

In this section, we'll introduce a hypothetical case study, Caesar's Gym, involving two entrepreneurs, John and Mary, who aspire to build a gym in their local community after retiring from a large financial company. Their objective is to facilitate fitness for the townsfolk and earn a reasonable income from about 100 members who would pay a monthly fee. After some research, they are able to outline the key steps involved in opening their new business. These include formulating a business plan, finding a suitable location within the town, applying for certification, getting insurance, purchasing equipment, and hiring staff. Of course, they know this list will evolve over time, but they are off to a good start.

As the project progresses, our entrepreneurs will need to invest in additional needs such as marketing to promote and advertise the gym and attract members. This step can include building a website, investing in email marketing, mailing flyers to local town citizens, and offering opening discounts. Finally, they will be excited to invest in their grand opening. This essential milestone will create buzz and attract new members.

John and Mary attend a project management course at a nearby university, where they gain a robust understanding of the predictive approach for effective project planning, organization, and control. They are also considering using it in their project. They acquaint themselves with the *Scrum Guide*[1] and delve into Jeff Sutherland's book, *Scrum: The Art of Doing Twice the Work in Half the Time*.[2] The iteration-based and value-driven strategy of Scrum as well as the potential for reduced time and cost appeals to them. They begin to understand

- Scrum roles (product owner, Scrum master, development team)
- Scrum events (planning, daily stand-up, review, and retrospective)
- Scrum artifacts (product backlog, sprint backlog, and the increment)

1 www.scrum.org/resources/scrum-guide

2 Sutherland, J. (2014). *Scrum: The Art of Doing Twice the Work in Half the Time*. Random House.

Their understanding of the Scrum framework, integrating the preceding, is illustrated in **Figure 6.3**.

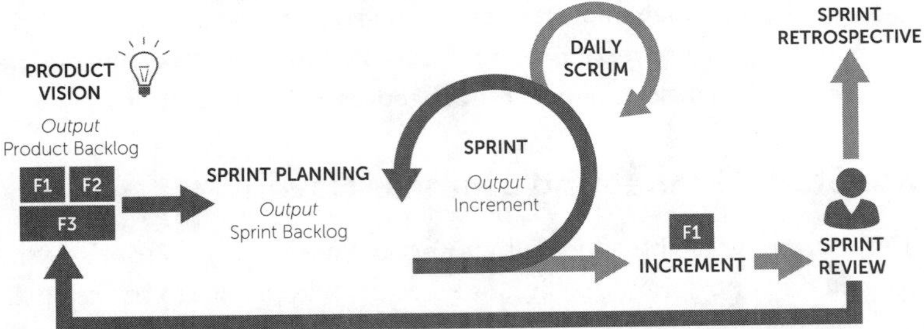

FIGURE 6.3 Scrum framework (we will refer to this figure throughout this section).

For the Caesar's Gym project, Figure 6.3 would translate to the following Scrum concepts:

- **Product Backlog:** Comprises the features and requirements desired for the gym.
- **Prioritize the Product Backlog:** Prioritize based on customer needs, cost, time, and overall strategic objectives. Procuring gym equipment might be a top priority (much higher than implementing a gym app).
- **Iterations/Sprints:** Break product backlog into small, manageable sprints, each focusing on a small portion of the overall product—for example, setting up the physical space.
- **Sprint Review:** At the end of each sprint, review, seek feedback, and adjust as necessary.
- **Retrospective:** Reflect on what can be improved for the next sprint.

Repeat these steps through the iterations, until the gym is fully functional and satisfies the vision.

In the context of project management for the gym construction venture, the focus is on delivering value to customers early. This means that even if the increment is a minimally viable product, it should be delivered to customers as soon as possible.

Mapping Predictive Concepts with Agile

Mary is curious how the adaptive approach compares with the predictive approach. Research using a search engine proves frustrating for her, so she uses ChatGPT:

"I will be using the Scrum framework for my project. I am familiar with the predictive approach. Can you tell me the corresponding adaptive approach processes or concepts in a tabular format?"

The response from AI comes in the form of a table:

NO.	ADAPTIVE APPROACH	RELATED PREDICTIVE APPROACH CONCEPTS
1	Project Vision and Objectives	Develop Project Charter
2	Create a Product Backlog	Collect Requirements
3	Sprint Planning	Plan Scope Management, Develop Project Management Plan
4	Incremental Development	Plan Schedule Management, Create WBS, Estimate Activity Durations, Identify Dependencies, Develop and Refine Schedule
5	Sprint Execution	Direct and Manage Project Work, Control Scope, Control Schedule, Control Costs, Control Quality, Control Resources
6	Daily Stand-up Meetings	Monitor and Control Project Work
7	Sprint Review	Validate Scope, Control Procurements
8	Sprint Retrospective	Monitor and Control Project Work
9	Continuous Customer Collaboration	Identify Stakeholders, Plan Communications Management, Monitor Communications
10	Adaptive Planning	Plan Risk Management, Perform Integrated Change Control

The results are exactly what Mary was looking for, except for control procurements, which she thought belonged to Sprint Execution.

Next, John and Mary are interested in understanding the broader concept of the life cycle of adaptive project management (APM). Formal life cycles exist for predictive projects for many industries, but with adaptive projects, it appears to be a fuzzy topic. They understand that agile projects go through three stages—Concept, Construct, and Close. To get more clarity, they prompt AI to display what activities might occur during these three agile project life-cycle phases.

"Consider the following three stages for convenience—Concept, Construct, and Close for our project. How would the above activities be grouped into this agile life cycle? Describe the APM phase, Steps, and Scrum Application in a tabular format."

Here's how those steps could be organized in the Adaptive Project Management (APM) phases and how Scrum could be applied within those phases:

APM PHASE	STEPS	SCRUM APPLICATION
Concept	Vision: Create a vision statement. Business Plan: Document target market, competition analysis, pricing strategy, and financial projections.	The vision statement and business plan serve as the foundation for the product backlog, with each component of the plan potentially translating to an item in the backlog. The Scrum team can review and refine these items in Sprint Planning meetings.
Construct	Location: Secure a suitable location. Equipment: Procure necessary equipment. Licenses and Permits: Obtain the required licenses. Insurance: Secure necessary insurance coverage. Hiring Staff: Hire necessary personnel.	Each of these steps could be a Sprint in itself, or even multiple Sprints, depending on their complexity. The Product Owner and Scrum team would need to prioritize these tasks in the product backlog and work through them in Sprints. The Scrum team would hold regular Scrum meetings to coordinate their efforts and address any issues.

continues

APM PHASE	STEPS	SCRUM APPLICATION
Construct (continued)	Software: Implement all gym management software such as the website, marketing, and membership system.	This could be a separate series of Sprints, with the team working closely with the software vendor or an internal IT team to configure and implement the software. Again, regular Scrum meetings would be crucial for coordination and issue resolution.
Close	Marketing: Launch marketing efforts to attract members. Opening: Plan and execute a grand opening event.	The marketing and opening tasks could be the final Sprints of the project. The Scrum team would need to work closely with marketing professionals to execute these tasks effectively. The Sprint Review at the end of these Sprints would be an opportunity to evaluate the success of the marketing and opening efforts and make any necessary adjustments for ongoing operations.

This output integrates all the business processes for Caesar's Gym. John and Mary now have a framework to introduce Scrum.

Scrum Prompts

In this section, we will introduce prompts to enlist the help of an AI tool with Scrum tasks. Refer to Figure 6.3 to see that the first step in the Scrum framework is articulating the project's vision.

Using AI for Setting the Vision for Caesar's Gym

As you know, the success of any project ultimately ties back to its vision. For Caesar's Gym, the first artifact (in Scrum terms) is a vision statement, a mandatory first step before the kickoff meeting. Agile philosophy believes in light documentation, so a charter is optional. John and Mary devise a prompt and ask an AI product for a well-rounded vision for their project:

> ***"Create a well-rounded vision statement for Caesar's Gym. Include references to the fitness and fitness excellence lifestyle and commitment to the customer."***
>
> Caesar's Gym is dedicated to cultivating a thriving fitness community where individuals are inspired to embrace an active lifestyle and pursue their health and wellness goals with passion and determination. We are committed to delivering fitness excellence, providing state-of-the-art facilities, expert guidance, and innovative programs to ensure our members experience the highest physical and mental well-being standards. At Caesar's Gym, we prioritize our customer's needs and aspirations, fostering a supportive and empowering environment that encourages personal growth and achievement. Our unwavering commitment to customer satisfaction is at the heart of our mission to shape lives and transform them into healthier, stronger, and happier versions of themselves.

Articulating a vision statement like this frequently cannot be completed even over a two-hour brain-storming session with stakeholders. Here we have a good start to tweak and edit, immediately delivered by ChatGPT. Of course, the key requirement is thoughtful composing of the prompt.

Creating a Product Backlog and Prioritizing It

Referring once again to Figure 6.3, you see that the second step is to create a product backlog.

AI will create a product backlog using a simple prompt such as

> ***"Create a product backlog."***
>
> A product backlog for the gym setup project might look something like this:
>
> - As a gym owner, I want to secure a lease for the gym location so that I can establish the gym in an accessible location.
>
> Tasks: Identify potential locations, negotiate lease terms, and sign lease.
>
> - As a gym owner, I want to design the gym layout so that equipment and facilities are organized for optimal use.
>
> Tasks: Collaborate with the interior designer and approve final layout.
>
> - As a gym owner, I want to procure high-quality gym equipment so that members have access to a variety of workout options.

Tasks: Research equipment options, place orders, oversee delivery and installation.

- As a gym owner, I want to hire and train staff so that members receive excellent customer service.

Tasks: Post job ads, interview candidates, hire staff, and provide training.

- As a gym owner, I want to implement a membership and billing system so that I can manage memberships effectively.

Tasks: Select the system, customize it as needed, and train staff on use.

Prioritization will also determine which tasks should be addressed first. For instance, marketing would be lower in order, as shown earlier. Customer needs, cost, time, and overall strategic objectives could constrain the order. Procuring gym equipment might be a top priority, whereas implementing a gym app might be lower. The product owners (John and Mary) make these decisions.

Building the Team

While this process can occur anywhere in the Scrum methodology, it would be good to identify the project team early.

"I need to identify the resources for the project. A good start would be to identify a team for the project."

The project team for Caesar's Gym project would typically include the following roles:

Project Owner or Product Owner: The key stakeholder responsible for maximizing the value delivered by the project, representing the interests of the business, and prioritizing the product backlog.

Scrum Master: Responsible for facilitating agile practices, ensuring the team adheres to Scrum principles, and removing any impediments that hinder progress.

Development Team: A cross-functional team of professionals from various disciplines such as gym management, fitness trainers, interior designers, equipment experts, marketing specialists, and administrative staff. They are responsible for delivering the product increments during each sprint.

Fitness Trainers: Trainers with expertise in different fitness disciplines, responsible for providing guidance and support to gym members and developing fitness programs.

Marketing Specialist: In charge of developing and implementing the gym's marketing strategy to attract members and promote the gym's services.

HR or Staffing Specialist: Responsible for hiring and training gym staff, ensuring they are equipped to deliver excellent customer service.

IT Specialist (if applicable): Manages implementing and customizing membership and billing systems or any other software tools needed for gym operations.

Finance Specialist: Provides financial expertise, manages the project budget, and ensures financial viability.

Being a small, startup venture, John decides to play the role of product owner and Mary the Scrum master. They also agree that they will use external experts and outsource the financial systems and customer membership payment systems components.

Other professionals from various disciplines will include gym management, fitness trainers, interior designers, equipment experts, marketing specialists, and administrative staff. These professionals will be responsible for delivering the product increments during each sprint.

It is worthwhile bringing the gym customer into the picture early—for example, to assess the intermediate products. An excellent way to begin thinking about customers is to identify personas.

PERSONAS Fictional yet realistic representations of users or stakeholders who will interact with the product.

"Identify customer personas for the Caesar's Gym project. They might be asked to review the deliverables at the end of specific releases and sprints."

Here are some potential customer personas for Caesar's Gym project who could be asked to review the deliverables at the end of specific releases and sprints:

- Fitness Enthusiast Emma: Emma is a dedicated fitness enthusiast who is passionate about leading a healthy lifestyle. She regularly visits gyms to work out and achieve her fitness goals. Emma will be interested in the gym's equipment variety, workout classes, and overall atmosphere.
- Busy Professional Alex: Alex is a busy professional with limited free time. They are looking for a gym with flexible membership options and convenient class schedules. Alex would appreciate features like easy online registration and mobile app access for booking classes.
- Senior Fitness Seeker Susan: Susan is a retiree looking to stay active and maintain her health. She is interested in gym facilities that are accessible and provide a safe and welcoming environment. Susan might also appreciate personalized fitness programs and support.

John and Mary's first reaction is how creative ChatGPT can be—it identifies interesting *labeled personas* like Fitness Enthusiast Emma and Busy Professional Alex. The development team and business analyst will focus on users throughout development. Personas will guide story refinement and sprint planning and create meaningful user stories. During user acceptance testing (UAT), live customers based on the personas will be selected to provide valuable feedback on the intermediate products and services.

Iterations and Sprints

The next step is to break the product backlog into iterations, also known as *sprints*. Each sprint will focus on delivering a small portion of the overall product. For example, the first sprint might focus on setting up the physical space and purchasing essential gym equipment.

With agile development, there is a natural gravitational pull to deliver value. In a Lean approach, the emphasis is on providing value to customers as quickly as possible while eliminating waste and focusing on continuous improvement. The release would prioritize the most valuable and impactful features, aiming to deliver them early to start generating revenue and gathering customer feedback.

ChatGPT is aware of Lean concepts and presents a release plan:

> ***"I want to be Lean and deliver value early. What would the releases look like?"***
>
> Here's what the initial Lean release for Caesar's Gym might look like:
>
> Lean Roadmap for Caesar's Gym:
>
> - Leased Gym Space and Basic Setup (Month 1):
>   - Secure the gym location through a lease agreement.
>   - Set up the basic gym layout with essential workout areas and equipment.
>   - Hire key staff members such as a receptionist and at least one fitness trainer.
> - Membership Management and Marketing Kickoff (Month 2):
>   - Implement a basic membership system to sign up and manage members.
>   - Launch initial marketing efforts to promote the gym's grand opening and attract initial members.
> - Grand Opening and Ongoing Operations (Month 3):
>   - Host a successful grand opening event to attract new members.
>   - Begin regular gym operations with essential services and class offerings.

    - Gather customer feedback and engage in continuous improvement.
- Iterative Enhancements (Month 4 and beyond):
    - Based on customer feedback and data, prioritize iterative enhancements to the gym's services and facilities.
    - Implement additional features and services that align with customer needs and preferences.

Note that investment in the gym, such as furnishing the group activity rooms, are delayed in Lean. This is because customer feedback might decide what kind of room and activities must be scheduled in month 4 or beyond.

Finally, John and Mary want to identify the critical product features their team will work on:

"For the gym project, what are the main features?"

- Physical Facilities
    - Workout area with various gym equipment (treadmills, weight machines, free weights, etc.)
    - Locker rooms and shower facilities
    - Designated areas for group classes (yoga, Zumba, spinning, etc.)
    - Reception and lounge area
- Services and Programs
    - Personal training services
    - Group fitness classes (yoga, Zumba, spinning, etc.)
    - Membership management (registration, subscription plans, etc.)
- Digital Features
    - A website with gym information, class schedule, and online membership signup
    - Mobile app for booking classes, tracking workouts, and communication

These features can be broken down further into individual user stories or backlog items. For example, the Workout Area feature could be split into several user stories, each detailing a specific aspect such as the arrangement of gym equipment, safety features, or cleanliness standards.

User Stories

User stories are widely used in agile project management because they vividly capture a description of a feature and the user goal.

USER STORIES **Short statements about a product feature written from a user's perspective. They describe who the user is, what they want, and why.**

When the development team writes user stories, an activity the product owner (John in the Caesar's Gym project) leads, they refer to the personas that were identified earlier.

"Give examples of user stories for the workout area."

Here are examples of user stories for the workout area of a gym:

- As a gym member, I want to have access to a variety of cardio machines so that I can choose different ways to complete my cardio workout.
  - This could lead to tasks like purchasing treadmills, stationary bikes, ellipticals, and rowing machines.
- As a gym member who lifts weights, I want a well-organized free weights section so I can easily find the weights I need.
  - Tasks might include planning the layout and organization of the free weights section and purchasing the necessary weight sets.
- As a gym member, I want clearly defined emergency procedures and easily accessible emergency equipment so that any injuries can be quickly and effectively dealt with.
  - Tasks could include developing emergency procedures, training staff, and installing first aid kits and other emergency equipment.
- As a gym member, I want the workout area to be clean and hygienic so that I can exercise in a pleasant and healthy environment.
  - This would involve creating a cleaning schedule, hiring cleaning staff, and maybe even providing sanitation stations for members to wipe down equipment.

Let's expand on this further. Acceptance criteria define what must be done for a user story to be considered complete. The criteria must be testable, clear, and specific conditions.

Here's an example of how John could establish acceptance criteria for each of their user stories:

"Given the user stories mentioned in the original prompt, what would be good acceptance criteria for each?"

- As a gym member, I want to have access to a variety of cardio machines.

—At least four different types of cardio machines (e.g., treadmills, stationary bikes, ellipticals, and rowing machines) are available.

—Each machine type has multiple units available to accommodate several users simultaneously.

- As a gym member who lifts weights, I want a well-organized free weights section.

—Free weights are sorted by weight and type in a clearly defined area.

—Signage is clear and easily visible, indicating the weight and type of the free weights

- As a gym member, I want the workout area to be clean and hygienic.

—A cleaning schedule is established and adhered to, with daily cleaning and sanitization of all gym equipment.

—Sanitation stations with cleaning materials are available near all workout areas for members to wipe down equipment before and after use.

—Regular inspections confirm that cleanliness standards are being maintained

The prompt results are helpful and appear to be comprehensive and complete.

Iteration Planning and Sprint Goals

Even though an adaptive project is flexible in order to accommodate surprises, that does not mean that the projects are mapped out with timelines, including a release plan for delivery of each iteration.

A formal, legal agreement, such as the gym's lease, would be handled using a predictive approach (little flexibility). It makes sense that securing the lease should be dealt with first, before the adaptive iterations begin. Also, since procuring equipment takes time, that aspect needs to be addressed early.

"I would like to create a release plan for the project. Present iterations and sprints consisting of two weeks."

- Pre-Sprint Work (Predictive Approach):
  - Secure Lease: Identify potential locations, negotiate lease terms, and sign a lease.
  - Procure Equipment: Research equipment options, and place orders.
- Sprint 1 (2 weeks):
  - Design Gym Layout: Collaborate with the interior designer and approve the final layout.
  - Start Staff Recruitment: Post job ads and start receiving and reviewing applications.

- Sprint 2 (2 weeks):
    - Procure Additional Resources: Research needs, e.g., mats, and place orders.
    - Continue Staff Recruitment: Interview candidates and start the hiring process.
- Sprint 3 (2 weeks):
    - Oversee Equipment Delivery and Installation: Ensure equipment is delivered and installed according to plan.
    - Finalize Staff Recruitment: Complete the hiring process and start staff training.
- Sprint 4 (2 weeks):
    - Implement Membership and Billing System: Select and customize the system and train staff on its use.
    - Start Marketing Strategy Development: Identify the target audience and develop a marketing plan.
- Sprint 5 (2 weeks):
    - Complete Staff Training: Ensure all staff are fully trained and ready for gym opening.
    - Finalize Marketing Strategy: Finalize the marketing plan and start creating marketing materials.
- Sprint 6 (2 weeks):
    - Complete Marketing Materials: Finalize and start distributing marketing materials.
    - Prepare for Gym Opening: Ensure all aspects of the gym are ready for opening.

The release plan is helpful for the following reasons:

Prioritization: It helps identify what needs to be done first based on the business value and dependencies.

Timeline Estimation: Although an agile schedule is flexible, it's still essential to have a rough timeline for when different features (user stories) will be developed.

Stakeholder Communication: It provides a roadmap that can be communicated to stakeholders so they have a clear idea of when they can expect various features to be ready.

In the adaptive approach, this release plan is not set in stone. It's expected that the plan will be revisited and revised throughout the project.

Story Map

A *story map* is an agile technique of ordering user stories along two independent dimensions. The map arranges user activities along the horizontal axis (or table columns) roughly in the order in which the user would perform the task. Down the vertical axis (or table rows), user stories are ordered by priority and increasing sophistication of the implementation. Given a story map arranged this way, the first horizontal row represents a "walking skeleton," a bare-bones but usable version of the product.

AI can create a story map for Caesar's Gym with the following prompt:

> ***"Create a story map display in table format."***
>
> A story map visually arranges user stories based on the order in which a user would interact with different product features. Here's a simple story map for the gym setup project, represented as a table.

Table 6.1 presents what ChatGPT provided, or as much as we can fit on this page!

TABLE 6.1 Story Map from Chat GPT

USER TASK	USER STORIES		
	SPRINT 1	**SPRINT 2**	**SPRINT 3**
Gym Layout	Collaborate with gym designers	Finalize gym layout	Oversee equipment installation
Equipment Procurement	Research equipment options	Place equipment orders	Oversee equipment delivery
Staff Recruitment & Training	Post job ads	Interview and hire candidates	Start staff training
Management Systems	–	–	Select membership and billing system
Marketing	–	Start developing marketing plan	–

Each row of the story map table provides additional details and functionality to complete Caesar's Gym on time.

Walking Skeleton

AI is aware of advanced concepts such as a *walking skeleton*, which is associated with minimum viable product (MVP) that provides very basic end-to-end functionality upon which further development can be built. It should be a simple, bare-bones version of the final product that is functional, deliverable, and valuable.

"Describe a possible walking skeleton based on the above story map."

For the gym project, the "walking skeleton" would likely include the following steps:

- Securing the lease (handled using the predictive approach outside of the Scrum sprints)
- Basic gym layout with essential workout areas (from Sprint 1)
- Procurement and installation of essential gym equipment like treadmills, weights, etc. (from Sprints 2 and 3)
- Hiring of minimum essential staff (from Sprints 2 and 3)
- A basic version of the membership and billing system (from Sprint 4)

This MVP can still deliver the core value proposition to the customers and allows for early testing and customer or staff feedback, which helps in iterating and improving the product over time.

Agile Estimation

Estimating agile projects is different from estimating predictive projects. The goal of estimation in agile is to improve planning and decision-making and build in a mechanism to handle risk and uncertainty. Estimation in agile can be done manually or with software programs but is widely done with story points.

STORY POINTS Units of measure used in agile estimation that express the overall effort required to fully implement a piece of work or a story.

Regardless of the method selected, you must involve the entire team in the estimation process to ensure shared understanding and accuracy, and you must adapt and learn with experience.

John and the Scrum team start with the following prompt to investigate agile estimation techniques:

"I need to estimate the sprints for my gym project. What is the best way to approach this?"

Break Down User Stories: Divide user stories within each sprint into smaller, manageable tasks for clear and accurate estimation.

Use Story Points: Consider using story points over time-based estimates.

Relative Sizing: Collaboratively compare user stories against a reference, assigning story points based on complexity.

Planning Poker: Utilize Planning Poker to estimate story points and collectively reach a consensus.

Agile estimating generally uses historical data. John and the Scrum team can refer to sprint data from completed iterations for better informed estimation.

"I would like to use Planning Poker. How does it work?"

1. Preparation: Gather the development team, Scrum master, and product owner for the estimation session. Ensure that user stories to be estimated are well defined and understood.
2. Estimation Cards: Create a set of Planning Poker cards, each displaying a Fibonacci sequence or t-shirt sizes (e.g., 1, 2, 3, 5, 8, 13, 20, etc.). These values represent the relative complexity or effort of each user story.
3. Facilitator: Designate a facilitator, often the Scrum master, to lead the estimation session and maintain focus.
4. Estimation Process:
    a. The facilitator presents one user story at a time to the team.
    b. Each team member privately selects a Planning Poker card representing their estimate for the complexity or effort of the user story.
    c. Once everyone has made their choice, all team members reveal their cards simultaneously.
5. Consensus and Discussion:
    a. If there is a clear consensus, the chosen estimate becomes the team's agreed-upon estimate.
    b. If there is a wide variation in estimates, the team engages in a discussion to understand the reasons behind each estimate.
6. Re-Estimation:
    a. After the discussion, team members privately choose a new card based on the insights gained.

   b. The estimation process is repeated until the team achieves consensus, typically after a few rounds of discussion.

7. Record the Estimate:

   a. The final agreed-upon estimate is recorded as the story points assigned to the user story.

   b. The estimates serve as a reference for sprint planning.

Planning Poker encourages active team participation and involvement in the estimation process. Product owner John and the Scrum team will need a list of user stories along with their descriptions, complexity, and risks. They will work collaboratively to assign story points based on their knowledge and experience. Next, ChatGPT simulates what the outcome will look like for the Caesar's Gym project.

> ***"Show estimates for user stories estimated in story points."***
>
> Here are three user stories for Caesar's Gym project, along with their estimated story points:
>
> - User Story: Sign Up for Membership
>   - As a potential member, I want to sign up for a gym membership online so I can access gym facilities and classes.
>   - Estimated Story Points: 5
> - User Story: Attend a Group Fitness Class
>   - As a gym member, I want to book and attend a group fitness class through the gym's mobile app so I can participate in my preferred classes conveniently.
>   - Estimated Story Points: 3
> - User Story: Personal Training Request
>   - As a gym member, I want to submit a request for a personal training session through the gym's website so I can receive personalized fitness guidance.
>   - Estimated Story Points: 8
>
> The story point values 5, 3, and 8 are relative measures of complexity and effort typically done with Fibonacci numbers.

During these estimation sessions, discussions about risks and uncertainties might come up (see Chapter 8, "The Role of AI in Risk Management"). Once the team considers their velocity, they can decide which stories to include in the upcoming sprint.

Project Execution

Planning and estimating the roles of the Scrum master and product owner becomes critical in leading the team through execution. Let's explore the unique nature of a development team in agile compared with teams on predictive projects.

Product Owner and Scrum Master

So far, we have not discussed the roles of product owner and Scrum master. In that capacity, let's document the roles John and Mary will be playing in the Caesar's Gym project.

"Describe the roles John and Mary will play in the Caesar's Gym project as product owner and Scrum master, respectively."

- John—Product Owner: As the product owner of Caesar's Gym project, John will play a crucial role in ensuring the project's success by representing the interests of the stakeholders and maximizing the value delivered by the team. His responsibilities include:
  - Vision and Prioritization: John will define the vision and overall goals for Caesar's Gym, ensuring that all development efforts align with the gym's strategic objectives. He will prioritize the product backlog based on customer needs and business value.
  - User Stories: John will work closely with stakeholders and the development team to write clear and concise user stories that effectively capture the requirements.
  - Acceptance Criteria: John will define the acceptance criteria for each user story, providing clear guidelines for the team to know when a user story is considered "done."
  - Sprint Review: John will actively participate in sprint reviews to provide feedback on the deliverables, ensuring they meet the intended business goals and customer needs.
  - Decision-Making: John will make informed decisions about the product based on data, customer feedback, and business priorities, helping the team stay focused and productive.
  - Backlog Refinement: John will regularly engage in backlog refinement sessions with the development team to clarify user stories, discuss potential changes, and ensure the backlog is ready for upcoming sprints.

- Mary—Scrum Master: As the Scrum master in the Caesar's Gym project, Mary will serve as a servant-leader, supporting the development team in embracing and implementing agile principles. Her key responsibilities include:
  - Scrum Framework: Mary will ensure that the Scrum framework is well understood and followed by the team, including facilitating Scrum events like sprint planning, daily stand-ups, sprint reviews, and retrospectives.
  - Obstacles Removal: Mary will proactively identify and remove impediments that hinder the team's progress, ensuring they have a conducive environment in which to work efficiently.
  - Empowering the Team: Mary will empower the development team to self-organize and make decisions collectively. She will encourage collaboration, transparency, and continuous improvement.
  - Facilitating Collaboration: Mary will promote effective communication and collaboration among team members, stakeholders, and the product owner, fostering a culture of openness and trust.
  - Metrics and Progress Tracking: Mary will track and communicate relevant project metrics (such as velocity or burndown charts) to provide insights into the team's performance and progress.

This succinctly describes the two key roles in leading the Caesar's Gym project toward success.

Development Team Role

The development team is a self-organized, cross-functional team with the proper skill set required to deliver business value defined by the product owner. They work together closely to have a potentially releasable increment product at the end of every sprint. They also uphold the five primary Scrum values: focus, commitment, openness, respect, and courage.

"Describe briefly the development team's role in the Caesar's Gym project."

1. Implements user stories, turning them into tangible products
2. Self-organizing and collaborating to achieve sprint goals
3. Possesses cross-functional expertise required for development
4. Commits to delivering a set of user stories within each sprint
5. Focuses on delivering high-quality and tested solutions
6. Actively participates in continuous improvement and retrospectives

Sprint Execution

The Caesar's Gym project team is ready to start sprint execution. Sprint execution deals with implementing selected user stories and creating product increments. Refer once again to Figure 6.3 to understand the key activities during the sprint execution phase. John and Mary list the following activities:

- **Sprint Planning:** Select user stories and define sprint goals.
- **Daily Stand-ups:** A short, daily meeting for the team to synchronize work, share progress, and identify potential blockers.
- **Product Owner Collaboration:** Validate work and answer questions.
- **User Acceptance Testing (UAT):** Ensure user stories meet acceptance criteria.
- **Sprint Review:** Demonstrate completed work and gather feedback.
- **Sprint Retrospective:** Reflect on performance and plan improvements.
- **Continuous Integration:** Regularly integrate and test the product.

AI can list the questions John and Mary must ask during sprint execution:

> ***"We are about to conduct and execute the sprint. What are some questions dealing with sprint planning, daily stand-ups, Scrum master facilitation, product owner collaboration, user acceptance testing, and sprint review that can come up and be addressed? Who should be asking those questions and researching those issues?"***
>
> Here are the prompts with the name of the Scrum role that might be asking these questions during the project execution of Caesar's Gym:
>
> - Sprint Planning: Product Owner
>   - What are the key user stories for the upcoming sprint?
>   - How do these user stories align with the sprint goal?
> - Sprint Execution: Scrum Master
>   - How is the Development Team collaborating on the implementation of user stories?
>   - What challenges or blockers are they facing during the execution?
> - Daily Stand-ups: Development Team
>   - What progress has been made since the last stand-up meeting?
>   - Are there any obstacles that need to be addressed by the team or Scrum master?

- Facilitation: Scrum Master
  - How is the Scrum master supporting the Development Team and removing impediments?
  - Are there any process improvements or adjustments that the Scrum master suggests?
- Collaboration: Product Owner
  - How is the product owner engaging with the development team during the sprint?
  - Is the product owner providing clear and timely feedback on user story implementations?
- Sprint Review: Product Owner
  - What feedback did stakeholders provide during the Sprint Review meeting?
  - Are there any new requirements or changes requested based on the delivered product increment? What impact will this feedback have on the product backlog or upcoming sprints?
- Sprint Retrospective: Scrum Master
  - What went well during the sprint that the team would like to continue doing?
  - What challenges or bottlenecks were encountered, and how can they be improved?
- Continuous Integration and Delivery: Development Team
  - How frequently are product increments being integrated and tested?
  - How is the team ensuring the quality and reliability of the product increment?

Prompts for Product Owners

If a product owner is inexperienced and playing the role for the first time, they can benefit from a quick primer on prompts to fully benefit from AI. We illustrate some simple prompts that will bring them up to speed on the core concepts. Let's demonstrate a scenario in which John, the product owner, is unaware of what happens during backlog refinement and wants to learn more of his responsibility:

> ***"Act as an experienced product owner; your role is to facilitate a backlog refinement session."***

- Preparation:
  - Review the product backlog and identify user stories that are likely to be included in the upcoming sprint. Ensure that each user story is written in a clear, concise, and understandable format.
- Schedule the Session:
  - Coordinate with the Development Team and other stakeholders to find a suitable time for the refinement session. Set aside enough time for a thorough discussion without rushing.
- Explain the Purpose:
  - Start the session by explaining the importance of backlog refinement in ensuring the team's shared understanding of the work ahead. Emphasize the need to clarify user stories and identify acceptance criteria.
- Story-by-Story Review:
  - Take each user story one by one and discuss it with the team. Encourage team members to ask questions, seek clarifications, and provide input.
- Acceptance Criteria Definition:
  - Collaboratively define clear and specific acceptance criteria for each user story. Ensure that the criteria are measurable and objectively verifiable.
- Estimation:
  - If needed, facilitate the estimation of user stories to provide the team with an idea of their complexity or effort. Ensure that the team understands the rationale behind the prioritization.
- Dependencies and Prioritization:
  - Discuss any dependencies between user stories and identify priorities for the upcoming sprint.
- Wrap-Up:
  - Summarize the key outcomes of the session and ensure that everyone is aligned on the refined user stories and acceptance criteria. Thank the team for their active participation and collaboration.

NOTE **The task identified in the prompt "your role is to facilitate a backlog refinement session" can be replaced with other activity items about which the product owner wants to learn more.**

Or, they could use the following comprehensive prompt:

> ***"Your role as an experienced product owner for the Caesar's Gym project is to guide the team in various activities, such as facilitating a backlog refinement session, defining a sprint goal, clarifying acceptance criteria, prioritizing user stories, reviewing technical considerations, collaborating on story estimation, and seeking stakeholder feedback. Please provide a detailed plan for conducting the session, including specific prompts and questions you will use to drive each activity effectively."***

- Activity: Define a Sprint Goal
  - Prompt 1: How can we collaboratively define a clear, achievable sprint goal aligning with the product vision?
  - Prompt 2: What key objectives and outcomes do we want to achieve in the upcoming sprint?
- Activity: Clarify Acceptance Criteria
  - Prompt 1: What steps can we take to ensure that acceptance criteria are specific, measurable, and well-defined for each user story?
  - Prompt 2: How do we ensure that acceptance criteria are agreed upon by the Development Team and stakeholders?
- Activity: Prioritize User Stories
  - Prompt 1: How can we collaboratively prioritize user stories based on business value and customer needs?
  - Prompt 2: Are there any dependencies or constraints that might influence the order of implementation?
- Activity: Review Technical Considerations
  - Prompt 1: What technical considerations or challenges do we need to be aware of for specific user stories?
  - Prompt 2: How can we involve the Development Team in discussing technical feasibility and potential solutions?
- Activity: Collaborate on Story Estimation
  - Prompt 1: How can we conduct effective story estimation to provide a shared understanding of the complexity of user stories?
  - Prompt 2: What estimation techniques or tools can we utilize to gain insights into the effort required?

- Activity: Seek Stakeholder Feedback
  - Prompt 1: How can we actively seek feedback from stakeholders on user stories to ensure alignment with their expectations?
  - Prompt 2: What channels or methods can we use to collect and incorporate feedback into the refinement process?

Through prompt engineering, John can learn more about the role of the product owner and perform all his tasks effectively.

Prompts for Scrum Masters

Similarly, novice Scrum masters (Mary in our example) can benefit from AI. Consider the following examples of prompts:

> ***"Act as an experienced Scrum master. Your assignment is to offer guidance and best practice advice to the development team to implement the Scrum methodology successfully."***
>
> ***"Act as an experienced Scrum master. Your role involves guiding the team on efficient retrospective conduct and practice."***
>
> ***"Act as an experienced Scrum master. Your role involves guiding the team on efficient retrospective conduct offering insights for continual improvement and providing best practice recommendations for optimizing work processes."***
>
> ***"Act as an experienced Scrum master. Your task is to guide the team on how to effectively design a Sprint board to enhance visibility, improve workflow, and increase overall productivity."***
>
> ***"Act as an experienced Scrum master. Your responsibility is to assist the team in explaining a comprehensive Definition of Done to ensure a clear understanding of work expectations and quality standards."***
>
> ***"Act as a seasoned Scrum master. Offer strategies and techniques to the team for improving communication and collaboration."***

By incorporating the activity items and corresponding prompts, Scrum master Mary can learn to perform all her tasks effectively.

Prompts for Development Team

Even the development team can benefit from AI. Consider the following examples of prompts:

> ***"Act as an experienced member of the Development Team. Your responsibility is to steer the team by sharing best practices for delivering outcomes successfully using the Scrum methodology."***

> ***"Act as an experienced member of the development team. Your responsibility is to lead a discussion on how to collaborate effectively to maximize productivity."***
>
> ***"Act as an experienced member of the development team. Your responsibility is to lead a discussion on techniques we can use to estimate the effort and complexity of user stories accurately during Sprint Planning."***
>
> ***"Act as an experienced member of the development team. Your responsibility is to address impediments and blockers raised during Daily Stand-ups efficiently to keep the sprint on track."***

The software developers and members of the IT team can utilize the following types of prompts to get high-quality responses from ChatGPT, by filling in the desired topic within the angled brackets:

> ***"Provide a quick-start tutorial on using <project software>."***
>
> ***"Write a code snippet that implements <functionality> using the <language> programming language."***
>
> ***"Analyze the following code to identify potential security vulnerabilities: <paste code snippet>."***
>
> ***"Identify common pitfalls and recommended best practices when using <language/framework>."***
>
> ***"Debug the <error> encountered when using <language/framework>—explain the cause and solutions."***

Project Measurement and Tracking

Now let's turn to the topic of progress tracking: how measurements are made with various techniques and indicators, and how the status of these indicators is communicated.

We know that Scrum projects are executed in fixed-length iterations called sprints, typically 2–4 weeks long. The Caesar's Gym project uses sprints with 2-week durations. The team commits to delivering user stories or backlog items at the start of each sprint. During spring execution, daily 15-minute stand-up meetings allow members to communicate what they've worked on, obstacles, and next steps. Product demo reviews at the sprint end will assess the completeness of user stories.

A culture that allows open communication about project risks, issues, and threats without fear of blame is essential. Make sure your team feels empowered to transparently share bad news early—a concept known as "failing fast"—so that feedback can be collected quickly and adjustments made to address the issue.

Burndown Charts

The burndown chart is a valuable tool for tracking the progress of a project and identifying whether your team is ahead, on, or behind schedule.

BURNDOWN CHART A visual presentation that tracks progress in a sprint, showing how much of the committed backlog is completed over time.

Your team might use this information to improve their planning and execution in future sprints. Work remaining might consist of a user story, associated tasks, remaining story points, responsible individuals' names, completion status, and acceptance status.

Table 6.2 presents data for the first six sprints, as that is what is currently planned for the Caesar's Gym project, with 2-week sprints using story points. Remember that a story point in agile methodology is a unit used to estimate the amount of work required to implement a story.

TABLE 6.2 Planned and Actual Productivity in Sprints

SPRINT	TOTAL STORY POINTS REMAINING (PLANNED)	TOTAL STORY POINTS REMAINING (ACTUAL)
Start	600	600
S1	500	520
S2	400	450
S3	300	300
S4	200	210
S5	100	120
S6	0	30
End	0	0

In this scenario, the project team starts with 600 story points. They complete 80 story points in the first sprint, leaving 520 story points. In the second sprint, the team completes 70 story points, reducing the total to 450 story points, and so on. This should result in a downward trending graph showing the decreasing amount of work remaining in the project.

When John asks ChatGPT to graph this data, he sees the result shown in **Figure 6.4**. It provides a clear visual indication of how quickly his team is working through the backlog and how much work remains. By comparing the *actual* burndown line with the *ideal* (planned) burndown line, he can gauge whether the project is on track.

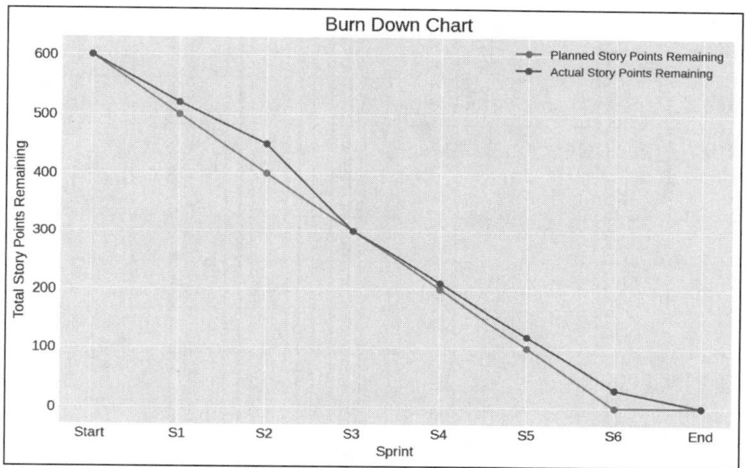

FIGURE 6.4 Burndown chart created by ChatGPT

John then asks ChatGPT:

> ***"Given the data and graph, what key observation can you tell me?"***
>
> The planned remaining work, shown by the "Planned Story Points Remaining" line, decreases steadily as you move from one sprint to the next. This suggests that the team planned to complete an equal amount of work in each sprint.
>
> The actual remaining work, shown by the "Actual Story Points Remaining" line, does not follow the planned line closely. The team was behind schedule in Sprints S1 and S2, caught up in Sprint S3, and again fell behind in Sprint S4.

When work is incomplete, the Sprint Review meeting is crucial. The team demonstrates finished work, discusses incomplete items, and gathers feedback. The focus is on completing the highest-value work first. Unfinished items return to the backlog for future prioritization.

As the project progresses, the team can view and update the burndown chart after each sprint. This helps them understand the project's trajectory, identify potential issues, and adjust the plan if needed.

Planned vs. Actual Velocity of Work

Velocity, in common usage, can be expressed as "miles per hour" or "feet per second." It's a unit of progress (commonly distance) per a unit of time. For agile projects, velocity is the number of story points completed per sprint.

Table 6.3 illustrates the data for the six sprints showing the planned versus the completed velocity in story points.

TABLE 6.3 Planned and Actual Velocity in Sprints

SPRINT	PLANNED VELOCITY	ACTUAL VELOCITY
S1	100	80
S2	100	70
S3	100	150
S4	100	90
S5	100	90
S6	100	90

ChatGPT can interpret the measurement data in the table:

> In Sprint 1, the team's actual velocity (80) was below the planned velocity (100). This could indicate that the team overestimated its capacity or ran into unforeseen challenges.
>
> In Sprint 2, the team's actual velocity fell further to 70. This could suggest ongoing issues with overestimation, increased difficulty or complexity of tasks, or other factors reducing the team's capacity.
>
> In Sprint 3, the team's actual velocity surged to 150, significantly above the planned velocity. This could be a result of an underestimation of the team's capacity, a decrease in task complexity, carryover from other sprints, increased efficiency or productivity, or other factors.
>
> In Sprints 4, 5, and 6, the team's actual velocity appears to have stabilized around 90, slightly below the planned velocity of 100.
>
> Overall, the team's performance appears to be fairly consistent, apart from the spike in Sprint 3. The trend toward stabilization in the latter half of the project suggests that the team may be becoming more accurate in their capacity estimation.
>
> To refine the process, it could be helpful to hold retrospectives after each sprint to discuss what went well, what didn't, and how the team can improve

moving forward. This is a common practice in agile project management that helps teams continually adapt and improve their processes.

Given the information in the table, John wants to see whether a different presentation gives him a better perspective (**Figure 6.5**).

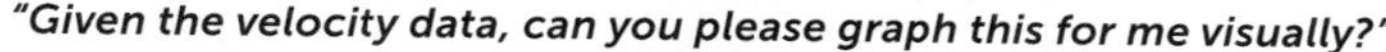

"Given the velocity data, can you please graph this for me visually?"

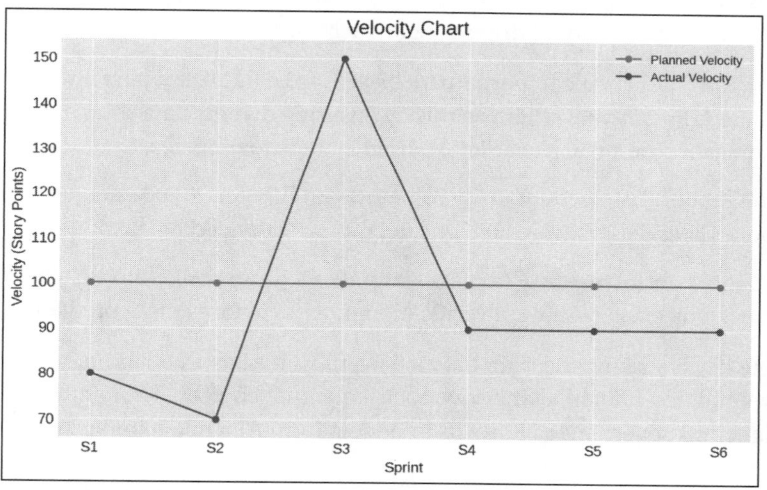

FIGURE 6.5 Velocity chart created by ChatGPT

The graphical representation of the data provides a clear perspective on the Caesar's Gym project team's velocity trends. For example, John notes that the significant spike in velocity during Sprint 3 (S3) warrants a closer examination. As highlighted previously by ChatGPT, potential explanations could range from increased productivity, perhaps due to improved collaboration or the removal of previous roadblocks, to the completion of carryover work from previous sprints.

For the Caesar's Gym project team, these possibilities underscore the complexity of their work and the factors influencing their productivity. By openly discussing such observations and their potential causes, agile teams can continually refine their understanding of their performance, which, in turn, will inform and improve their planning, estimation, and overall project execution in the future.

TECHNICAL GUIDE **See the Technical Guide at the end of this chapter for additional details on using ChatGPT Advanced Data Analysis feature to generate a burndown chart, burnup chart, or velocity chart.**

Ethical Considerations and Professional Responsibility

We have used several tools in this chapter including ChatGPT. While such tools can provide helpful information, human oversight is essential. At the time of this writing, ChatGPT's historical knowledge cuts off as of January 2022, so it lacks current context that might lead to providing incorrect costs and expenses. Moreover, AI cannot match human judgment and intuition, which should drive critical decisions.

Be mindful that AI can perpetuate biases in the data on which it was trained. Proactively minimize this by ensuring diverse data sources and monitoring outputs. Never let AI disadvantage teammates.

Remember that accountability remains with humans even when using AI tools. Clearly establish who owns decisions influenced by AI.

Quality control matters. AI makes mistakes. Users should know its limits, check outputs, and have a verification process before acting on them.

The key is striking the right balance —utilizing AI as a collaborator but maintaining human agency over consequential choices. Thoughtful oversight and governance allows us to benefit from AI while minimizing risks.

Key Points to Remember

Generative AI can provide support in various ways when it comes to learning and implementing Scrum:

- **Theoretical Learning:** Detailed explanations about Scrum principles, roles, events, and artifacts.
- **Practical Guidance:** Advice on implementing Scrum practices in the project, such as Sprint Planning, Daily Scrum, and managing the Product Backlog.
- **Scenario-based Learning:** Providing solutions or approaches based on Scrum methodology for specific challenges in the project.
- **Reflection and Improvement:** Generating topics or advice for productive Sprint Review meetings, and Retrospective meetings.
- **Focus on Customer's Needs:** Deliver value from the start by identifying features that can be released early.

Technical Guide

Using Advanced Data Analysis to Create Burndown, Burnup, and Velocity Charts

The following prompts are designed for the analysis of key agile metrics: burndown, burnup, and velocity charts. These charts provide valuable insights into a team's progress and performance over time.

The burndown chart illustrates the remaining work against time, the burnup chart shows the cumulative work completed over time, and the velocity chart measures the amount of work a team completes during a sprint (versus expected rate of completion).

To dive into the analysis of these metrics using ChatGPT Advanced Data Analysis, follow these steps:

1. Start a new chat with Advanced Data Analysis.
2. Use the Upload File feature to provide your Excel data.
3. Once your data is uploaded, use one of the following prompt templates to guide your analysis.

Burn Chart Prompt:

> ***"Act as a Scrum master and agile coach. Analyzing a project, you are provided with Excel data for the project's sprints, including 'Total Story Points Remaining (Planned)' and 'Total Story Points Remaining (Actual)'. Using the Advanced Data Analysis features, your task is to:***
>
> ***Construct a burndown (and/or burnup) chart that visually outlines the project's progress against the planned trajectory.***
>
> ***Formulate an analysis that details observed trends, deviations, and pacing of the team.***
>
> ***Identify potential reasons for any discrepancies between planned and actual story points and propose strategies for future improvement."***

Velocity Chart Prompt:

> ***"Act as an agile coach and consultant brought in to review a project. You are presented with Excel data that includes 'Sprint,' 'Planned Velocity,' and 'Actual Velocity.' Using your Advanced Data Analysis features, your mission is to:***
>
> ***Design a velocity chart that clearly shows the planned versus actual velocity across the sprints.***

Deliver a comprehensive report on the team's performance consistency, planning accuracy, and any remarkable shifts in velocity.

Extrapolate possible causes for any significant velocity variations and advise on potential strategies for better velocity management in future sprints."

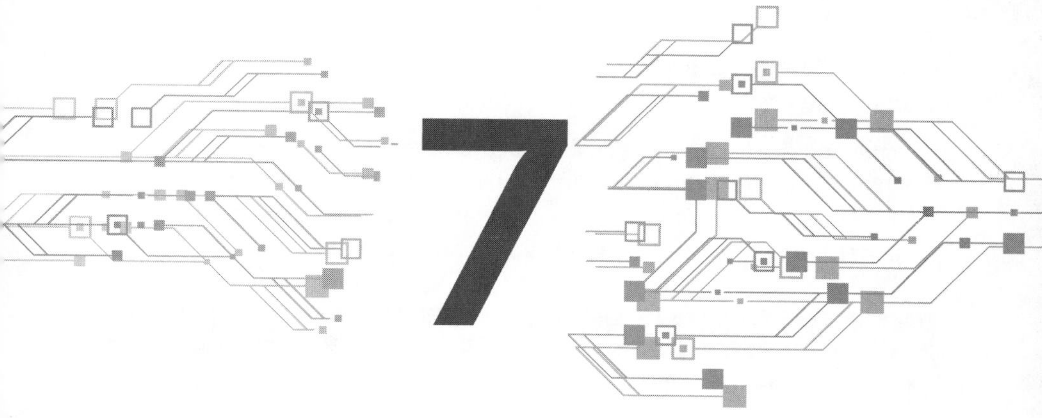

Monitoring Project Work Performance with AI

This chapter delves into integrating generative artificial intelligence (AI) into the Executing stage and the Monitoring and Controlling stage of project management. Powerful AI tools can process vast amounts of data, make predictions, generate reports, and converse using natural human language. We begin by showing how AI can be leveraged in the Executing phase of a project—for example, how you can use AI for task allocation and resource management.

We then investigate the role of AI in monitoring scope and schedules, controlling costs, and maintaining quality.

By the end of this chapter, you'll have a comprehensive understanding of how AI can be leveraged to enhance project management's effectiveness and efficiency. You'll see how maintaining a keen focus on ethical standards and professional responsibility is also essential.

AI IN ACTION: AI TOOLS BATTLE MEETING OVERLOAD

Keeping meetings productive is a common problem for many professionals today. This is where AI tools such as Otter.ai's new products OtterPilot and Otter AI Chat can help.

OtterPilot is an AI-powered virtual assistant that can automatically join online meetings and take notes. It transcribes the conversation in real time and summarizes key points, action items, and decisions. Users can invite OtterPilot to any meeting on their calendar or set it to attend all meetings automatically. It can also join multiple meetings concurrently so that you can obtain insights from more than one meeting using this AI tool.

OtterPilot captures meeting conversations reasonably accurately. It highlights crucial details such as names, dates, numbers, and links in the transcript. While not perfect, the automated transcripts are detailed enough that readers can easily understand what was discussed. None of us can retain everything that is said in every meeting we attend, and OtterPilot provides a quick refresher. The product is a huge time-saver for busy professionals who cannot always devote their full attention to meetings.

Complementing OtterPilot is Otter AI Chat, which leverages AI to answer questions about meetings attended by OtterPilot. You can ask for specifics like "What did John say about the budget?" or "When is the next project deadline?" Otter AI Chat can also synthesize meeting transcripts into useful follow-up content such as emails, summaries, and reports.

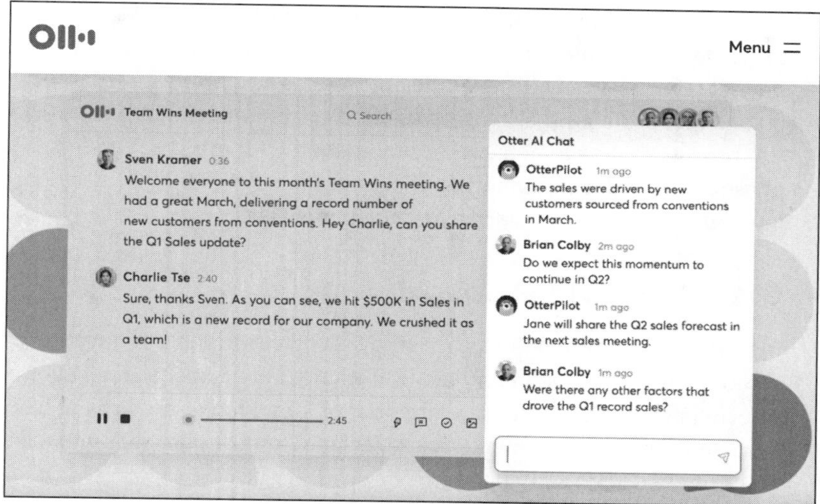

This example demonstrates the potential of AI to augment human capabilities in the workplace. However, as with any new technology, there are challenges around ethical use, privacy, and unintended consequences. Meeting data requires thoughtful handling, especially when sensitive company or proprietary information is involved.

Otter.ai's meeting assistant tools showcase promising productivity applications for AI technology. Although open questions remain, the capabilities they unlock for documenting conversations and extracting insights can empower professionals to maximize their meeting time. These AI assistants may provide welcome relief for organizations struggling with meeting overload.

Direct and Manage Project Work

The Executing stage of a project involves multiple critical tasks to keep the project on track. The *Project Management Body of Knowledge* (PMBOK)[1] groups these tasks under a new project performance domain called Project Work Performance. This domain centers on the process by which you, the project manager, can manage and control the work necessary to deliver your project's products, services, or results. This process keeps the project on track and helps ensure that the project's objectives align with stakeholder expectations.

1 From the Project Management Institute: www.pmi.org.

This process includes managing the flow and delivery of tasks, adapting to changes, and ensuring your team's focus. A key element is leading your project team and establishing efficient systems and processes that result in a quality product. It also involves clear communication with stakeholders, resource management, and coordination with external vendors. This phase requires keen monitoring of changes and promoting project learning and knowledge transfer among team members.

Case Study—Hotel Bougie

In this chapter, our fictitious case study revolves around a renovation project for Hotel Bougie, a luxury hotel. With the hotel expected to become a cornerstone of high-end accommodation downtown, the project has attracted significant attention due to its ambitious design, top-tier facilities, and prime location.

As the project manager for the Hotel Bougie renovation, you lead an internationally diverse team of architects, engineers, contractors, and designers. The goal is to renovate the building and ensure it meets stringent quality standards, complies with all local regulations, and aligns with the hotel's vision of excellence for its guests.

Automating Task Assignments with AI

Properly allocating tasks to team members is critical to project success. You must consider your team members' skill sets, availability, and workloads. Task allocation can be a complex and time-consuming process, especially in large teams as in your Hotel Bougie project.

Generative AI products like ChatGPT can play a pivotal role in simplifying this process. As the project manager, you can use ChatGPT to help automate task assignments, a crucial aspect of the Direct and Manage Project Work process.

> ***"ChatGPT, based on the skills matrix and current workload of the team, who should we assign the interior design task to in the Hotel Bougie renovation project?"***
>
> Based on the skills matrix and workload data you've shared, Laura Johnson, your interior designer based in London, is the best fit. She has the necessary expertise, and her current workload suggests she can take on this task. However, confirm this with her and the rest of your team to ensure she has the capacity.

Reflecting on this interaction, we can see AI's value in task allocation. It can process complex data like skills matrixes and workload schedules much faster and more precisely than manual methods. This allows you, as project manager, to make informed decisions.

Task Scheduling with AI

Task scheduling in a complex project such as the Hotel Bougie renovation requires a thorough understanding of each task, its dependencies, the resource needs, and the time it will take. Constraints such as the availability of resources, their working hours, and the hotel's ongoing operations must also be considered. (The items in the angle brackets would be supplied in your prompt.)

> ***"Here are the main tasks for the Hotel Bougie renovation project, their dependencies, estimated durations, and resources required:***
>
> ***<List of tasks, dependencies, durations, and resources>***
>
> ***Can you help generate an optimal schedule for these tasks considering a 5-day workweek?"***
>
> Certainly. Here's a proposed schedule considering the dependencies, durations, and resource constraints:
>
> Task 1: Interior Design Review and Approval
>
> Start: Day 1
>
> End: Day 10
>
> Resources involved: Project Manager, Design Team, Client Representative
>
> Task 2: Structural Assessment and Planning
>
> Start: Day 11 (dependent on the completion of Task 1)
>
> End: Day 26
>
> Resources involved: Structural Engineer, Project Manager
>
> ...
>
> *{Response continues with detailed scheduling of the remaining tasks, truncated for brevity and relevance.}*

The ability of AI to process such vast information quickly and propose an optimal schedule provides a significant advantage, particularly in large and complex projects. AI can help ensure that all tasks are scheduled to minimize delays and conflicts and allow project managers to identify potential bottlenecks and take preventive action. This makes the project scheduling process more dynamic and responsive.

As part of the Hotel Bougie renovation project, you continue to use AI to monitor communications across various platforms like Slack or Microsoft Teams. This monitoring allows AI to identify any new tasks mentioned during your team's discussions and automatically add them to the project schedule, ensuring they do not get overlooked.

Prompting AI for Task Addition

Let's say you've set up an automation integration that is triggered when you react to a specific message in your team's Slack or Microsoft Teams communication with an emoji. The AI software then processes this alert to read the message, summarize it, generate action items, and add the new task to your project schedule and a specific team member's to-do list in the project management information system (PMIS).

TECHNICAL GUIDE See Technical Guide 7.1 on how to use Zapier and ChatGPT to automate tasks from communication platforms and integrate them into your PMIS.

Perhaps you receive a message from the interior designer on the project's Slack channel: "We have a new task; we need to add vintage chandeliers in the main lobby. It will take about a week."

From here, you decide to add the "✔" (check mark) emoji to send it to your project PMIS.

"I received a new task to add vintage chandeliers in the main lobby. The task will take about a week. Could you help me assess where this new task fits best within our current schedule and resources?"

To integrate this new task into your project, we must consider its dependencies, resources required, and potential impact on the current schedule.

Based on the current schedule and the task dependencies, I suggest inserting the new task after the Lobby Renovation task. This is because installing the chandeliers should happen after the overall renovation of the lobby.

Regarding resources, the interior designer is leading this task, so we need to check their availability. If they are engaged with another task during the proposed period, we may need to reallocate resources or reschedule other tasks.

Please confirm the dependency and resource availability so I can help you update the project schedule accordingly.

By integrating AI with your team's communication channels, you ensure every update, every new task, is captured and scheduled efficiently and that everything runs smoothly. Furthermore, using AI for such activities frees up more time for you as project manager to focus primarily on critical decision-making tasks.

Let's assume you've just concluded a highly productive meeting filled with crucial discussions. Numerous key risks, actions, issues, and decisions were discussed. Fortunately, you had an AI assistant in attendance. This assistant recorded the meeting minutes with time stamps, speakers, and more. However, you've forgotten some of the topics discussed.

"Please review the meeting minutes and provide an executive summary. In addition, outline an analysis of the identified Risks, Actions/Assumptions, Issues, and Decisions (RAID) from the meeting into a table. In this table, be sure to list the owners of each and time stamps where mentioned. Additionally, please tell me which specific follow-up items are assigned to me and the specific time from the meeting recording they are assigned."

After reviewing the meeting minutes, it is clear that several key points were discussed. The main risks identified were potential delays in project timelines due to unforeseen circumstances and the potential for budget overruns. The actions and assumptions made included the belief that all team members will complete their tasks on time, and the effort to conduct regular check-ins to monitor progress. The main issues were the lack of resources and potential conflicts in team schedules. Decisions made include allocating additional resources to ensure project completion and adjusting team schedules to avoid conflicts.

In terms of the RAID analysis, here is the table:

RAID	DESCRIPTION	SEVERITY/PRIORITY	STATUS	RESOLUTION DATE
Risks	Potential delays in project timelines	High	Open	-
Actions/ Assumptions	Regular check-ins to monitor progress	Medium	In Progress	-
Issues	Lack of resources and potential conflicts in team schedules	High	Open	–
Decisions	Allocation of additional resources and adjustment of team schedules	High	Closed	2023-08-02

{Some columns deleted from table due to limited space.}

As for your specific follow-up items, you have been assigned to oversee allocating additional resources at the time stamp 00:45:50.

"Perform a sentiment analysis on the meeting minutes."

The sentiment analysis of the meeting minutes indicates a generally positive tone, with team members expressing optimism about the project's progress and confidence in overcoming identified risks and issues. However, there were also expressions of concern about potential delays and resource allocation, indicating areas that may need additional attention moving forward.

TECHNICAL GUIDE In Technical Guide 7.2, you'll discover how you can use the Transcription feature in Microsoft Word to upload or transcribe audio. You can then input the transcription into an AI tool called Anthropic's Claude for AI-driven summaries, action items, insights, and sentiment analysis.

Instead of rewatching and listening to the entire meeting, the AI assistant can provide the key highlights. To take it a step further, you ask for the specific time stamps at which the topics were discussed. You can also ask it to list all the action items assigned to you. You may want to add the items to the project schedule and to-do list via automations and plug-ins using AI. Popular communication platforms such as Slack are also integrating AI services where users can interact directly with automated agents such as Anthropic's Claude.

TECHNICAL GUIDE See Technical Guide 7.3 to learn some capabilities of using Claude in Slack.

Resource Allocation and Optimization with AI

In the subsequent phase of the Hotel Bougie renovation project, you encounter a common challenge in project management: resource allocation and optimization. This process is easier said than done due to the complexity and dynamic nature of the project.

Imagine there's a need to adjust the team allocation due to changes in project requirements, or perhaps a team member becomes unavailable for a time. Manually figuring out how to reallocate resources and adjust schedules can significantly eat up your time. Also, it's difficult to keep all parameters in view, which can lead to suboptimal decisions. That's where you can leverage AI to optimize this process.

Let's say that one of your critical team members, the lead engineer, falls ill and will be unavailable for two weeks. AI can lend a helping hand, as shown in the following prompt.

"The lead engineer is out for two weeks. Could you help me reassess the project schedule and suggest optimal reallocation of tasks and resources?"

Based on the engineer's current task assignments, we have a few tasks that will be impacted:

- Finalize Lobby Structural Changes
- Review Safety Protocols for the Kitchen Renovation

For the task Finalize Lobby Structural Changes, we should consider reallocating this task to the assistant engineer, given their previous involvement with the project and skill set. However, this will also require moving their Patio Renovation task to a later date or assigning it to another team member.

Shall I draft a revised schedule considering these changes?

Effective resource allocation is not just about filling a gap in the team when someone is unavailable. It is a dynamic process that requires ongoing adjustments and reallocation to account for project conditions, priorities, and resource availability changes. Therefore, the true value of AI in resource allocation is its ability to optimize resource allocation to maximize efficiency continually.

Because of updated building codes, let's assume an unplanned task pops up: Redesigning the Front Porch. You must allocate this task to a team member as a project manager. This is where AI can provide valuable assistance.

"I need to add a new task to the project: Redesigning the Front Porch. This task requires architectural and regulatory knowledge. Can you suggest the best team member to assign this task to?"

Based on the team's current workload and the required skill sets, I recommend assigning Redesigning the Front Porch to the Assistant Architect. They have both architectural and regulatory knowledge and are currently working under capacity. The addition of this task should not disrupt their current workload. However, consider reprioritizing their task Inspecting Interior Walls, which is of lower priority and can be postponed or reassigned without significant impact on the project.

AI can thus provide a data-backed decision, factoring in the task requirements, the skill sets, and the team's current workload. This ensures an optimal and balanced distribution of tasks among your team.

AI-powered project management tools can allow you to dynamically reallocate resources, ensuring minimal disruption to project schedule.

Quality Management with AI

Project quality management ensures that the project will satisfy the needs for which it was undertaken. It includes all activities of the overall management function that determine the quality policy, objectives, and responsibilities and implements them within the quality system.

Long after the project is complete, the stakeholders will remember only one thing—the quality of the work performed. So, it is important that all project managers pay particular attention to this topic. Now you can count on AI to assist you, as project manager, in developing and monitoring quality standards and suggesting improvements based on data-driven insights.

Quality Planning with AI

Quality planning involves defining the quality standards for a project and comparing the actual results to these standards to optimize the overall project quality. AI can play a significant role in helping project managers develop and monitor these standards while also preventing defects and inconsistencies throughout the project's life cycle.

Establishing clear and measurable quality benchmarks and standards is integral to quality planning. These benchmarks give your project team a target to aim for, while the standards outline the practices to be followed to achieve these benchmarks.

An AI product such as ChatGPT can assist you in establishing benchmarks and standards. For instance, in the Hotel Bougie project, two quality benchmarks are crucial: preserving the aesthetic appeal of the original architecture and ensuring a superior level of comfort and luxury.

> ***"We aim to maintain the original architectural aesthetics of Hotel Bougie during our renovation while maintaining a high standard of comfort and luxury. Could you help me draft a detailed quality standard for this benchmark?"***
>
> The renovation of Hotel Bougie should incorporate modern amenities and facilities without compromising the original architectural aesthetics, such as the Victorian-era stonework, the ornate woodwork in the lobby, and the unique stained-glass windows in the dining hall. All added elements should complement these features. The overall design should respect the original spatial proportions and layout to maintain the historical ambiance. All guest rooms should have state-of-the-art climate control systems, plush bedding, and high-end bathroom fixtures to provide guests with a luxurious experience. Common areas like the lobby and dining hall should feature comfortable seating, elegant lighting, and tasteful decor that enhances the hotel's historical charm. High-grade materials and finishes are essential in all areas of the hotel to ensure durability and a sense of luxury.

AI's ability to provide such detailed and context-specific responses could significantly ease the task of setting quality standards, ensuring they are well defined and clear to all project stakeholders.

Quality Assurance with AI

Quality assurance (QA) is a proactive process that seeks to prevent defects by ensuring that a project's planned standards and procedures are followed accurately. In the context of Hotel Bougie, QA would involve regular checks and audits to ensure adherence to the quality standards for maintaining the original architectural aesthetics and luxury.

> ***"We need to implement a proactive quality assurance process to ensure that our renovation project respects the original architectural aesthetics of Hotel Bougie and maintains a high standard of comfort and luxury. How can we ensure this?"***
>
> To ensure that the renovation of Hotel Bougie adheres to the established quality standards, a multipronged quality assurance strategy should be implemented.
>
> First, a dedicated quality team should be established, consisting of individuals who have a deep understanding of the hotel's architectural style and luxury standards. This team should conduct regular audits of the renovation process to ensure that the original architectural aesthetics are respected.
>
> Second, a detailed checklist should be developed that outlines the specific elements that need to be preserved, such as the Victorian-era stonework, the ornate woodwork in the lobby, and the unique stained-glass windows in the dining hall. This checklist should be used during the audits to ensure these elements are preserved and enhanced.
>
> Third, training sessions should be held for all project team members to ensure they understand the importance of preserving architectural aesthetics and maintaining luxury standards. These sessions can also reinforce the procedures and practices that must be followed.
>
> Any deviations from the established standards should be documented and reviewed by the project manager and the quality team. Corrective actions should be taken promptly to rectify any issues.

The key takeaway is that ChatGPT can assist project managers with quality assurance by providing detailed and context-specific guidance. You can use AI to help you brainstorm and develop a series of steps, actions, and plans to preserve the quality benchmarks and standards for your project.

Quality Control with AI

Quality control involves monitoring the project outcomes to determine if they comply with the relevant quality standards and identifying ways to eliminate causes of unsatisfactory performance. ChatGPT can aid in framing the approach for quality control as well:

> ***"We have completed a set of rooms in the Hotel Bougie as per the planned high standard of comfort and luxury. We need to ensure the quality of work before we move on to the rest of the rooms. What should be on our quality control checklist?"***
>
> A quality control checklist is a great way to ensure that the rooms meet the desired standards.
>
> Here's a sample checklist:
>
> - Furnishings: Check each piece of furniture for its design, comfort, and material quality. Ensure they match the specified criteria. Pay attention to details like the bed's comfort, the chairs' ergonomic design, and the drapes' quality.
> - Amenities: Test all the modern amenities. The Smart TV should function correctly with access to streaming services and high-speed Wi-Fi connectivity, the temperature control system should work accurately, and the mini fridge should function adequately and be stocked as planned.
> - Color Palette: Assess the overall aesthetic of the room. Check if the color palette of the room aligns with the defined scheme, and ensure that the textures and patterns blend well without breaking the color scheme.
> - Overall Impression: Lastly, walk into the room as if you're the guest. Does it give an impression of high-standard comfort and luxury? Does everything work as it should? Is there anything that's out of place or that could be improved?

You can also leverage AI to analyze data and create visual tools such as Pareto charts. These charts are particularly useful in identifying a project's most common sources of problems. For example, you could ask ChatGPT to create a Pareto chart from a set of quality control data using the Advanced Data Analysis tool:

> ***"ChatGPT, I've collected quality control data from our refurbishment project. Several issues have cropped up multiple times. Can you help me create a Pareto chart to identify the most frequent problems?***
>
> Here is a Pareto chart that shows the most frequent problems in the project.

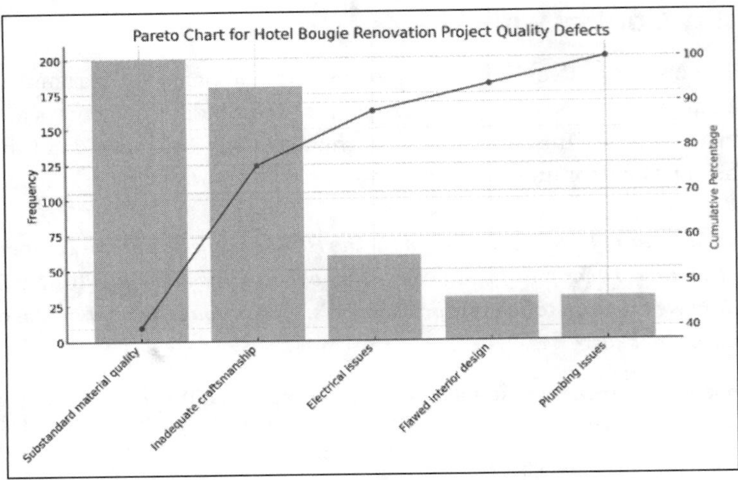

From the data provided, ChatGPT might generate a Pareto chart highlighting the most common issues, such as delays in material deliveries, changes in interior design plans, or issues with contractors. With this visual tool, you can focus your efforts on mitigating the most significant problems first.

TECHNICAL GUIDE **In Technical Guide 7.4, you'll find a prompt template that can be used for quality control.**

Leveraging AI for Continuous Quality Control and Improvement

Quality control in a project involves continuously monitoring the project outcomes to ensure they meet the defined quality standards. Any deviation can then be corrected promptly, ensuring continuous improvement. AI tools can support this by tracking project outcomes against specified criteria and providing alerts in case of any deviations.

Let's imagine that ChatGPT has been given access to a database of historical renovation projects, including images of before and after renovations, associated quality benchmarks, and the outcomes achieved. Here's how you can prompt AI to inspect completed work:

"We have just finished renovating the first set of rooms at Hotel Bougie. Here are the images of the renovated rooms. Could you compare them with our quality standards and let me know if there are any deviations?"

The image could be analyzed by ChatGPT's Vision feature (or similar AI with image prompts such as Google's Bard or Microsoft's Bing AI). The AI would compare them with the defined standards, and provide a response highlighting potential deviations and recommending corrective actions. This unbiased feedback would enable you to take quick corrective action.

AI in Monitoring and Controlling Project Work

AI tools, such as ChatGPT, can be a game-changer in monitoring and controlling project work. By leveraging AI, you can automate tasks that would usually consume significant amounts of your time and get insights for proactive adjustments. Let's explore this further through the lens of the Hotel Bougie renovation project.

Project Performance Monitoring with AI

Of course, as project manager for the Hotel Bougie renovation, you have maintained diligent records of the project's progress. You've logged the hours worked by each team member, tracked material usage, documented costs, and maintained a record of each task's status.

Now, you can turn to ChatGPT to help digest this data and generate a performance report. In this example, we'll assume the data has been pre-processed into a format that ChatGPT can understand, or you can upload a spreadsheet using the ChatGPT Advanced Data Analysis feature.

"ChatGPT, here's the collected data from our ongoing renovation project at Hotel Bougie:

<Insert project data here>

Task List:<Insert a list of tasks with their planned and actual completion dates.>

Time Logs: <Insert hours of each team member's hours spent on each task.>

Material Logs: <Insert quantities of each type of material used so far.>

Cost Logs: <Insert labor and material costs for each task.>

Quality Reports: <Insert QA results for each completed task.>

Could you analyze this data and provide a brief project performance report?"

Based on the provided data, here's a hypothetical overview of the project's performance:

Schedule Performance: With the provided task list and completion dates, the project is running three days behind schedule. Notably, the delay is primarily due to Task 7, which took longer than anticipated.

Cost Performance: The project is slightly over budget. The total actual cost is 4% higher than the budgeted cost. Labor costs are on target, but material costs are higher than expected, especially for Task 5.

Quality Performance: The quality reports show that 90% of the completed tasks have met the set quality standards, which is a good indicator. However, three tasks did not meet the required standards and had to be redone, contributing to the schedule delay.

This interaction with ChatGPT gives you a high-level overview of the project status in terms of schedule, cost, and quality. The example provided did not use actual data, but using real datasets about your project will yield a more specific and detailed response for your project.

Now let's see how ChatGPT can assist you in performing an earned value management (EVM) analysis:

"Using the same data from the Hotel Bougie renovation project, could you provide an EVM analysis?"

Indeed, here's a simple Earned Value Management (EVM) analysis based on your data, showing planned value (PV), earned value (EV) and actual cost (AC):

MONTH	PV	EV	AC
1	$50,000	$47,500	$49,400
2	$100,000	$95,000	$98,800
3	$150,000	$142,500	$148,200

Schedule Performance Index (SPI): Considering the data you've provided, the SPI is 0.95, which indicates that for each hour of work, you're only completing 95% of what you had planned. This supports the observation that the project is slightly behind schedule.

Cost Performance Index (CPI): Your CPI is 0.96, meaning you're getting 96 cents worth of work for every dollar spent. This indicates that you're slightly over budget, aligning with the cost overrun observed earlier.

This analysis confirms the earlier findings that the project is running slightly behind schedule and over budget.

AI enables efficient and accurate project performance monitoring and provides valuable insights for decision-making.

Proactive Project Adjustments with AI

Project management is a dynamic field, and project managers often need to adjust their strategies on the fly in response to unexpected changes or issues. The ability to anticipate these changes and make adjustments in advance can significantly impact the overall success of a project.

AI can help generate various alternative scenarios or action plans based on the data fed into it, enabling you to make proactive decisions. It can suggest corrective actions based on project performance metrics, offer suggestions on reallocating resources, or propose adjustments to the project schedule.

For example, based on the EVM analysis for the Hotel Bougie renovation project, it's clear that the project is slightly behind schedule and over budget due to unforeseen issues. Use AI to explore various strategies for getting the project back on track.

> ***"Given the current project status, what strategies could we employ to bring the Hotel Bougie renovation project back on schedule and budget? Can you perform an impact analysis?"***
>
> Reallocating resources: Reallocating some resources from less critical tasks to the ones causing the delay. For instance, if the lobby and restaurant renovation delay is due to electrical issues, you could allocate more electricians to this task to expedite the process.
>
> Revising the project schedule: Some tasks that aren't dependent on the lobby and restaurant renovations could be moved up. This would allow other parts of the project to move forward without being held up by the delay.
>
> Negotiating with vendors: It could be beneficial to negotiate with vendors for faster delivery of materials or even discounts to help control the costs. However, this must be done without compromising on the quality.

These strategies can be evaluated and fine-tuned based on the project's specific circumstances. You can then implement the most suitable approach to bring your project back on track. The advantage is that the AI offers options that you might have yet to consider, providing a more holistic view of the project and increasing the chances of success. AI helps you understand the potential consequences of your decisions by conducting a detailed impact analysis.

TECHNICAL GUIDE Technical Guide 7.5 shows how you can use exported project data from PMIS products such as Asana, Jira, or Trello to import into the ChatGPT Advanced Data Analysis tool to conduct impact analyses and what-if scenarios for your project.

Validating and Controlling Scope, Schedule, and Cost with AI

Managing a project effectively requires careful consideration of the triple constraint—cost, scope, and time—while maintaining quality. It's crucial to clearly understand the project scope, keep a close eye on budget allocation, identify schedule constraints, and define what quality means in the project context. Balancing these constraints may shift during the project, but having a clear grasp of how each constraint impacts the others will help you make informed decisions.

Scope Validation

In project management, scope validation involves the customer accepting the completed project deliverables. It ensures that each deliverable is complete and satisfactory according to the project scope. AI can enhance the scope validation process by automating many routine checks and providing an objective assessment. For instance, in the Hotel Bougie project, the scope includes "high-standard comfort and luxury." Several quality checks and customer reviews must be considered to validate this scope.

"I have customer reviews for our newly renovated rooms in a CSV file. We asked customers to rate the rooms based on comfort, luxury, and overall satisfaction on a scale from 1 to 5. I'd like to understand the overall trend and any specific issues or highlights mentioned by the customers. Can you assist?"

Certainly, first take a look at this table from the CSV file:

CUSTOMER ID	COMFORT RATING	LUXURY RATING	OVERALL SATISFACTION RATING	COMMENTS
001	4	5	5	"Excellent service and room conditions. Very comfortable and luxurious."
002	4	3	4	"Very comfortable, but I expected more luxurious details."
003	5	4	5	"The room was very comfortable. The luxury aspect was good, but there's room for improvement."
004	3	5	4	"The luxury aspect was top-notch, but the bed could be more comfortable."
005	4	4	4	"Good balance between comfort and luxury. Keep it up!"

Overall Trend: Overall Satisfaction: The average overall satisfaction rating is 4.4 out of 5, indicating high levels of satisfaction among customers.

Specific Issues:

One customer (Customer ID 004) mentioned that the bed could be more comfortable. This may be an area to look into, as it could enhance the comfort rating.

Another customer (Customer ID 002) expected more luxurious details. It might be beneficial to obtain more specific feedback to understand which areas could be improved to increase the luxury rating.

Highlights:

Several customers mentioned that they found the rooms both comfortable and luxurious, which aligns with the project's scope.

The service was praised as excellent by one customer (Customer ID 001).

AI can interpret the data and extract the key information, giving an overall picture of customer satisfaction and any specific concerns or praises. With this insight, you can determine whether the project scope (high-standard comfort and luxury) is being met as perceived by the customers.

Such automation reduces manual work and minimizes human bias and error. As you progress in the project life cycle, it's essential to keep validating your work against the defined project scope to stay on the right track.

Scope Control with AI

Controlling the project scope is another crucial aspect of project management. It involves monitoring the status of the project and product scope and managing changes to the scope baseline. Using AI, you can keep track of your project's progression and ensure that it aligns with the original scope. By feeding project data into an AI like ChatGPT, you can keep tabs on the project scope and be alerted if it starts to deviate.

Now the Hotel Bougie project is well under way, and as is often the case, new suggestions and ideas are continually cropping up. This is where AI can help you, as project manager, remain vigilant about the project's scope.

"Here's the latest round of updates from our various stakeholder groups. I must know if we're staying within our initial project scope of 'high-standard comfort and luxury.' Can you help identify any potential scope creep?

Architectural Team: The renovation is moving ahead as planned, but due to supply chain issues, we're considering changing the fixtures in the bathrooms to a different, slightly less premium brand.

Culinary Team: The team has prepared a new room service menu. It now includes several luxury dishes based on the latest culinary trends. However, they also want to introduce a 'farm to table' concept, where we'd source fresh, organic produce from local farms.

IT Team: The team has suggested upgrading the hotel's Wi-Fi system to provide faster Internet service. This wasn't in our original plan, but the team believes it's a critical step in ensuring high-standard comfort for our guests."

Based on your provided updates, here are some potential deviations that could lead to scope creep:

1. Architectural Team: Changing the bathroom fixtures to a different brand might not align with the project's original "high-standard comfort and luxury" scope. You'll need to ensure that the quality of the new fixtures matches the expected standards.

2. Culinary Team: The "farm to table" concept proposed by the team is a great idea for enhancing luxury, but it was not included in the initial scope. This could increase project costs and require additional resources to manage.
3. IT Team: The team's suggestion to upgrade the entire hotel's Wi-Fi system is crucial for providing comfort. However, since it was not part of the original plan, this could increase project cost and time.

This shows that by regularly engaging with AI like ChatGPT, you can obtain valuable insights that help you promptly identify and mitigate potential scope creep. You can make informed decisions about accepting or rejecting changes based on their alignment with your project's original objectives and constraints. Based on the prompt response above, as a project manager, you should use your judgment and coordination with stakeholder expectations to guarantee quality and be wary of the triple constraint.

TECHNICAL GUIDE Technical Guide 7.6 provides a prompt template to address scope control.

Schedule Control with AI

The hotel renovation project is in full swing, and everything appears to be on track. The Room Redesign phase has been finished on schedule, taking the planned 30 days. Following this, the Plumbing Installation phase was supposed to start immediately, estimated to last 45 days. After the plumbing work, the Electrical Setup phase, which depends on the completion of the plumbing phase, would commence.

However, an unforeseen delay occurred—the delivery of the plumbing materials has been postponed by a week, causing a late start to the Plumbing Installation phase and extending it by an additional week. Naturally, the Electrical Setup phase is also affected, but to what extent? How will this delay impact the overall project schedule?

"Our Hotel Bougie Renovation project is facing some delays. The Room Redesign phase took 30 days, but we've hit a snag with the Plumbing Installation phase. A delay in material delivery caused us to start a week late and extended the phase by an additional week. Given that the Electrical Setup phase was supposed to start immediately after the plumbing work, it's also delayed. Can you help analyze the schedule variance and explain the potential impacts on our project?"

AI can calculate and provide a detailed schedule variance analysis. Utilizing AI in such a manner allows you to stay on top of your project timelines and make informed decisions when deviations occur, as you can see in this response from ChatGPT:

> I can help with that. The initial delay in the Plumbing Installation phase affects this phase as well as the subsequent Electrical Setup phase. Here's how the delay impacts the overall schedule:
>
> Plumbing Installation Phase: This phase was initially supposed to last 45 days, but with the delay in the material delivery and the subsequent start, it now takes 52 days. This results in a schedule variance of +7 days for this phase.
>
> Electrical Setup Phase: This phase can start only after the Plumbing Installation phase is complete. Thus, the delay has a ripple effect, pushing the start of the Electrical Setup phase back by 7 days. If we assume that no extra resources are added, and the duration of this phase remains unchanged, this phase will also end 7 days later than initially planned. This results in a schedule variance of +7 days for this phase.
>
> Overall Project: Considering these variances, your project schedule has been extended by 14 days. This delay may impact other dependent tasks and stakeholder expectations and may also have cost implications.
>
> However, it's important to note that these projections are based on the current situation and assume there won't be any further disruptions or resource changes. You should promptly communicate this delay to all stakeholders and start exploring strategies to mitigate its impact. This could include rescheduling tasks, reallocating resources, or adjusting the project scope if necessary.

This detailed response from ChatGPT provides an analysis of the schedule variance and gives actionable insights on how to communicate this delay and potential strategies to mitigate its impact.

Project Timeline Forecasting with AI

Artificial intelligence offers an array of predictive capabilities that can significantly aid in forecasting project timelines. The ability to process large volumes of data, learn from historical project data, and analyze current trends can provide project managers with invaluable insights.

For instance, in the Hotel Bougie renovation project, you can use ChatGPT to analyze data and provide insights at each stage:

- **Data Collection and Organization:** Initially, as a project manager, you need to collect and organize relevant project data. This includes historical project timeline data, data on current progress, and details about any delays or changes in the schedule.
- **AI-Powered Analysis:** Once you have all relevant data, you can use the ChatGPT Advanced Data Analysis tool to upload your dataset. The AI can process this data, identify trends, compare progress with historical timelines, and analyze deviations.
- **Prediction and Forecasting:** Based on the data analysis, you can ask ChatGPT to forecast the potential completion date of the project. This might resemble the following interaction:

  "Given the organized project timeline data, the current progress, and the delays we have experienced, can you help me forecast the probable completion date of our project?"

  Analyzing the provided data, I see the Designing and Procurement phases are completed. The Renovation Work is running two weeks behind due to unexpected structural complications. Given the historical data and current pace, and assuming no significant delays, the project will likely take two more weeks to complete. Please note that this is a prediction, and actual timelines may vary. Continuous monitoring and adjustment is advised.

- **Review and Plan Accordingly:** You can then review these AI-generated forecasts, and based on your expertise and understanding of the project, devise strategies to recover the lost time or adjust your stakeholders' expectations.
- **Project Management Systems:** Most organizations use some form of project management system to track the progress of their projects. Systems such as Microsoft Project, Jira, Trello, or Monday are popular examples. These systems can provide a wealth of data about task completion, dependencies, and timeline adjustments and usually support exporting data to formats such as comma-separated values (CSV) or Excel.
- **Team Input:** The most up-to-date information is often obtained directly from the team members working on the tasks. Regular project update meetings or written status updates can provide additional context and details about progress and potential delays.

- **Risk Registers:** Project managers track potential risks and issues impacting the project timeline. Incorporating this data can improve the accuracy of predictions.

Once all the necessary data is collected, it can be organized in a suitable format (such as CSV or Excel) and then uploaded into ChatGPT Advanced Data Analysis tool for analysis.

Ethical Considerations and Professional Responsibility

Integrating AI into project management presents vital ethical considerations. In planning, adjusting, reporting, or decision-making, levering AI benefits without lowering ethical standards is paramount.

AI can suggest proactive project adjustments and provide real-time monitoring, but we must validate its insights. Blind trust and neglect of human elements raise ethical concerns, as do the transparency and accuracy of AI predictions.

AI can expedite insightful decision-making through rapid reporting, but we must ensure input data is accurate and unbiased. AI-generated reports must be verified. We must be transparent about when and how they are used. When using AI for calculations, such as EVM metrics, it's crucial to check for possible errors, remembering that report quality depends on input data.

AI can boost performance monitoring, yet it doesn't replace human oversight. It's our ethical duty to consistently review and validate AI outputs.

The core principles of project management ethics—responsibility, respect, fairness, honesty—should steer AI use.

Key Points to Remember

- **AI in Project Work Performance and Execution:** AI can facilitate better-informed decisions in the execution phase of a project by assisting in task allocation, resource management, and managing knowledge.
- **Schedule Monitoring with AI:** AI can process vast amounts of schedule-related data and help identify potential bottlenecks and issues, providing proactive problem-solving opportunities.

- **AI and Cost Management:** Project managers can improve accuracy and efficiency by integrating AI into cost estimation and control. ChatGPT can work with large datasets and perform complex calculations.
- **Quality Control via AI:** ChatGPT can assist project managers in maintaining quality standards, from analyzing past performance data to identifying potential quality issues.
- **The Role of AI in Scope Management:** AI can help identify and control scope creep by analyzing project trends and providing early warnings. Still, project managers should avoid overreliance on AI.
- **Ethical Considerations and Professional Responsibility:** As we leverage AI in project management, it's essential to uphold ethical principles such as data privacy, accuracy, fairness, and transparency. AI should not replace human decision-making with respect to monitoring and controlling projects.

Technical Guide

7.1 Automating Tasks from Communication Platforms into a Project Management Information System (PMIS) Using Zapier and ChatGPT

Zapier, a powerful automation tool, can seamlessly integrate with Slack, Teams, or other supported communication platforms to streamline project management tasks. By setting up a Zap, you can react to a message and trigger an automation. This automation uses OpenAI's ChatGPT to generate a succinct message summary and identify key action items. These action items are automatically parsed and sent to a PMIS like Asana. This process results in a more efficient workflow, reducing manual data entry and ensuring tasks are tracked and managed effectively.

Integrate Slack with Zapier

1. Log in to your Zapier account or create a new account if you don't have one.
2. Once logged in, click **Make A Zap**.
3. Set the trigger app as Slack (or the communication platform of your choice).
4. Select the **New Reaction Added** trigger.
5. Connect your Slack account to Zapier if it isn't already connected.
6. Set the specific emoji reaction to trigger the Zap and Slack Channel. Click **Continue**.

Integrate Zapier with ChatGPT

1. Click **Add A Step** and then **Action/Search**. Select **OpenAI ChatGPT** as your action app.
2. Choose the **Conversation In ChatGPT** action event.
3. Connect your OpenAI account to Zapier if it's not already connected.
4. Under App & Event, choose an Event Type of **Conversation**.
5. Click **Continue**.
6. Under Action, in the User Message (Required) field, instruct ChatGPT with a prompt.
   a. To customize this prompt using variables from the previous inputs, under the Insert Data fields, select the variable Message Text under New Reaction Added In Slack. This is taking the original message from Slack and asking ChatGPT to review the text (**Figure 7.1**).

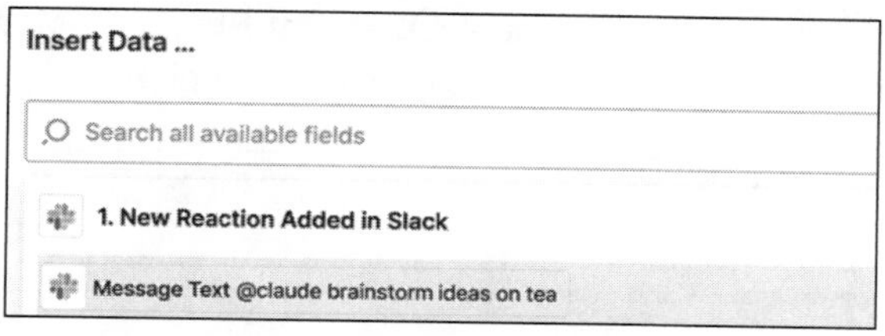

Insert Data ...
Search all available fields
1. New Reaction Added in Slack
Message Text @claude brainstorm ideas on tea

FIGURE 7.1 Zapier inserting data from Slack

b. Provide ChatGPT with your prompt, asking it to review "Message Text:" (the variable) and to provide a title, summary of the message, and any action items. It should look similar to **Figure 7.2**.

* User Message (required)
Review 1. Message Text: @claude brainst...rm ideas on tea and provide the following:
1. A title for the message
2. Summary of the message.
3. Action items

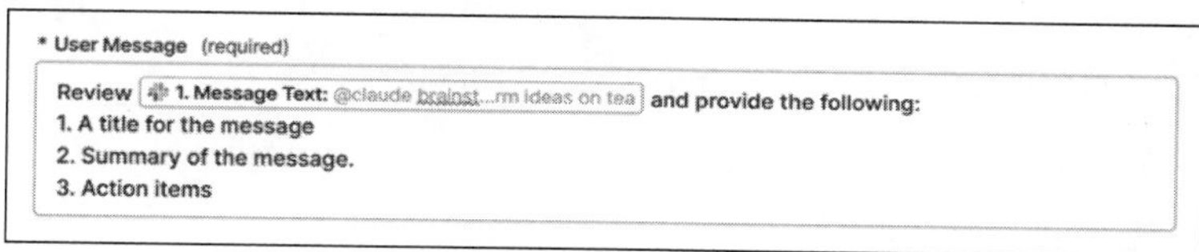

FIGURE 7.2 Zapier ChatGPT user message

7. Set the Model, Max Tokens, Temperature, and other fields according to your preference.
8. Click **Continue**.

Send Actions to Asana

1. Click **Add A Step** and then **Action/Search**.
2. Choose **Asana** as the app.
3. Select the action **Create Task**.
4. Connect your Asana account to Zapier if it's not already connected.
5. Set up the task by selecting the workspace, project, and section.
6. Under Name, give the incoming Asana Task a name (**Figure 7.3**).

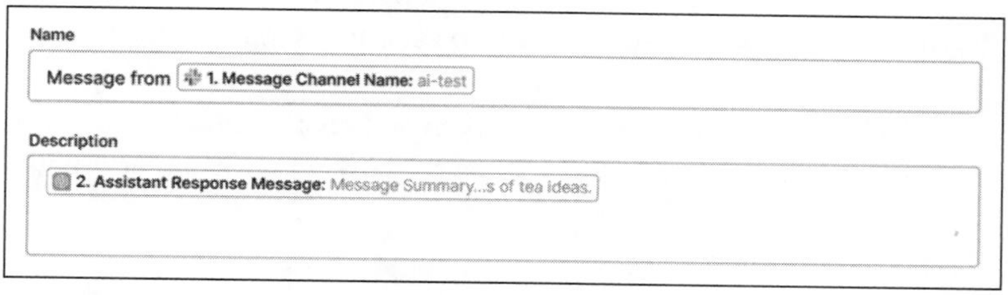

Name
Message from 1. Message Channel Name: ai-test
Description
2. Assistant Response Message: Message Summary...s of tea ideas.

FIGURE 7.3 Zapier sending task to Asana

7. Under Description, select the variable **Assistant Response Message** from the Conversation In ChatGPT Insert Data field picker (**Figure 7.4**)

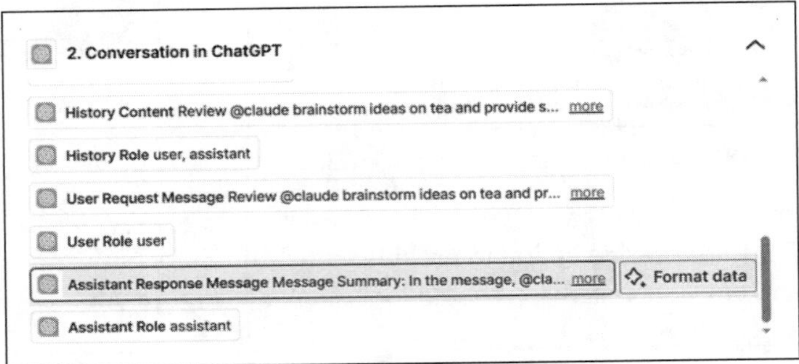

FIGURE 7.4 Zapier sending ChatGPT output to Asana

8. Fill out any other Asana field based on your preference.
9. Click **Continue**.
10. Remember to test your Zap before turning it on. You can do this by clicking **Test & Review** at each step and finally clicking **Test & Continue**. If everything is set up correctly, you can then select **Turn On Zap**.

Putting It All Together: Reacting to a Message in Slack

1. Open the Slack workspace and navigate to the message you want to react to.
2. Hover over the message. A set of icons will appear on the top-right corner of the message.
3. Click the **Add Reaction** icon (a smiley face with a plus sign).
4. Select the reaction emoji from the menu. The reaction will be added to the message.
5. From here, the automation should have taken place where Zapier sends the reacted Slack message to ChatGPT to review and create the title, summary, and action items to send to Asana.

NOTE These steps may need adjustment based on the specific requirements and setup of your Slack, Zapier, ChatGPT, and Asana accounts.

7.2 Getting AI-Generated Meeting Minutes by Uploading Meeting Transcripts

Project management involves managing several moving parts, and meetings are critical for successful communication, planning, and execution. But how do you ensure you've captured every detail discussed in those meetings? More important, how do you generate actionable insights from these discussions?

Enter Microsoft Word's Transcribe feature and Claude AI. The Transcribe feature converts spoken words from your project meetings into written text, creating a precise record that can be referred to later. But the real magic happens when these transcriptions are fed into Claude, an advanced AI tool.

Since Claude has a large token limit (100k—roughly the size of a 200-page novel), it can intelligently review this raw data, generating actionable insights, follow-up tasks, sentiment analysis, and comprehensive meeting summaries. This synergy between Word's Transcribe and Claude reduces the manual work involved in note-taking and minute-writing and significantly enhances your project management capabilities. This tutorial will guide you through this process step by step.

Starting a Transcription in Microsoft Word:

1. Open Microsoft Word and create a new document.
2. From the top menu, select **Home**, then click the **Dictate** drop-down menu on the right side of the toolbar and select **Transcribe**.
3. In the Transcribe pane, you'll see two options: Upload Audio and Start Recording.
   a. You'll use the **Upload Audio** option if you already have a recorded audio file. Click that option and select the audio file from your device.
   b. If you want to record the meeting in real time, select the **Start Recording** option, and the recording will start. Remember to stop the recording once the meeting is over.
4. After completing the transcription process, you'll see the transcribed text in the pane. You have the option to edit any part of the transcription if necessary.
5. Once you're satisfied with the transcription, click **Add To Document** at the bottom of the Transcribe pane. The transcription will be added to your Word document.
6. Save this document as a DOCX or TXT file. You will copy and paste the information from here into Claude.

Note: Ensure that you have the necessary permissions to record and transcribe meetings, and inform all participants beforehand. Word's Transcribe feature may be restricted to certain licenses and subscription models. Check with your version and Microsoft 365 subscription plan to determine whether this functionality is available to you.

Feeding Transcriptions into Claude:

1. Log in to your Claude account and navigate to a new chat.
2. Copy the transcript from the Word file you saved previously. Paste the content into Claude.
3. Prompt Claude to generate meeting insights, identify action items from the meeting, conduct a sentiment analysis, and more.

7.3 Using Slack with Claude Integration

Claude AI, developed by Anthropic, is an AI competitor to OpenAI's ChatGPT, is a chatbot that you can use in Slack to help you with various tasks, such as summarizing, writing, and brainstorming. You can add Claude AI to your Slack workspace for free and communicate with it directly or in a group chat. Claude AI can remember your conversation history and follow links that you share with it. However, Claude AI also has some limitations, such as making mistakes or "hallucinating" information.

Adding Claude AI to your Slack workspace

Follow these steps:

1. Go to the Claude page on the Slack App Directory and click **Add To Slack**. Or open Slack, click Apps, select Add Apps, and search for **Claude**.
2. Make sure you are adding Claude to the right workspace and follow the screens to complete the process.
3. To chat with Claude, select it from the Apps list and type your message in the Message Claude field. You can reference previous comments by entering **/reset** to start a new thread.
4. To include Claude in a channel conversation, type **@Claude** and your message. Invite Claude to the channel if prompted. Anyone in the channel can also mention Claude and get a response.
5. You can learn more about Claude AI and its features by visiting Anthropic's Claude in Slack page or sending feedback to support@anthropic.com.

Project Management Use Cases

- Suppose you have a long conversation with your team members about a project deliverable in a Slack channel. You want to get a summary of the main points and action items from the discussion. You can mention Claude in your message and then ask Claude to summarize the conversation with bullet points and priorities. Claude will then scan the thread and generate a concise summary for you.
- Say you want to write a project status report based on some information you have collected. You can share the data and information with Claude in a direct message or a group chat and ask it to write a draft for you. Claude will then use its creative and collaborative writing skills to produce a draft you can review and edit.
- Say you are stuck with a project problem or challenge and need fresh ideas or solutions. You can brainstorm with Claude and your team members in a Slack channel by mentioning Claude and asking it to generate some suggestions or alternatives. Claude will then use its AI smarts to develop some possible ideas or solutions you can then discuss and evaluate.

7.4 Quality Control Prompt Template

Quality control is vital in project management. However, setting these benchmarks and communicating them effectively to your team can be challenging. Our quality control prompts aim to guide you in defining detailed quality standards, navigating critical factors for project success, and formulating a clear training plan. These prompts simplify your approach to project management and help you achieve your project-specific quality objectives.

> ***"We're in the process of outlining the quality metrics for our [project_name]. We're seeking to ensure [project_specific_quality_objectives]. Can you help me draft detailed quality standards for these benchmarks?***
>
> ***For our [project_name], we need to balance cost, scope, and time to deliver our project adequately. Can you guide me on critical factors I should consider to achieve the desired [specific_quality_standard]?***
>
> ***We're finding difficultly in communicating the quality standards of our [project_name] to our team. Could you help us create a training plan or guidelines to ensure everyone understands the required [specific_quality_standard]?"***

7.5 Using ChatGPT Advanced Data Analysis to Review Project Data and Conduct What-If Scenarios

Project management often involves dealing with complex schedules and making decisions that could significantly impact a project's timeline. In such scenarios, having a tool that can quickly analyze project data and perform predictive forecasting can be immensely beneficial. ChatGPT, with its Advanced Data Analysis feature, can assist project managers in conducting detailed project schedule analysis and facilitating what-if scenarios for predictive forecasting. This guide illustrates a step-by-step process for utilizing this AI tool to manage and predict project outcomes. You'll start by uploading your project data—exported from your PMIS such as Asana, Jira, or Smartsheet—to gain insights from hypothetical changes. This guide walks you through leveraging ChatGPT for your project management needs.

Upload the Project Schedule File

1. The first step is to upload the Excel file containing your project schedule. This file could be an export from your PMIS, such as Asana, Jira, Smartsheet, or any other tool you use to manage your projects. These tools can often export project data into an Excel or CSV format that ChatGPT can easily interpret. To upload the file, click the "+" icon in the chat interface.
2. Navigate to the location of your file in your device's file explorer, select your file, and click **Open** to upload it.
3. The assistant will confirm that the file has been successfully uploaded. This file will be used to conduct predictive forecasting, analysis, and what-if scenarios in subsequent steps.

Ensure that your Excel file is formatted correctly and that the project schedule is clear and well structured so that the assistant can accurately interpret and analyze the data. For example, the file should contain columns for task names, durations, start and finish dates, dependencies, and so forth.

Read and Review the Data

1. Once the file is uploaded, prompt ChatGPT to

   "Read and analyze the project schedule data from the uploaded file."
2. ChatGPT will provide an initial analysis of the project schedule, including the project's duration, the earliest and latest start and finish dates, and other important details.
3. Revise the prompt if needed to refine results.

Conduct a What-If Scenario

1. To conduct a what-if scenario, provide the assistant with the necessary information about the new task, such as its name, duration, dependencies, and where it fits into the schedule.
2. For example, you might say,

"Perform a what-if scenario by adding a new task named Task X that is 10 days long and dependent on Task A."

ChatGPT will add the new task to the project schedule, adjust the project's timeline accordingly, and provide an updated analysis.

Compare the Results

1. Once the what-if scenario is completed, ask the assistant to compare the new schedule with the original one.
2. You can say,

"Compare the new schedule with the original."

ChatGPT will compare the two schedules, highlighting the changes in project duration, start and finish dates, and other relevant metrics.

Draw Insights

1. Finally, ask ChatGPT for its insights on the impact of the new task on the project schedule.
2. You can say,

"Provide insights on the impact of the new task on the project."

ChatGPT will then provide its insights, such as how the new task affects the project's timeline, its dependencies, and whether it introduces any risks or issues.

7.6 Scope Control Prompt Template

AI can provide an objective analysis of these changes by mapping them against the initially agreed-on project scope and objectives. It can flag potential scope deviations and analyze how these deviations could impact other areas of the project.

Here's an example of a customizable template that project managers across different domains and industries can use:

> ***"Act as a project manager skilled in scope control and change management. We have received several requests from stakeholders about possible changes/additions to our project. I'd like you to analyze these suggestions in light of our initially agreed project scope and objectives and let me know if these would lead to deviations from our planned scope. Our primary goal is <project's main goal>, and the scope was defined as <description of project scope>. Here are the requests:***
>
> 1. ***<Request 1>.***
> 2. ***<Request 2>.***
> 3. ***<Request 3>.***
>
> ***Please ask any clarification questions to ensure you have the appropriate amount of information to make an objective analysis of the requests."***

This template can be adapted for any project across different industries. You must replace the placeholders with the relevant project details and suggestions received from your stakeholders. With this prompt, ChatGPT can objectively analyze the suggestions, giving you the necessary insight to make informed decisions.

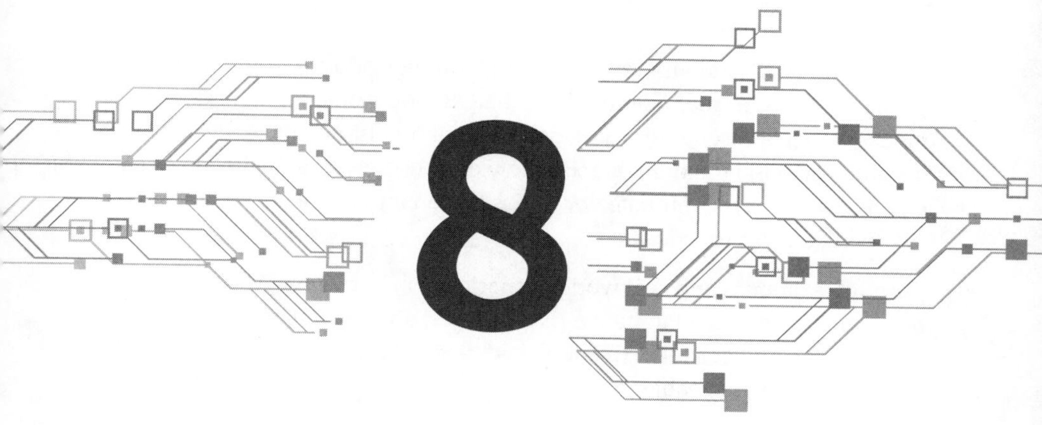

The Role of AI in Risk Management

Managing project uncertainty, or risk management, is at the core of any successful project. Whether building a state-of-the-art skyscraper or launching a groundbreaking software application, project managers face myriad uncertainties that can make or break the project. In an ever-changing world, traditional risk management practices often fall short. Enter generative artificial intelligence (AI), it simply excels at project risk management.

From identifying and analyzing risks to planning responses and monitoring progress, AI technologies like ChatGPT are reshaping the risk management landscape. They bring a level of precision, efficiency, and insight previously unattainable. But how exactly does AI achieve this? This chapter explores the intricate ways AI is woven into the fabric of modern risk management practices.

Through examples and real-world scenarios, you'll see how AI tools support qualitative and quantitative risk analyses; analyze impact, likelihood, correlations, and cost-effectiveness; and turn "known unknowns" into well-defined, manageable risks.

AI shines in risk response planning and implementation, allowing project managers to create robust strategies and contingency plans. Whether developing targeted response strategies or automating alerts, AI provides a framework for agile decision-making.

Clear communication with stakeholders is vital. AI takes this further, generating precise risk reports and executive summaries tailored to various stakeholders. From detailed risk item tracking forms to succinct executive insights, AI's reporting capabilities are a game changer.

In this chapter, we'll consider the many facets of AI in risk management, uncovering how it enhances productivity and fosters a culture of informed decision-making and proactive risk handling.

AI IN ACTION: MANAGING RISKS IN THE BANKING SECTOR

The banking industry is increasingly harnessing the capabilities of AI. Many banks are capitalizing on intelligent chats as a standout application and offering round-the-clock customer service. This proves invaluable for customers seeking help beyond standard business hours. Banks can tailor customer interactions through AI by discerning their needs and inclinations, leading to banking product suggestions rooted in individual profile insights.

Fraud detection through transactional pattern analysis presents another promising avenue. While in its early stages, several banks are delving into AI's potential to sift through vast financial datasets to pinpoint potential fraud indicators. AI can produce synthetic data mimicking fraudulent transactions, which can then refine machine learning models for more precise fraud detection.

Risk management stands as a domain where AI offers significant advantages. Through AI, synthetic data mirroring various risk situations can be produced. Banks can leverage this data to refine risk evaluation models, leading to more informed lending and investment choices without using actual customer data.

Furthermore, AI aids banks in regulatory adherence by producing synthetic data to evaluate compliance mechanisms. However, with synthetic data, there's a potential pitfall that AI might not be fully capturing the complexity of real-world scenarios. Hence, businesses should prioritize transparency when employing AI-driven tools for content generation for compliance purposes and disclose the limitations and biases that may exist in the synthetic data.

Here are some specific examples of how generative AI is being used in the banking sector today:

- Bank of America is using AI to create synthetic data that can be used to train its fraud detection models. This has helped the bank reduce fraud losses by 20 percent.[1]
- JPMorgan Chase uses AI to create personalized financial advice for its customers. The bank's AI system analyzes customer data to identify their financial goals and recommends products and services to help them achieve those goals.

The customer service chat feature continues to be AI's most successful and mature application. There are many reasons for that:

- The modern customer expects instant support and 24x7 customer service.
- The technology supporting AI in customer service is well established, with many ready-to-use solutions at a reasonable cost.
- Vast data from customer interactions is a rich resource for training AI models, ensuring they're effective and personalized.

As AI technology evolves, we anticipate banks will unveil more innovative strategies to enhance their operations and offerings using AI.

---

1 www.wsj.com/articles/bank-of-america-confronts-ais-black-box-with-fraud-detection-effort-1526062763

Risk Identification with AI: Understanding Threats and Opportunities

In the modern, fast-paced world of project management, the ability to leverage the capabilities of AI as a collaborator in risk management can be a game changer. AI platforms like ChatGPT provide a dynamic environment for project managers to brainstorm, analyze, and explore various scenarios. It also enables a more interactive approach to risk identification by simulating humanlike conversations, making it possible to uncover hidden pitfalls and discover unexplored opportunities. Whether it's probing the intricate web of factors affecting a project or devising innovative solutions, the collaborative nature of AI adds a new dimension to risk management. Let's delve into this collaborative process, starting with a clear understanding of the two fundamental aspects of risks: threats and opportunities.

Case Study—Constructing a Steel-Based Skyscraper

Our fictional case study for this chapter is Skyline Soaring Construction, a leading construction firm known for its daring architectural feats and sustainable building designs. With a reputation for pushing boundaries, they took on their most ambitious project yet: the SteelNexus Tower, a 100-story skyscraper designed to be an iconic structure in the city's skyline. The project vision was not merely about constructing a building but about crafting an enduring monument, a testament to human ingenuity, and a symbol of sustainable urban development (**Figure 8.1**).

FIGURE 8.1 SteelNexus Tower image created by OpenAI's DALL•E

Steel was chosen as the primary building material for its strength, sustainability, and aesthetic appeal. However, the large-scale use of steel also presented many risks, from procurement and pricing fluctuations to construction methodologies and safety protocols.

Skyline Soaring Construction opted to incorporate AI-driven risk management into their planning, construction, and monitoring phases to tackle these challenges. The SteelNexus Tower project was in the spotlight from day one. Investors, city officials, and the public eagerly watched its progress, adding pressure to the complex undertaking. Risks were abundant: the volatile price of steel, potential delays in procurement, complexities in designing with steel, the potential for structural issues, weather-related delays, and safety concerns. Throughout this chapter, we'll explore how AI became integral to the SteelNexus Tower project, helping Skyline Soaring Construction identify potential pitfalls, analyze risks, adapt to unforeseen challenges, and ensure the majestic tower's timely and successful completion.

Threats: Recognizing Potential Pitfalls

You, as project manager, know that threats are events or conditions that could adversely impact a project. Let's see how a conversation with ChatGPT can uncover threats and guide you toward mitigation strategies.

> ***"We're concerned about the fluctuating steel prices affecting the SteelNexus Tower project. How can we identify potential threats linked to this issue?"***
>
> The threats related to steel price fluctuations may include budget overruns, potential delays in construction, and contractual issues with suppliers. Monitoring global market trends and supplier agreements will be essential.
>
> ***"What about geological instability in the chosen site? Could that pose threats as well?"***
>
> Geological instability can lead to threats such as foundation failures, structural weaknesses, and legal compliance challenges. Consult with geological experts and consider alternate sites if the risks outweigh the benefits.

The conversation with ChatGPT reveals the potential threats related to the SteelNexus Tower project. It's clear that a project of this magnitude carries significant risks. The AI's suggestions to monitor market trends and consult with geological experts underscore the importance of proactive risk management in ensuring project success.

Opportunities: Embracing Potential Advantages

Conversely, opportunities are favorable conditions that you can exploit to meet or even exceed your project objectives. Identifying and seizing these opportunities is as important as uncovering risks.

> ***"The SteelNexus Tower project has a chance to use new eco-friendly materials that are becoming available. Could this be an opportunity?"***
>
> Utilizing eco-friendly materials could provide significant opportunities, such as enhancing your brand image and attracting eco-conscious investors. Conducting a thorough analysis of these materials would be the first step.
>
> ***"There are also local government incentives for projects incorporating community spaces. How can we take advantage of this?"***
>
> This presents an excellent opportunity for enhancing the community value of the SteelNexus Tower. Consider designing spaces that serve local needs, such as parks, cultural centers, or recreational areas. Collaborating with local authorities and community leaders will ensure alignment with community expectations and enable you to take advantage of the incentives.

The identification of threats and opportunities is a dynamic process requiring insight, vigilance, and adaptability. Through tailored conversations with ChatGPT, you and your team can explore potential scenarios, weigh the pros and cons, and craft strategies that turn risks into manageable factors.

Enhancing Traditional Risk Identification Methods with AI

While traditional risk identification methods have proven effective over the years, the integration of AI can significantly enhance these practices. AI can streamline the risk identification, provide deeper insights, and offer more accurate predictions. Let's explore how AI can be incorporated into your traditional risk identification methods such as brainstorming, the Delphi technique, predictive models, and creating a risk register.

Brainstorming Risks with AI

You have probably conducted brainstorming sessions, a popular method for identifying potential risks. AI tools like ChatGPT can facilitate brainstorming sessions, offer unbiased input, suggest innovative ideas, and provide real-time analysis of the discussed risks. As we've seen in many areas, AI can bring a new level of efficiency and effectiveness.

For a project manager, the ambition to create an iconic skyscraper is inspiring but also overwhelming. From the early planning stages, you are acutely aware that the extensive use of steel presents complex risks that demand meticulous attention. How do you even begin to identify the potential challenges? You decide to engage with AI to brainstorm the risks. It's like having a conversation with an expert in the room:

> ***"Act as a Construction Project Management Expert. We're about to embark on the SteelNexus Tower, a 100-story steel structure. Utilizing your expertise in construction methodologies, procurement strategies, and safety protocols, can you help me identify and analyze the potential risks? Please consider industry best practices and provide examples where relevant."***
>
> Let's break down the potential risks into categories and explore them in detail, considering common challenges and unique factors associated with the SteelNexus Tower project. Here's how we can approach it.
>
> Procurement Risks: Fluctuations in steel prices, potential delays in delivery, and quality inconsistencies
>
> Construction Methodologies: Complexities in steel design, potential for structural issues, reliance on specialized labor and equipment
>
> Safety Protocols: Safety regulations related to steel construction, potential hazards with handling heavy materials, and measures to ensure worker safety
>
> Would you like me to delve deeper into any specific area?
>
> ***"Yes, please elaborate on the potential for structural issues and the measures we can take to ensure worker safety."***

So your conversation continues, with AI providing detailed insights and examples tailored to your SteelNexus Tower project.

This AI brainstorming exercise does more than jump-start the risk identification process; it propels it forward with well-informed insights. By leveraging AI, you can craft an initial list of risks that not only addresses immediate concerns but also paves the way for identifying secondary and residual risks. Recognizing that comprehensive risk identification is an ongoing endeavor throughout the entirety of a project, you can deploy AI incrementally and iteratively at various stages. Already, you've started to unravel design complexities with steel, highlighting potential structural issues, safety concerns, and more.

Delphi Technique for Risk Identification

Building on the insights from your brainstorming session with AI, it's time to tap into the wisdom of experts. The Delphi technique is a structured communication process used to gather information and judgments from a panel of experts. The SteelNexus Tower project's complexity calls for additional perspectives. How can AI augment this process?

Incorporating AI into the Delphi Technique

The integration of AI streamlines the Delphi technique's execution. Let's follow the flow, starting with the development of a questionnaire with ChatGPT:

> ***"Act as a Construction Project Management Expert. I need to design a questionnaire to gather expert opinions on the potential structural and safety risks for the SteelNexus Tower. Can you create a draft tailored to explore steel design complexities, potential structural issues, and safety concerns?"***
>
> Here's a draft questionnaire to explore steel design complexities, potential structural issues, and safety concerns.
>
> Steel Design Complexities:
>
> - What are the primary challenges in steel design for a project like the SteelNexus Tower?
> - How would you rate the complexity of incorporating modern steel designs into existing structural guidelines?
> - Are there specific industry standards that need special consideration?
>
> Potential Structural Issues:
>
> - What potential structural risks could arise during construction?
> - How would you assess the stability of innovative structural designs?
> - Can you identify essential methods to prevent structural failure?
>
> Safety Concerns:
>
> - How can safety be ensured during the construction phase?
> - What safety protocols must be implemented?
> - Are there unique safety considerations for a project of this magnitude?

Next, you will send the AI-generated questionnaire to a panel of construction and safety experts. After gathering the expert responses, your next step is to analyze and synthesize the data. This is where AI can streamline the process.

"ChatGPT, analyze the responses and synthesize the insights into a summarized report, highlighting key risks and identifying consensus."

Steel Design Complexities: Both perspectives highlight the need for proper integration and standards, but the structural engineer emphasizes technical complexities, while the safety consultant focuses on training and safety compliance.

Potential Structural Issues: Consensus on risks such as structural integrity and compliance but different angles on prevention and assessment.

Safety Concerns: Agreement on the necessity of safety protocols, emphasizing training and constant supervision.

You will want to conduct successive rounds of questioning of experts, refining questions based on prior responses until a consensus is reached.

"The structural engineer's response mentioned 'lack of clear standards.' Can you elaborate on this in the context of steel design?"

Certainly! The lack of clear standards refers to the absence or ambiguity in universal guidelines for complex steel designs. This could include the absence of best practices for integrating new materials or methodologies, the need for clarity in compliance with local building codes, or gaps in current engineering guidelines that may not cover innovative design elements. The challenge lies in navigating these uncertainties while ensuring structural integrity, safety, and compliance with legal requirements.

Combining human expertise with AI-driven tools like ChatGPT offers more than just risk identification; it provides nuanced insights, tapping into the collective wisdom of experts. The Delphi approach requires anonymity, and the demonstrated approach can provide it.

AI-Driven Delphi Technique: AI as Expert

Expanding upon the integration of AI with the Delphi technique, you could choose to pioneer a new model entirely driven by artificial intelligence. Leveraging ChatGPT's capabilities as a panel of experts instead of humans, the process could look as follows:

"Using the questionnaire we generated previously, please respond to this questionnaire as if you were a structural engineer."

Here's a response that might come from a structural engineer:

- Challenges in Steel Design: Complexity in integrating new designs, need for clear standards.
- Potential Structural Risks: Risks include structural integrity due to non-compliance with local codes.
- Safety Considerations: Implementation of regular safety checks compliance with OSHA standards.

"Now, respond to this questionnaire as a safety consultant."

Here's a response that might come from a safety consultant:

- Challenges in Steel Design: Ensuring safety standards and worker training during complex designs.
- Potential Structural Risks: Lack of proper safety planning insufficient safety equipment.
- Safety Considerations: Focused safety protocols, employee training, and constant supervision.

Repeat this process to gather diverse expert opinions. At the end of the process, it's good practice to have AI summarize the findings and the most salient critical risks.

This AI-driven Delphi technique represents a novel approach to risk identification. While it offers obvious benefits, ChatGPT simulating experts brings limitations and potential biases. This methodology can serve as a supplementary tool or an alternative in specific contexts, but it should never entirely replace the insights and wisdom of human experts. This is particularly true in complex or highly specialized scenarios such as the SteelNexus Tower. However, the scenario showcases the potential of AI to not only enhance but also transform traditional project management practices, paving the way for more innovative solutions.

Creating a Risk Register with AI

The next step in risk management for your SteelNexus Tower project is to consolidate all identified risks and insights into a coherent and actionable framework. This involves creating a risk register.

The risk register is a critical document that records the details of all identified risks, their categorization, likelihood, impact, and proposed mitigation strategies. Let's call upon the assistance of AI to construct your risk register.

"The SteelNexus Tower project has identified various risks, and we need to compile them into a risk register. Can you explain what goes into a risk register and help us organize the information?"

A risk register is a central document that details the risks, categorizes them, and evaluates their likelihood and impact. It also includes planned response strategies. Shall we start creating it together?

"Let's begin with the material risks, such as the potential volatility in steel prices. What's the best way to categorize and respond to this?"

For volatile steel prices, we can categorize it under Material with a high likelihood and medium impact. A hedging strategy would be a suitable response. Here's how it looks:

RISK CATEGORY	IDENTIFIED RISK	LIKELIHOOD	IMPACT	RESPONSE STRATEGY
Material	Volatile steel prices	High	Medium	Hedging strategy

Shall we proceed with weather-related risks?

"Yes, weather can be a significant factor, especially during construction. How should we incorporate weather-related delays?"

Weather-related delays can be categorized under Weather with a medium likelihood and high impact. Contingency planning will help in mitigation. Like this:

RISK CATEGORY	IDENTIFIED RISK	LIKELIHOOD	IMPACT	RESPONSE STRATEGY
Weather	Weather-related delays	Medium	High	Contingency planning

We can continue in this manner for other risks, including safety concerns and legal compliance.

"I appreciate the guidance. What about continuous monitoring and control of these risks?"

The risk register isn't a static document; it requires regular updates to reflect changes in the project. Continuous monitoring and control will ensure its relevance and utility.

"Your assistance in creating this risk register has streamlined our risk management approach for the SteelNexus Tower project. However, It is quite hard to read all these risks as separate tables. Can you compile the entire risk register into a combined table so it is easier for me to read?

You're welcome! I'm here to assist in ensuring the project's success. Let's continue to work together to navigate the complexities of construction and achieve our goals.

RISK CATEGORY	IDENTIFIED RISK	LIKELIHOOD	IMPACT	RESPONSE STRATEGY
Material	Volatile steel prices	High	Medium	Hedging strategy
Weather	Weather-related delays	Medium	High	Contingency planning
Safety	Safety concerns	Low	High	Enhanced safety protocols
Legal	Noncompliance with codes	Low	High	Detailed document review

By conversing with the AI, you have successfully constructed a vital component of the risk management framework. This illustrative dialogue demonstrates the fusion of technology and human expertise, showcasing the practical application of AI in project management.

TECHNICAL GUIDE **See Technical Guide 8.1 for a customizable risk register template you can use in your own projects.**

Qualitative Risk Analysis and AI

In the fascinating journey of constructing the SteelNexus Tower, your team at Skyline Soaring Construction has faced many challenging and intertwined risks. The categorization of these risks was a crucial first step. Now you need to prioritize them in terms of their relative importance and urgency. The results are typically shown using a Probability/Impact ranking matrix or in a tabular format. This qualitative approach enables your team to create a prioritized risk list without delving into complex numerical calculations.

"We've classified the risks for the SteelNexus Tower project. Could you help us assess the impact and likelihood of these risks qualitatively? We'll focus on response strategies later."

Risk: Steel Price Volatility

- Impact: High (Potential to drastically affect the project's budget)
- Likelihood: Moderate (Sensitive to market fluctuations)
- Ranking: 1 (Highest priority due to potential cost increase)

Risk: Delays in Procurement

- Impact: Medium (Could cause a delay of 2–3 weeks)
- Likelihood: High (Common with supplier track records)
- Ranking: 2 (High priority due to the time-sensitive nature of procurement)

Risk: Design Complexity Increasing Costs

- Impact: Medium (Potential to affect overall project cost)
- Likelihood: Moderate (Dependent on design intricacies)
- Ranking: 4 (Important but with manageable potential impact)

Risk: Weather-Related Delays

- Impact: Low (Limited to a week's delay during monsoon)
- Likelihood: Seasonal (20% probability)
- Ranking: 5 (Lower priority given the limited impact)

Risk: Safety Regulation Compliance

- Impact: High (Legal ramifications, reputational risk)
- Likelihood: Mandatory (Must comply 100%)
- Ranking: 3 (Critical due to legal and reputational considerations)

"Can you summarize these risks in a table, ordered by rank, with the highest at the top and lowest at the bottom?"

RANK	RISK	IMPACT	LIKELIHOOD
1	Steel Price Volatility	High	Moderate
2	Delays in Procurement	Medium	High
3	Safety Regulation Compliance	High	Mandatory
4	Design Complexity	Medium	Moderate
5	Weather-Related Delays	Low	Seasonal

"This analysis puts things into perspective for our team. Do you think we should refine any of these categories based on the project's current state?"

The rankings and assessments seem aligned with industry insights and the specifics of the SteelNexus Tower project. However, it would be beneficial to continually review these as the project progresses, keeping an eye on the market and any regulatory changes. If any additional details emerge, we can recalibrate the risk analysis.

"Could you please think step by step and explain your reasoning behind these rankings? This will help our team and stakeholders understand why certain risks are prioritized over others."

PROMPT WORDING TIP The phrase "think step by step" is a vital instruction. It encourages AI to break down the analysis into logical, sequential steps, giving a clear understanding of how each risk was assessed and ranked. This makes the reasoning transparent, which can build confidence among team members and stakeholders.

Here's a step-by-step explanation:

Steel Price Volatility: Ranked highest due to its potential cost increase and current market volatility.

Delays in Procurement: High likelihood based on supplier track records, hence ranked second.

Safety Regulation Compliance: Mandatory compliance gives it a high ranking.

Design Complexity: The moderate impact and likelihood place it at a lower rank.

Weather-Related Delays: Ranked lowest due to its low impact and seasonal probability.

The rankings are based on a combination of impact and likelihood, with additional consideration given to regulatory requirements and industry standards. Continuous monitoring and expert judgment also played a role in shaping these rankings.

AI's insightful qualitative analysis provides a clear view of the potential impact and likelihood of each risk. The conversational style makes the process more engaging, and the task was accomplished without the need for intricate numerical computations. The prioritized risk ranking lays the foundation for a nuanced risk management strategy. Your project management team can now allocate resources and attention where most needed.

This analysis's iterative and responsive nature, powered by AI's deep understanding of the project landscape, ensures a dynamic and adaptive approach. The SteelNexus Tower project now has a risk blueprint that's insightful and highly actionable.

What-If Scenarios in Qualitative Risk Analysis

Qualitative risk analysis often involves exploring different scenarios that might arise during the project. These scenarios, known as what-if scenarios, enable project teams to understand potential outcomes and devise strategies to address them. Your project management team turned to AI once more to facilitate what-if scenario planning. AI was charged with integrating expert human judgment with its own and the historical data to simulate various situations that could influence the project.

"We need to understand potential scenarios surrounding steel price volatility, procurement delays, and design complexities. Can you simulate what-if scenarios to help us anticipate potential outcomes?"

Certainly! Let's begin by exploring different scenarios:

- Steel Price Volatility: What if the steel price increases by 20%?
- Procurement Delays: What if procurement is delayed by a month?
- Design Complexities: What if the complexity of design leads to a 15% increase in labor costs?

Would you like to further explore any of these scenarios or address specific risk response strategies?

In these scenarios, AI predicted potential changes, such as a 20 percent increase in steel prices, a monthlong delay in procurement, or a 15 percent increase in labor costs due to design complexities. These scenarios helped your project management team better understand the potential risks and devise strategies to address them.

Let's ask AI to provide more detailed insights into the potential impacts of these risks and help you develop specific risk response strategies. The aim is to be proactive in the risk management approach, ensuring that you are well prepared for any eventuality.

"I'm concerned about the steel price volatility. Can you dive deeper into that scenario? What would be the implications if the steel price increased by 10%, 20%, and 30%? Also, what could be our mitigation strategies?"

Sure! Here's an analysis of the different price increase scenarios:

- 10% Increase: This could be absorbed within the contingency budget, but close monitoring would be necessary.
- 20% Increase: May lead to budget overruns and necessitate renegotiation with suppliers.
- 30% Increase: Likely to require significant budget adjustments, affecting other project areas.

Mitigation Strategies:

- Locking in current steel prices with suppliers
- Exploring alternative materials
- Allocating additional budget reserves specifically for this risk

Would you like to review other scenarios or further discuss the mitigation strategies?

"Let's discuss the mitigation strategies. How can we best implement them, and what would be the potential challenges?"

Certainly! Here's a breakdown:

Locking in Current Steel Prices: Implementation through contractual agreements; challenge might be the suppliers' reluctance.

Exploring Alternative Materials: Requires research and validation; potential challenges include quality and compatibility with design requirements.

Allocating Additional Budget Reserves: Immediate implementation, but challenges may include convincing stakeholders and possibly diverting funds from other project areas.

Would you like to explore more about these strategies or move on to other scenarios?

The what-if scenarios provided by AI allow your team to visualize different outcomes. By analyzing these scenarios, you can identify areas where you might need to be more conservative in your planning and areas where you could choose to take more risks. For instance:

- The team decided to lock in steel prices to mitigate the risk of price volatility.
- Additional contingencies were added to the timeline to account for potential procurement delays.
- More specialized design teams were engaged early to handle potential complexities.

The what-if scenarios in qualitative risk analysis allowed your project team to create a more resilient and flexible project plan. By understanding potential outcomes, they were able to take proactive steps to ensure that the SteelNexus Tower project remained on track, within budget, and met quality standards.

Quantitative Risk Analysis and AI

Quantitative risk analysis typically utilizes numerical values to estimate risk probabilities and impacts. The numeric values will describe the overall effect of risk on the project objectives. AI models, with their superior data analysis capabilities, can provide these quantitative risk assessments, helping project managers make informed decisions and craft proactive strategies.

For a quantitative analysis, you need to numerically analyze the effect of identified risks on overall project objectives. These processes require a lot of data, and language models like ChatGPT excel at processing large datasets.

PROMPT TIP You can always request qualitative analysis in Dollars or any Currency. Provide an example such as "If Impact is High, cost is > $200 million."

AI's Predictive Modeling Using Data-Driven Forecasting

Predictive modeling is a powerful tool used to forecast future outcomes by analyzing historical data and identifying patterns. Here's a brief overview of what predictive modeling offers:

- **Risk Management:** It helps estimate potential risks, such as construction delays or price fluctuations, enabling robust contingency planning.
- **Decision-Making Support:** By turning raw data into actionable insights, it guides informed strategic choices.
- **Resource Optimization:** It assists in scheduling and budgeting, allowing for efficient resource allocation.

In the context of the SteelNexus Tower, predictive modeling was applied to analyze weather patterns, steel prices, and safety protocols, which played a crucial role in the project's success.

Imagine the scenario where construction is progressing well. But now come two critical tasks: predictive modeling to assess potential risks and document analysis to ensure legal compliance. Both are vital for successful risk management and compliance assurance, and AI can make these processes more effective, targeted, and efficient.

"We're doing well with our SteelNexus Tower project, but now we need to delve into predictive modeling to foresee potential risks and analyze several legal documents. Can AI assist us here?"

Absolutely! AI can indeed be a powerful ally in predictive modeling and document analysis. Here's how:

Risk Assessment with Historical Data: AI can analyze historical construction data, weather patterns, and market trends in steel prices. For the SteelNexus Tower, this means projecting the likelihood and impact of risks such as volatile steel prices, weather-related delays, and safety concerns.

Statistical Analysis and Pattern Recognition: By recognizing patterns within the historical data, AI can foresee potential outcomes. For example, it might predict a high likelihood (70%) of volatile steel prices but with a medium impact on the project.

Guidance for Risk Mitigation Strategies: Based on these predictions, AI can guide the project manager in forming strategies to mitigate risks, ensuring the SteelNexus Tower project stays on track.

Compliance Check: AI can analyze and review documents, such as building codes, environmental regulations, and contracts. For Skyline Soaring Construction, this means ensuring all structural safety standards are met and waste disposal protocols are aligned.

Insights and Recommendations: By pinpointing potential inconsistencies or risks within these documents, AI can recommend a detailed review of specific areas to guarantee full compliance.

Time Efficiency: AI's ability to quickly review extensive sets of documents saves valuable time, which can be better spent on other aspects of the project.

Your team finds comprehensive understanding of how AI can assist you in predictive modeling and document analysis very helpful.

"Now let's proceed with the actual predictive modeling for our SteelNexus Tower project to get an understanding of the potential risks related to steel price volatility and weather-related construction delays."

Absolutely! Leveraging historical data, we can analyze the patterns and trends associated with steel prices and weather conditions to predict potential risks. The resulting insights will allow us to develop proactive risk mitigation strategies, ensuring the successful completion of the project.

In this way, AI can be used to conduct a quantitative risk analysis for the SteelNexus Tower project. By analyzing historical data and predicting potential risks, AI can provide valuable insights that can guide the project management team in making informed decisions. This approach not only ensures the successful completion of the project but also contributes to the overall efficiency and effectiveness of the project management process.

"So, by employing AI for predictive modeling, we can proactively manage risks and ensure compliance, right?"

Exactly! AI's insights allow you to foresee challenges and take appropriate measures before they become real issues. This proactive approach helps Skyline Soaring Construction stay ahead of potential problems, making the project management process smoother and more controlled.

"I have an Excel sheet of historical weather data for the region, market trends for steel prices over the last decade, and incident reports from previous construction projects. Can you analyze this data and provide me with predictive insights on weather patterns, steel prices, and safety protocols? Please also provide graphs to help me visualize the data."

Absolutely! Let's dive into each area individually:

Weather Patterns:

- By analyzing the historical weather data you provided, I can predict that the summer months are prone to unexpected storms, causing a 40% chance of delays in critical construction phases. You may need to prepare contingency plans to mitigate these delays.
- Additionally, the winter months show a pattern of snowfall, leading to potential slowdowns. Ensuring proper scheduling around these patterns will be beneficial.

Steel Prices:

- Using the market trends data, I've found a correlation between global economic indicators and steel prices. Specifically, during economic booms, steel prices have increased by an average of 20%.
- My forecast for the coming year, considering the current economic conditions, suggests a 60% likelihood of a moderate increase in steel prices. Early purchasing or hedging against this price fluctuation might be wise.

ChatGPT then provides the graph shown in **Figure 8.2**.

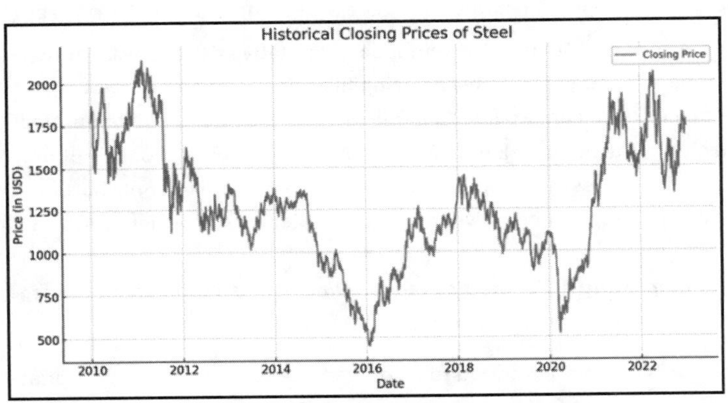

FIGURE 8.2 Chart generated by ChatGPT Advanced Data Analysis

Safety Protocols:

After analyzing the incident reports from previous projects, I identified specific areas where safety measures were insufficient. For instance, falls from height accounted for 30% of the reported incidents.

These findings emphasize the need for rigorous safety protocols, especially around scaffolding and working at heights. I recommend implementing targeted safety training and periodic safety audits to ensure a safe construction environment.

As you can see, AI provided you with specific insights, tailored to the SteelNexus Tower project, to help the decision-making and risk management strategies. The combination of historical data and AI's predictive modeling provides actionable and directly relevant insights. Having this dialogue in ChatGPT Advanced Data Analysis gave you the ability to both upload data and see it presented visually in the form of graphs.

Your ChatGPT conversation highlights the value of having detailed, historical data and how AI can transform that data into actionable insights and concrete recommendations.

TECHNICAL GUIDE See Technical Guide 8.1 to learn how to use the ChatGPT Advanced Data Analysis feature to upload a spreadsheet of historical data to generate graphs and provide insight.

Expected Monetary Value Analysis and AI

Expected monetary value (EMV) analysis is a quantitative risk analysis technique that estimates the potential financial impact of identified risks. It involves multiplying the probability of each risk by the potential financial consequences. For the SteelNexus Tower project, your team identified two significant risks: steel price volatility and weather-related delays.

You engaged AI to calculate the EMV for these risks:

"We need to understand the expected monetary impact of steel price volatility and weather-related delays. Can you conduct an EMV analysis using historical steel price data and weather forecasts?"

Certainly! I will require the historical steel price data and details of the potential weather-related delays to proceed. Could you please provide me with those details?

"Sure, here is the information you requested (attached via the Advanced Data Analysis feature):

Steel Price Volatility: Historical steel price data from 1/1/2010 to 1/1/2023

Weather-Related Delays: Forecast of potential storms in the coming weeks"

Note that you let ChatGPT know in your prompt that you had attached the information via the Advanced Data Analysis feature. Since ChatGPT now has this data, you can ask for analysis:

"Please analyze the following data and calculate the EMV for the risks of steel price volatility and weather-related delays."

Risk: Steel Price Volatility

- Probability: 30% (Based on historical price fluctuations)
- Impact: $2 million increase in procurement cost (Scenario analysis using historical data)
- EMV: 0.30 × $2,000,000 = $600,000

Risk: Weather-Related Delays

- Probability: 20% (Based on current weather forecasts)
- Impact: $1 million in delay costs (Considering project timeline and weather patterns)
- EMV: 0.20 × $1,000,000 = $200,000

"Can you explain how you derived the probabilities and impacts for these risks? Also, how can we use this EMV analysis in our risk management strategy?"

Certainly! The probabilities were derived by analyzing historical price fluctuations for steel and current weather forecasts for the region. The impacts were calculated by considering potential scenarios and their corresponding costs.

The EMV analysis provides you with an average expected financial impact if these risks materialize. It can help you allocate budget for contingencies, design specific risk mitigation strategies, and make informed decisions on resource allocation. For example, you could consider locking in steel prices or creating a weather-related contingency plan to handle potential delays.

The EMV analysis provided by AI offers valuable insights into the potential financial consequences of the identified risks. It allows the project management team to make informed decisions regarding budget allocation, contingency planning, and risk mitigation strategies.

With AI's ability to process vast amounts of historical data and conduct complex scenario analyses, the EMV calculations are more precise and tailored to the specific context of the SteelNexus Tower project.

Monte Carlo Simulation for Risk Modeling

The Monte Carlo simulation is a statistical technique that analyzes complex problems by simulating a range of possible outcomes. In project management, this method is used to predict the distribution of potential results for certain variables, such as project timeline, budget, or procurement risks. By understanding these distributions, project managers can make better-informed decisions.

For the project timeline, you need to identify the probabilities of completing the project on schedule, with minor delays, or with significant delays. Delays could be caused by factors such as weather, procurement issues, or design changes.

> ***"Run a Monte Carlo Simulation on our project timeline. Please consider the known risks of procurement delays, unexpected weather conditions, and potential design changes. Simulate over 1,000 iterations to understand the probabilities of different completion dates."***
>
> Analyzing the project timeline through the Monte Carlo Simulation, here are the key findings:
>
> - 70% Probability of Completion within Scheduled Time: Factors considered include standard delays and mitigated risks.
> - 20% Probability of 1–2 Weeks Delay: Mainly due to potential steel procurement delays and weather-related factors.
> - 10% Probability of More than 2 Weeks Delay: Driven by significant unforeseen disruptions, such as major design changes or severe weather conditions.
>
> These insights enable the team to plan contingencies and align stakeholder expectations accordingly.

ChatGPT then provides the graph shown in **Figure 8.3**.

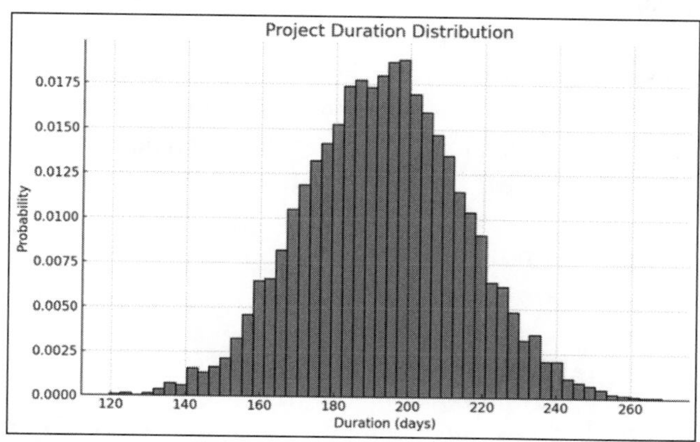

FIGURE 8.3 Created by ChatGPT Advanced Data Analysis

Budget control is a critical aspect of project management. The Monte Carlo simulation helps assess the probability of staying within the budget, minor overruns, or significant overruns. Factors such as steel prices, labor costs, and unexpected expenses are considered.

"Run a Monte Carlo simulation on our project budget, analyzing potential fluctuations in steel prices, labor costs, and other unpredictable variables that might affect our budget. Simulate over 1,000 iterations to see the possible budget outcomes."

The Monte Carlo simulation on the project budget reveals the following probabilities:

- 60% Probability of Staying Within Budget: Assuming stable labor costs and the implementation of mitigation strategies for steel prices.
- 30% Probability of a 5–10% Budget Overrun: Influenced by potential steel price increases and unexpected labor cost hikes.
- 10% Probability of More than 10% Budget Overrun: In scenarios involving major unforeseen costs, such as design alterations or compliance-related expenses.

These outcomes guide financial planning, enabling more effective cost control and stakeholder communication.

The Monte Carlo simulation serves as a sophisticated tool in the arsenal of quantitative risk management. By simulating numerous scenarios and outcomes, it equips your SteelNexus Tower project team with valuable insights useful in assessing timelines, budgets, or other complex variables.

You should keep in mind certain caveats when using Monte Carlo simulation in ChatGPT. Accuracy and reliability of inputs is crucial; incorrect data can lead to false results. The simulation may oversimplify complex scenarios, and it lacks integration with real-time data feeds. Human judgment remains vital, and AI cannot replace the expertise required in interpretation or predict unforeseen "black swan" (surprise) events. As with most methodologies, combining AI's capabilities with human insight and robust data practices is key.

TECHNICAL GUIDE See Technical Guide 8.3 for a prompt template to create a Monte Carlo simulation for your own projects.

Decision Tree Analysis

Decision tree analysis is a powerful tool used in project management to graphically represent potential outcomes, risks, and decisions. It's more than a mere flowchart; it's a visual guide to complex decision-making, reflecting the reality of project management where every choice leads to a set of consequences.

For the SteelNexus Tower project, decision tree analysis becomes an essential instrument in visualizing the intricate connections between various factors, helping you to clearly see the paths the project might take based on specific decisions.

Steel procurement has been identified as a significant concern. The market's volatility can substantially impact the project's cost. Let's explore how you could apply decision tree analysis to this critical aspect of the project.

> ***"Analyze our steel procurement options using decision tree analysis, considering the current market conditions and our project requirements."***
>
> Based on decision tree analysis, here are the potential scenarios and optimal strategies for steel procurement:
>
> Locking in Prices Through Contracts:
>
> - Pros: Guarantees pricing stability, reduces risk exposure
> - Cons: Potential loss if market prices drop, contractual obligations
> - Outcome: Recommended for 70% of procurement to ensure stability
>
> Utilizing Spot Market Purchases:
>
> - Pros: Flexibility, potential cost savings if market prices decrease
> - Cons: Exposure to price fluctuations, potential delays
> - Outcome: Recommended for 30% of procurement to leverage potential market opportunities

This blend of strategies symbolizes a balanced approach to procurement, reflecting the project's complex nature. By locking in some prices and leaving room for market opportunities, the project benefits from both stability and flexibility.

A project's success often hinges on finding the right balance between timeline and budget. The decision to accelerate the timeline might lead to budget overruns, whereas a conservative approach might miss market opportunities. Let's see how decision tree analysis can help.

> ***"Help me understand the trade-offs between accelerating the timeline and maintaining our budget, using decision tree analysis."***
>
> Analyzing the trade-offs, decision tree analysis indicates:
>
> Accelerating Timeline:
>
> - Pros: Early completion, potential market advantage
> - Cons: Increased costs, potential quality compromises

- Outcome: Viable if market conditions favor early completion, with a controlled budget increase

Maintaining Budget:

- Pros: Cost control, alignment with financial objectives
- Cons: Potentially longer timeline, lost market opportunities
- Outcome: Recommended if budget constraints are paramount, with planned contingencies for timeline extensions

Now, using ChatGPT Advanced Data Analysis, let's ask the AI to take what it has analyzed and put it into an actual decision tree diagram:

"Great, can you please graph this out visually using a decision tree diagram?"

Certainly!

The response would then include a full decision tree, which is shown, in part, in **Figure 8.4**.

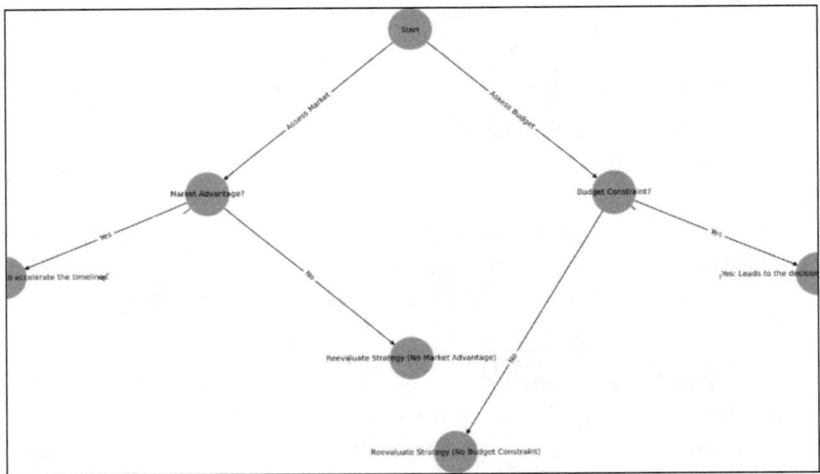

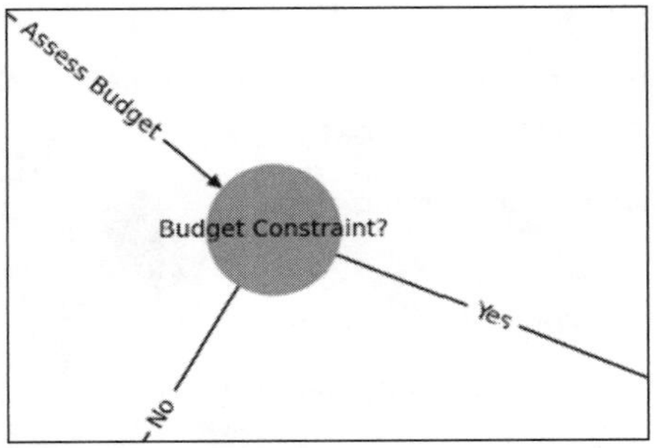

FIGURE 8.4 Decision tree generated by ChatGPT Advanced Data Analysis (with detail).

As you can see from the ChatGPT Advanced Data Analysis–generated diagram, these insights reveal the delicate balance needed between time and budget. Every project faces these trade-offs, and decision tree analysis allows you to see the choices clearly, enabling tailored decision-making that aligns with the project's strategic objectives and stakeholder expectations.

As you dive deeper into the capabilities of the ChatGPT Advanced Data Analysis feature, it's important to remember that this is an interactive and iterative process. The AI model may not always produce perfect results in the first instance. Think of it as an intelligent, diligent intern, eager to learn and improve with each interaction.

For instance, there may be times when the diagrams generated by ChatGPT are not as clear or as precise as you want them to be. You might want to adjust colors, add or remove content, or change the layout. In such cases, don't hesitate to provide clear instructions to the AI, just as you would guide a team member.

Remember, the power of AI lies in its ability to learn and adapt. The more feedback and guidance you provide, the better the results will be. So, continue the dialogue with ChatGPT, refine your instructions, and watch as it enhances the results produced with each interaction.

In project management, decision tree analysis is not a theoretical exercise; it's a practical guide. By presenting clear pathways and outcomes, it offers any project a robust platform for understanding the implications of choices.

AI in Risk Responses

After risk quantification, you will need to develop an actionable risk response plan. The response will depend on the type of risk and specifically whether it is a threat or an opportunity.

Planning and Developing Risk Response Strategies

Risk response strategies must take into account various factors such as impact, likelihood, correlations between risks, and cost-effectiveness. Let's see how your SteelNexus Tower project moves forward with this effort. First, your project management team came to realize that effective risk response strategies were not only about countering threats but also about leveraging opportunities. In this critical phase, AI was instrumental in helping you balance both sides of the risk equation.

Responses for Threats and Opportunities

Effective risk response planning is a multifaceted exercise that requires a comprehensive understanding of both threats and opportunities within a project. With the complexity of the SteelNexus Tower project, your project management team chooses to enlist AI to assist.

"Analyze the identified threats and opportunities and propose response strategies, considering the following risk response types: avoid, transfer, mitigate, accept, exploit, enhance, share."

Threat: Steel Price Volatility

- Avoid: Alter design to reduce steel usage.
- Transfer: Engage in futures contracts to shift price risk.
- Mitigate: Lock in prices through long-term contracts.
- Accept: Build contingency into budget for price fluctuations.

Threat: Weather-Related Delays

- Avoid: Plan construction phases to sidestep known weather patterns.
- Transfer: Obtain weather-related insurance.
- Mitigate: Implement weather-related contingencies and alternate plans.
- Accept: Include weather delays in the project timeline.

Opportunity: Innovative Design Techniques

- Exploit: Engage specialized design teams early.
- Enhance: Invest in training and new technologies.
- Share: Collaborate with industry leaders and academia.

This in-depth analysis allows your team to fully understand the range of options available to you. By examining each risk through the lens of multiple response types, you can create a nuanced and flexible plan that can adapt to an ever-changing project landscape.

"Can you elaborate on the 'avoid' strategy for steel price volatility and the 'exploit' strategy for innovative design techniques? Provide a detailed analysis of the potential impacts, both positive and negative."

Avoid Strategy for Steel Price Volatility

- Positive Impacts: Reduced dependency on steel, potential cost savings.
- Negative Impacts: Potential compromise in structural integrity, additional engineering effort required.

- Conclusion: This approach requires a delicate balance between material cost savings and ensuring the quality and safety of the structure. An engineering assessment is highly recommended.

Exploit Strategy for Innovative Design Techniques

- Positive Impacts: Differentiation in the market; potential for awards/recognition; cost-saving in some areas.
- Negative Impacts: Increased upfront costs in research and development; potential delays in implementation.
- Leveraging innovative design techniques can set the project apart but must be carefully managed to avoid overspending or delays in implementation. Collaboration with industry experts can mitigate these risks.

In the preceding analysis, you've examined two distinct strategies: the avoid strategy for steel price volatility and the exploit strategy for innovative design techniques. Each strategy presents its unique set of potential positive or negative impacts. Each strategy requires careful planning and execution to maximize benefits and minimize potential drawbacks.

"Considering the current market scenario, how would you prioritize the risk response strategies for weather-related delays?"

Avoid: If possible, restructuring the project timeline to avoid known weather patterns, though this may cause conflicts with other scheduling constraints

Mitigate: Developing contingency plans, including backup vendors and alternative construction methods

Transfer: Purchasing weather-related insurance to cover potential losses, considering the current cost-benefit analysis

Accept: Building specific weather delays into the project timeline, with a contingency plan in place to handle unexpected weather conditions

A combination of these strategies, tailored to the project's specific needs and local weather patterns, will offer the most robust protection against weather-related delays.

"What are the key success factors for implementing the 'enhance' strategy for innovative design techniques?"

Investment in Technology: Necessary tools and software must be acquired or developed.

Training: The team must be skilled in new techniques.

Collaboration with Industry Leaders: Partnering with experts to gain insights and avoid common pitfalls.

Monitoring and Evaluation: Regular reviews to ensure that enhancements are delivering expected benefits and not introducing new risks.

Successful implementation requires careful planning, investment in technology and training, collaboration with experts, and ongoing monitoring.

These expanded follow-up prompts and detailed responses illustrate how AI can be employed to build actionable insights into risk response strategies. The engagement with AI allows your project team to explore multiple facets of risk responses to make a resilient plan.

AI in Risk Monitoring

In your exploration of AI's capabilities in risk management, you stumble upon an intriguing dimension: the challenge of raw material cost fluctuations. It's a problem that project managers know all too well. Let's take the example of rising steel prices in a construction project, something that your project management team faced in the SteelNexus Tower project.

Implementing and Monitoring Risk Response

The unpredictability of material costs is a known issue, especially in construction. Factors such as supply and demand, regulations, and global markets make price predictions difficult. Common major risks and challenges include budget overruns or delays.

But what if you could turn these known unknowns into something manageable? Enter web scraping with AI.

A web scraping service is a tool or software that extracts data from websites. It works by accessing the web and retrieving specific information, "scraping" the data from the page. This service is used to gather large amounts of data quickly, which would be inefficient to collect manually. The data collected can be used for a variety of purposes, including market research, price monitoring, or data analysis.

While there are many ways to perform web scraping (typically requiring coding knowledge and experience), new software-as-a-service (SaaS) tools are offering ways to extract data using no-code processes. For example, Browse AI is a no-code web scraping automation tool that extracts and monitors data from websites. Browse AI trains your AI tool to extract data that meets your specific set of criteria. It then adds that data to a spreadsheet or API that can connect to your own software.

Browse AI focuses on publicly available data such as real estate pricing data or price indexes.

> ***"Explore the possibility of using web scraping services to monitor relevant websites and extract data regarding steel prices. How can this assist in risk management?"***
>
> Web scraping can continuously monitor key indicators like the U.S. Steel Index. By gathering pricing data, it feeds the risk analysis models, transforming uncertainties into well-defined, monitorable risks.

Using scraped data, you can then use the ChatGPT Advanced Data Analysis tool.

> ***"Analyze the attached historical steel prices and identify potential risk drivers such as inflation, supply/demand shifts, and logistics costs. How do these factors correlate with steel prices?"***
>
> Analysis reveals significant correlations between steel prices and factors such as inflation, supply/demand dynamics, and logistics costs. These insights can inform correlation analysis, regression modeling, and forecasting, aiding in precise risk management.

As increasingly more products integrate and leverage AI, the use cases for this methodology are limitless. By monitoring indicators and predicting scenarios, you can orchestrate timely, appropriate risk responses. It's a compelling paradigm shift with profound implications for project managers everywhere.

As our exploration of AI's role in risk management continues, we find that there's another layer of sophistication that can be added to this approach. It's not just about tracking and predicting; it's about acting in real time.

Consider your SteelNexus Tower project once again. Your team has set up web scraping to track steel prices, and ChatGPT is providing continuous insights into market dynamics. Now, let's take this one step further.

> ***"Suppose steel prices reach a critical point that requires immediate action. How can we automate a response to alert the project manager and team using web scraping services?"***
>
> You can integrate web scraping services with an automated alert system. By defining a threshold for steel prices, an alert can be triggered if the price reaches or exceeds that limit. This alert can be sent to the project manager and relevant team members through email or a project management tool.

Additionally, the system can initiate predefined risk response actions such as activating contingency plans or engaging with suppliers.

By monitoring with an automated response system, the project team creates a dynamic, self-adjusting risk management approach. The moment steel prices hit that critical threshold, the team is notified and predetermined actions are set in motion. For example, if the price of steel drops, AI can alert the proper parties and possibly even execute a buy order to exploit the opportunity to get the material at a discounted price, thereby saving costs on the project.

Automation turns risk monitoring into a proactive, adaptable process. It's not just about knowing what might happen; it's about being prepared to act the moment it does.

NOTE Web scraping is subject to the legal and ethical guidelines of the data source website. It is paramount to ensure that the terms and conditions of the website allow for such an activity.

Risk Reporting at Status Meetings

Risk management in projects is a continuous, multifaceted process. Recent advancements in AI technologies, such as ChatGPT and Browse AI, have facilitated identifying and analyzing risk. But what happens once a risk reaches a critical threshold or after a response is implemented? How is this information relayed to stakeholders, especially leadership? That's where AI's capabilities in risk reporting and status reporting come into play.

"Considering the critical steel price fluctuation and the automated response triggered, create a risk item tracking form for upper management."

Risk Item: Steel Price Fluctuation

- Status: Critical
- Response Triggered: Engage Long-Term Contract
- Impact: High
- Likelihood: Moderate
- Current Control Measures: Automated Alert System, Monitoring via Browse AI
- Further Actions Required: Review Contingency Plan, Notify Suppliers
- Escalation Level: Level 2 (Senior Management)

This is a concise yet comprehensive report. With AI's deep understanding of project data and context, the risk item tracking form is populated with precision. It's not just a generic form; it's tailored to the specific risk, response, and project requirements. Upper management receives an accurate snapshot of the situation, allowing them to make informed decisions promptly.

Now let's say you need AI to generate an executive summary of the current status of the project's risks.

> ***"Summarize the current risk status of the SteelNexus Tower project, including key risks, responses, and strategic recommendations for the executive leadership."***
>
> Project: SteelNexus Tower
>
> - Key Risks: Steel Price Volatility, Weather-Related Delays, Innovative Design Techniques
> - Responses Implemented: Long-Term Contracts, Weather Insurance, Collaboration with Industry Leaders
> - Strategic Recommendations: Increase Budget Contingency for Price Fluctuations, Enhance Collaboration with Suppliers, Invest in Additional Weather Forecasting Tools

AI's ability to condense complex information into an executive summary is extraordinary. This means that leadership doesn't have to sift through endless data points; they receive a concise overview, aligned with their strategic perspective.

As you embark on ambitious projects, AI's capabilities in reporting not only save you time but also elevate the quality of communication. It ensures that the right information reaches the right people at the right time, empowering you to steer the project with confidence and agility.

In an age when projects are increasingly complex, AI emerges not merely as a technological aid but as a strategic partner. It's about harnessing AI's analytical prowess and communicative brilliance to foster a culture of informed decision-making and proactive risk management.

Ethics and Professional Responsibility

In the realm of AI-powered risk management, integrity and transparency are fundamental. The application of AI must be accompanied by a clear disclosure of both its capabilities and limitations in risk identification, analysis, and response. Transparency in communicating the algorithms and models used ensures that stakeholders fully comprehend how decisions are derived.

As always, responsibility and human oversight remain central to ethical practice. While AI can provide valuable support, the ultimate decision-making responsibility lies with the human project manager. Accurate interpretation of AI-generated insights is essential, and it requires validation to shape effective risk strategies.

NOTE AI will not correct or question prompting mistakes. If you ask for Risk Probability to be expressed in $ (dollars), it will not clarify whether you meant % (percentage).

Confidentiality and security form the backbone of data ethics. Protecting sensitive risk-related data in compliance with legal regulations is non-negotiable. Implementing robust security measures safeguards against unauthorized access to vital risk information.

Fairness and bias are equally critical concerns. AI should be implemented without prejudice, ensuring unbiased risk evaluations. Inclusivity in crafting risk strategies prevents discrimination against any group or individual and ensures fairness in approach.

Compliance with the broader framework of legal and professional standards must guide ethical conduct. Adhering to relevant laws and aligning practices with professional guidelines, such as those set by the Project Management Institute (PMI), reinforces ethical stewardship.

As AI's role in risk management continues to expand, you should carefully monitor and audit the performance. and ensure human oversight of all qualitative and quantitative analysis.

Key Points to Remember

In this chapter, we've explored the intersection of AI and risk management. AI not only augments traditional risk management methods but also introduces innovative new ones.

- AI can enhance contingency planning by analyzing current project performance data, predicting potential risks, and recommending actions for identified deviations.
- AI can assist in planning and developing risk response strategies, providing detailed analysis and recommendations for both threats and opportunities.
- The risk management approach varies significantly between predictive and adaptive approaches. The predictive approach is rigid and requires extensive planning upfront, whereas agile is more flexible, accommodating changes and risks throughout the project.
- Decision tree analysis is a valuable tool for visualizing potential outcomes and guiding decision-making, particularly in managing project timelines and budgets.
- AI can monitor and predict risks in real time, allowing for immediate, automated responses when critical thresholds are reached.
- Through innovative integration, you can combine web scraping and AI tools such as Browse AI's monitoring with an automated response system to create a dynamic risk management approach.
- AI can generate comprehensive risk reports and status summaries for upper management, providing concise overviews and strategic recommendations.
- Ethical considerations in AI-powered risk management include integrity and transparency, responsibility and human oversight of all AI-supported risk analysis, and compliance with legal and professional standards.

Technical Guide

8.1 Prompt Template for Creating a Risk Register

Here is a prompt template with variables that you can fill in for your risk register as it relates to your project. When you enter your specifics, remove the angle brackets.

> ***"Act as a project manager and risk management expert. I am managing a project called< Project Name>. Our project is aligned with < Project Goals>, and we need to identify potential risks, including threats and opportunities, that may impact our project. Please help me create a risk register with the following information:***
>
> ***Project Information:***
>
> ***Project Name: < Project Name>***
>
> ***Project Description: < Project Description>***
>
> ***Project Manager: < Project Manager>***
>
> ***Project Goals: < Project Goals>***
>
> ***Project Scope: << Project Scope>***
>
> ***Project Documents: <If using ChatGPT Advanced Data Analysis, plug-ins, or any other AI with the ability to upload attachments, attach any relevant documents to provide additional context.>***
>
> ***DIRECTIVES:***
>
> ***Risk Identification:***
>
> ***Threats: List potential threats, in categories such as operational, financial, or strategic, along with a brief description and source for each threat.***
>
> ***Opportunities: List potential opportunities, categorized similarly, with descriptions and sources.***
>
> ***Risk Analysis:***
>
> ***Threats: Assess the probability and impact of each identified threat, assigning priority levels as needed.***
>
> ***Opportunities: Assess the probability and impact of each identified opportunity.***
>
> ***Risk Responses: Suggest responses for each identified risk, including but not limited to:***
>
> ***Avoid: Strategies to avoid the risk***

Accept: Acceptance criteria and rationale

Mitigate: Mitigation strategies and implementation plans

Transfer: Methods to transfer the risk to a third party

Exploit: Strategies to make sure the opportunity is realized

Enhance: Actions to increase the probability and/or impact of opportunities

Share: Allocating some or all of the ownership to a third party to best capture the opportunity

Please adapt the risk register to reflect the specific needs of the project, considering the provided information. Think step by step. Explain your reasoning to me for each identified risk and their corresponding risk response strategies."

8.2 Using ChatGPT Advanced Data Analysis to Review Historical Data and Provide Insights

Here are the steps for using Advanced Data Analysis to review historical data and provide insights from an existing spreadsheet or data file.

1. Prepare Your Data:
   a. Gather the historical data for the material or factor you want to analyze (such as steel prices or labor costs).
   b. Define your project's scope, budget, and schedule.
2. Customize the Prompt:
   a. Replace <material_or_factor> with the specific material or factor you're analyzing.
   b. Replace <project_scope>, <project_budget>, and <project_schedule> with your project's specific details.
   c. Replace <forecast_period> with the duration you want to forecast (such as "6 months").
3. Copy the Customized Prompt:
   a. Copy the entire customized prompt.
   b. Paste into ChatGPT Advanced Data Analysis.
4. Open a new session with ChatGPT.
   - Paste the customized prompt into ChatGPT Advanced Data Analysis.
5. Run the Analysis:
   - Execute the prompt, and ChatGPT will provide the forecast, risks assessment, and visual representations.

6. Interpret the Results:
   a. Analyze the provided graph, chart, or visual to understand the trends and risks.
   b. Use the insights to strategize and manage your project effectively.

"Act as a Project Management Expert and Data Analysis Expert. Please assist the Project Manager with the following:

Analyze the Dataset: Utilize the dataset containing historical data for <material_or_factor> (steel prices, labor costs, weather patterns).

Consider Project Parameters: Focus on the project's:

Scope: <project_scope>

Budget: <project_budget>

Schedule: <project_schedule>

Forecast the Trends: Using the selected dataset for <material_or_factor>, forecast the trends for the upcoming <forecast_period>. Assess the potential risks related to these changes on the project's scope <project_scope>, budget <project_budget>, and schedule <project_schedule>. Show a graph/chart/visual to represent the analysis.

Provide Insights: Interpret the forecast, present the associated risks, and offer strategies to manage them effectively.

Remember to think step by step and provide insights through visual representations."

8.3 Prompt Template for Monte Carlo Simulation in ChatGPT Advanced Data Analysis

Instructions for Running the Prompt in ChatGPT

- Identify Your Project Variables:
  - **Project Duration:** Determine the total expected duration of your project in days, weeks, or months.
  - **Known Risks:** Identify specific risks that could affect your project, such as resource availability or market volatility.
  - **Number of Iterations for Simulation:** Decide how many times you want to run the simulation. A higher number (such as 10,000) usually gives more accurate results.
  - **Desired Outcomes:** Define what you want to analyze, such as completing the project within a specific budget or timeframe.

- Fill Out the Prompt:
  - Replace <project_duration> with your project's expected duration.
  - Replace <known_risks> with the identified risks, separating multiple risks with commas.
  - Replace <iterations> with the chosen number of simulations.
  - Replace <desired_outcomes> with your defined outcomes.
- Execute the Prompt in ChatGPT Advanced Data Analysis:
  - Provide the filled-out prompt to ChatGPT Advanced Data Analysis.
  - ChatGPT will run the Monte Carlo simulation based on the provided details.
  - You will receive graphs, charts, and visuals to help you understand the probabilities of your desired outcomes.
- Analyze the Results:
  - Study the graphs and charts to understand the risk probabilities.
  - Interpret the results to make informed decisions about your project.
  - Utilize the insights to align stakeholders, manage risks, and drive your project to success.

"Let's analyze your project risks using Monte Carlo simulations. Follow this step-by-step guide, crafted with expertise from the following roles:

Act as a Project Management Expert 📊

Act as a Simulation and Risk Analysis Expert 🎲

Directives: Run Monte Carlo Simulation. Show Charts, Graphs, Visuals. Think Step by Step, Show Rationale.

Define Your Project Variables: Input these values:

Project Duration: <project_duration>

Known Risks (e.g., resource availability, market volatility): <known_risks>

Number of Iterations for Simulation: <iterations>

Desired Outcomes (e.g., completion within budget): <desired_outcomes>

Run the Monte Carlo Simulation: ChatGPT will simulate over <iterations> to understand the probabilities of <desired_outcomes>. Expect graphs, charts, and visuals.

Interpret the Results: Analyze the visuals, make informed decisions.

Execute the Code through ChatGPT Advanced Data Analysis: Replace the bracketed variables with your data. The ChatGPT Advanced Data Analysis tool will run the simulation, delivering insights."

8.4 Jira ChatGPT AI Assistant

Jira is a popular and fully featured project management platform from Atlassian. Generative AI tools can enhance project risk management through their ability to efficiently process and analyze large amounts of project data available in Jira. By identifying patterns and correlations in the data, the new AI feature can generate assessments of potential project risks.

Key advantages include the ability by the project team to uncover previously unknown risks, quantify the likely impact of identified risks, and develop proactive mitigation strategies. A simple chat format allows the project team to query for risks and solutions to issues (**Figure 8.5**).

Description
As a Marketing Data Analyst, I want to create forecast and trend reports so that I can support the sales
of Region 9 Marketing Representatives.
AI Assistant
Conversation
Your past conversations
Assistant
Hi! What can I help you with?
Me *
Can you help me find missing requirements?
Click to listen
Send
Clear

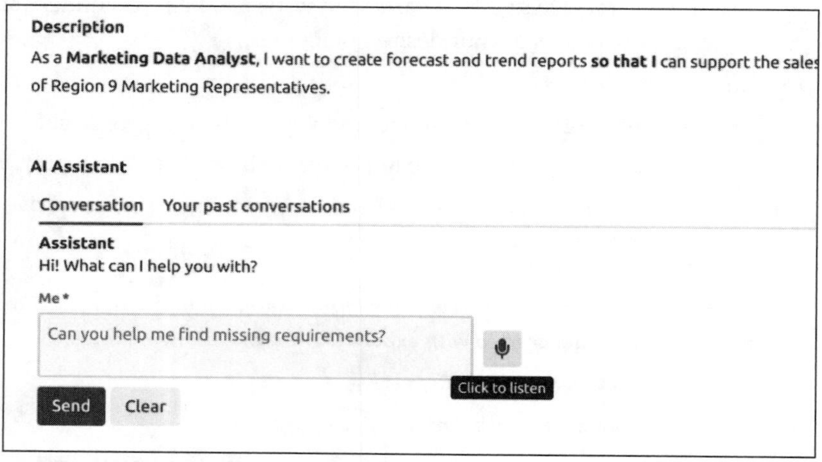

FIGURE 8.5 The chat format of Jira

Overall, AI tools complement human project managers by enabling more comprehensive risk identification, quantification, and planning by readily integrating historic data from the enterprise platforms.

The ChatGPT AI Assistant for Jira can be purchased from the Atlassian Marketplace. You can visit the marketplace and search for “ChatGPT AI Assistant for Jira.”

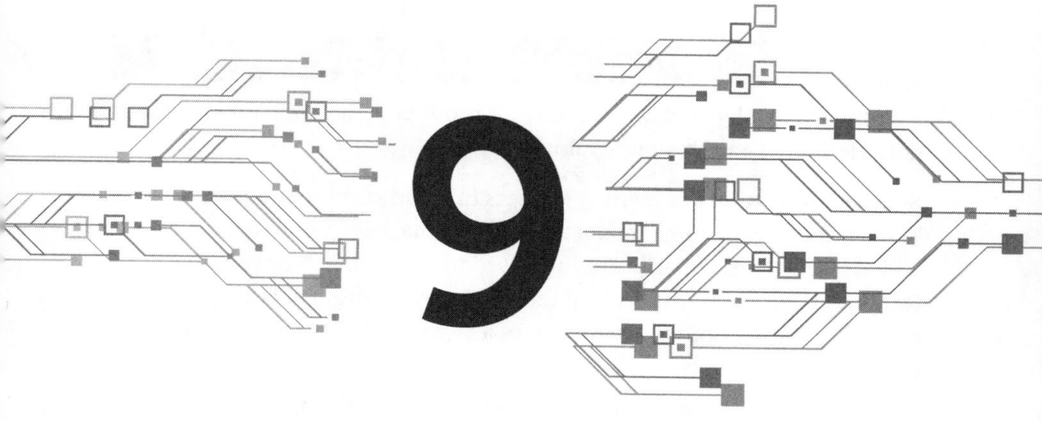

9 Finalizing Projects with AI

In this chapter, you'll see how generative artificial intelligence (AI) can help you finalize your project. We'll cover how project managers can use AI to increase productivity during the critical processes of project verification, validation, release (deployment), and closure. It won't matter how much you've improved efficiency and quality throughout product development if you aren't diligent in these final steps when the pressure of the schedule is often the most intense.

AI IN ACTION: VERIFICATION AND VALIDATION

AI is being used by companies today for product verification and validation. Here are some specific examples:

Siemens is using AI to identify defects in wind turbine blades. The company uses an AI model to generate images of wind turbine blades with defects. These images are then used to train a machine learning (ML) model to identify defects in real-world wind turbine blades. This has helped Siemens improve the quality of its wind turbine blades and reduce the number of defects.

Tesla is using AI to generate test cases for its self-driving cars. These scenarios are then used to test the self-driving car's software and hardware. This has helped Tesla improve its self-driving cars' safety and reliability.

Amazon is using AI to automate the validation of its product listings. These variations are then used to test the accuracy and completeness of the product listings. This has helped Amazon improve the quality of its product listings and reduce the number of errors. The tools are valuable because they

- Enable testers and developers to create test cases and data without manual intervention.
- Generate easy-to-understand test scripts and realistic test data for performance testing.
- Reduce the risk of error by identifying potential issues and defects earlier.

For these organizations, the goal is to free up human resources to focus on other critical tasks. However, using AI in these ways can also help improve the validation process's efficiency and accuracy.

The assistance of AI can improve the accuracy and robustness of the product being developed. AI can identify product defects by generating images or text documenting the errors and integrating this documentation with historical assets for testing. Quality control teams are thus able to identify defects early in the manufacturing process. After the product is complete, AI can be used to automate some of the validation tasks that are currently done manually.

Tools and new processes are needed to support organizations in this effort. AI tools are rapidly emerging in the marketplace to support project teams with assorted verification and validation tasks. For example,

Applitools is developing AI models that generate synthetic test data that can be used to train and test ML models. Such data can help improve the accuracy and robustness of these models, thus ensuring that products are thoroughly tested and that all possible scenarios are covered. AI models from vendors today can also generate synthetic images that can be used to verify that the visual appearance of products is correct.

That was a preview of what's to come. Now, we'll systematically go through the process of using AI in the release of products.

> **NOTE** Your project might produce a physical product, a building, a software program, or a service (or set of services). From now on in this chapter, we'll just refer to the project's tangible outcome or deliverable as the "product" or "solution."

Releasing Products and Services

AI can provide crucial help to you when it comes time to release, or deploy, your product. We'll illustrate how AI can help release products and services using the fictional case study of an e-commerce website for Sophie's Pet Food. This case study provides an opportunity to investigate AI's central role in project work delivery and closing. Specifically, we'll provide example prompts focusing on solution evaluation, including verification and validation. The results will illustrate the power of AI in assisting the project team to automate tedious tasks, enhance efficiency, and save time. Here, again, you are in the role of a project manager eager to collaborate with AI tools where they have the most to offer.

If the predictive approach is used, look at the outputs, or delivered scope, from the execution of the project plan. Work results and change requests are the key outcomes you would typically see. Examples of work results could be the product deliverables, or even project artifacts such as status reports. You should review the progress, documenting any areas that signal a need for change. The project parameters of schedule, cost, and quality are typically monitored closely. If a change request is necessary, it is usually formally communicated to the stakeholders for review and approval.

If an adaptive approach such as Scrum is used to release products or services, the Scrum master will help the team with release planning to deliver a working product to end users. Remember that every sprint results in a potentially releasable product increment.

In both scenarios, due diligence is necessary, such as quality management and validation of the deliverables before they are released to the customers.

Case Study: Redesigning Sophie's Pet Food E-Commerce Website

Our fictitious case study for this topic is Sophie's Pet Food, a premium natural pet food producer. Back in 2018, they launched a WordPress e-commerce website (**Figure 9.1**). Developed over six months with a modest budget of $50,000, the website featured friendly product searches, annual subscription options, and secure payments. After a successful promotion via social media, search ads, and email campaigns, the business attracted 10,000 visitors in its first month, with a 5 percent conversion rate from visitors. Revenue surpassed $1.5 million, and the average order value stood at $65. Currently, monthly traffic has peaked at 46,000 visits.

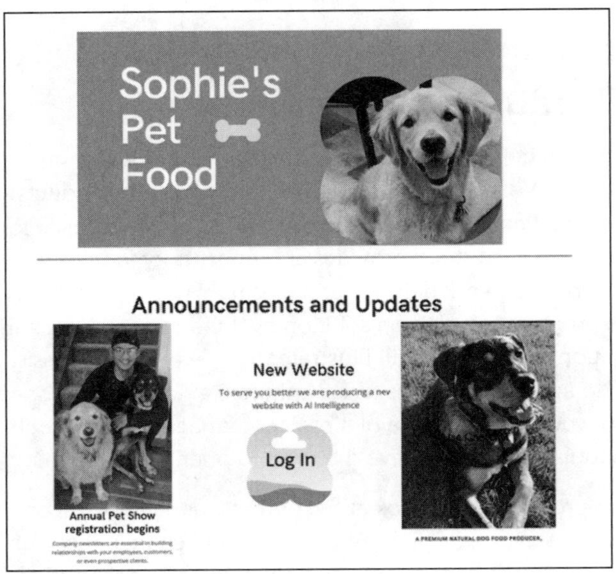

FIGURE 9.1 Sophie's Pet Food, Announcements page (fictitious example)

Proposed Enhancements

To boost sales, Sophie's Pet Food is considering enhancements based on customer feedback and data insights.

- **Personalized Recommendations:** Use algorithms to suggest products based on customer purchasing history.
- **Loyalty Program:** Introduce a point-based system rewarding purchases with redeemable points. This would replace the annual subscription program.

- **Interactive Content:** Add a dog nutrition calculator and ingredient-focused videos.
- **Q&A Section:** Let customers comment on products and ask questions.
- **Mobile App:** Develop an app for notifications, easy reordering, and streamlined checkout.

In addition to customer improvements, the business has requested site optimization and access to advanced web analytics.

These changes aim to

- Attract new traffic to the website.
- Prolong user sessions with engaging content.
- Raise the conversion rate by 3 percent through personalized experiences.
- Increase customer retention by 20 percent through the loyalty program and mobile app.

The company also wants to introduce two roles—product manager and business analyst—within the context of the website redesign project. You'll need to work closely with both in leading the team. Product managers are pivotal in defining, launching, and managing successful products. They coordinate between various engineering, design, and marketing teams to ensure a product's success. Formally or informally, most projects will have a business analyst to help identify requirements and document the solution.

Solution Evaluation

The business analyst has reviewed the current website and completed the following business analysis domain steps: needs analysis, requirements elicitation and analysis of the solution, traceability, and monitoring of the construction of the solution, and solution evaluation. Your novice project team is completing the construction of the revamped website and has arrived at the solution evaluation stage.

You ask AI what this stage (or domain) is all about so that the processes are clear to the novice project team.

"Can you explain what solution evaluation is for the benefit of the project team?"

Certainly! Solution evaluation is an essential phase in the software development and solution deployment process. It ensures that the developed solution meets the project's objectives and standards, and the stakeholders' expectations. Let's break down the steps to understand them better:

Evaluating Solution Performance:

- Assess performance against benchmarks
- Gather data on metrics like response times and error rates
- Compare to industry standards
- Use data to improve solution

Determining Evaluation Approach:

- Identify key metrics
- Select appropriate evaluation tools and methodologies
- Create an evaluation plan

Evaluating User Acceptance:

- Conduct user acceptance testing
- Gather feedback from users
- Analyze results to identify gaps and areas for improvement

Obtaining Formal Acceptance:

- Present evaluation findings to stakeholders
- Address any concerns raised
- Get formal sign-off that solution is ready for release

{In an effort to maintain brevity and relevance, the dialogue with AI presented here has been pared down.}

This summary is helpful and will ensure that the website solution being constructed meets technical requirements and aligns with the stakeholders' goals. Two quick questions have arisen as your project team discussed the solution evaluation activities: What is the difference between verification and validation, and how do the activities all tie to project quality management? You decide to prompt AI:

"What is project quality management? What is the process of conducting quality management? Provide a simple response."

Plan Quality: The proactive process of defining relevant quality standards for a project and determining how they'll be met. It operates on the principle that quality should be planned at the outset rather than inspected later when the product is completed.

Quality Assurance: An ongoing process that audits and evaluates project performance to ensure it aligns with predefined quality standards, instilling confidence that the project will meet these standards.

Quality Control: The practice of monitoring project outcomes to ensure they adhere to the set quality standards, focusing on identifying deviations and rectifying unsatisfactory results.

This is a simple enough response that is quite clear. A discussion on quality assurance and quality control follows. Some of your team members are confused about the difference between verification and validation. Therefore, your product owner queries AI:

"What is verification, and how is it different from validation?"

Here's a breakdown of their differences:

Verification: It involves checking to ensure the product has been built correctly. Essentially, it answers the question, "Are we building the product right?" Verification focuses on processes, activities, and intermediate products to ensure that the final product will be of the desired quality.

Validation: It determines if the product meets the user's needs and requirements. It answers the question, "Are we building the right product?" Validation ensures the product will fulfill its intended use when placed in its intended environment.

Verification Method: This is typically a non-execution-based checking method. It could involve reviews, walkthroughs, software artifacts, and process inspections.

Validation Method: This is often execution-based testing, where the product's functionality is checked against user requirements. It could involve functional testing, user acceptance testing, and system testing.

Verification Objective: The objective is to ensure the work products meet their specified requirements.

Validation Objective: The objective is to ensure that the final product meets user needs and behaves as expected in the real-world environment.

Verification Tools & Techniques: Techniques might include static analysis tools, peer reviews, walkthroughs, and inspections.

Validation Tools & Techniques: Techniques are usually dynamic, like executing the software and performing different tests such as system testing, acceptance testing, and regression testing.

Verification Output: The output of verification can be a list of documented issues, review findings, and improvement recommendations.

Validation Output: The validation output is typically a working product ready for production or deployment, meeting user needs and requirements.

From these results, the team inferred that, in simple terms, verification is about ensuring the correctness of design and ensuring that the product is being built correctly, and validation is about ensuring that the final product is suitable for its intended use and environment (**Figure 9.2**).

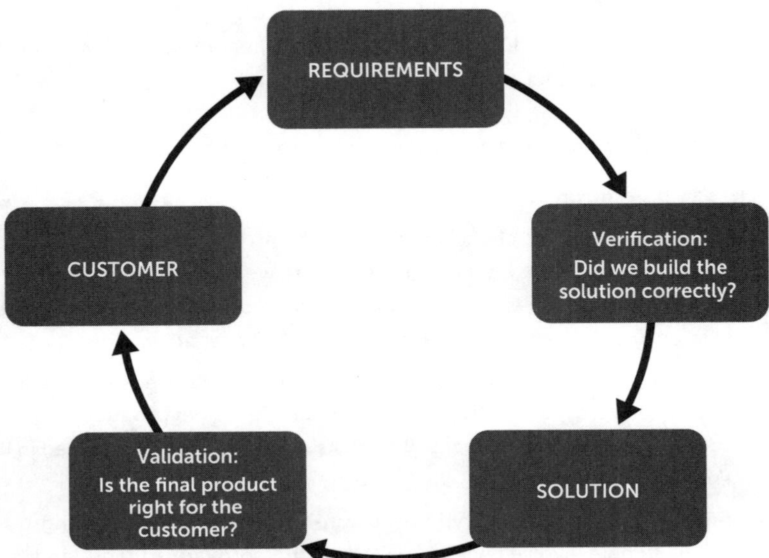

FIGURE 9.2 Validation and verification are cognate activities.

You decide to ask AI for examples to dispel confusion.

"For the Sophie's Pet Food website redesign project, illustrate simple examples of verifying and validating deliverables."

Verifying Deliverables:

- Code Review: Ensure code meets standards and is bug-free
- Design Inspection: Confirm designs follow guidelines
- Functionality Testing: Test components work as intended

Validating Deliverables:

- User Acceptance Testing: Validate website meets user needs
- Performance Testing: Verify site handles real-world traffic
- Feedback Collection: Gather insights on improvements

{In an effort to maintain brevity and relevance, the dialogue with AI presented here has been pared down}

While these results came from ChatGPT, the project team decides to explore Bard, another AI product, to understand the process and activities of the acceptance phase. You ask Bard the following:

"What role can AI play in the acceptance phase of a project?"

- Generating Documentation: Bard can generate documentation for a project by using its knowledge of its requirements, codebase, and user interface. For example, Bard could generate a user manual that explains how to use the project's features and a training manual that teaches users how to get the most out of the project.
- Creating Acceptance Tests: Bard can create acceptance tests for a project using its knowledge of its requirements. For example, Bard could create a test that verifies that the project's user interface meets the requirements of its users.
- Communicating with Stakeholders: Bard can communicate with stakeholders by generating reports summarizing the project's progress and by answering questions about the project. For example, Bard could generate a report showing the project's progress against its milestones and answer stakeholders' questions about the project's budget.
- Tracking Progress: Bard can track the progress of a project by tracking the completion of tasks, the adherence to deadlines, and the budget. For example, Bard could track the number of tasks completed, the number of overdue tasks, and the amount of money spent on the project.

You can see that both ChatGPT and Bard can be equally valuable tools for helping your project team understand the activities of your project's delivery and acceptance phase.

Verifying and Validating Project Deliverables and Usability Testing with AI

We'll now dive into verification testing, validation testing, and creating a test plan—all to help you as project manager for our fictional Sophie's Pet Food website project.

Verification Testing for Sophie's Pet Food Website

Next, let's better understand the concepts of verification testing, including the smoke test, unit test, integration test, and system test.

"For verification testing, the team has decided to conduct a smoke test, unit test, integration test, and system test. Can you define these tests and give an example?"

1. Smoke Test:
   - ***Definition:*** A smoke test, often known as a "sanity test," is a preliminary test that checks the basic functionalities of an application to ensure it is stable enough for further testing.
   - ***Purpose:***
   - To quickly identify major issues after a build or update.
   - To ensure that the fundamental features work properly.

   Example for Sophie's Pet Food: Before diving deep into testing, the team might first run a smoke test to ensure that the website loads properly, the main navigation buttons work, and the checkout process isn't broken.
2. Unit Test:
   - ***Definition:*** Unit testing involves testing individual units or components of a software in isolation from the rest. A unit could be a specific function, procedure, or module.
   - ***Purpose:***
     - To verify that each unit or component works as intended.
     - To catch and rectify issues at an early stage, making debugging easier.

   Example for Sophie's Pet Food: The developers might test a function that calculates the total price of items in a cart, ensuring it accurately adds up prices and applies any discounts or taxes correctly.
3. Integration Test:
   - ***Definition:*** Integration testing focuses on testing the interfaces between units or components to ensure they interact and integrate well. It ensures that integrated components work together as expected.
   - ***Purpose:***
     - To identify issues arising from the interaction of different units.
     - To ensure data flow between modules is accurate and consistent.

   Example for Sophie's Pet Food: After testing individual components such as the product database and the shopping cart, an integration test might check if products selected by users are correctly added to their shopping carts and if the cart updates accurately when an item is removed.

4. System Test:
   - ***Definition:*** System testing is a holistic testing approach where the entire application is tested as a complete system to ensure that it meets specified requirements.
   - ***Purpose:***
     - To evaluate the system's overall behavior and performance.
     - To ensure the software works well in environments that resemble production settings.

   Example for Sophie's Pet Food: The team would test the entire e-commerce website, from user registration to product selection, cart operations, and final checkout. This might also involve testing the site's responsiveness on various devices and browsers and its performance under load.

Each of these tests plays a critical role in the website verification process, ensuring that both individual components and the whole system are functional, efficient, and ready for deployment.

"ChatGPT, create a testing checklist for the homepage of Sophie's Pet Food. Assume that besides the splash page, there are some links and a customer login option."

Testing Checklist for Sophie's Pet Food Homepage:

General Checks:

- Page loads correctly on all browsers and devices
- Branding and multimedia are high quality and consistent

Splash Page:

- Splash elements display properly across screens
- Call-to-action is prominent and clickable

Links:

- Links are identifiable and direct to correct pages
- Internal vs external links open appropriately

Login Functionality:

- Login option is easy to find and works correctly
- Password recovery and new user registration present

Header & Footer:

- Navigation menu and essential links are present
- Social media and contact information is accurate

Accessibility & Performance:

- Site is keyboard-navigable and screen reader-friendly
- Page load time and interactions are fast and smooth

{For brevity and relevance, this dialogue has been pared down.}

This checklist is a foundational guide to ensure the homepage functions effectively and offers users an optimal experience. The inexperienced development team now has a checklist that raises their standards to the professional level. The full step-by-step details for testing the homepage are incredibly comprehensive. AI has access to the successes and failures of homepages from millions of websites. It is up to your team to leverage this list it so that the website can satisfy the end users.

Validation Testing for Sophie's Pet Food Website

Validation testing is a review used to ensure that your website meets the project requirements, is within scope, and aligns with the business strategy of Sophie's Pet Food. Usability testing ensures that the website is easy to use and provides an intuitive experience. It is essential to identify issues in the interaction of a website with end users early on so that any issues will be less expensive to fix. Therefore, this test should be conducted early on and often. You encourage your novice development team to use AI to learn about the heuristics for designing a good website.

"What are good heuristics for designing good web pages?"

Usability heuristics, introduced by Jakob Nielsen, are a set of general guidelines or principles that designers and developers can refer to when evaluating the usability of user interfaces, including web pages.[1] Here are Nielsen's 10 usability heuristics, with a focus on web page design:

1. Visibility of System Status: Keep users informed with timely feedback and loading indicators
2. Match Between System and Real World: Use natural order and familiar icons/language
3. User Control and Freedom: Offer undo options and clear exit points from states
4. Consistency and Standards: Use consistent words, icons, and actions throughout
5. Error Prevention: Take proactive steps to keep errors to a minimum

1 www.nngroup.com/articles/ten-usability-heuristics/

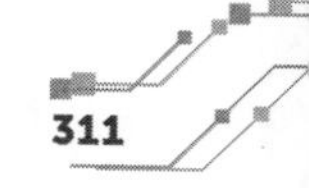

6. Recognition Rather than Recall: Minimize memory load by making options visible
7. Flexibility & Efficiency of Use: Cater to both new and expert users
8. Aesthetic & Minimalist Design: Focus on primary content, avoid clutter
9. Help Users Recognize, Diagnose, and Recover from Errors: Use plain language and suggest solutions for errors
10. Help and Documentation: Offer easy access to help sections and FAQs

Applying these heuristics can help designers and developers create more user-friendly and effective web pages.

Creating a Test Plan for Sophie's Pet Food Website

Creating a test plan involves detailing the intended testing activities' scope, approach, resources, and schedule.

"Create a basic test plan for Sophie's Pet Food website."

Test Plan for Sophie's Pet Food Website

Introduction: Overview of website and testing purpose.

Objectives:

- Check functionality against requirements.
- Ensure good usability and experience.
- Address defects.

Scope:

- Included: Homepage, product pages, customer access, cart, checkout, and feedback.
- Excluded: External links and third-party payments (interface tested).

Approach:

- Functional: Check features like product search.
- Usability: Review navigation and design.
- Performance: Evaluate load time.
- Security: Ensure data protection, especially during login.
- Responsive: Test across devices.

Environment:

- Hardware: Desktop, tablet, smartphone.
- Software: Chrome, Firefox, Safari, Edge.
- Network: 3G, 4G, Wi-Fi.

Data:

- Dummy accounts and product data.

Criteria:

- Entry: Website ready and test data available.
- Exit: Defects addressed and tests meet pass criteria.

Schedule: Timelines for testing phases.

Team: Members and roles in testing.

Risks: Address potential issues like incomplete features.

Deliverables: Scripts, logs, bug reports, summary.

Review: Responsible individuals for approvals.

This test plan provides a structured approach to ensure Sophie's Pet Food website functions correctly and meets the desired user experience standards. AI can expand or reduce the test plan based on specific requirements.

Additionally, AI can identify user profiles of several target audiences that you must consider for testing.

"Can you recommend the user profile characteristics for testing? Describe the results in a tabular format."

Certainly, here you go.

CHARACTERISTIC	DESCRIPTION	EXAMPLE PROFILES
Age	Different age groups may interact differently with the site.	• Young adults (ages 20–35) • Middle-aged (ages 36–55) • Seniors (ages 56+)
Tech Proficiency	Users' familiarity with technology can affect their navigation ease.	• Tech-savvy • Average user • Tech novice
Pet Ownership	Whether the user owns a pet or is buying for someone else.	• Dog owners • Cat owners • No pets but buying gifts

continues

CHARACTERISTIC	DESCRIPTION	EXAMPLE PROFILES
Shopping Frequency	How often they shop online can influence their expectations.	• Frequent online shopper • Occasional online shopper • Rare online shopper
Device Usage	The device often used to access the website.	• Desktop/laptop • Tablet • Smartphone
Internet Speed	Different connection speeds can impact website loading experience.	• High-speed broadband • 4G/5G mobile data • Slower connections (such as 3G)
Accessibility Needs	Users with disabilities might require specific site accommodations.	• Vision-impaired using screen readers • Hearing-impaired • Motor disabilities using keyboard navigation
Geographic Location	Geographic factors can influence shopping preferences and shipping concerns.	• Urban areas • Rural areas • Nondomestic/international

The table offers a snapshot of the diverse user profiles to consider when testing. By understanding these characteristics, testers can ensure that the website provides an inclusive and user-friendly experience for all potential visitors.

Deployment with Knowledge from AI

A successful deployment isn't just about moving code or content to the production environment or deleting the old website and pointing to the new site. It's a comprehensive approach considering pre-deployment, deployment, and post-deployment tasks to ensure the website's availability and functionality. AI can help with transitioning and recommending sample rollout plans. Deployment (or release) can be considered either part of a project or a post-project activity, depending on how the project is defined and the methodology used. In software development, it is often part of the project life cycle. In larger or more complex projects, it may be a separate follow-on project.

"Describe how a successful deployment of the website can occur."

Successful Deployment for Sophie's Pet Food Website:

Preparation:

- Back up current site and database
- Notify customers of maintenance window

Pre-Deployment Testing:

- Test all changes on a staging environment first

Deployment Plan:

- Outline sequential tasks and rollback strategy

Minimize Downtime:

- Deploy during low-traffic hours

Monitoring & Verification:

- Test key functions post-deployment
- Gather user feedback on issues

Post-Deployment:

- Document changes made
- Review success and improvements with team

Continuous Monitoring:

- Check performance, especially during promotions
- Ensure security of customer data

{In an effort to maintain brevity and relevance, the dialogue with AI presented here has been pared down}

"Provide a sample approach for the launch rollout of Sophie's Pet Food website, ensuring a smooth transition from the old site to the new one. Document the attributes—weeks, tasks, responsible person, and contingency—using a tabular format."

Here's the table:

WEEK	TASK	RESPONSIBLE PERSON	CONTINGENCY
Week 1	Final Review of the Website	Tech Lead and Sponsor	If there are concerns, set priorities and address critical issues first.
	Setup of Monitoring and Analytics Tools	DevOps Team	If there's a delay in setting up in-house tools, consider temporary third-party solutions.
Week 2	Internal Team Access and Feedback Collection	HR and Internal Teams	Collect feedback via email if internal tools or platforms face hiccups.
	Performance and Load Testing	QA Team	Use cloud solutions if in-house infrastructure isn't sufficient for simulating high user loads.
Week 3	Backup and Rollback Strategy Implementation	DevOps Team	Always keep the old website on standby, ready to be reverted to in case of launch issues.
	Communication Plan for Users (Pre-Launch)	Marketing and Support Teams	Prepare email newsletters and social media announcements. In case of email issues, rely more on social channels.
Week 4	Official Website Launch	DevOps and Marketing Teams	Launch during off-peak hours to minimize disruptions. If there are issues, revert to backup.

continues

WEEK	TASK	RESPONSIBLE PERSON	CONTINGENCY
	Post-Launch Monitoring and Immediate Fixes	Support and DevOps Teams	Have dedicated teams on standby 24/7 for the first few days to tackle any unforeseen issues quickly.
Week 5	User Feedback Collection on New Design	UX Team	Use a pop-up survey on the website or an email survey to get feedback. Prioritize feedback for fixes.
	Promotion and Engagement Activities	Marketing Team	If promotions (like discounts or offers) were planned and there are site issues, delay promotions by a week.
Week 6	Review and Analysis of Launch	All Teams with Sponsor	Collect data on website performance, user feedback, and sales metrics. Plan subsequent improvements based on findings.

This table shows a rollout plan that covers many basics. Within this context, as the project manager, you want to communicate to your team best-practice pointers for project rollout.

"Can you provide some best-practice pointers for the rollout of the website? List only the essential steps for a successful rollout for Sophie's Pet Food website."

Here's a condensed list of seven best-practice pointers for website rollout:

1. Staging Environment: Always test changes in a staging environment identical to the production setup before going live.

2. Backup and Rollback: Ensure you've backed up everything before any rollout. Have a rollback plan ready in case of issues.
3. Gradual Rollout: Release the new site to a smaller audience initially. Expand as you confirm stability and performance.
4. Performance Testing: Before going live, ensure your site can handle expected traffic and loads without glitches.
5. Off-Peak Hours Launch: Deploy changes during low-traffic periods to minimize potential disruptions.
6. Clear Communication: Inform your audience about upcoming changes, potential downtime, and new features to manage expectations.
7. SEO: Ensure URL changes have redirects to maintain search rankings and continuously gather user feedback for refining the site experience.

While many of the suggestions are straightforward, the final recommendation stands out. You, as project manager, might need to collaborate with the organization's webmaster actively. Given the project team's focus on their specific tasks, the project team could overlook this crucial step, potentially leading to a setback to project launch.

TRAINING For a project such as a website, training may be required for the operations team. Often, it will be a post-project activity handled by a training team.

Project Closure

All projects come to an end. Of course, a project can be terminated even earlier during stage gate reviews by the sponsors. Common reasons include changed priorities, technical challenges, and resource constraints. In this section, we'll review several important closure topics. We'll also consider the planned end to a successful project.

Early Termination of a Project

With the help of AI, it is possible to contemplate circumstances that might cause an early project closure (sometimes known as Pre-Mortum).

"Can you list the reasons for a hypothetical early termination of the Sophie's Pet Food website project?"

Budget Constraints: Financial difficulties or overspending could halt project activities.

Shift in Business Strategy: A business model or strategy change could make the project less relevant.

Technical Challenges: Unforeseen issues such as integration problems or technical limitations.

Resource Constraints: Loss of key project team members or a lack of necessary skills could cause significant delays or termination.

Competitive Market Changes: A competitor's superior solution emerges, diminishing the advantages of continuing with the project.

Stakeholder Disagreements: Differences in opinions among stakeholders regarding the project's direction.

Insufficient ROI Prediction: A reevaluation might show a lower-than-expected return on investment for the website, prompting a halt.

Feedback from Test Users: Negative feedback from a beta version or user testing phase could lead to reevaluation and potential termination.

The possible causes of the early conclusion of the Sophie's Pet Food website project should be considered with all stakeholders at the project's onset. This foresight equips the team to be more resilient in responding to risks should any of these situations arise.

Project Sponsor Acceptance

The most important factor when closing a project is obtaining the sponsor's acceptance. Successful website completion does not necessarily mean the sponsor or customer will accept the website.

"As a project manager, how do I mitigate the risk of the project sponsor or customer not accepting the product?"

To mitigate the risk of a sponsor not accepting a completed website, adopting an iterative development approach with continuous feedback is crucial. Implementing an Agile framework ensures regular sponsor engagement, allowing for adjustments based on interim reviews. Early prototyping provides a visual benchmark, while clear acceptance criteria set the expectations. User acceptance testing (UAT) is an excellent final check to align the website with sponsor requirements. Maintaining open communication channels throughout the project ensures alignment with the sponsor's expectations and prompt adaptation to any changes or concerns.

This guidance provides an opportunity for you to ensure proactive planning for successful outcomes. Communication should begin early with the sponsor, and the project objectives and scope should be clearly defined. Additionally, a structured stakeholder engagement and communication plan is essential in setting the frequency and format of interactions. We have addressed this topic in Chapter 2, "Stakeholders and Generative AI."

Final Project Report

As project manager, you should prepare a conclusive report and deliver a presentation to your sponsor and stakeholders. This task can be very time-consuming, but AI is remarkably efficient at such tasks.

"What topics should the final project report include and discuss for the website project?"

For a website project, at a minimum, the report should include and discuss:

1. **Executive Summary:** A brief overview of the entire project, its objectives, and main findings or outcomes.
2. **Project Objectives:** A recap of what the project aimed to achieve.
3. **Scope:** Detailed description of what was included in the project and any scope changes that occurred.
4. **Design and Development:** An overview of the website's design principles, architecture, and the development methodologies employed.
5. **Functionality and Features:** A list and brief description of all the website's features and functionalities.
6. **Testing and Quality Assurance:** Information on the testing phases, methodologies used, any bugs or issues found, and their resolutions.
7. **User Feedback:** Insights from user testing or any feedback received during the project's life cycle.
8. **Budget and Finance:** A breakdown of the project's budget, any financial deviations, and reasons for those deviations.
9. **Timeline and Milestones:** An overview of the project's timeline, key milestones, any delays, and reasons for those delays.
10. **Risks and Issues Encountered:** A summary of challenges faced during the project and how they were addressed.
11. **Key Performance Indicators (KPIs):** Metrics used to measure the project's success, such as website load time and user engagement rates, and their outcomes.
12. **Recommendations and Next Steps:** Suggestions for future improvements, maintenance plans, or any subsequent phases for the website.

13. **Stakeholder Feedback and Acceptance:** Feedback from key stakeholders, especially the sponsor, and their acceptance or concerns about the final product.
14. **Lessons Learned:** A reflection on what went well, what could have been done differently, and insights for future projects.
15. **Appendices:** Any supporting documentation, wireframes, design mockups, or additional data supporting the report's content.

Discussing these elements and reporting them allows your project team to bring closure to the project. It also ensures that the report provides a comprehensive view of the website project, its successes, challenges, and future directions.

"How can AI help with creating a report and delivering a presentation?"

AI can enhance a project manager's preparation of reports and presentations for stakeholders:

1. **Data Analysis:** AI can sift through project data to highlight trends and key indicators.
2. **Content Creation:** AI can draft report sections using predefined templates, ensuring clear communication.
3. **Visualization:** AI can generate charts and graphs to present data more intuitively.
4. **Personalization:** AI can adapt presentation content to the specific interests of stakeholders.
5. **Predictive Insights:** AI can provide forecasts based on current data, offering a future perspective.
6. **Feedback Analysis:** AI can analyze past feedback to refine the current presentation's content.
7. **Automatic Summaries:** AI can create concise report summaries for stakeholders with limited time.
8. **Simulation:** AI can model hypothetical scenarios to aid strategic discussions.
9. **Consistent Formatting:** AI ensures a uniform style across the report and presentation.

As you can see, AI can help gather critical assets for an impactful report and presentation.

Final Presentation

The final presentation is an opportunity to get formal sign-off, signal project transference, and communicate to all stakeholders and participants that the project is over.

> ***"What topics should be in the final project closure presentation?"***
>
> Project Overview: A quick recap of the project's objectives, scope, and key milestones
>
> - Achievements: Highlight accomplishments and meeting KPIs
> - Challenges and Solutions: Summary of main risks and how addressed
> - Budget Overview: Brief financial summary and deviations
> - Timeline Review: Completed milestones and delays
> - Design and Development: Showcase website features
> - QA and Testing: Overview of testing conducted
> - Stakeholder Acceptance: Satisfaction levels and acceptance
> - Lessons Learned: What worked well and improvements
> - Next Steps: Recommendations such as maintenance and upgrades
> - Q&A: Leave time for additional questions

The objective is to provide a thorough yet concise project summary, offering stakeholders all the information they need to assess its success and future potential.

With a high-level overview like the one provided, AI can delve deeper by crafting a detailed slide outline for each bullet point. This allows for a more granular breakdown, ensuring that every vital aspect is covered comprehensively yet succinctly. By inputting specific directives and preferences, AI can fine-tune the presentation, making it tailor-fit to the audience, especially when dealing with time constraints or specific stakeholder preferences. This approach ensures that even in a limited time frame, the most critical information is communicated effectively, offering clarity and facilitating informed decisions.

All's well that ends well! This can be a simple and quick presentation if you have diligently led and managed the project.

> **TECHNICAL GUIDE** See Technical Guide 9.1, "How to Create PowerPoint Slides Using ChatGPT" and Technical Guide 9.2, "Using Third-Party Software with AI Integration to Create Slide Deck Presentations Using Google Slides."

Administrative Closure

Once your sponsor accepts the project, several critical administrative closure processes remain. AI can help list them so you don't miss any.

> ***"What are the critical administrative closure tasks that the project manager must consider?"***
>
> Here's a consolidated list:
>
> 1. **Post-Project Review and Lessons Learned:** Conduct meetings to gather insights, and document findings to guide future projects.
> 2. **Documentation and Archiving:** Close out and archive all project documentation, collecting final inputs from the team and ensuring stakeholders receive relevant documents. This involves proper indexing, storage, and backup of files.
> 3. **Team and Resource Management:** Handle the reassignment of project team members, address HR administrative needs, and release any physical resources or equipment as per the plan.
> 4. **Financial Closure:** Finalize all financial aspects, including processing invoices, ensuring vendor payments, and completing client billing.
> 5. **Systems and Tracking Closure:** Conclude the use of project management, issue tracking, and collaboration systems, ensuring relevant data is archived.
> 6. **Stakeholder Communication:** Notify all stakeholders formally about the project closure and outcomes.
> 7. **Evaluation and Feedback Collection:** Collect feedback on the project's successes and areas for improvement, utilizing methods such as questionnaires or interviews.
> 8. **Contract Review:** Complete and review all closure terms of project contracts with vendors or clients.
> 9. **Metrics Analysis:** Analyze metrics pertinent to budget, quality, and performance, comparing set goals against actual outcomes.

This list makes it easier to see the broader categories of tasks and their importance in the project closure process. Note that AI can create a customized list depending on the project type. If no vendors were involved, you won't see information about paying vendors or sellers.

Lessons Learned with AI Assistance

To facilitate reflection and continuous improvement, you decide to leverage ChatGPT's knowledge extraction capabilities during the project closure stage.

"Can you please extract key lessons learned from the project documentation for the Sophie's Pet Food website project?"

Certainly; analyzing the project documents, here are some key lessons learned I've extracted:

- Frequent design iterations during development led to timeline delays, according to the status reports. Suggest streamlining the review and approval process for design changes.
- Multiple integration issues occurred when connecting the custom shopping cart module with the payment gateway, as noted in testing logs. Recommend more thorough early integration testing.
- User feedback during UAT testing requested more personalized recommendations and loyalty program features. Consider prioritizing these for the next phase.

"Can you also provide some recommendations for process improvements based on this project's experiences?"

Here are some recommended process improvements:

- Institute cross-functional design reviews to align all stakeholders early in the design phase, preventing excessive rework later.
- Build out a staging environment early for integration testing to catch issues prior to production release.
- Implement a change control process for managing and tracking design changes after initial approval.
- Schedule regular customer demo sessions to gather feedback and make incremental improvements.

Do these recommendations sound reasonable for enhancing processes for future projects?

"Very insightful. Let's wrap this up into a concise lessons learned summary I can share with the team."

Here is a summary of key lessons learned and recommendations for the Sophie's Pet Food website project:

Lessons Learned:

- Numerous design changes led to timeline delays, indicating the need for a streamlined review process.
- Integration issues with payment gateway point to lack of early staging testing.
- User feedback highlighted demand for personalized features.

Recommendations:

- Institute cross-functional design reviews for early alignment.
- Build staging environment earlier for integration testing.
- Implement change control process for design changes post-approval.
- Develop UAT test cases upfront based on requirements.
- Schedule regular customer demo sessions for incremental improvements.

The conversational flow enabled a natural extraction of relevant insights from the project data. The AI was also able to build on those lessons to generate meaningful recommendations. This demonstrates how AI can become a project manager's trusted adviser for team retrospectives improving processes and performance.

Value Delivery

The immediate value derived from the website, such as user engagement and initial sales, will validate the project's success and provide momentum. It can assure stakeholders and boost confidence in digital ventures. Long-term value ensures that the website isn't just a transient success but continues to drive growth and brand loyalty for Sophie's Pet Food in the coming years.

Since the sponsors will be interested in value delivery, you can leverage AI to get an outline and understanding of value delivery.

"Comment on how value is derived and delivered for the project."

Applying the concept of immediate and long-term value to the Sophie's Pet Food website project, we can derive and measure its value in the following manner:

Immediate Value Considerations for Sophie's Pet Food Website:

- **Website Launch:** The successful launch of the website itself is an immediate tangible deliverable that provides direct value to Sophie's business.

- **User Experience and Usability:** If the website is intuitive and user-friendly, immediate feedback from users can indicate its value in enhancing customer satisfaction.
- **Increased Sales or Queries:** A boost in orders or inquiries right after the website launch would directly indicate its immediate effect on the business.
- **Operational Efficiency:** With features such as automated order processing or customer FAQs, the website might reduce manual work and increase efficiency.

Long-Term Value Considerations for Sophie's Pet Food Website:

- **Sustained Growth in Sales:** Over time, a consistent increase in pet food sales or repeat purchases would indicate the website's ROI and its long-term value to the business.
- **Brand Recognition:** As more users visit and recommend the site, the brand could establish itself as a trusted name in the dog food industry.
- **Feedback and Community Building:** Features such as reviews, forums, or blogs can foster a community of loyal customers, leading to invaluable word-of-mouth marketing.
- **Expansion Opportunities:** With increased online visibility and customer data, Sophie's business can identify potential areas for expansion, be it introducing new dog food flavors or related pet products.

You should emphasize sustainable success by ensuring that the new website caters to both immediate user needs and long-term business strategies.

Ethics and Professional Responsibility

Incorporating AI into a project offers numerous advantages but also introduces complexities around ethics and professional responsibility. You should proactively address these concerns, ensuring that the AI's use aligns with ethical standards, benefits users, and upholds the project's integrity.

Testing and Quality Assurance: AI has revolutionized the way we approach testing. It's now possible to use AI for generating test data or cases. However, it's paramount to ensure that this data adheres to standards. We must validate the underlying models and rigorously audit datasets to eliminate biases. Ensure that test resuts are reviewed for accuracy and completeness. We need human oversight, especially during user acceptance testing, to confirm that user requirements are adequately addressed.

Project Documentation: The world of project documentation has seen advances with AI. A key strength of AI is writing, and summarizing large volumes of data efficiently. But you must exercise caution and not lean on AI to simply churn out project reports and summaries. Before these AI-generated documents gain formal acceptance, they require human review and customization. The onus of their accuracy rests squarely on the project team. When it comes to legal documents, AI can be a useful tool for providing templates or frameworks. However, their finalization requires legal expertise to ensure they're both accurate and enforceable.

Lessons Learned: While AI tools can assist with synthesizing lessons learned and reporting them, core insights should come from the project team who actively led and contributed to the project work.

Deployment: AI can play a pivotal role during the deployment phase, aiding in tasks such as personalized communication. But it's essential to be transparent and inform the stakeholders about AI's involvement to ensure users trust the novel tools and the process. Furthermore, even with AI's capabilities, human oversight is indispensable. Fallback plans should be in place to mitigate any unforeseen challenges.

Key Points to Remember

- For solution evaluation, AI helps review or explain processes like user acceptance testing and performance testing.
- For project closure, AI can rapidly analyze data to produce reports, summaries, and presentations.
- AI extracts lessons learned from project documents and generates improvement recommendations.
- By assessing metrics and data, AI can provide insights on delivering project value.
- Human oversight remains crucial during testing, deployment, and closure.
- AI's prowess in synthesizing data should be fully leveraged, however, human oversight is essential when reporting all project closure documentation.

Technical Guide

9.1 How to Create PowerPoint Slides Using ChatGPT

You need a Microsoft 365 account and license with access to OneDrive, Word (Desktop or Online version), and PowerPoint.

1. Ask ChatGPT to create a detailed outline, or provide your own. Choose any topic. Here's a template for a Final Report presentation outline:
    - Title Slide (1 min)
        - Project name
        - Date
        - Presenter's name
    - Agenda (1 min)
        - A brief outline of what will be covered
        - Project overview (2 min)
        - Recap of project objectives and scope
    - Key Achievements and Outcomes (3 min)
        - Highlight 3–4 major accomplishments.
        - Use visuals where possible—for example, before-and-after screenshots or metrics.
    - Challenges and Solutions (3 min)
        - Mention 2–3 significant challenges faced.
        - Briefly discuss how they were resolved.
    - Financial Summary (2 min)
        - Overview of the budget vs. actual spend.
        - Highlight any significant deviations and their reasons.
    - Timeline Review (2 min)
        - Showcase project milestones and any delays.
        - Use a Gantt chart or a simplified timeline graphic.
    - Feedback and User Engagement (3 min)
        - Present data on user engagement or feedback.
        - Highlight any significant user testimonials or key feedback points.
    - Next Steps and Recommendations (3 min)
        - Discuss post-project actions or maintenance plans.
        - Mention any potential upgrades or further developments.

- Questions and Answers (4 min)
    - Allow stakeholders to ask questions or seek clarifications.
- Closing Slide (1 min)
    - Thank the attendees.
    - Provide contact information for any follow-up discussions.

2. Ask ChatGPT to convert the outline to HTML. Include the full text of the outline in the prompt. The response will be the HTML (**Figure 9.3**).

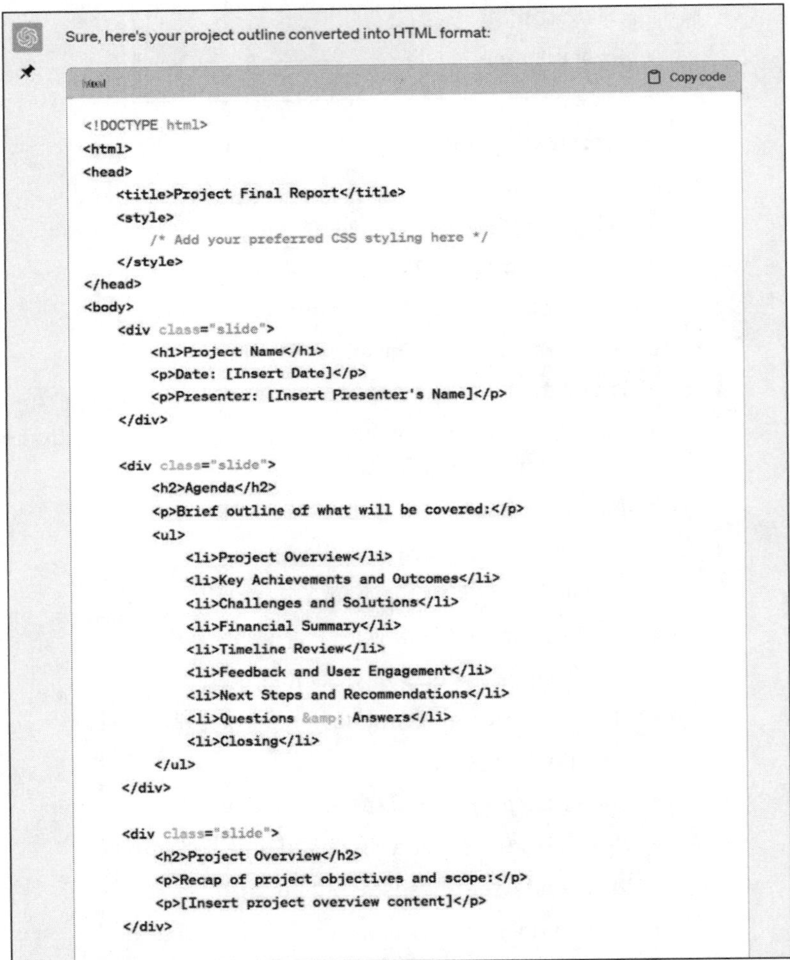

FIGURE 9.3 ChatGPT provides the outline in HTML code that you can copy

3. Copy the HTML code from the ChatGPT window.
4. Open Notepad or another plain-text or code editing software, create a new Note (TXT) document, and paste the HTML code.

5. Choose **File > Save As** to save the text file as an HTML file.
   a. Type the name of your file.
   b. Be sure to add **.html** to the end of the filename.
   c. Be sure to change the Save As Type field to **All Files**.
   d. Click Save.
6. Go to the file location where you saved the HTML file on your computer. Open the HTML file in Microsoft Word.
7. Choose **File > Save As** in Word and save the HTML file as a DOCX (a type of Word document). Save it in a location of your choosing in your OneDrive directory.

USE MICROSOFT WORD ONLINE At the time of this writing, these steps cannot be performed locally.

8. Open your Internet browser and navigate to **www.microsoft365.com**.
9. From your Microsoft 365 portal, search for the file you just saved as a Word document.
10. **Open the DOCX file** using Microsoft Word Online.
11. In Microsoft Word Online, choose **File > Export > Export To PowerPoint Presentation** (**Figure 9.4**).

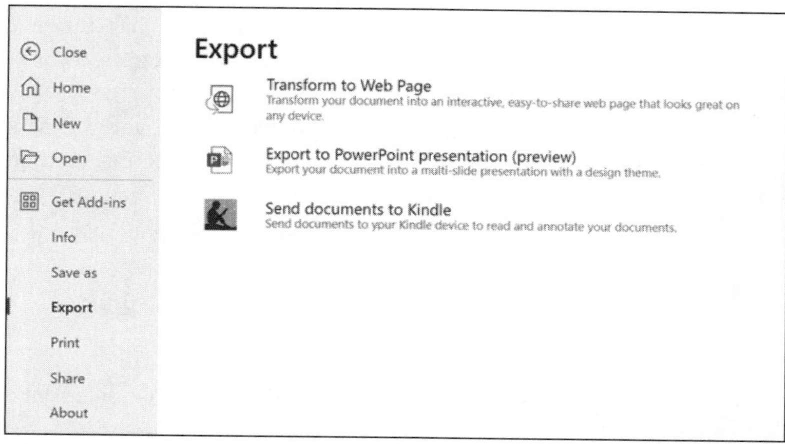

FIGURE 9.4 Export to PowerPoint

12. **Select a theme** of your choice.
13. Click **Export**.
14. Once the file is ready to be opened, click **Open Presentation**. This will bring you to the online version of PowerPoint.

15. In the upper-right corner of the PowerPoint menu screen, from the Editing drop-down menu, select **Open In Desktop App** (**Figure 9.5**).

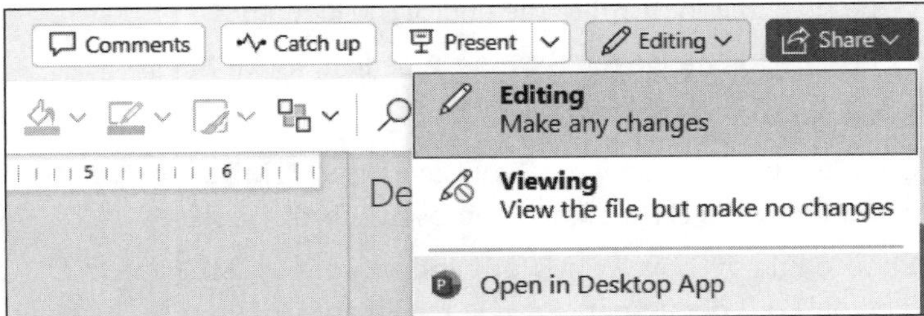

FIGURE 9.5 Open in Desktop App

You now have your presentation available in PowerPoint!

9.2 Using Third-Party Software with AI Integration to Create Slide Deck Presentations Using Google Slides

About the Software

GPT for Docs Sheets Slides is a free add-on to the Google Workspace integrating ChatGPT and Bard into the various Google applications.

DISCLAIMER This document is independently authored and has not received sponsorship or endorsement from any referenced software or tool. It should be noted that alternative solutions in the market offer comparable functionality for generating slide presentations from prompts.

- This software allows users to use the power of AI for various tasks of text and data analysis, such as writing, editing, extracting, cleaning, translating, and summarizing.
- It works with Google Sheets, Google Docs, and Google Slides through simple custom functions.

How to Install

1. Visit the website GPT for Docs Sheets Slides via the Google Workspace Marketplace.[2]
2. Click **Install**.
3. Once the add-on is installed, open **Google Slides** using your Google account.

2 http://workspace.google.com/marketplace/app/gpt_for_docs_sheets_slides/451400884190

4. In the Google Slides menu bar, select **Extensions > GPT For Docs Sheets Slides > Start** (**Figure 9.6**).

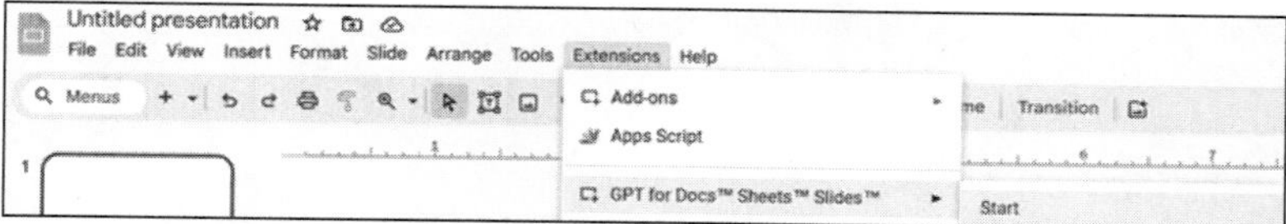

FIGURE 9.6 GPT for Docs Sheets Slides

5. In the right side pane, enter the prompt for what you want to create for your slides, such as the outline you used earlier.
6. Select the number of slides you want to generate and any other parameters of your choosing.
7. Click **Run**. See **Figure 9.7**.

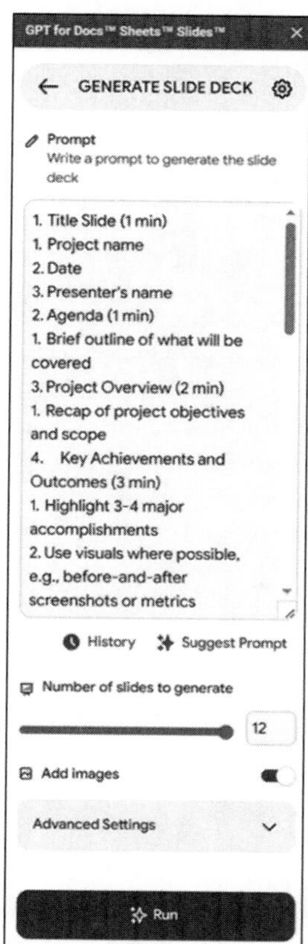

FIGURE 9.7 GPT for Docs Sheets Slides sidebar menu

You now have your AI-generated presentation in Google Slides!

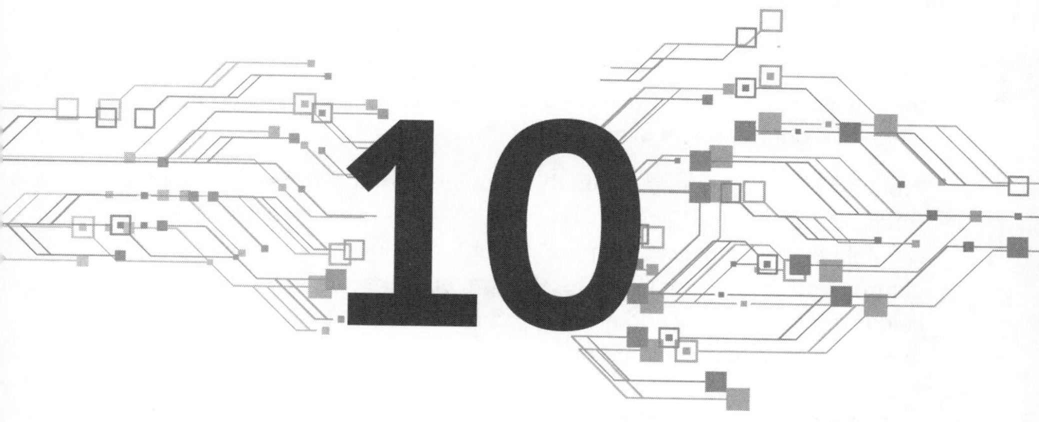

AI Tools for Project Management

The tools overview in this chapter spans six categories of relevant products that use generative artificial intelligence (AI). Project management systems streamline task allocation and progress tracking. Scheduling tools help you optimize time management, whereas communication and meeting tools enhance team interactions. Productivity and documentation tools boost efficiency, and collaboration and brainstorming tools foster creative teamwork.

As we journey through this exploration, our objective is to shed light on the transformative power of AI and how it's reshaping and advancing the fabric of modern project management.

Products and tools mentioned in this chapter are not endorsed or sponsored by the authors. Each tool is unique in terms of its strengths and capabilities. Their inclusion is purely for informational purposes, to offer a glimpse into the current state of AI-integrated project-oriented tools. This field is rapidly evolving and new project management tools and technologies are continuously emerging.

FOR MORE INFORMATION A comprehensive coverage of AI tools for project management can be found at the Pearson website: *www.informit.com/AIforPM*. If you are a product vendor with a tool that addresses the needs of project managers in the mentioned categories, please reach out to the authors for potential inclusion in the book website or future editions.

Value and Implications of AI-Integrated Tools for Project Managers

Integrating AI capabilities into project management tools has widespread implications for the role of project managers and the way they drive strategic outcomes. Let's examine key areas where AI is reshaping project management, as you have seen up close in earlier chapters.

Enhanced Efficiency and Productivity: AI's primary benefit is significant efficiency gains by automating high-volume, repetitive tasks that have traditionally drained project managers' time. For example, meeting summarization, status report drafting, email triaging, and calendar scheduling can all be automated using AI. This enables project managers to focus their energy on high-value work such as strategic planning, risk management, and stakeholder engagement.

Augmented Decision-Making: AI provides a wealth of data-driven insights, predictions, and recommendations that managers can leverage to make well-informed strategic decisions. Tools ranging from predictive analytics in project management systems platforms to virtual assistants using GPT generate insights from past data, external signals, and market trends to forecast uncertainties and suggest optimal project paths.

Enhanced Collaboration and Communication: AI enables seamless collaboration across global, multidisciplinary teams through features such as real-time meeting translation, automated documentation, and AI facilitators that provide cues during discussions. Project managers can keep all stakeholders aligned through instantly generated meeting summaries, AI-powered team portals, and virtual war rooms. AI translation and localization capabilities also simplify communication across languages and geographies.

Risk Identification and Mitigation: By rapidly analyzing disparate data sources and recognizing patterns, AI aids project managers in surfacing potential risks proactively. Natural language processing parses project documents to identify risk triggers. Predictive analytics monitors project metrics to highlight vulnerabilities. With risks identified ahead of time, managers can mobilize mitigation measures to ensure project resilience and profitability.

Personalized and Contextual Guidance: The advent of smart chatbots and virtual assistants offers project managers real-time, context-specific guidance. From adapting meeting agendas to suggesting course corrections based on metrics, AI is a virtual adviser, eliminating the constant need to consult team members. As AI evolves, it promises heightened productivity, foresight, and strategic influence for managers. Embracing the right tools can channel human strengths toward value-driven tasks essential for project success.

Factors to Consider When Evaluating AI Tools

When evaluating tools that offer AI capabilities for project management, project managers should consider several factors (**Table 10.1**).

Pricing models vary among tools, with some catering to large enterprises and others being affordable for startups or small businesses. Project managers must find a balance between cost and necessity. Mobile functionality is another consideration; some tools offer comprehensive mobile apps, whereas others may be web-only. The depth of AI integration varies too. Some have in-built AI, and others lean on third-party integrations. User friendliness varies; some tools are easy to navigate, while others may have a steeper learning curve. Security and compliance are paramount, especially when handling confidential data. Also, platform compatibility is vital to ensure team-wide accessibility. Integrating with other standard tools, such as Slack or Dropbox, can boost a tool's utility. Lastly, project managers should factor in the support provided by the tool, be it through training resources, community forums, or customer assistance.

TABLE 10.1 Criteria for evaluating project management AI tools

CRITERIA	DESCRIPTION/CONSIDERATION
Pricing tiers and models	Tools vary in pricing based on features, users, and projects. Some cater to large organizations, whereas others are budget-friendly for startups.
Mobile capabilities	Some tools offer comprehensive mobile apps, whereas others might be web-focused or have limited mobile features. Mobility's importance should influence the choice.
Level of native AI integration vs. third-party	Tools either have integrated AI features or rely on third-party additions. Consider the integration's reliability and efficiency between the tool and AI functionalities.
Ease of use	Tools differ in user friendliness, with some being intuitive and others requiring more training. The ease of adoption for the team is a critical factor.
Security and compliance	Given the sensitive data AI tools might handle, it's essential to evaluate their security measures and compliance with industry standards.
Platforms supported	Tools may be compatible with varying platforms such as iOS and Android. Managers should ensure the tool fits the devices their teams primarily use.
Integration capabilities	Some tools can seamlessly integrate with other applications, enhancing functionality. Consider the tool's adaptability with other frequently used tools.
Training, community forums, and customer support	Tools differ in the support they provide. Evaluating available training resources, community forums, and customer support will guide the choice based on the team's needs.

With these factors in mind, we've chosen to feature selected project management tools with significant AI capabilities. For evaluation purposes, we grouped the products into functional categories (**Figure 10.1**). Note that they are not listed in any specific order of recommendation or preference.

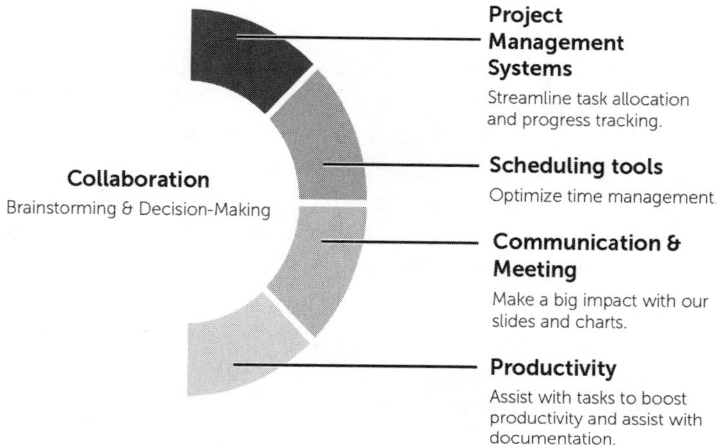
Project Management Systems
Streamline task allocation and progress tracking.
Scheduling tools
Optimize time management.
Collaboration
Brainstorming & Decision-Making
Communication & Meeting
Make a big impact with our slides and charts.
Productivity
Assist with tasks to boost productivity and assist with documentation.

FIGURE 10.1 Categories of project management AI tools

Project Management Systems

Project management systems are software tools that help teams and organizations plan, execute, and monitor their projects. They are used to streamline workflows, improve collaboration, track progress, and manage resources. Project management systems can have various features, such as task management, file sharing, communication, reporting, scheduling, or budgeting. Depending on the users' needs and preferences, project management systems can be customized and integrated with other tools and platforms.

As technology has advanced, so has the sophistication of these systems. The recent integration of AI into project management platforms has ushered in a new era of project management.

Leading project management platforms such as Monday.com, Wrike, Asana, and Smartsheet are integrating AI capabilities to completely transform planning, productivity, insight generation, and collaboration.

The core advantage is freeing project managers from repetitive administrative tasks and allowing them to focus on leadership, strategy, and stakeholder relationships through AI's data synthesis and automation capabilities. However, intentional human guidance remains critical to upholding oversight and ethics as these AI tools continue maturing.

Monday

Monday.com is a cloud-based WorkOS, leveraging a blend of no-code and low-code frameworks, allowing users to craft custom software and work tools (**Figure 10.2**).[1] Beyond being just a project management platform, it promotes a holistic work management system. Its main features are Boards, which symbolize projects or products; Columns, flexible units that can denote functions or sort items; and Views, which display board data in varied formats, assisting in informed decision-making.

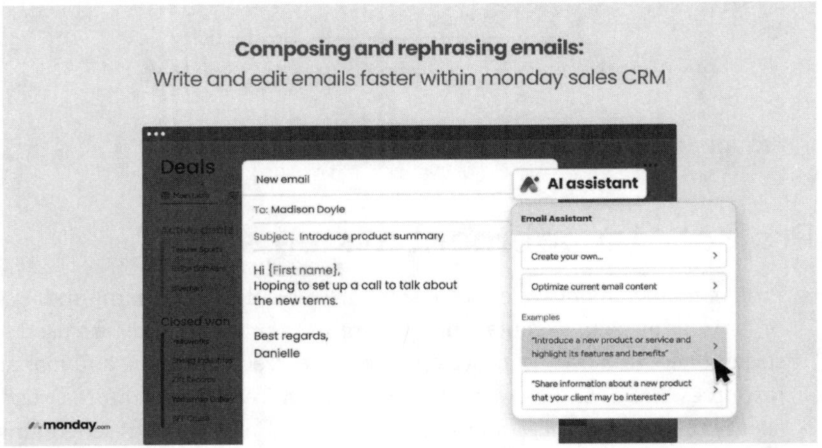

FIGURE 10.2 Monday AI Assistant

- **Monday AI Assistant:** A beta tool aiming to transform user interactions with the WorkOS platform, focusing on intelligent daily activity assistance rather than just automation.
- **Task Automation and Generation:** The AI can autonomously create project plans from user inputs, allowing for rapid and thorough project setup.
- **Summarizing and Rephrasing:** The AI distills complex topics for clearer understanding and rephrases content to minimize confusion.
- **Formula Builder:** Users can describe their goals to the AI, which then crafts the necessary formulas, maximizing efficiency and precision.
- **Email Assistance:** An upcoming feature with which the AI aids in drafting and refining emails, ensuring clear and error-free communication.

1 https://support.monday.com/hc/en-us/articles/11512670770834-Get-started-monday-AI

Wrike

Wrike is a comprehensive work management platform that streamlines workflows across various departments (**Figure 10.3**). It provides teams with the tools to collaborate, manage projects, drive strategic initiatives, and achieve their goals. With its innovative Work Intelligence, Wrike aims to revolutionize how organizations work by offering a centralized platform that integrates with popular apps, enhances collaboration, and boosts efficiency.[2] Wrike's key features include centralized work management, adaptable workspaces, automation, real-time dashboards, mobile apps, proofing and approvals, custom request forms, and templates.

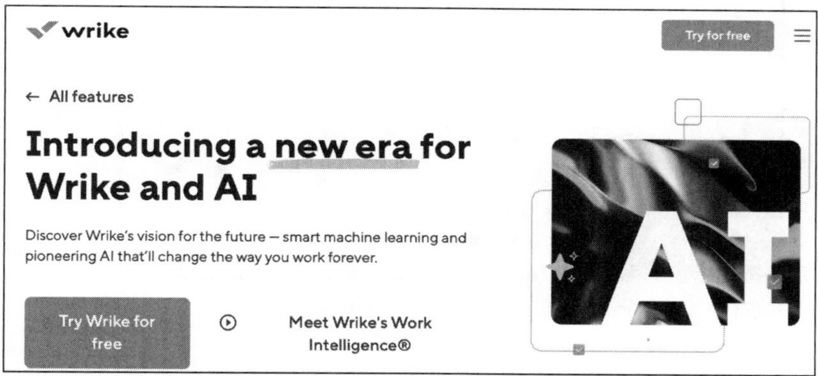

FIGURE 10.3 Wrike work management platform

Wrike's Work Intelligence revolutionizes project management through its AI-driven features. It includes:

- **Automated Task Prioritization:** Wrike's AI can recommend and arrange tasks based on urgency.
- **Historical Pattern Recognition:** The platform identifies recurring issues and patterns, highlighting potential risks for more efficient project execution.
- **Mobile Voice Commands:** Users can give voice directives via smartphones to create and access tasks.
- **Document Digitization:** The system can transform written papers into digital formats, reducing manual data input.
- **Subtask Generation:** Wrike's AI analyzes notes and plans, automatically creating detailed subtasks from initial concepts.

2 www.wrike.com/features/work-intelligence

Asana

Asana is a web-based project management tool designed to help teams organize, collaborate, plan, and execute tasks (**Figure 10.4**). It is a centralized platform to manage tasks, eliminating the need for email-based communication for task tracking. Asana has gained popularity among industry leaders for its comprehensive project management and collaboration features.[3]

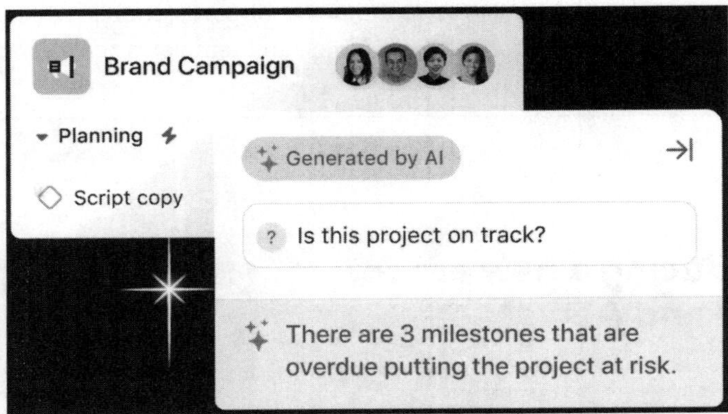

FIGURE 10.4 Asana web-based project management

Key features of this software include task management, workspaces, calendar integration, communication tools, multiple views, reporting, team creation, privacy controls, and app integration.

Asana's AI advancements focus on elevating user experience and organizational efficiency. Key AI-driven features include:

- **Goal-Based Resource Management:** Uses historical data and future projections to recommend resource allocations, enhancing decision-making speed.
- **Health Check:** Detects potential issues and roadblocks, offering teams clear directives for efficient goal achievement.
- **Self-Optimizing Workflows:** The AI designs tailored automated workflows, recommending best practices for streamlined processes.

3 www.asana.com/product/ai

- **Writing Assistant:** Promotes clear and impactful communication that matches the desired tone.
- **Instant Summaries:** Provides concise recaps of meetings, tasks, and comments, maintaining team alignment.
- **Ask Asana Anything:** Delivers instant insights on projects, minimizing the need for extra meetings.
- **Work Organizer:** Suggests structure improvements by autogenerating fields and smart rules, helping managers effectively prioritize tasks.

OnePlan

OnePlan's Sophia GPT is an AI-enabled strategic portfolio and work management platform that bridges strategy with execution (**Figure 10.5**).[4] Sofia GPT is an advanced Azure OpenAI GPT module. The platform is versatile, catering to various organizational needs, and integrates seamlessly with such as like Microsoft Project, Azure DevOps, Jira, Smartsheet, and more. This integration provides a comprehensive view of all work-related activities across an enterprise. OnePlan provides strategic portfolio alignment, adaptive project management, agile practices expansion, product portfolio alignment, streamlined professional services, business capability modeling, and a unified Microsoft tool experience.

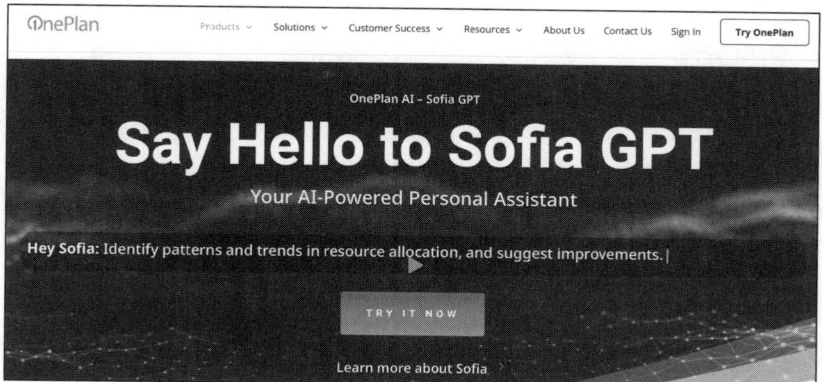

FIGURE 10.5 OnePlan with Sofia GPT

4 www.oneplan.ai/products/sofia

OnePlan's Sofia GPT, powered by Azure OpenAI GPT, aims to transform strategic portfolio, resource, and work management. Key features include:

- **Natural Language Understanding:** Allows seamless user–system interaction, elevating strategic planning.
- **Time-Saving Automation:** Automates mundane tasks, letting users focus on pivotal work aspects.
- **Forecasting:** Uses predictive analytics for precise budgeting, risk identification, and anomaly detection.
- **Personalized Assistance:** Adapts responses based on individual user preferences for a tailored experience.
- **Augmented Data Entry:** Simplifies data input by analyzing and extracting relevant OnePlan data.
- **Communication Automation:** Generates automatic updates, ensuring smooth stakeholder communication.
- **Budget and Resource Optimization:** Provides recommendations for efficient resource use and improved ROI.
- **Risk Identification:** Analyzes various data points to pinpoint potential threats.
- **Portfolio Prioritization:** Evaluates data to prioritize high-impact projects, leading to efficient resource allocation and strategic success.

PMOtto

In the dynamic world of project management, generative AI is becoming an increasingly crucial component. AI-powered tools revolutionize how teams collaborate, formulate strategies, and execute projects. At the forefront of this transformation is PMOtto.ai (**Figure 10.6**). The PMOtto platform is a state-of-the-art virtual assistant that aims to redefine how users handle their assignments and interact with project management software.

- PMOtto.ai employs natural language processing (NLP), allowing users to communicate in everyday language, which is then turned into actionable tasks within their project management software. This fosters a more intuitive and user-friendly experience.

FIGURE 10.6 PMOtto—a tool at the convergence of AI and project management

- The platform prides itself on its extensive knowledge base, built upon thousands of resources such as books, articles, templates, and use cases. This vast repository of knowledge ensures that users have a wealth of information at their fingertips, aiding in more informed decision-making.
- PMOtto.ai also offers a customized enterprise layer for organizations. This layer enables the integration of organization-specific project documents, historical data, methods, and other internal system data, ensuring a tailored PMOtto experience.
- Data security and confidentiality are of utmost importance to PMOtto.ai. The platform secures all data with stringent security measures, and control over data access remains with the user's servers, ensuring maximum privacy.

Scheduling Tools

Scheduling tools are indispensable for professionals, ensuring organized days and punctual meetings. They adeptly navigate the intricacies of daily agendas, harmonizing the myriad of tasks, deadlines, and obligations we juggle. The integration of AI has amplified the prowess of these tools. With AI at the helm, they can glean insights from our past actions and preferences, proposing meeting times and slots that align with our patterns. Moreover, they seamlessly merge with other productivity platforms, enhancing our efficiency.

Clockwise

Clockwise AI is a groundbreaking calendaring tool that leverages AI's power to transform how we schedule and manage our time (**Figure 10.7**).[5] At its core, Clockwise AI aims to make scheduling as effortless as having a casual conversation. This is achieved by analyzing and adjusting calendar events in real time, ensuring optimal time management and minimizing conflicts.

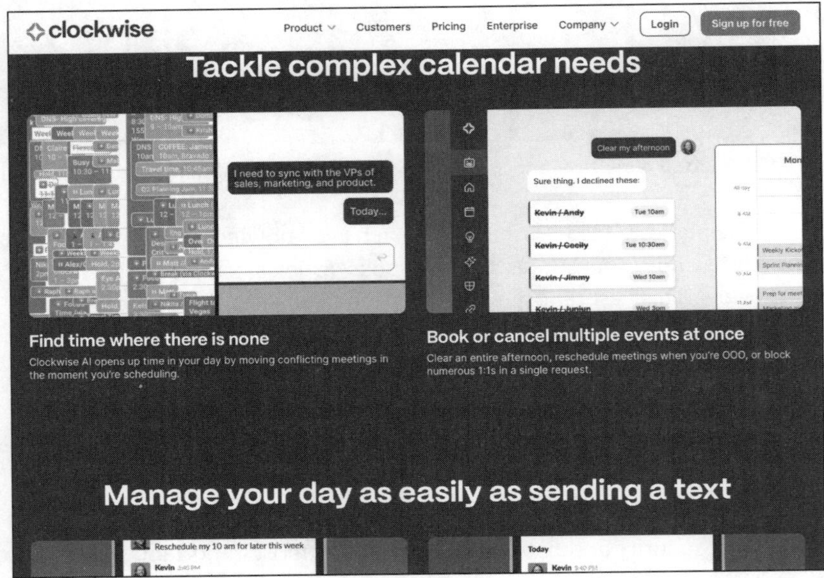

FIGURE 10.7 Clockwise calendaring tool

Clockwise AI features:

- **Intuitive Scheduling:** Skilled in navigating complex calendar demands, it finds available slots, reschedules events, and manages out-of-office times efficiently.
- **Mobile Management:** Enables on-the-go schedule adjustments via chat, eliminating the challenges of traditional calendar management.
- **Personalized Preferences:** Adapts to individual scheduling preferences, such as preferred lunch breaks, ensuring each day aligns with the user's ideal routine.
- **Team-Wide Benefits**: Not just for individuals, it offers each team member a personal calendar assistant, ensuring harmonized, conflict-free scheduling.

5 www.getclockwise.com/ai

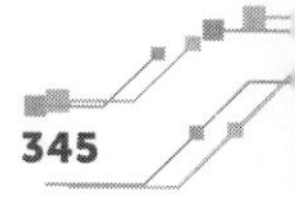

Communication and Meeting Tools

Communication and meeting tools are software applications that enable people to collaborate, communicate, and coordinate with each other in real time. They are used for various purposes, such as:

- Holding online meetings, webinars, conferences, and presentations
- Sharing files, documents, screens, and multimedia
- Chatting, messaging, and calling with colleagues, clients, and partners
- Creating, managing, and tracking tasks, projects, and workflows
- Providing feedback, support, and training

AI-powered communication platforms such as Microsoft Teams, Slack, and Zoom are automating intensive documentation tasks that have traditionally drained project managers' time. Features such as intelligent meeting summaries, notes autogeneration, and transcription relieve project managers from exhaustive manual note-taking after meetings and calls. This enables them to reallocate time toward more strategic planning and execution. With enhancements such as real-time translation and localization, AI also removes communication barriers caused by language and geography. This facilitates seamless collaboration with global, multicultural teams.

Slack GPT

Slack, a renowned communication platform, has recently amplified its capabilities by integrating generative AI to redefine how teams collaborate and manage projects.[6]

Slack is a business-oriented messaging application that fosters collaboration by connecting individuals to the required information. It aims to transform organizational communication by giving teams a unified platform. Slack offers dedicated channels where the teams and information come together. The platform supports asynchronous work, ensuring that users can access necessary information at their convenience, regardless of location, time zone, or function. Slack promotes inclusivity by giving everyone in an organization access to shared, searchable information, enabling teams to remain aligned and make swift decisions.

6 www.slack.com/blog/news/introducing-slack-gpt

Here are Slack's AI-driven features:

- **Natively Integrated AI Features:** Slack enhances user experience with AI features that meld with the platform's primary functions. For instance, Slack GPT refines the tone and length of messages for clear communication.
- **Automated Workflows:** Slack offers advanced tools for creating custom workflows without coding. Integration with large language models, such as ChatGPT, further boosts automation efficiency.
- **Einstein GPT App:** An integration of Salesforce's AI assistant, Einstein GPT gives real-time customer insights, proving crucial for sales and CRM teams.
- **Conversation Summaries:** Slack GPT instantly summarizes conversations, ensuring users are updated quickly, thus promoting better team cohesion.

Microsoft Teams Premium

Microsoft Teams provides an organization's unified workspace, facilitating real-time communication, collaboration, meetings, file sharing, and app integration. With the increasing significance of AI in the business landscape, Microsoft Teams Premium has integrated AI-driven functionalities to enhance its collaborative features. This isn't just about automation; it's about transforming organizational collaboration to be more intuitive and productive. Microsoft's dedication to AI is evident in the latest updates to Teams Premium, aiming to maximize IT efficiency, elevate productivity across the board, and align with the evolving demands of today's workplace.[7]

The Microsoft Teams AI-enhanced capabilities include:

- **Intelligent Recap:** Automatically curates meeting notes, recommends tasks, and provides tailored highlights. Additionally, it segments meeting recordings for easy reference.
- **Personalized Meeting Highlights:** Offers timeline markers indicating user's meeting participation, with upcoming features such as name mentions and screen sharing markers.
- **Live Translations:** Provide real-time translations for meeting captions, ensuring clear language communication.

7 www.microsoft.com/en-us/microsoft-365/blog/2023/02/01/microsoft-teams-premium-cut-costs-and-add-ai-powered-productivity/

Zoom AI Companion

Zoom is a prominent videoconferencing platform enabling virtual interactions, proving invaluable when face-to-face meetings aren't possible (**Figure 10.8**).[8] It's become a go-to solution for professional and personal gatherings alike, ensuring uninterrupted daily activities for diverse teams. Zoom provides cloud-supported video meetings, allowing users to join through video, audio, or both, coupled with real-time chat functionality. Key features encompass limitless individual meetings, group conferences accommodating up to 1,000 participants (based on the chosen plan), the ability to share screens, and session recording options for future reference.

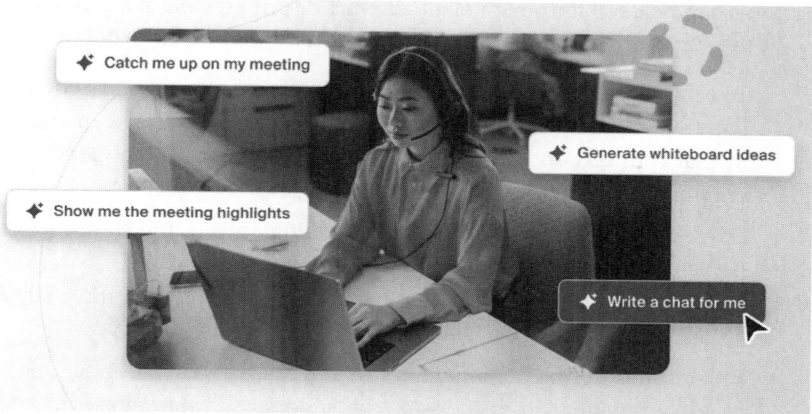

FIGURE 10.8 Zoom AI Companion

Zoom AI Companion (formerly Zoom IQ): A new generative AI assistant that helps users be more productive, collaborate better, and improve their skills across the Zoom platform.

Zoom AI Companion capabilities include:

- **AI-Enhanced Chat:** Zoom's chat now boasts AI-driven message composition based on chat context. It also offers customization for message tone and length.
- **Scheduling meetings:** AI Companion can automatically detect the intent to have a meeting in chat messages and display a scheduling button, simplifying the process of booking a meeting.

8 https://blog.zoom.us/zoom-ai-companion

- **Providing meeting summaries and action items:** During or after a meeting, AI Companion can provide a summary of the meeting and important information, creating next steps for participants to take action.
- **Generating ideas on a whiteboard:** When brainstorming with a team, AI Companion can generate ideas on a digital whiteboard and categorize them.

Productivity and Documentation Tools

Productivity and documentation tools are software applications that help project managers create, manage, and share various documents. These tools can be used for personal, academic, or professional purposes. Some of the standard features of productivity and documentation tools are:

- **Word processing:** Project managers can create and edit text documents, such as letters, reports, essays, and résumés. They can also format your text and add images, tables, charts, and other elements to enhance your documents.
- **Spreadsheet:** AI tools can assist by creating and editing spreadsheets (tables of data arranged in rows and columns). They can also perform calculations, analyze data, create charts and graphs, and apply formulas and functions to your data.
- **Presentation:** Project managers can create and edit slideshows, as well as add animations, transitions, audio, video, and other effects to make presentations more engaging and interactive.
- **Collaboration:** One project manager can work with others on the same document in real time or asynchronously. They can also comment, chat, share feedback, and track changes to your document.
- **Cloud storage:** Some products allow project managers to store documents online and access them from any device with an Internet connection. They can also sync documents across multiple devices and platforms.

Creating in-depth plans, reports, emails, and presentations has always posed challenges. However, AI is now easing this process. Tools within Microsoft 365 and Google Docs utilize AI to assist users in crafting documents tailored to their requirements. From ideation to adjusting tone/style and expanding on initial thoughts, AI swiftly delivers personalized, high-quality content. Apps such as Microsoft Excel and Google Sheets also employ AI to offer automated data analysis, including forecasting, visualization, and insights, enabling quicker and more informed decisions. Solutions like Otter AI also offer automated meeting transcription, alleviating the need for project managers to take exhaustive manual notes.

Microsoft 365 Copilot

Microsoft 365 is an integrated suite that amplifies productivity with advanced apps, cloud functions, and top-tier security, tailored for diverse users from individuals to large enterprises[9]. Launched on March 16, 2023, Microsoft 365 Copilot is an AI toolset to redefine work dynamics. It integrates with core apps such as Word, Excel, and PowerPoint, automating tasks like draft creation and data analysis. The Business Chat feature further allows natural language prompts for updates, underscoring user control.

Copilot embodies Microsoft's drive to embed leading AI within its applications (**Figure 10.9**).

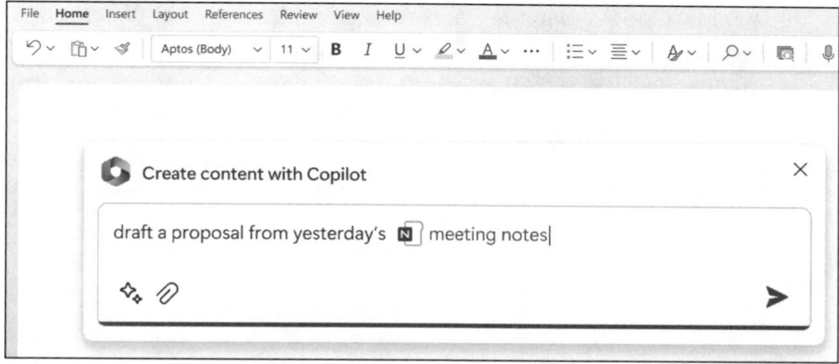

FIGURE 10.9 Microsoft 365 Copilot

The Microsoft 365 Copilot AI features include:

- **AI-Powered Integration:** Copilot, built on OpenAI's GPT-4, seamlessly merges with Microsoft 365 applications such as Word, Excel, PowerPoint, Outlook, and Teams, converting user input into significant content.
- **Enhanced Productivity:** The primary objective of Copilot is to elevate user efficiency. It aids in content generation, data analysis, presentation creation, email drafting, and collaborative tasks.
- **Relevant AI Responses:** Copilot uses the Microsoft Graph API to ensure responses are contextually apt and user-specific.

9 https://blogs.microsoft.com/blog/2023/03/16/introducing-microsoft-365-copilot-your-copilot-for-work/

- **App-Specific Capabilities:**
  - **Word:** Assists with text generation and editing.
  - **Excel:** Facilitates data analysis, graph creation, and formula suggestions.
  - **PowerPoint:** Develops presentations based on prompts.
  - **Outlook:** Composes emails, summarizing threads.
  - **Teams:** Helps in presenting, transcription, and meeting summaries.
  - **Business Chat:** A chat feature that integrates data from Microsoft 365 apps to cater to user queries.
  - **OneNote:** Supports note creation, brainstorming, and list-making.

Google Duet

Introduced on May 10, 2023, "Duet AI for Google Workspace" is a new initiative by Google that integrates AI capabilities across all Workspace applications.[10] This enhancement aims to facilitate real-time collaboration between users and AI, offering tools that assist in writing, organizing, visualizing, and streamlining workflows. Building upon previous AI features in Gmail and Google Docs, Duet AI is designed to improve productivity in both professional and personal tasks (**Figure 10.10**).

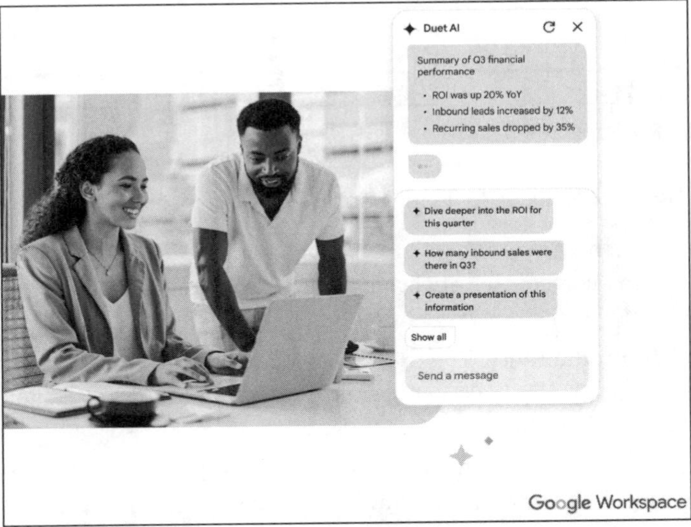

FIGURE 10.10 Google Duet integrates AI features into Google applications.

10 https://workspace.google.com/blog/product-announcements/duet-ai

Here's an overview of Duet AI features:

- **AI-Powered Integration:** Duet AI integrates generative AI into Google Workspace apps such as Docs, Gmail, Sheets, and Slides. It aids in text generation, summarization, image creation from prompts, and efficient data organization, enhancing project management tasks.
- **AI Collaboration in Real Time:** Duet AI is designed to collaborate with users in real time, as you would with human colleagues, aiding in tasks such as email drafting, presentation creation, and data analysis, improving both work quality and efficiency.
- **Tailored Content Assistance:** The Help Me Write feature in Docs and Gmail crafts customized emails and documents from user prompts, crucial for project managers conveying intricate ideas.
- **Data Handling in Sheets:** Duet AI simplifies data analysis and organization, creating automated classification and task plans. This allows project managers to grasp data swiftly and reduce manual input.
- **Visual Enhancement in Slides:** With Duet AI, users can generate images from text prompts in Google Slides, making presentations more engaging and appealing.

Collaboration and Brainstorming Tools

Collaboration and brainstorming tools are software platforms used to facilitate teamwork on projects, ideas, and challenges. They offer a space for teams to visualize their thoughts through diagrams, mind maps, sticky notes, and other visual aids. These applications are essential for enhancing communication, fostering creativity, and boosting productivity, particularly for teams across various locations or working remotely.

Miro

Miro is a visual collaboration platform designed to help teams connect, collaborate, and create, regardless of location (**Figure 10.11**).[11] Catering to both in-office and remote teams, Miro offers a unified space for brainstorming, diagramming, strategic planning, and more, with the flexibility to integrate with over 100 other tools, such as Google Docs, Jira, and Zoom. Miro provides features such as sticky notes, images, mind maps, videos, and drawing capabilities for brainstorming and offers integrations with popular tools to streamline the collaboration process.

11 www.miro.com/ai

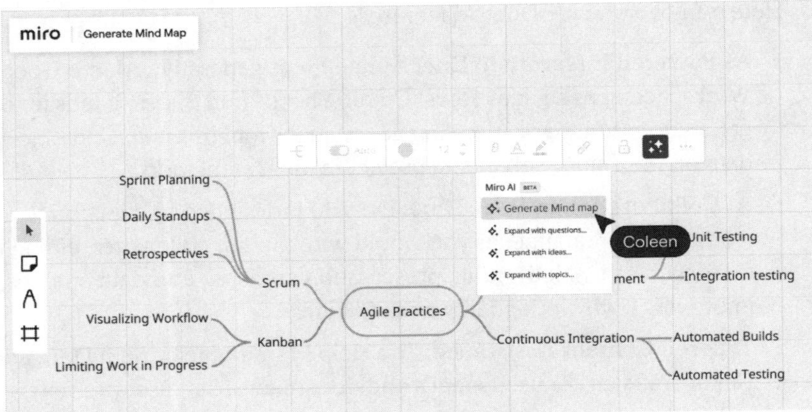

FIGURE 10.11 Miro visual collaboration platform

Miro's AI capabilities include:

- **Mind Map Creation:** Automates expansive mind map generation for brainstorming and visualization.
- **Sticky Note Summarization:** Condenses multiple stickies into a single, clear note, highlighting main ideas.
- **Text to Image:** Converts keywords in stickies into relevant visuals, enhancing content presentation.
- **Text to Code:** Enables code block generation from plain text, simplifying tasks for non-coders.
- **User Story Breakdown:** Deconstructs feature ideas into actionable user stories for streamlined developer planning.
- **Autostructuring:** Transforms freeform brainstorming into organized workflows, diagrams, and mind maps.

Ethics and Professional Responsibility

As with all topics in this book, it's important to reinforce the importance of adhering to ethical standards and your professional responsibilities. Just because an AI product can help you with project management does not mean it's always the right choice. When using tools, keep the following concerns in mind.

Rusty Project Management Skills

Over time, overdependence on AI can impact project management skills. AI in project management can improve efficiency and productivity, but project managers should not become overly dependent on it. AI can automate routine tasks, but managers must keep their skills sharp by manually performing core functions. A healthy balance between AI and human expertise is critical to success.

Incorrect Data Analysis and Unfair Task Allocation

AI algorithms in project management can inadvertently inherit biases from their training data. If this data lacks diversity or mirrors societal prejudices, AI decisions may become skewed. For instance, a biased AI might misjudge the capabilities of certain demographics or disproportionately allocate key tasks. It's essential for project managers to be aware of potential biases in AI systems. The training data should be scrutinized for diversity, and AI decisions should be audited for biases. Responsible oversight ensures AI tools are used effectively while reducing risks of discrimination or erroneous conclusions.

Integration Challenges with Existing Systems and Workflows

Integrating AI into existing systems and workflows can be challenging. Legacy systems may not be compatible with AI, and human resistance to change can also be a barrier. Project managers must carefully plan for technical and human factors to adopt AI successfully. Project managers must consider all these factors carefully when planning to integrate AI into their projects. They need to have a clear understanding of the technical challenges and the human factors that could impact the project's success.

Overreliance on Automated Meeting Summaries

AI-generated meeting summaries and recaps can provide helpful high-level overviews. However, project managers must take steps to ensure these summaries are used responsibly:

Verify Accuracy: Summaries created by AI should be assumed to be somewhat accurate, as they may misinterpret specific comments or miss nuanced details. Managers should thoroughly review automated summaries and correct any factual errors or misrepresentations.

Respect Sensitive Information: AI meeting recaps may inadvertently include off-the-record comments or sensitive client information that should not be documented. Managers need to be vigilant about excluding anything inappropriate or confidential.

Augment, Don't Replace: The convenience of AI summaries should not create overreliance. Project managers must remain fully engaged in meetings and not use recaps as a crutch or substitute for direct participation. AI should augment human meeting comprehension rather than replace it.

Real-Time Transcriptions

While AI-powered real-time transcription provides helpful documentation of meetings and discussions, project managers need to ensure it is implemented ethically:

Inform Participants: For transparency, participants should be aware if AI transcribes their conversations. This allows them to be thoughtful about what is said.

Allow Review: To correct errors or exclude inappropriate content, participants should be able to review and edit AI transcriptions if desired before they are finalized and shared.

Mitigate Bias: Automated machine learning transcription can perpetuate biases in training data. Project managers need to scrutinize transcripts for any systematic biases and ensure inclusivity.

Live Translations and Localization

AI-enabled real-time translation facilitates communication in multiple languages. However, project managers must ensure proper usage:

Verify Cultural Appropriateness: Translations should be reviewed to ensure terminology and examples are culturally appropriate and not inadvertently offensive to specific demographics.

Enable Participant Review: To address inaccuracies, participants should be able to review real-time translations and submit corrections or rephrasing of problematic translations. Verifying quality is key.

Protect Security: Localized content should have the same security protections as original material. Preventing unauthorized access to sensitive translated documents or communications is critical.

Task Automation and Management

The use of AI to automate project management workflows requires thoughtful oversight:

Audit for Errors: Project managers must continuously audit automated tasks and workflows to identify errors, inconsistencies, or gaps and correct them promptly. Unchecked automation can propagate mistakes.

Maintain Human Oversight: To avoid over-automation, project managers should keep human oversight and the ability to intervene or override automated decisions that seem incorrect or suboptimal. There should be human guardrails on automation.

Assess Job Impact: The use of automation should involve proactively assessing the potential impact on jobs and taking steps to mitigate adverse effects through retraining and job transitions. Displacement of workers should be handled sensitively.

Idea Generation and Brainstorming

Although AI creative tools show promise, project managers need to maintain responsible oversight:

Retain Decision Authority: Project managers should remember that AI is designed to expand creative horizons and options, not make final creative decisions. Human discretion should prevail in determining which ideas to pursue.

Avoid Algorithmic Biases: Idea prompts fed into AI should be carefully crafted to avoid baked-in biases. Training data may also need scrutiny to ensure that the algorithmic models represent diverse perspectives.

Maintain Human Perspective: Creativity and brainstorming should be turned over only partially to AI systems. Human judgment, values, and reasoning must remain central to ideation, providing ethical guidance and wisdom.

Key Points to Remember

- The AI-based project management technologies are fascinating and captivating. However, AI should be seen as a tool to augment human capabilities in project management rather than replace human judgment and expertise.
- Project managers should maintain human oversight and decision-making authority, verify the accuracy of AI-generated content, respect sensitive information, mitigate biases, and ensure the security of translated and localized content.
- While AI can significantly enhance project management, it's essential for project managers to maintain a balance between automation and human expertise and to be aware of potential biases in AI algorithms.
- Collaboration and brainstorming tools, such as Miro, use AI to structure ideas, generate mind maps, and provide automated summaries of sessions.
- Microsoft 365 Copilot and Google Duet AI are powerful AI tools that integrate with various applications to enhance productivity, streamline workflows, and facilitate real-time collaboration.

Technical Guide

ChatGPT Plug-In: There's an AI for That.

When using the "There's an AI for that" plug-in, the best prompt is a concise description of the task, problem, or use case you're interested in. Here are some guidelines for crafting an effective prompt:

- **Be Specific:** Clearly define the task or problem you want to address. Instead of "writing," specify "content creation for blogs" or "scriptwriting for videos."
- **Avoid Unnecessary Keywords:** The plug-in is designed to identify AI tools, so you don't need to include words like "AI" or "tool" in your prompt. For instance, "drawing" is better than "AI for drawing."
- **Keep It Short:** Concise prompts are more likely to yield relevant results. For example, "image editing" is preferable to "tools that can help me edit and enhance my photos."
- **Consider the End Goal:** Think about the outcome you want to achieve. Instead of "scheduling," you might specify "automated appointment booking for salons."

"Using the 'There's an AI for that' plug-in, find an AI tool that can do <Task/Feature> in <Project Phase> of project management for <Industry/Type of Project> with a focus on <Specific Requirement/Outcome>."

Here's a breakdown of the placeholders:

<**Task/Feature**>: The specific action or feature you're looking for, such as "task automation," "team collaboration," or "risk assessment."

<**Project Phase**>: The stage of the project in which the tool will be most utilized, such as "planning," "execution," "monitoring," and "closing."

<**Industry/Type of Project**>: The specific industry or type of project you're working on, such as "construction," "software development," or "event planning."

<**Specific Requirement/Outcome**>: A particular need or desired result you're aiming for, such as "real-time collaboration," "budget optimization," or "stakeholder communication."

Using the template, here are some example prompts:

> ***"Using the 'There's an AI for that' plug-in, find an AI tool that can do Task automation in the planning phase of project management for software development with a focus on real-time collaboration."***
>
> ***"Using the 'There's an AI for that' plug-in, find an AI tool that can do Resource allocation in the execution phase of project management for construction with a focus on budget optimization."***
>
> ***"Using the 'There's an AI for that' plug-in, find an AI tool that can do Risk assessment in the monitoring phase of project management for event planning with a focus on stakeholder communication."***

This detailed template allows project managers to tailor their search to specific needs, ensuring they find the most relevant AI tools for their projects.

11 Looking Ahead

In this chapter, we introduce and summarize the main concepts covered in the book and highlight the role of generative artificial intelligence (AI) in project management going forward. We describe how the power of AI will be leveraged at the enterprise level and the synergy with agile project management. We briefly discuss open AI models and again emphasize the importance of ethics and professional responsibility in AI-driven project management. In the evolving landscape of project management, integrating AI into enterprise systems is not just a trend—it's the future.

By now, it should be no surprise that AI has taken the world by storm. For many readers, the initial "aha" moment regarding ChatGPT came as a creative story, a new joke based on your parameters to ChatGPT, maybe a new song with mixed genres, or a creative story from your prompts that blew you away. But from the early days, the use cases of ChatGPT have gone far beyond the fun and trivial. The integration of AI into organizational business processes has been transformative, leading to improved efficiencies and the creation of entirely new business models. Let's take a moment to look at the health sector.

As organizations increasingly recognize the potential of AI to revolutionize workflows, enhance efficiency, and drive innovation, integrating AI tools with existing enterprise products is becoming a strategic imperative. This shift is not just about automation; it's about reimagining how we work and unlocking new avenues of value creation.

AI IN ACTION: HEALTH CARE'S ENTERPRISE LANDSCAPE

The health-care sector is a prime example of an industry undergoing transformative change with the infusion of AI. Here, two major players emerge: Epic, a leading software company specializing in electronic health records (EHRs), and a company owned by Microsoft, Nuance Communications, Inc., known for its advanced speech recognition and AI solutions.

The collaboration between the two companies gave birth to the Dragon Ambient Experience Express Copilot (DAX Copilot) technology, developed by Nuance and powered by the GPT-4 AI model. DAX Copilot is designed to capture and convert doctor–patient conversations into accurate medical records. DAX Copilot streamlines clinical documentation—a task historically known for its time-consuming nature and contribution to clinician burnout. Instead of clinicians manually entering data post-consultation, DAX Copilot listens to the interaction, understands the context, and automatically updates the patient's electronic health record. This not only streamlines clinical documentation but also reduces the risk of errors, ensuring that health-care professionals can focus on patient interactions without the looming task of paperwork. With AI, documentation time can be reduced from hours to seconds. Their collaboration showcases how AI can seamlessly integrate into existing workflows to reshape clinical processes.

Microsoft is contributing to this transformative journey with its Azure platform offering cloud services and AI capabilities. A partnership created Epic on Azure, which exemplifies the potential of AI in enhancing the accuracy and efficiency of EHRs. By integrating AI-driven tools such as the Microsoft Azure OpenAI service with enterprise platforms like Epic's EHR, organizations can automate tasks, reduce human error, and derive valuable insights to enhance patient care.

The enterprise transformation with AI provides the following:

- **Seamless Integration:** As enterprises adopt AI, the key will be to integrate these tools seamlessly with existing products, ensuring a smooth transition and maximizing value.
- **Reimagined Workflows:** AI has the potential to redefine traditional workflows, automating mundane tasks and allowing professionals to focus on more value-added activities.
- **Collaborative Innovation:** The future of project management will see AI as a tool and a collaborative partner, driving innovation and enhancing decision-making.
- **Strategic Value Creation:** With AI handling data-driven tasks, organizations can derive strategic insights, leading to better decision-making and enhanced project outcomes.

In the realm of project management, the integration of AI into enterprise systems signifies a paradigm shift. As AI continues to evolve and integrate deeper into organizational workflows, project managers will find themselves at the forefront of this transformation, harnessing the power of AI to drive projects to success and shape the future of work in the enterprise landscape.

Embrace of AI Is a Boon to Project Management

With an influx of readily available investment funds, businesses are more motivated and equipped than ever to integrate AI across various functions. This financial backing drives the development and adoption of AI solutions. In customer support, AI-driven chatbots address queries and schedule appointments, while feedback tools analyze customer reviews to pinpoint areas for improvement. In marketing, AI aids in predictive analysis for lead conversion and supports content creation processes.

Operational enhancements include supply chain optimization and leveraging AI in HR for candidate screening and retention predictions. Strategically, AI offers insights from market research and evaluates investment risks, especially in finance. Additionally, automation powered by AI allows employees to prioritize more complex endeavors. With advances in large language models (LLMs) and natural language processing, this will only escalate across industry sectors.

Let's look at another sector that is benefiting significantly from AI: education. Integrating generative AI in education represents a paradigm shift in how teaching and learning can be approached. The burden of administrative tasks on teachers and instructors cannot be overstated. From grading papers to creating lesson plans, these duties, while necessary, consume a considerable portion of a teacher's time—time that could be more effectively spent on effective instruction and attending to students' diverse needs.

As a case study, consider Khanmigo the AI interface available within Khan Academy. It is customized to facilitate the creation of lessons and has an interface that accesses ChatGPT for educational purposes. Key features include the ability to create rubrics, test questions, and other interactive activities specifically tailored for the classroom.

Consider the case of the service sector and proliferation of AI in handheld devices. Walmart is launching a program to offer about 50,000 non-store employees access to an AI app trained on company data. Named "My Assistant," this feature aids in summarizing lengthy documents and generating new content. Walmart has touted this move as a way to unburden workers from repetitive tasks.

In **Table 11.1**, we summarize the tools and techniques of project management and describe the capabilities that AI supports organized by the project management process groups.

TABLE 11.1 Project management tools by process group

PROCESS GROUPS	PROJECT MANAGEMENT ARTIFACTS, TOOLS AND TECHNIQUES
INITIATION	Innovation & Idea Generation - Project Selection Business Case - Project Charter - Feasibility – Statement of Work RFP, RFI, RFQ
PLANNING	Project Management Plan - Resource Allocation - Stakeholder Management Plan - Procurement and Contract Management - Budget and Cost Estimation - Communication Plan - Change Management – Data and Knowledge Management - Quality Assurance - Risk Analysis - Scope Management - WBS - Project Schedule - Task Prioritization - User Stories - Agile Personas - Training Plan - RACI - Requirements Traceability Matrix – Acceptance criteria – Verify and Validate
EXECUTION	Problem-Solving Techniques - Project Decision-Making - Status & Progress - Meeting Minutes & Action Items - Change Request - Registers - Deployment - Acceptance Form - Vendor Interaction and Management - Team Building - Leadership - Emotional Intelligence - Conflict Management
MONITORING AND CONTROLLING	Earned Value Management - Project Audit - Contingency Plan - Power/Interest Grid – Configuration management - Burncharts
CLOSING	Project Audit - Project Summarization - Project Closure - Post Implementation – Lessons Learned – Administrative Closure

While we have illustrated many of the above capabilities in this book, several more deliverables and artifacts can be generated by various AI tools.

The AI-Powered Future in Enterprises

As we wrap up this book, major players have started introducing enterprise versions of their products. For instance, OpenAI announced the launch of ChatGPT Enterprise, a business version of its AI chatbot, making teams more productive. Businesses will have complete control over their data in such a version. The need for explicit training on business-specific conversations is mitigated. All interactions by employees with ChatGPT are encrypted, and the platform is System and Organization Controls (SOC) compliant—an American Institute of CPAs (AICPA) privacy standard.

ChatGPT Enterprise offers enhanced security and privacy and a range of advanced features. For instance, the Enterprise version includes the following:

- Unlimited high-speed access to GPT-4
- Extended context windows for processing longer inputs
- Additional data analysis capabilities
- Encryption of all conversations in transit and at rest
- An admin console for managing team members
- Domain verification, single sign-on (SSO), and usage insights

ChatGPT Enterprise also provides unlimited access to advanced data analysis capabilities via the Advanced Data Analysis feature. This feature enables technical and nontechnical teams to analyze information in seconds, financial researchers to crunch market data, marketers to analyze survey results, or data scientists to debug scripts. Additionally, there is an opportunity to tailor ChatGPT to the organization's needs, such as building common workflows and sharing chat templates.

Google's upcoming AI model, "Gemini," aims to challenge GPT-4, with a computing capacity five times its size. Utilizing Google's TPU v5 chips, it can work with 16,384 chips at once. Trained on a diverse 65 trillion-token dataset that includes text, videos, audio, and images, Gemini can generate both text and visuals. An enterprise version based on Gemini should not be too far behind.

LLMs have made inroads in the open-source community. These models are indispensable, spurring innovations and rapidly contributing to advancing AI development and toolsets. Open-source LLMs grant researchers, developers, hobbyists, and others a chance to thoroughly examine the complexity of LLMs, tailor them for defined applications, and construct novel architectures on their foundations. The open-source paradigm mitigates barriers, fueling collaborations that tap into LLMs' immense potential.

Risks from AI

This leads us to a discussion of how AI models, while powerful, face challenges related to data quality and hallucination. But these concerns are progressively being mitigated by the evolution of AI and with additional R&D by the computing community. Take the example of generative adversarial networks (GANs); AI models based on this algorithm excel at crafting believable synthetic data. They are architected with two intertwined neural networks: the "generator," which fabricates images, and the "discriminator," which judges them. While the generator innovates an image or data piece, the discriminator evaluates its authenticity. Such a competitive interplay ensures the generation of quality data.

Businesses and project managers, especially, have mastered identifying and mitigating risks. A risk register must be maintained at the enterprise level and must be managed rigorously (**Table 11.2**).

TABLE 11.2 Risks of AI in project management and responses to mitigate risk

RISKS	MITIGATING RESPONSES
POTENTIAL FOR WRONGDOING AND MALFEASANCE	Improved data collection, refining algorithms, increased transparency,
MISINFORMATION AND BIAS RISK	AI-driven tools are in development to authenticate information and detect AI-generated content to trace "should" messages. Improved data collection, refining algorithms, increased transparency, and introducing diverse AI teams can help reduce biases in AI models.
LOSS OF LITERACY	The education approach needs to change and focus on critical thinking. Platforms will use markers to indicate AI-generated content to prevent rampant issues of plagiarism.
EMPLOYMENT CONCERNS	Introducing new technologies can lead to job shifts rather than job losses. Investments in reskilling and upskilling can prepare the workforce for new roles and industries.
LEGAL AND ETHICAL CHALLENGES	Active dialogue between stakeholders can lead to comprehensive legal frameworks. Existing intellectual property laws can be adapted to cater to AI-generated content.

Introduce AI Solutions Only to Address a Need

While we have been enthusiastic about AI throughout this book, we want to step back. The idea that businesses should use AI solutions simply for the sake of technology or to keep up with a trend is the most significant risk of all. There should be a clear business need or opportunity that drives the adoption of AI. Project managers and business analysts are aware of the structured approach to take. The following issues must be addressed before AI solutions are introduced in an organization:

- **Needs Analysis:** For any technology adoption, alignment with the overall business strategy is crucial. At the heart of every business decision should be a well-defined problem or opportunity, and the solution must align with the business strategy. Without this clarity, it's easy to become enamored with the latest technology (like AI) and see it as a solution to a problem. This can lead to misplaced investments and suboptimal results. A sound needs analysis must be conducted as a first step.
- **Business Case:** Implementing AI solutions is not a trivial task. It often involves costs related to data collection; infrastructure; talent recruitment, such as data scientists and AI experts; and training. Without a clearly articulated business case, an organization might spend valuable resources on a solution that doesn't deliver meaningful value financially.
- **Change Management:** Introducing AI can require significant changes in processes, roles, and workflows. Employees may need to be trained or even reskilled. Without a strong business case justifying these changes, organizations may face resistance from employees and stakeholders, undermining the successful implementation of the technology.
- **Ethical and Social Considerations:** AI systems can sometimes unintentionally introduce biases, infringe on privacy, or make decisions that are hard to explain. Such risks should be identified and mitigated.
- **Sustainability:** AI models may require frequent updates and refinements. If the environment changes, they can become obsolete. Implementing AI without a clear business case can lead to unsustainable solutions that demand ongoing resources without delivering commensurate value.

Closing Remarks

AI's rapid evolution and adoption across various industries—such as education, illustrated in this chapter—necessitates continuous investment in AI. Correspondingly, this surge in AI-centric projects has thrust the discipline of project management itself into the limelight. With the intricate nature of AI projects—encompassing data ethics, technological complexities, and often uncharted territories of innovation—the demand for skilled project managers has skyrocketed. These professionals are now tasked not just with traditional project execution but also with navigating the multifaceted challenges posed by AI. As a result, project management methodologies, tools, and techniques are necessarily evolving to meet the unique needs of AI projects, leading to the enhancement and specialization of the discipline. Chapter 10, "AI Tools for Project Management," describes such products. An important point to note is that with the increasing adoption of AI across industries, the demand for project managers who are comfortable planning and leading AI projects will continue to grow.

There is a lot of merit in investing in this type of a transformation in the practice of project management. Numerous research studies demonstrate the considerable productivity increases due to AI.[1] Similar productivity increases in project management and enhanced quality are likely to materialize when the project work scope falls within the abilities of AI.

We've come to the end of our journey exploring how AI is transforming project management. Thank you again for your time and interest in this important topic. We are confident you have gained valuable insights into how AI can enhance productivity. This will help you professionally as a project manager and will help your organization. The possibilities are endless—whether it's using AI tools for status updates, leveraging its strengths in predictive analytics, anticipating risks, or automating routine tasks. Don't be afraid to experiment and innovate. The projects of tomorrow will be managed differently because of AI. We encourage you to start with a single concept from what you've learned in this book and actively apply it in your project environment.

1 Fabrizio, D., McFowland, E., Mollick, E. R., Lifshitz-Assaf, H., Kellogg, K., Rajendran, S., Candelon, F., & Lakhani, K. R. (2023). "Navigating the Jagged Technological Frontier: Field Experimental Evidence of the Effects of AI on Knowledge Worker Productivity and Quality," *Harvard Business School Working Paper*, No. 24-013.

Do not forget to leverage the tools and practices described on the book's website, which has much more information about AI tools and techniques and useful links. The resources will guide project managers and professionals to prepare for AI's increasing role and offer an opportunity to stay updated and relevant in the field. We will update it with the latest, so make sure you bookmark it for future reference. By starting today, you can lead that change.

Index

H

I

J

K

L

M

S

T